Attracting
BIRDS
to Your Backyard

536
Ways to Turn Your Yard and Garden into a Haven for Your Favorite Birds

Sally Roth

Rodale Press, Inc.
Emmaus, Pennsylvania

OUR PURPOSE

"We inspire and enable people to improve their lives and the world around them."

The information in this book has been carefully researched, and all efforts have been made to ensure accuracy. The author and Rodale Inc. assume no responsibility for any injuries suffered or for damages or losses incurred during the use of or as a result of following this information. It is important to study all directions carefully before taking any action based on the information and advice presented in this book. When using any commercial product, always read and follow label directions. Where trade names are used, no discrimination is intended and no endorsement by Rodale Inc. is implied.

Printed in the United States of America on acid-free ∞, recycled ♲ paper

We're always happy to hear from you. For questions or comments concerning the editorial content of this book, please write to:

Rodale Book Readers' Service
33 East Minor Street
Emmaus, PA 18098

Look for other Rodale books wherever books are sold. Or call us at (800) 848-4735.

For more information about Rodale Organic Gardening magazine and books, visit us at
www.organicgardening.com

Editor: **Fern Marshall Bradley**
Contributing Editors: **Deborah L. Martin, Delilah Smittle, Nancy J. Ondra**
Senior Research Associate: **Heidi Stonehill**
Cover and Interior Book Designer: **Diane Ness Shaw**
Layout Designer: **Keith Biery**
Interior Illustrators: **Randy Hamblin, Maureen A. Logan**
Assistant Illustrator: **Brian Swisher**
Cover Illustrator: **Randy Hamblin**
Copy Editors: **Durrae Johanek, Ann Snyder**
Manufacturing Coordinator: **Patrick Smith**
Indexer: **Nanette Bendyna**
Editorial Assistance: **Jodi Guiducci, Sarah Wolfgang Heffner, Susan L. Nickol**

Rodale Organic Gardening Books

Managing Editor: **Fern Marshall Bradley**
Executive Creative Director: **Christin Gangi**
Art Director: **Patricia Field**
Production Manager: **Robert V. Anderson Jr.**
Studio Manager: **Leslie M. Keefe**
Associate Copy Manager: **Jennifer Hornsby**
Manufacturing Manager: **Mark Krahforst**

**Library of Congress
Cataloging-in-Publication Data**

Roth, Sally.
    Attracting birds to your backyard : 536 ways to turn your yard and garden into a haven for your favorite birds / Sally Roth.
        p.   cm.
    Includes bibliographical references and index.
    ISBN 0-87596-790-6 hardcover
    1. Gardening to attract birds.   2. Bird watching.   I. Title.
QL676.5 .R668 1998
598'.07'234—ddc21   98-19764

Distributed in the book trade by St. Martin's Press

11   12   13   14   15   16   17   18   hardcover
          8   9   10   11   paperback

Attracting BIRDS to Your Backyard

For Jan,
who knew how to be quiet

For Clay,
who loved beauty and life

For Jimmy,
who shares his secrets—
the walking fern, the hermit thrush,
and the joy of living simply

CONTENTS

INTRODUCTION

To me, a yard without birds is like a half-finished picture. Plants and birds are just a natural combination, and I love them both. No matter how picture-perfect my garden may (or may not) be, I always enjoy it most when it's filled with bird song as well as flowers.

Whether you're a gardener who also enjoys birdwatching, or a backyard birdwatcher who wants to know more about gardening for birds, you'll find that I've written this book for you. I've designed it so you can skip around easily, reading about what interests you most first. You'll find it's lots of fun to sample whatever catches your eye as you flip through the pages. If you have a specific question about backyard birds, I'm sure there's an entry that will provide an answer.

Attracting Birds to Your Backyard covers backyard birding and bird gardening A to Z—literally! Whatever your area of interest may be, there's probably an entry that covers it. For example, let's say you want to attract more chickadees to your yard. Just look up Chickadees, and you can read all about them. Or perhaps you want to know what kind of birdseed to use in a tube feeder. Turn to Birdseed, where you'll find the answers you need, plus a rundown of all the best seeds for birds and fun recipes for birdseed treats. After perusing Birdseed, you may find your curiosity stirred by my entries on Bird Feeders or Birdseed Gardens.

Advice for Beginners

If bird feeding and bird gardening are new hobbies for you, you'll find plenty in this book to help you get started. I suggest that you start with Bird Feeding, which describes all the basics of setting up a bird café that will attract every bird within eating distance. Then turn to Bird Feeders to see what kind of furnishings your backyard diner should have. Check out Birdbaths to learn how to use a simple bowl of water to bring even more birds to visit. Then, browse through some of the short topics on special foods for birds, including Dog Food, Doughnuts, and Peanuts and Peanut Butter.

There's a rhythm to the seasonal activities of birds, and you can learn about it by turning to the Spring Almanac, Summer Almanac, Fall Almanac, and Winter Almanac entries.

All about Birds

Birds are fascinating to watch, and it's lots of fun to learn about how and why birds do the things they do. To start learning more about birds, turn to Behavior, an introduction to the daily lives of backyard birds. During nesting season, read Courtship, Nesting, Eggs, and Baby Birds, for a greater appreciation of the everyday miracles that are taking place all around you. And, of course, there are profiles of all the best-loved birds, including special tips on how to attract them to your yard: Just check the entries on Bluebirds, Goldfinches, Robins, Woodpeckers, and many more.

Let's Hear It for Hummingbirds!

You hummingbird lovers—and who isn't!—will find lots of suggestions for keeping your hummers happy, including a special garden just for them. Start with Hummingbirds and move on to Coral Bells, Fuchsias, Impatiens, and other great nectar plants. The Annuals, Perennials, Vines, and Wildflowers entries will also give you the inspiration to squeeze just one more hummingbird-attracting plant into your yard. If you've ever been dazzled by the loop-de-loop courtship flight of hummingbirds, read all about it in Courtship.

Branching Out with Bird Gardening

When you're ready to start dreaming about what to plant in your bird-friendly garden, turn to Annuals, Evergreens, Groundcovers, Perennials, Shrubs, or Trees to pick up some pointers on plants that will bring in the most birds for your buck (as well as being beautiful to boot). Turn to Water Gardens to learn why every bird garden should have one. From there, you can move on to more in-depth reading about particular bird-attracting plants in entries such as Sunflowers or Bee Balm.

Once you're hooked (and be warned: birds and gardens are passions that are hard to resist), you can have fun skipping about in the book to sample anything that catches your eye.

As you sample all the great ideas in this book, you'll find that each one leads you to learn a bit more, then another bit more, about the family of birds and the fancy of gardening. If it's Christmastime when you pick up the book, indulge yourself with Christmas for the Birds. If it's a spring morning and bird song is filling the air around you while you sip your morning coffee on the deck, find out what those arias are all about in the Bird Songs and Calls entry.

Just for Fun

Bird lovers share their best stories of the weird and wonderful things birds do in "The Wild World of Backyard Birds" features scattered here and there throughout these pages. Gardeners from novice to expert tell about what works for them in "Homegrown Wisdom." As your garden grows and the time you spend watching birds increases—a natural outcome, and a good one—you'll experience your own special moments with your bird friends, and learn your own tricks in the garden. Pass them along to your friends and family. Maybe they'll pick up the bug, too!

Spending time in a garden full of birds is the kind of therapy I like best. It calms my mind, erases the everyday woes and busyness of the workaday world for a few hours, and makes me remember what brings true happiness. A sprouting seed, a swelling bud, a new flower every morning; bluebirds in the nest box, a chickadee on my shoulder, the fluting of a wood thrush at dusk— nothing money can buy comes close to those treasures. Bringing the pleasures of plants and the lively antics of birds to your backyard will give you new surprises every day. A garden full of life is a garden full of love.

ACORNS

Highly nutritious, protein-rich acorns are prized bird food. Birds will pluck acorns from oak trees, pick acorns off the ground, or search among crushed shells on sidewalks and streets for exposed nut meats. Some birds, especially nutcrackers and jays, bury acorns and other nuts in the ground for safe storage. Many of the nuts survive the winter without being eaten. In spring they sprout into young, vigorous trees that will bear acorns themselves in a few years.

An oak tree to supply acorns is a great addition to a backyard bird garden, but you don't have to rely on birds to plant acorns for you! Instead, plant a young oak tree—they're excellent shade trees. To learn more about which oaks are best for your region, turn to Oaks on page 183.

Winter Feeder Treats

If you already have an oak tree, you may have noticed that some years the acorn crop is too heavy for the birds to keep up with. Don't let those extra acorns go to waste—store them to use as winter feeder treats. Before the fallen acorns start to sprout, collect them in paper bags and store them in sealed containers in a dry, cool place that stays between 35° and 65°F. In winter, put a few handfuls of acorns in a sock, pound the sock a few times with a hammer, then pour out the broken nut meats into a tray feeder.

Acorn Eaters

A mature oak can host dozens of birds in its branches. Whether they're downy woodpeckers, acorn woodpeckers, or yellow-shafted flickers, woodpeckers never met an acorn they didn't like. These birds will shell nuts in the tree or feed from the ground. Jays of all kinds, and their relatives the magpies and Clark's nutcracker, are just as fond of acorns as woodpeckers.

Other acorn lovers working in the branches might include chickadees, titmice, or nuthatches, along with pine grosbeaks and band-tailed pigeons or mourning doves. At ground level, watch for brown thrashers, juncos, and native sparrows. Depending on where you live, you may also be lucky enough to spot quail and grouse, wood ducks, or the regal ring-necked pheasant and wild turkey dining on acorns.

In fall, watch the branches of backyard oak trees. You may spot a tufted titmouse or other nut-eating birds whacking small holes in acorn shells to reach the nut meat inside.

ANNUALS

After I started watching birds in my garden, I discovered that my annual gardens were great bird attractors! A pair of common yellow-throats collected caterpillars among the flower stems to feed to their babies. And my Mexican sunflowers, with their countless orange-red daisies, drew hummingbirds like a neon "Eat at Joe's" sign.

Annuals are so fast and easy to grow that everyone should plant at least a few in their garden. If you don't want to bother planting annual seeds, just visit your local garden center. You're sure to find your favorites available in pots or flats, ready to plant. See "Favorite Annuals for Birds" on page 4 for a start.

The colors and scents of annual flowers are a season-long delight. When you grow annuals, you can cut armloads of beautiful blossoms for indoor bouquets. And even if you sometimes forget to water and weed, your annuals will often bloom nonstop until frost.

The bright colors of annual flowers draw hummingbirds and butterflies. Dozens of songbirds flock to the plants to hunt for insects or to feast at the seedheads.

Seeds for Winter Feeding

Annuals become even more attractive to birds as summer ends. When cosmos and zinnias go to seed, they become a feeding station for many beautiful birds. Goldfinches will hang from the tips of cosmos, stretching to nibble the slim black seeds.

An old-fashioned annual called love-lies-bleeding (*Amaranthus caudatus*) has unusual dangling "ropes" of deep pink flowers that look like fat lengths of fuzzy yarn. After the flowers mature, they yield thousands of tiny oil-rich seeds that native sparrows and finches adore. Another old-time favorite, the humble bachelor's-button (*Centaurea cyanus*), attracts finches, buntings, and native sparrows when its flowers go to seed. Because bachelor's-button flowers mature at different times, you're apt to see goldfinches and other birds foraging for seeds even while the plant is still blooming.

When the garden season ends, don't be too quick to cut back your annuals. Leave them standing in the garden during the winter. Juncos and native sparrows will scratch beneath them, gleaning leftover seed that has dropped to the ground.

Tickseed sunflower

Zinnia

Mexican sunflower

Planting Annuals for Birds

Once you discover how easy it is to attract birds to your garden with an inexpensive planting of annuals, you'll want to add more of these easy-care flowers every year. Experiment with new kinds. Birds may ignore some, but others—especially those in the huge daisy family—will draw them like magic. And even if the birds don't eat the seeds, they find other food on the plants, of the live variety: caterpillars, beetles, wasps, and assorted tidbits.

Plant annuals densely, because birds feel more at home in thick growth. You can plant transplants or sow seeds directly in the garden. To plant seeds, first scratch the soil surface with a claw-type hand tool, then scatter the seeds and crumble a few handfuls of soil over them. Annuals sprout quickly and grow rapidly, but you'll need to keep the seedbed moist until the seedlings are established. The one essential for most annuals is sun.

Mulch your annuals with compost before they start to flower. This will give them an extra boost of nutrients to stimulate flowering and will cut down on the need to weed and water. Don't spend a lot of time fussing over weeds or tending the plants, because birds prefer to visit an undisturbed garden.

Homegrown WISDOM

ZINNIA SEEDS, PLEASE!

"If I could plant only one thing for the birds," says Marie Bedics of Whitehall, Pennsylvania, "it would be zinnias. I love watching goldfinches come for my zinnia seeds."

Marie sows a zinnia hedge between her yard and her neighbor's garage. She plants a 3-foot-wide strip of tall dahlia- and cactus-flowered types that have 4-inch flowers in red, salmon, rose-pink, canary yellow, and glowing magenta—even green! "The birds visit that hedge from Labor Day until Christmas," Marie says. "In 1996 when we had snow after snow, cardinals were under the plants every day, finding whatever seeds they could."

Bachelor's-buttons Garden balsam Cosmos Love-lies-bleeding

FAVORITE ANNUALS FOR BIRDS

Here are seven of my favorite bird-attracting annuals. Sunflowers are another annual that birds love; to learn more about growing sunflowers, turn to Sunflowers on page 236.

PLANT NAMES	BIRDS ATTRACTED	PLANT DESCRIPTION	CULTURE	COMMENTS
Bachelor's-button (*Centaurea cyanus*)	Finches, buntings, sparrows	2' to 3' branching plants with 1½" fringed flowers in blue, pink, rose, purple, and white from spring to fall	Sow in fall or early spring in full sun in average soil.	Sow seeds or plant transplants every four weeks for season-long bloom. Self-sows after the first year.
Garden balsam (*Impatiens balsamina*)	Flowers attract hummingbirds; seeds attract grosbeaks, cardinals, sparrows	1' to 2' succulent plants with pretty ruffled 2" flowers in pink, purple-pink, or white in mid- to late summer	Sow in early spring in full sun to shade in average soil.	Self-sows, but flower color changes to soft magenta purple.
Cosmos (*Cosmos* spp.)	Finches, sparrows, juncos, buntings	Airy 2' to 4' branching plants with fine foliage and lovely 3" to 4" flowers in a range of pinks, reds, yellow, and orange	Sow in spring in full sun in average soil.	Try unusual cultivars like 'Seashell', with rolled petals, and look for interesting edgings of contrasting color on flowers of self-sown plants.
Love-lies-bleeding (*Amaranthus caudatus*)	Finches, sparrows	Bushy 3' to 4' plants, often with vivid magenta stems; with velvety-soft tiny flowers on dangling tassels up to 1' long in summer to fall	Sow in full sun in midspring when soil is warm, in average to poor soil.	Leave plants in the garden into winter to feed sparrows and other small seed-eating birds.
Mexican sunflower (*Tithonia rotundifolia*)	Flowers attract hummingbirds; seeds attract finches, buntings, cardinals, jays, titmice, chickadees, nuthatches	4' to 8' branching plants with large leaves and velvety stems; brilliant orange-red daisylike flowers from midsummer to early fall	Sow in full sun in average soil. Leave plenty of space for plants to spread their branches.	Try planting an entire bed or a hedge of these fabulous flowers.
Tickseed sunflower (*Bidens aristosa*)	Finches, buntings, chickadees, titmice, sparrows	2' to 5' airy, branching plants with ferny foliage, covered in buttery yellow daisylike flowers in mid- to late summer	Sow in early spring in full sun in average soil. Thrives in wet soil, too.	Self-sows very generously. Mulch to control seedlings or hoe lightly to uproot them.
Zinnias (*Zinnia* spp.)	Finches, sparrows, buntings, chickadees, titmice	Bright or pastel, flat or mounded flowers on bushy, branching plants. Flowers and plants vary widely in size, depending on species and cultivar.	Sow in midspring in full sun in average soil.	Produces plenty of seeds for birds through fall and early winter. Powdery mildew may mar the foliage; plant lower-growing annuals in front to hide the mildewed zinnia leaves.

BABY BIRDS

When baby birds hatch in a nest in your back-yard, you may feel as delighted and protective as a doting grandparent. As the nestlings grow, they become irresistibly cute, with fuzzy heads and bright eyes.

Be a Wise Watcher

The best way to locate a nest around your yard is to keep your ears wide open, because baby birds are little loudmouths. When Mom or Dad visits the nest, the babies pipe up as loudly as they can to make sure they get something to eat. Listen carefully in spring for the soft, repeated cheeping of bird babies. Older nestlings can be so loud you can hear them 200 feet away.

Although it's fun to watch bird families, avoid the temptation to get too closely involved. Many songbirds will abandon a nest-building project if they realize they're being observed. Watch from a discreet distance, and don't touch the nest or pull down a branch for a close look. Even if the parents aren't scared off, you'd be laying down a scent trail for any curious four-legged predator to investigate.

Encounters with Baby Birds

If you find what seems to be an abandoned or helpless baby bird in your yard, look but don't touch—at least at first. Try to figure out whether the baby is old enough to have left the nest. Newborn birds are naked, featherless, and squirmy. Fledglings will have stubby wing feathers, and their tail feathers will be about halfway grown.

If you've found a baby bird that has fallen from the nest, pick the bird up and pop it back in the nest. (Don't worry—it's an old wives' tale that birds will abandon a baby because they detect human scent on it.)

Songbird fledglings typically leave the nest before they can truly fly. After making that great leap over the edge of the nest, they hide in sheltering plants for a few days until they earn their wings. This fledgling stage is a vulnerable time for baby songbirds. The parents usually stay close by or check in frequently. If you've spotted a fledgling on the ground, chances are you'll see a parent arrive shortly. But if several hours pass and the bird is truly unable to fly, you may have an adoptee on your hands. If so, you'll need to care for the bird temporarily while you contact a wildlife rehabilitator. See First Aid for Birds on page 110 for instructions on what to do.

Baby songbirds spend about 8 to 14 days in the nest, changing from spindly hatchlings to bottom-heavy nestlings. Their shape serves a purpose: The heavy bottom keeps them securely weighted in the nest.

BANDING

Where do birds go when they migrate, and how do they get there? How long do wild birds live? If we could talk to birds, these are some of the questions we'd like to ask them.

Since most birds can't speak English, scientists have figured out another way to collect information about them. Since 1920, the U.S. Fish and Wildlife Service has run a program of bird banding. When a bird band is recovered and returned to the service (per the instructions on the band), scientists can gain insights into the details of bird life.

Bird banders trap birds in mist nets of very fine fiber, attach a tiny metal band to the bird's leg, record data on the bird's sex and weight, and then release the bird. Each band has a number that identifies the bird. If the bird is later recaptured, the band is checked. If you find a dead bird that is banded, remove the band and send it to the service.

Ornithologists often band birds at major migration points, such as Hawk Mountain in Pennsylvania and Cape May in New Jersey, but thousands of other banders work right in their own backyards.

To become a bander you must be top-notch at identifying birds and at record keeping. You'll need to apprentice under an experienced, federally licensed bander. To find a bander, call your chapter of the National Audubon Society, which can put you in touch with someone willing to train a beginner.

BAYBERRIES

Bayberry (*Myrica pensylvanica*) is a beauty in the garden, thanks to its glossy narrow leaves and waxy blue-gray berries, which remain on the shrub through the winter. Yellow-rumped warblers, bluebirds, and other birds may feast on a backyard bayberry's fruits.

Some of the spicy-scented leaves of bayberries will cling to the shrubs through the winter. The berries are also aromatic.

Bayberries may be shrubby or grow into a small tree up to 9 feet tall. They thrive in any soil unless it's alkaline, need no fertilizing, tolerate drought, and grow well in Zones 2 to 7. Be sure to plant a male shrub along with your female shrubs for best fruit production.

Wax myrtle (*Myrica cerifera*) is a similar southern species that's good for gardens in Zones 8 and 9. California wax myrtle (*M. californica*), a West Coast species (Zones 7 to 10), grows to about 20 feet tall.

Bayberry shrubs are almost guaranteed to draw handsome yellow-rumped warblers to gardens in the eastern half of the United States and along the West Coast.

BEE BALM

Whenever a friend tells me she can't get hummingbirds to visit her garden, I offer her a homely gift and a guarantee. Handing over a messy clump of roots and soil wrapped in a sheet of wet newspaper, I promise that this starter plant of bee balm will bring hummingbirds to the garden by the end of summer. It hasn't failed yet.

Bee Balm Basics

Bee balm (*Monarda didyma*) belongs to the mint family, and you know what that means: This plant is pushy. It's a spreading perennial that can quickly shoulder aside its neighbors. Plant a small division or pot of bee balm in spring, and by season's end it will have spread to 2 feet or more. If you have loose, fertile soil, you may have a 6-foot circle of bee balm by the end of its second year of growth.

The spreading habit of this hummingbird-attracting plant is a virtue, not a flaw, as far as I'm concerned. It's easy enough to keep bee balm in place if need be—its knotted, lateral roots pull up like a rug.

Bee balm is a native of eastern North America and grows wild along woodland streams. In gardens it thrives in Zones 4 to 8, growing well in sun or partial shade and in almost any soil. The unusual mop-head flowers often have a tiered arrangement, each tier made up of a circle of individual tubular flowers.

Choosing bee balms. If you don't have any hummers frequenting your garden yet, plant a red bee balm such as 'Cambridge Scarlet', 'Adam', or 'Gardenview Scarlet'. Their brilliant color will draw hummingbirds like magic. Once hummingbirds find your garden, they'll also linger at bee balms of other colors. Try 'Croftway Pink', purplish 'Prairie Night' and 'Violet Queen', or creamy 'Snow White'.

More Bee Balms

Wild bergamot (*M. fistulosa*) is a native bee balm of dry, open fields. It has pale purple-pink flowers, grows well in dry soils in Zones 3 to 9, and is lovely in a meadow garden. Spotted bee balm (*M. punctata*) is another good hummingbird plant that thrives in Zones 3 to 9. It has light yellow flowers with purple spots.

Anise hyssop (*Agastache foeniculum*) makes a good perennial companion for bee balm in a hummingbird garden. It's strong enough to resist being swallowed up by the bee balm, and its vertical spikes of strong blue-purple flowers are a good contrast to the bushy bee balm heads. Anise hyssop is hardy in Zones 4 to 9, and, like bee balm, its foliage is intensely aromatic, with a distinctive licorice scent.

Plant bee balm and enjoy long visits from ruby-throated hummingbirds. The hummers circle round and round the flower heads, dipping their beaks in each individual flower.

BEHAVIOR

Learning to understand bird behavior is like learning another language—a fascinating language not just of bird calls, but of body position and movement. When you get to know your backyard birds by their behavior, you'll gain a much deeper understanding of the feathered creatures that share your garden. Watch a bird for a few minutes and you'll be able to tell whether he's contented or feisty, healthy or sick, and singing to his lady love or issuing a challenge to trespassers.

Birds at Mealtime

One easy way to start observing bird behavior is to watch birds at your feeders. You can usually do this from the comfort of your home, looking through a window. When you watch birds at feeders, you'll see more than just birds eating. Observe closely and you'll see them jockeying for position, interacting with other birds, and even engaging in courtship.

Pecking order. "Pecking order" isn't just a turn of phrase—it refers to the barnyard hierarchy of chickens: The rooster eats first, then the dominant hens get their turn, and the more timid chickens eat last.

There's also a pecking order at your feeders, or even at a berry bush or other food source in your yard. The most aggressive birds eat first and get the lion's share. Small birds like chickadees or titmice can dart in and snatch a beakful while a large bird like a blue jay is dining, but they wouldn't dream of challenging the jay for possession of the feeder.

The exception to the big-birds-rule routine is the hummingbird. These little guys aren't afraid to match their swordlike beak and fast, agile flight against any comers. If your hummingbird nectar feeder is located too close to your seed feeders, you'll probably see hummingbirds making threatening rushes toward other birds. For that matter, hummingbirds may bully whomever happens to wander near their food source—dogs, cats, and humans included.

Thirsty birds. We expect birds to spend lots of time eating, but sometimes we forget that

Reading the Signs

Figuring out bird behavior takes a little intuition. If you spot a chickadee sitting at the feeder with fluffed-up feathers, it could mean that the chickadee is cold or sick or trying to intimidate another feeder visitor. How can you decide what's going on? Look for other clues to narrow the possibilities. For example, if the temperature is 5° below zero, most likely the bird is just trying to keep warm. But if it's not a cold day and the bird stays in one place for a long time without showing the typical jerky movements of a chickadee, it's probably sick. If you watch awhile and notice the chickadee making a quick jab with its beak toward the bird beside it, its fluffed feathers are a sign of aggression.

Another clue to interpreting a bird's behavior is to check what other nearby birds are doing. For example, if a junco suddenly dives into the protective cover of your pine tree, and all the other birds in the area skedaddle too, you can bet there's a predator approaching. Scan the sky and see if you can spot a hawk nearby.

they need water, too. Birds that can't get enough to drink will suffer, and their behavior sometimes reveals the problem. When a bird is thirsty, you may see it sitting on a branch or on the ground panting, with its beak half open. Hot weather will also cause a bird to pant. Thirsty birds will investigate containers around your yard that might hold water and even follow you when you water the garden to drink from pools that collect around plants.

Sick, or just cold? In the winter, you may spot birds at or near your feeders that aren't eating. That doesn't automatically mean they're sick. If the weather is chilly, the bird may just be cold. Cold birds will shiver, puff up their feathers, hunker down so that their belly feathers cover their legs and feet, or draw a leg up into their belly feathers.

Sick birds do show symptoms that you can spot if you're observant. One telltale sign is a bird that remains at the feeder when all the rest dive away in panic. If the bird is puffed up and looks dull, it's probably sick. Avian illnesses are often swift and fatal. A bird that's hopping listlessly in your yard one day may be gone to the great bird feeder in the sky the next.

If you find a sick bird that has died, slip your hand inside a plastic sandwich bag before you pick up the body. Dispose of the body in the trash so that the illness doesn't spread, or dig a hole in your yard at least 6 inches deep and bury the body. If a sick bird was visiting your feeders before it died, clean out the remaining seed and scrub the feeders with a 10 percent bleach solution to kill germs.

Battling Birds

Birds are always squabbling over something, it seems. If it's not food, it's birdhouses, nesting territory, or the attentions of a female. Even

Nuthatches are sweet-looking, mild-mannered birds, but when they're roused, they spread their wings and tail feathers to make themselves look threatening.

loving bird parents can show a mean streak when it's time to "encourage" the youngsters to fend for themselves.

Look for these clues to find out when a bird feels feisty:

◆ Puffed feathers
◆ Lowered head
◆ Drooping wings
◆ Threatening jabs or feints with beak
◆ Chasing
◆ Shrieks, sharp chips, or loud chirps, or in the case of wrens and a few other birds, a chattering scolding call

Most bird battles are more show than actual fight, so you don't need to worry if you see birds squabbling at your feeders.

Birds in Love

Birdwatching is loads of fun when it's mating time. Birds in love can act just as silly as lovestruck humans. The male bombards the female with love songs, edging closer and closer to her as he warbles, no matter how disinterested she appears to be. He contorts his body to flash his snazzy wing patches or struts his bright-colored self before her. Some songbirds, including buntings, larks, and hummingbirds, even perform a courtship flight, when the male soars aloft to pour out his heart in song while looping, diving, or swinging like a pendulum above his intended mate. You can learn more about the courtship rituals of backyard birds in Courtship; see also Bird Songs and Calls.

Bird Families

Nesting season is an ideal time to observe the behavior of your birds. You're bound to catch a glimpse of exciting events in the world of birds. If you spot a bird flying with a piece of grass dangling or a twig crosswise in its beak, it's a sign that he or she is building a nest. You have two options for observation: You can try to track down where the bird took the material (be discreet!), or you can watch the place where you think the bird collected the grass or twig until it returns for more. Then you can see exactly how the bird pulls out the blade of grass or picks up or breaks off the twig.

Making a nest usually takes a few days, giving you plenty of time to spy on how the bird accomplishes the task. Use binoculars and observe from a distance to avoid alarming the bird, or it may abandon the nest midway through construction.

Stay away from the nest during egg-laying time, which lasts several days as the female deposits her eggs one by one into their new home. But find a bird's-eye view for the incubation period, when the female (and sometimes the male) sits quietly for hours at a stretch to keep the eggs cozy.

The Wild World of Backyard Birds

Pay attention to what the birds are saying when you're in your garden, advises Rick Mark of Evansville, Indiana. "When I hear a bird making chipping noises from the bushes or a brushy spot, there's a good chance that its warning is aimed at me," Rick says. "Most likely it's because I'm getting a little too close to a nest for comfort. When the bird is really excited, I know the nest is probably within arm's length." Once Rick has gotten a response like that from a bird, he just stands still and looks around. He usually spots the nest, and then he backs off so he won't alarm the birds too much.

Once a song sparrow began scolding Rick as he worked in his strawberry patch. "That was before I knew that there are birds that build their nests on the ground," Rick says. "I figured the sparrow was trying to chase me away from the berries, so I kept on working. I almost stepped on the nest! It was tucked in between two strawberry plants."

When the eggs hatch, things get really interesting. The parents travel back and forth to the nest with food for their hungry children from sunup to sundown. Watch how the nestlings jostle for position when the parent arrives with a fat caterpillar or other treat, and see if you can tell whether they get fed equally or whether the pushiest babies get the most.

If you're interested in learning more about how and when birds build nests, turn to Nesting on page 176.

Birds on the Move

The most amazing thing about birds is their ability to fly. Each species of bird has its own way of flapping, gliding, soaring, and otherwise maneuvering. A crow is stately in flight, while a tree sparrow zips and twists quickly across stretches of open space. There's usually a reason for such differences: The crow has no fear of attack, so it can take its time and fly out in the open. The tree sparrow knows that it's vulnerable to attack, so it hugs the brush and flies in an erratic, random pattern of twists and turns to throw off possible pursuers.

Bird flight is amazing enough in itself, but birds don't just fly—they travel, or migrate, following a seasonal pattern. Once you start paying attention to backyard birds, you'll be quick to spot any newcomers and quick to notice any regulars that depart. It's all part of learning the rhythms of migration. North with the spring, south with the frost—it's a routine that most songbirds have followed for thousands of years. Migration is fascinating: To learn more about it, turn to Migration on page 164.

Bathing Birds

Keeping feathers clean isn't just a matter of tidiness for birds. Clean feathers are as vital for birds as de-iced wings are for airplanes. Gunk and grime on feathers can slow down a bird or interfere with its ability to maneuver in flight.

Removing dust also helps feathers remain waterproof so that rain rolls right off. When a bird uses its beak to preen, it's smoothing the tiny barbs that lock the feathers together back into perfect position, just as you might do with your clumsy human fingers when you try to straighten out the gaps in that feather on your hat (for an illustration of feather barbs, turn to page 106).

Birds are also meticulous about removing parasites like fleas and mites. As they preen their feathers, they pick out these pests, which keeps them healthy and untroubled by itches or bites. They also fluff dust under their feathers to help control parasites.

You can help birds stay clean by setting up birdbaths and a dustbath area in your yard. To learn how, see Birdbaths and Dustbaths.

One of the most bizarre bird-cleaning rituals is "anting," in which birds hold ants in their beak and wipe the insects along their

Blue jays and other birds sometimes smear ants under their wings and among their feathers, which may help to repel fleas and other pests.

feathers. It's a behavior I haven't seen often, but it's immediately recognizable—it looks like the bird is giving itself a sponge bath. Birds may also wriggle themselves into an anthill, letting the ants crawl over them.

One explanation for anting is that ants contain formic acid—a tangy substance that repels pests. Tanagers, towhees, starlings, jays, robins, and cardinals, among others, have been observed anting.

Bird Games

Birds lead such busy lives—build the nest, sit on the eggs, feed the young, feed the young, feed the young—that when they stop to play, it's utterly endearing. Here are some of the playful behaviors you may see.

Mock attacks. Many birds, especially young ones, engage in mock combat, sparring with each other like kittens or puppies while they learn to sharpen their self-defense skills.

Chasing. Woodpeckers often play what looks like a game of tag, following each other from tree to tree and usually making a lot of noise doing so.

Flight. Crows, hawks, and kestrels are the masters of the air. They delight in playing games of chase while they fly.

Hide-and-seek. Crows, ravens, and jays are fond of shiny objects. Sometimes one bird will snatch up a desired plaything and tuck it into a hiding place like the crotch of a tree. Then the bird's companions do their best to search out the toy.

Pass-the-berry. Waxwings often sit in a row on a branch of a cherry or other fruit tree, and pass a berry from one bird to the next.

Drop-the-stick. Hawks enjoy this game, which they can play alone or with other birds. The hawk flies aloft with a stick clenched in its talons, drops it, then swoops down to snatch it up again. Hawks will often repeat this game for several minutes at a time.

The Wild World of Backyard Birds

Midnight blue Steller's jays may look elegant, says Tom Williams of Florence, Oregon, but they're clowns at heart. "Steller's jays started coming to the feeder on my deck for the sunflower seeds," says Tom, "but they'd soon fly away into the woods. I wanted to keep them around a little longer, so I started laying out toys for them on the deck rail."

Tom lined his railing with bright new quarters and dimes, large safety pins, and shiny trinkets he picked up at thrift shops or discount stores. Sequins and spangles are favorites, he notes. To complicate the game, Tom attached the glittery toys to the rail with sticky putty, but the birds quickly learned to peel the toys off the rail anyway.

"I don't know where the toys finally end up," says Tom, "but the jays can spend hours playing and pretend-fighting over them." Occasionally, though, a raven would become interested, and that ended all arguments, Tom says. Ravens are twice as big as jays, so they get what they want.

Birds on Alert

Birds must be constantly alert for danger: a hawk flying above the feeder, a cat eyeing nestlings, or a person who's too close for comfort. Doves often "appoint" a lookout, who keeps an eye on things while the rest of the group is feeding. False alarms are commonplace, especially at the feeder, where a single alarm chip from a cardinal can make 50 birds fly off in a panic. Birds depend on each other to give signals—whoever spots trouble says so. Nobody stops to question an alarm call!

Once you begin watching how birds respond to alarm notes, you'll see that they respond to both the calls of their own species and every other bird in the area. A group of birds is quick to rush to the offensive when they can drive off a predator like a cat or snake, for instance. But only the bravest birds are willing to tangle with a hawk or owl. Less aggressive birds go into hiding at the first hint of a bird of prey.

How do you know what's exciting your backyard birds? See where their heads are turned and look in that direction yourself. If the wren you're watching is giving a scolding rattle and hopping about excitedly on its birdhouse roof, peering toward the ground, take a peek yourself. Chances are you'll find a cat or maybe a snake in the nearby bushes.

Birds Asleep

Birds need a safe place to sleep, where they'll be protected from nighttime raids of raccoons, owls, prowling cats, and snakes. They also need a cozy place where they'll be sheltered from rain and heavy dew. Shelter is especially important in the ice, snow, and cold to help birds preserve their precious body heat.

Birds roost, or retire for the night, long before dark. By dusk, songbirds are safe in their nighttime havens. They're out and about at the first rays of the sun, or even before. In breeding season, you can hear robins tuning up their dawn chorus before the first streaks of color appear in the eastern sky. If a sleeping bird is disturbed at night, it may break into a snatch of song before it rouses itself enough to respond with the more expected alarm call.

Dense evergreens like hemlocks and rhododendrons are favorite sleeping haunts in both summer and winter. Cavity-nesting birds, like woodpeckers, chickadees, and bluebirds, seek out holes in dead trees or bird boxes to snore away in. In the coldest nights of winter, several birds may share a single cavity, piled together to keep warm and snug.

At dusk, step under the low-hanging branches of a pine or other evergreen tree and look up. You may spot birds roosting shoulder to shoulder on a branch.

BERRIES

Whenever I add a new shrub to my garden, I try to select one that produces berries. No matter where you plant a shrub—in a perennial flowerbed, as an accent plant for the lawn, in a hedge along the road, or as part of a barricade against trespassing dogs—choosing one that produces berries gives you a living bird feeder as well.

Of course, before the berries come the flowers, and often very showy ones, so you'll get at least two seasons of ornament from berry-bearing shrubs and other berry-producing plants like perennial vines and groundcovers.

A garden full of berries is irresistible to birds, especially during fall migration and in winter, when high-energy food is vital. Once I added berried shrubs to my yard, I started adding new names to the checklist of birds that I've spotted in my backyard. Gray-cheeked thrushes came to visit the spicebush (*Lindera benzoin*); catbirds came for the European cranberrybush viburnum (*Viburnum opulus*), and everybody

and their brother came for the arrowwood viburnum (*V. dentatum*).

Experienced birdwatchers seek out patches of wild elderberries, pokeweed, and other berried plants when they're afield, knowing that birds will soon be visiting these treasures. Even a small flock, like three or four bluebirds, can erase every berry from a small to middling-size shrub in a day or two. Because berries disappear in such a hurry once birds discover them, try planting shrubs that ripen at different times of the season. For example, you could plant a hedge of a dozen kinds of viburnum, drawing birds from September to December as the fruits ripen, rather than a single-species hedge that would be picked clean in a week.

Strawberry

Black currant

Juneberry

American cranberrybush

Berries are bound to bring birds flocking to your yard, so plant plenty of berry-producing shrubs like juneberries. If you plant berries like strawberries to eat yourself, keep the plants covered with netting or you may have to share the harvest with your bird friends.

BEST BERRY PLANTS FOR BIRDS

Berries attract a slew of birds, including gorgeous bright-colored tanagers, orioles, and grosbeaks. Here I've listed several of my favorite berry-producing plants for the bird garden. To learn more about berry-producing plants for birds, turn to Bayberries, Brambles, Grapes, Groundcovers, Hollies, Mulberries, Native Plants, Shrubs, Sumac, Viburnums, Vines, and Virginia Creeper.

PLANT NAMES	BIRDS ATTRACTED	PLANT DESCRIPTION	CULTURE	COMMENTS
American cranberry-bush (*Viburnum trilobum*)	Robins, thrushes, bluebirds, and many others	Rounded shrub to 12' tall, with three-lobed leaves. Flat-topped clusters of white flowers in late spring; shining red fruits in early fall.	Grow in well-drained, moist soil, in sun to partial shade; irrigate during droughts. Zones 2 to 8 (grows best in cool-summer areas)	Looks best planted as a hedge or a privacy screen.
Arrowwood (*Viburnum dentatum*)	A very wide range of berry-eating birds	Multistemmed shrub 8' to 15' tall expands slowly from base to form a large clump. Clusters of small creamy flowers in early summer; oval blue-black fruits in fall.	Grow in well-drained soil, in sun to partial shade. Zones 2 to 8	Buy in the fall, when you can see the fall color; only some plants turn rich red.
Barberries (*Berberis* spp.)	Catbirds, mockingbirds, and many others	Thorny, very dense, rounded shrubs varying in size from 18"-tall 'Crimson Pygmy' to 6'-tall 'Red Chief'. Yellow flowers followed by bright red or orange berries.	Grow this adaptable, drought-tolerant shrub in well-drained soil in full sun. Zones 4 to 8	Reddish purple-leaved cultivars like 'Crimson Velvet' or 'Helmond Pilla' add color to the garden. Try grouping barberries and maiden grasses.
Black currant (*Ribes nigrum*)	Robins, mockingbirds, jays, and many others	Twiggy shrub to 6' tall, with lobed leaves. Clusters of greenish white flowers followed by edible black fruits.	Grow in full sun to light shade, in well-drained soil. Zones 4 to 8	Sale of currants is restricted in some states because they host white pine blister rust disease. Ask your extension agent about restrictions before planting. Use currants in a mixed hedge for cover, nesting, and food.
Elderberries (*Sambucus* spp.)	A very wide range of berry-eating birds	6' to 10' multistemmed shrubs with white flowers and abundant clusters of tiny berries	Grow in well-drained soil, in sun to part shade. Zones 4 to 8	Try *S. canadensis*, the common garden variety with purple-black fruits, or grow American red elderberry (*S. pubens*), Pacific Coast red elderberry (*S. callicarpa*), or European red elderberry (*S. racemosa*).
Juneberries (*Amelanchier* spp.)	Waxwings, bluebirds, and many others	Shrubs or small trees with white flowers in early spring, followed by fruits that turn red, then blue-black or purple. Leaves turn yellow to deep red in fall.	Grow in well-drained, moist, acidic soil, in sun to shade. Zones 4 to 9 (some species are hardy to Zone 2)	'Autumn Brilliance' and 'Autumn Sunset' are graceful small trees; 'Prince William' is shrubby; 'Cumulus' grows 20' to 30' tall. *A. canadensis* is a suckering shrub that is a great choice for a wild garden.
Strawberries (*Fragaria* spp. and hybrids)	Robins, catbirds, thrashers, and many others	Groundcovers with clumps of three-lobed leaves. White or pink flowers in spring followed by delectable red berries.	Grow in full sun in well-drained soil rich in organic matter. Zones 4 to 9	Choose cultivars that you like, or try the tiny, sweet clusters of wild strawberry (*F. virginiana*). Western beach strawberry (*F. chiloensis*) is hardy to Zone 7 and has beautiful, glossy leaves. Plant some strawberries as a groundcover around shrubs, where birds can forage for them safely.

BINOCULARS

Binoculars bring the fascinating details of the lives of backyard birds into sharp view. With binoculars, you can see how an oriole pokes a piece of string through the fibers of its nest. Colors are brighter and you can admire all the small touches that make birds so beautiful—dabs of bright yellow at the throat, perfect round speckles on the belly, elegant bits of blue on wing edges.

Basic Binoculars

Although the best binoculars cost a bundle, you can find good-quality binoculars for about $100 and serviceable discount-store glasses for as little as $25.

The two most important features of a pair of binoculars are their magnification power and their light-gathering capability. One standard type is 7 × 35. The "7" tells you the magnifying power: These glasses multiply your vision by

seven times. The "35" tells you the diameter of the large lens: 35 millimeters across. This size allows a lot of light to enter the glasses, so the image you see is bright, an important consideration when you're watching birds in dimly lit areas like among shade trees and woods. If you're a novice birder, 7 × 35s are a good first choice.

The size of the lens (the "35" in 7 × 35, for instance) also means a bigger field of view. A wide field of view lets you look at a bigger area at one glance, so you're more likely to spot birds on the move. Reputable manufacturers like Bushnell, Orion, and Nikon often combine an 8-power lens with a 42-mm lens for a great view. Keep in mind that a wider lens means a bigger pair of binocs, because the tubes must be sized to fit the lenses.

Binocular Shopping Tips

Conventional wisdom advises trying out binoculars before you buy them. Ask your dealer to let you take the glasses outside into the real

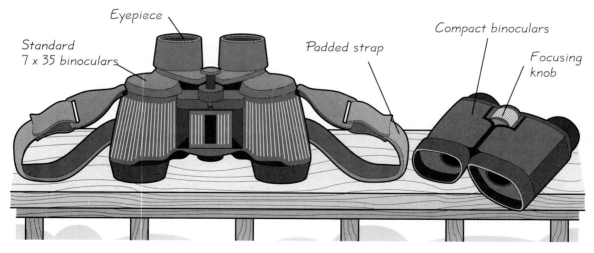

Eyepiece

Standard 7 x 35 binoculars

Padded strap

Compact binoculars

Focusing knob

For beginning birdwatchers, a basic pair of compact or standard binoculars is a good choice. Most modern binocs have coated lenses that cut down on reflection and glare. Look for "armored" binoculars plated with rubber or other protection that won't break when you drop them—as you inevitably will.

world, even if all you zero in on is a car license plate. With a well-known brand of binoculars you can be sure that you're getting good quality, but you need to test how easy the glasses are to use. Make sure the eyecups fit your eyes comfortably, and that the focus knob responds quickly and easily. And remember: The binoculars you buy will be hanging around your neck for years to come. Be sure the pair you choose isn't too heavy for you.

Going High Power

If your purse strings can expand a bit, try a pair of 10 × 50 binoculars, which may cost about $500. It can be tricky to use 10-power binoculars—every tremor of your hands translates to the lens, so it's hard to get a steady view of your image.

If you plan any birding trips to areas with large stretches of water or other hard-to-reach areas, you'll want to invest in a spotting scope.

Expect to pay $400 and up for a good-quality scope, plus $50 and up for the necessary tripod. Meade, Celestron, and Orion are deservedly popular brands.

Getting in Practice

It takes some practice to find and keep small birds or moving birds in your lenses and in focus. Here are a few things to zoom in on with your new binoculars.

◆ Locate a bird on the ground or in a tree. Focus your binoculars on it, and try to follow it with your binoculars as it moves about.
◆ Find a bird in flight with your binoculars, adjust the focus, and follow it to its landing place. See how long it takes you to identify it.
◆ Focus on birds at your feeders; admire the carefully layered arrangement and overlapping edges of wing feathers, check out the eye colors of your birds, or examine the intricacies of head markings.

Spotting scope

10 x 50 binoculars

As you get more serious about birdwatching, you may want to graduate to high-power binoculars or a spotting scope. These let you see birds in sharp detail even when they're 100 feet away.

BIRDBATHS

If you've ever watched a bunch of starlings splashing in a roadside puddle, you know that birdbaths don't need to be fancy. Birds will bathe in or drink from any kind of shallow container filled with fresh water. On hot summer days, a crowd of house finches often lines the rim of my dogs' water bucket! So take a close look at a puddle of bathing birds—it has all the characteristics of an appealing birdbath.

◆ Shallow water: Birds prefer bathing in 1 or 2 inches of water; anything deeper than 3 inches spells danger, and birds will avoid it.
◆ Rough bottom surface: Birds like solid footing when they wallow in the water. A slick-bottomed birdbath won't attract many repeat customers.
◆ Open site: A bathing bird is vulnerable to predators because it can't fly well when its feathers are wet and heavy. A clear view of approaching predators is vital. If neighborhood cats prowl in your yard, set up your birdbath in an area where it's not close to clumps of plants. Allow at least 2 feet of open space on all sides of the bath.
◆ Clean water: Algae, mud, or droppings can quickly make bathwater unappealing. It's important to scrub your birdbaths daily and refill them with clean water.
◆ Perches nearby: Position your bath within a few yards of a small tree so birds have a convenient place to sit and preen after bathing.

Birdbath Choices

Birdbaths can be quite an investment. A good-quality terra-cotta birdbath may cost more than $50, and antique replicas or special pottery birdbaths may have price tags in the hundreds.

If your budget is limited, you can use any shallow, wide container you have on hand. Remove the handle of an old frying pan and you've got a great watering hole for birds. Or use an old pie plate, a turkey platter, or a trash can lid. Thrift shops are a great source of inspiration! You can also buy just the top of a traditional concrete pedestal-model birdbath at garden centers or discount stores and settle it on a stump or rock. Backyard bird lovers who like make-it-yourself projects will enjoy making a built-in bathing pool for birds, like the one described in "A Pleasant Pool for the Birds" on page 21.

Attracting Birds to Birdbaths

If you want immediate activity at your birdbath, try placing it near your feeding station— the birds will notice it more quickly. Also, choose a pedestal-style birdbath. I've observed that birds seem to take to them more easily than to other containers.

A tree stump makes a great natural birdbath pedestal. Top it with a large clay saucer for the bath, and the birds will love it.

The most reliable way to attract birds to your birdbath is to create the sound of dripping or running water. If you have an outside electrical outlet, a small, inexpensive recirculating pump is worth its weight in warblers.

Another easy way to create a dripping sound is to rig a bucket with holes in it over your birdbath. Punch a few small nail holes in the bottom of a gallon jug or plastic household bucket, fill it with water, and check the drip. What you're aiming for is a slow drip-drip-drip that will be music to a bird's ears. You can hang the bucket from an iron shepherd's-crook pole or from an overhanging tree branch.

Keeping a drip bucket going can be a frustrating task (the bucket empties faster than you'd expect, even with a slow drip), but you'll need to fill it only once a day. The dripping sound will lure some birds, and after that their presence alone will attract other customers to the bath. I use this trick only during spring migration, when I want to entice passers-through to linger in my garden. On April and May mornings, when migration is at its peak, I fill the bucket and let 'er drip. By the time it's empty, I'll have had a wonderful morning watching unexpected guests drop in.

The Birdbath Birding Scene

A birdbath is a year-round attraction for birds, but the crowd that partakes will vary depending on the season. Here are some of the seasonal highlights to watch for at your birdbath.

Winter. Drinking water is at a premium for birds in winter in cold areas of the country, where many natural water sources freeze over. Lay an inexpensive heating element or de-icer in your birdbath to keep the water accessible (you'll need to plug the de-icer into an outdoor outlet). Or, try the low-tech method of carrying out a saucer of warm water at regular

Homegrown **WISDOM**

CLEAN YOUR BIRDBATH WITH HORSETAILS

You can clean your birdbaths with a plastic scouring pad, or you can take a tip from Native Americans and use a plant to do your cleaning.

Common horsetail, or scouring rush (*Equisetum hyemale*), is an unusual perennial plant with leafless evergreen stems that grow thick and fast. Native Americans used it to scrub their clay pots. The hollow, jointed stems are loaded with tiny grains of silica (which is also the main ingredient of sand). Every day I snap off a stem or two, wad them up into a loose clump, and do a quick scrub of my birdbath. They cut through grime and slippery algae faster than any commercial product I've tried. When your cleaning supplies are growing in easy reach, keeping the birdbath clean is a cinch.

Hardy to Zone 5, scouring rush thrives in wet places, so it will enjoy the daily dousing it gets as birds visit your birdbath. Scouring rush spreads and is difficult to keep under control, so either contain it with a sunken barrier or grow it in a big clay pot.

times each day so the birds get accustomed to your schedule: Morning and noon are busy bathing and drinking times.

Drinking, not bathing, is the main activity at winter birdbaths in cold regions, although occasionally a starling will enjoy a splattering good time in the warm water. Though an icy shower makes our teeth chatter, birds don't mind bathing in cold water a bit. The layer of down feathers next to their skin stays dry and keeps them cozy while they clean their outer feathers. Birdbaths with built-in heating elements are the ultimate in deluxe bird bathing. They'll keep the water ice-free even on the coldest days, with no thought or care from you. You may want to invest in such a model if your winters are long and frigid.

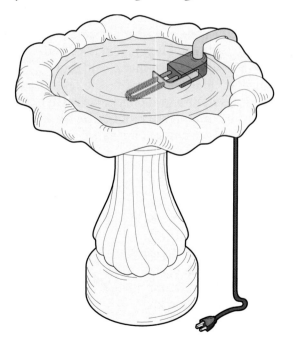

A simple de-icer will keep birdbath water thawed in most conditions. De-icers come in several sizes; read the packaging to see how much water a particular model will heat.

Spring. Look for both resident birds and migrating birds that are passing through. Vireos, wood warblers, and other insect-eating birds that won't stop at your feeder will stop at your birdbath. Because birds move in and out of an area so rapidly during spring migration, delightful surprises are a daily pleasure. One gentle April morning I looked out the window to find a scarlet tanager and an indigo bunting drinking from adjoining saucers. Then a rose-breasted grosbeak fluttered down from the trees in a flurry of black-and-white wings and settled himself on the rim of another saucer.

Summer. When the weather gets hot, watch for resident songbirds like robins, orioles, catbirds, and tanagers seeking respite from the heat and dust with a cooling bath. Be sure to add a shallow dish of water near to the ground for birds like towhees and thrushes that like to stay low. Watch for family groups showing up at the bath as fledglings leave the nest. The young birds are fun to watch, especially when they line up on the rim of the basin like a bunch of kids waiting their turn in the tub. If summer brings drought, expect to see the unexpected. That's when birds that might not ordinarily visit your garden will come in for a drink. Meadowlarks, crows, blackbirds, and many of the shier sparrows, including grasshopper sparrows and field sparrows, will venture into unfamiliar territory to get a drink when a dry spell has its grip on the countryside.

Fall. Birdbath traffic often dies down in the fall as songbirds leave for warmer climes. House finches and house sparrows are still regular bathers, and titmice and chickadees visit for drinks though they don't usually stay to splash. In areas with abundant fall rains, natural water is plentiful, so birds can find natural puddles more easily.

A PLEASANT POOL FOR THE BIRDS

For a fun afternoon project, try making an in-ground bathing pool for birds. This is a pool for spring, summer, and fall use; if the water freezes, it may crack the concrete.

Two 80-pound bags quick-setting cement
Recirculating pump
Black landscape plastic
River gravel

1. Choose a sunny site in an open area at least 10 feet across. Use a spade to dig a shallow oval, circular, or free-form hole about 3 feet in diameter. Make the hole 6 inches deep at the center and taper it to 4 inches deep at the edges.

2. For a more natural look, remove the turf around the hole to create a "beach" area about 18 inches wide.

3. Mix the cement with water according to the directions, and trowel it into place in the depression, making a 3-inch-thick layer.

4. Drag a stiff scrub brush over the cement to create a slightly ridged surface.

5. After the cement sets, you can install a recirculating pump, burying the electrical cord as shown on the package. Set the pump to burble at the water's surface, just enough to create the gurgle of moving water.

6. Cover the beach area with black landscape plastic to block weeds and top it with a layer of river gravel. Add a few rocks at the edge of the bath, fill it with fresh water, and retreat to your favorite lawn chair to watch the show!

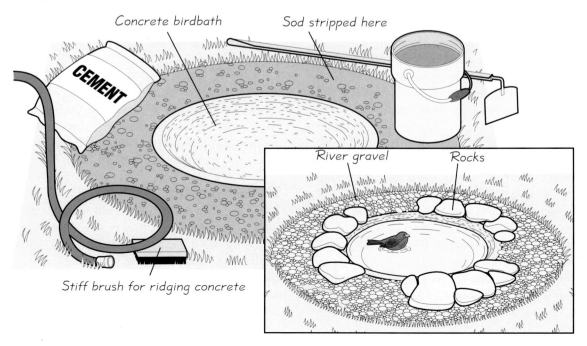

Concrete birdbath

Sod stripped here

CEMENT

Stiff brush for ridging concrete

River gravel

Rocks

BIRD COUNTS

At Christmastime, millions of folks take a break from shopping and celebrating to spend a day counting birds in fields, woods, and even along city streets. They're taking part in the Christmas Bird Count sponsored by the National Audubon Society and the U.S. Fish and Wildlife Service.

The Christmas Bird Count gives a quick snapshot of winter birdlife so researchers can track which species are declining or increasing and how their ranges are shifting. The count happens in all 50 states plus Canada, Central America, Mexico, and South America.

Getting Involved

This hemisphere-wide count is a grassroots effort, and it comes at the worst time of year. If you're like me, your calendar is already crammed with performances, parties, cookie baking, shopping, and decorating. Taking a day off to count birds sounds like the height of madness, but it's really a healthy dose of sanity. Counts may be scheduled for two weeks before or after Christmas, usually on a Saturday.

To get involved with a bird count, contact your local chapter of the Audubon Society. They'll tell you the dates of the counts in your area. They'll also put you in touch with a small group of counters to tag along with (novices are warmly welcomed—every pair of eyes counts!) and send you general instructions, tally sheets, and a map of your count area. You can also count with your own friends or alone, if you like, though groups tend to get a more complete count.

On the count day, you'll rise at the crack of dawn and head out to your designated count area. For the next several hours, you'll tramp around peering for birds in bushes and trees. Every count has its special moment. One year it may be a flock of 50 cardinals filling a

Watch Birds for Science

Tens of thousands of dedicated backyard birders track feeder birds in winter for Project Feederwatch (PFW), a joint project of the Cornell Laboratory of Ornithology, the National Audubon Society, Bird Studies Canada, and the Canadian Nature Federation.

It's easy to become a part of Project Feederwatch. All you do is survey your feeders on specified dates, plus describe your backyard plantings and the foods you offer. In return, you'll get lots of great information, have the fun of seeing how your observations match up with others', and know the satisfaction of contributing to science. To learn more, contact the Cornell Lab of Ornithology (see phone number and address on page 290) or visit the web site at http://birdsource.cornell.edu/pfw. Membership in PFW is $15.

thicket; the next, a single bluebird in a sunny valley. Sometimes there's a rarity, such as a Harlan's hawk (an unusual type of red-tailed hawk) spotted hundreds of miles from home, or a catbird mewing in December.

Other Counts

While the Christmas Bird Count is the biggest, there are censuses at other times of the year, including nesting season and spring migration. Then, some fanatic birders pull a Big Day count, tallying every bird they find from dawn through dark in a fierce competition.

BIRD FEEDERS

The fastest, most surefire way to a bird's heart is definitely via the stomach. Put up a backyard bird feeder and birds will certainly come to feed in your yard. Where you live determines what you'll see because of differences in birds' range and habitat preferences. But I guarantee you (no money back, though!) that at least one of the top five most common feeder birds in North America—blue jay, house finch, downy woodpecker, goldfinch, and junco—will be there, no doubt with his friends and family.

As word spreads about your feeder, the kinds of birds and the size of the crowd will increase. Even if you live in the city where it seems pigeons and house sparrows are the only birds on earth, you'll get surprises every year as more unusual birds like evening grosbeaks find your food or stop in on migration.

Bird-Feeder Basics

Putting out a bird feeder is a fun and easy project. Discount stores, garden centers, and bird-supply shops stock a multitude of feeders. Making a simple bird feeder is easy and fun, too (even for klutzes like me), and it can be a great family project.

When you shop for bird feeders, you'll find your choices are almost limitless. You may wonder how to decide what to buy. Here are some hints.

Ease of use. The most important factor in choosing a feeder is how easy it is to use—for both me and the birds. Test out the feeder in the store. Is the feeder easy to open to pour in seed? I once had a beautiful pagoda-style feeder that required two hands to open, leaving zero hands for pouring in birdseed. As a result, that feeder sat empty a lot. You'll

Whether you opt for a fine and fancy bird feeder or a simple homemade feeder fashioned from a coffee can wrapped with twine, you're sure to enjoy watching the birds who come to sample feeder treats.

want a feeder that's easy to fill and that holds a reasonable amount of seed (at least a quart).

If you're just getting started, look for a feeder that displays seed in full view because birds are attracted by the sight of food and by the sight of other birds eating. An open tray is great for starters.

Make sure your feeder has plenty of room for birds to eat without protrusions or decorations getting in the way. Birds also like a feeder with a raised ledge or perch that they can grasp while dining.

Check whether you can take the feeder apart to clean it. Are there corners and crannies that are hard to reach? If so, you can be sure that seed will end up stuck there, and old seed can mold and cause birds to get sick.

Size. When birds come to a feeder, they want food, and they want it fast. I suggest choosing a main tray feeder that's big enough for at least a dozen birds to eat at once. Supplement that with hopper- and tube-type feeders. Domed feeders are great for small birds like chickadees. Feeders inside wire cages give small birds a place to eat in peace without competition from starlings or other larger birds.

Once you have one or two large feeders you can add as many smaller ones as you like. One of my favorite feeders is a single-chickadee-size clear plastic feeder that attaches to my window with a suction cup and brings the bird right to my eye level when I'm working at my desk.

Quality. Make sure your feeder is well made. Reject any with cracks or splits in the wood, especially where it's nailed or stapled together. Thin, flimsy wood will be less durable than thicker wood or well-made plastic or metal. The birds don't care about the construction—

they'd be happy to eat right off the ground—but feeders can be costly, so get one that lasts.

A sturdy, simple, but beautiful, feeder costs more than you'd think. Expect to pay $20 to $60 for a feeder that will last for years. You can also pay that price or more for trendily decorated or otherwise fancified feeders. Gussied-up feeders may be fun, but check to be sure the flashy details don't hide a shoddy feeder.

Tray Feeders

I have a multitude of feeders in my yard, but there's only one I couldn't do without: my all-purpose simple wooden tray feeder. It's big, it's easy to fill, and it accommodates a slew of birds. The other feeders pick up the overflow and I can stock them with select treats, but it's the big tray that's the main draw.

Cardinals, finches, jays, grosbeaks, bluebirds, blackbirds, nuthatches, chickadees, titmice, and buntings all prefer an open tray feeder. The only birds reluctant to use a tray feeder mounted on a post are ground-feeding birds. A very low tray on stumpy legs will accommodate these birds, which include native sparrows, quail, towhees, and doves. You can put any kind of seed in a tray except for tiny niger, lettuce, and grass seeds, which are apt to blow away or get wasted (put these in a tube feeder instead). Tray feeders are also good places to put out doughnuts, bread crumbs, and fruit.

You can buy commercially made tray feeders, but the prices I've seen are high: almost $20 for a feeder about the size of a sheet of legal paper. But tray feeders are easy to make. All you need to do is nail a wood frame together, staple window screen and hardware cloth to the frame, and mount it on a post, as shown on the opposite page.

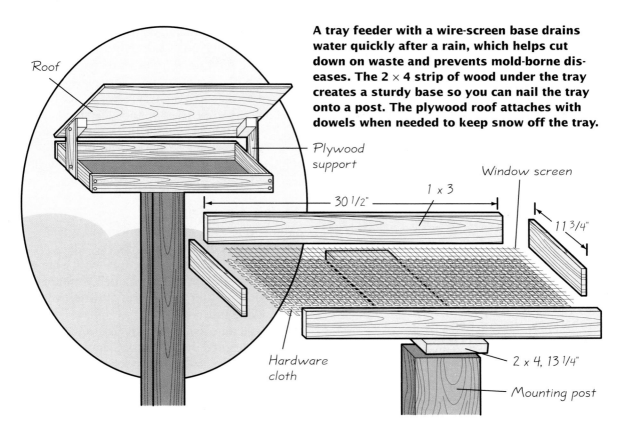

A tray feeder with a wire-screen base drains water quickly after a rain, which helps cut down on waste and prevents mold-borne diseases. The 2 × 4 strip of wood under the tray creates a sturdy base so you can nail the tray onto a post. The plywood roof attaches with dowels when needed to keep snow off the tray.

Roof

Plywood support

Window screen

30 1/2"

1 x 3

11 3/4"

Hardware cloth

2 x 4, 13 1/4"

Mounting post

Hopper Feeders

Hopper-style feeders, with plastic or glass enclosures that dole out seeds as they're needed, are an efficient choice because seed is used as needed and large amounts aren't exposed to wet or snowy weather, or kicked out by scratching birds. Many birds, including chickadees, nuthatches, titmice, cardinals, jays, and woodpeckers, eat eagerly at a hopper feeder. Make sure the tray of a hopper-style feeder has enough room for more than two or three birds to gather and eat, and check to see if the feeder will be easy to clean if seed spoils in bad weather.

Be especially careful if you mount your hopper feeder permanently in the garden. If the hopper or frame blocks the tray, the feeder may be very hard to clean. I've found myself reduced to scraping out the seed from hard-to-reach corners with a teaspoon.

Windowsill Feeders

Years ago, before the days of fancy screens and storm windows, many folks simply scattered a handful of crumbs or seeds for the birds on their windowsills. This is still a great idea, especially if you find it difficult to get outside to fill feeders. My friends call it the lazy woman's bird feeder (I'm sure they mean nothing personal), but I call it smart.

You can mount a simple shallow tray feeder on the outside of a window, mounting it like a window box (but higher and closer to

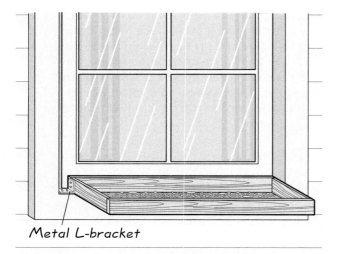

Metal L-bracket

The best view in the house is yours when you put up a windowsill feeder. Chickadees, nuthatches, titmice, and grosbeaks are generally brave enough to feed there, even when you're just on the other side of the glass.

the pane). You can use wooden or metal brackets that attach below the sill or on the sill, as shown in the illustration on this page.

To fill the feeder I simply open the window and pour in a scoop of seeds from a covered metal bucket that I keep beside my chair. I use hulled sunflowers in my windowsill feeder so there's no mess from shells, and I dole them out in small amounts so the feeder is picked clean between refills.

It's great to be able to watch the chickadees and other visitors up close. Though they're skittish at first, they soon become used to the presence of an observer, as long as you don't make any sudden movements.

Feeders that attach to your window with suction cups are also a great invention. I use only small stick-on feeders because I've had one too many incidents when the whole she-

bang let loose, either all on its own or when a large bird landed on it. Not only did it scare the daylights out of me, it frightened my window-friendly birds away for days. Clear plastic stick-on feeders that are about the size of cage-bird feeding cups are perfect for a chickadee, goldfinch, titmouse, nuthatch, or other small bird. I keep a flurry of them—four in all—on the window at my desk, above the windowsill tray feeder, and they're constantly in use.

Tube Feeders

Simple tube feeders are a perfect example of form matching function. They're self-contained, so seed stays dry; they hold a good quantity of seed, so they don't need refilling too often; and they can accommodate several birds at one time.

Not all tube feeders are created equal, though. I learned the hard way to invest a few extra dollars in the more expensive models, such as those made by Duncraft or Droll Yankees. The tube itself is sturdier, the feeding holes are designed better so there's less spillage of seeds as birds eat, and the heavier metal used on top and bottom makes the feeder more stable. (Lightweight plastic models may swing easily in the wind, scattering seed on the ground.)

Tube feeders are welcomed by goldfinches, purple finches, pine siskins, chickadees, and house finches, who seem to know they can eat in peace there without being disturbed by the "big guys." Read the label to find out what kind of seed your tube feeder was designed for. The size of the hole determines whether you have a feeder that should be filled with niger, birdseed mix, or sunflower seeds.

Fruit Feeders

Fruit feeders are fun to make and fun to watch, as mockingbirds, chickadees, orioles, and other

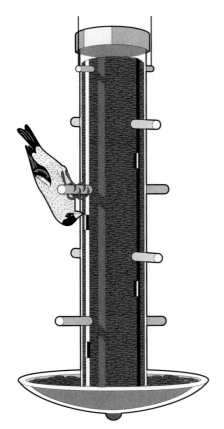

To give goldfinches preferred status, try a tube feeder with perches above the holes. The acrobatic goldfinches feed easily from these feeders, but house finches won't be able to get at the openings, so they'll go elsewhere.

birds work at the grapes, oranges, and other fruits you stock them with. Most fruit feeders consist of a board back with spikes or hooks for mounting the fruit and perches for the birds. Fruit feeders are a perfect do-it-yourself project. A piece of scrap wood for a backing and a handful of big nails and cup hooks are all the supplies you'll need. For an example, check the illustration on page 118.

Nectar Feeders

Sweet sugar water, or nectar, is a huge draw for hummingbirds. Put up a nectar feeder and you're practically guaranteed to get hummers. The birds search for red and deep orange-red flowers, and anything that color will bring them in for a closer look. Your nectar feeder may also attract other birds with a sweet tooth, including orioles, house finches, and woodpeckers. In the wild these birds would satisfy that craving with real nectar from flowers, or a sip of sugary tree sap or fruit juice. The sugar boost gives them quick calories and the energy needed to live that fast-paced bird life. See Nectar on page 175 for more on this sweet treat.

I'm a big fan of "natural," so the first nectar feeder I bought was a ceramic feeder in lovely tones of blue and beige. But it didn't attract any birds, so I gritted my teeth and bought a plastic nectar feeder with lots of red on it. Less than an hour after I hung the feeder, it was buzzing with hummingbirds.

As with other feeders, look for a nectar feeder that's easy to fill and easy to clean. Make sure you can remove the base to clean out the feeding holes. Bee guards of gridded plastic over the feeder openings are a necessity unless you like to watch constant battles between wasps and hummers. Insects can be just as territorial as hummingbirds when it comes to defending a food source.

Maintaining Your Feeders

Good housekeeping counts when it comes to bird feeders. Because a feeding station is an unnatural situation, with so many birds crowded into a small space, all eating from the same tray, illnesses can spread like wildfire. Basic cleanliness will keep your birds healthy and prevent disease from spreading through the flock you've invited to your yard. Regular maintenance will also make your feeders last longer; wet seed that accumulates in the feeder can cause the wood to decay.

You'll quickly get a feel for how much seed your birds eat. Plan to refill every morning, as early as possible, so that there's fresh seed waiting when birds come looking for it. For a feeder in which the seed is exposed to the elements, start with a small amount and see how long it takes birds to polish it off. Your aim is to put out the amount that is eaten daily. Piling an open feeder full of seed may save you time in refilling, but it's inviting trouble. Dew, rain, or snow can make the seed unusable and even unhealthy once mold sets it. Sweep out your feeders before refilling. A whisk broom makes quick work of the job; a plastic pancake turner is surprisingly effective, too.

You can mount flat-bottomed feeders on a 4 × 4 post by nailing them in place. Try nailing flat-backed feeders to a post in the garden or on your front porch. Or you can hang feeders from tree branches, wrought-iron shepherd's crooks, or other hangers.

Place your feeder in an open area with cover that's only a couple of feet away, so birds can dive for safety if threatened. If you put your feeder in a wide-open area of lawn, you'll attract fewer birds because they'll be reluctant to expose themselves to possible predator attack. Choose a site protected from strong winds, or erect a fence or hedge to break the force of gusts.

If your neighborhood is home to squirrels, you can bet they'll soon show up for a handout. Baffles and special squirrel-deterring feeders are worth the time and trouble, because squirrels can use up seed like a vacuum cleaner. See Squirrels on page 228 for more tips on keeping feeders safe from squirrels.

Cover the area beneath your feeders with bark chips or shredded bark mulch. When

Keep It Clean

Good housekeeping is essential when you use bird feeders. Inviting dozens (or hundreds) of birds to gather in such close quarters creates an unnatural situation where disease can spread like wildfire.

To make sure problems don't start at your feeders, keep your seed and nectar fresh. Damp or wet birdseed can sprout *Aspergillus* mold, which can infect birds when the fungus releases its spores into the air. As sick birds huddle at the feeders, their droppings contaminate the seed and spread the disease to other birds.

If seed gets wet, scoop it out of the feeders (I find a stiff, thin piece of hard plastic or a wide spatula works well) and dispose of it. Let the feeder dry before you refill it. If old seed accumulates beneath your feeders, rake it up or cover it with a 2-inch layer of wood chips to prevent problems.

Once a month, scrub all feeders with a 10:1 solution of water and bleach and rinse them well with clean water. Again, let the feeder dry before you put fresh seed in it.

shells reach the messy stage, turn over the mulch to hide them and add a new topping of mulch. Or keep the area bare and rake the shells periodically. This helps to cut down on disease, too, which may be lingering in contaminated seed or bird droppings.

BIRD FEEDING

Who benefits the most from feeding wild birds—the birds or us? I tend to think we get the best end of the deal. The pleasure of feeding birds is twofold: We enjoy feeling connected with wild creatures that otherwise would take no notice of us, and we get the daily wonders of a yard filled with feathered life.

Learning about the basic foods and the treats that bring wild birds flocking is an education all by itself. Knowing what to feed will help you fine-tune the offerings at your backyard bird café so that the guests you can expect will be provided for with little waste. Finding out what plants work the best for birds makes us better gardeners, too.

Knowing when to feed is vital for the birds who will quickly become regulars at your feeding station. Though it's not true that birds will wither away if you neglect to feed them, it is a fact that birds go to their accustomed places to find food first. If the cupboard is bare they will soon head off to seek sustenance elsewhere. So at critical times—during the winter and nesting season—you'll want to make sure you're keeping up with your feeders.

You'll attract more birds, and more variety of birds, if you combine plants with feeders. Bird feeders are the quickest way to draw a crowd to your yard, but bird-favored plants will attract a different clientele—the

Depending on the size, shape, and strength of their beaks, birds can shell sunflower seeds, scissor between scales of a pinecone, chisel into wood after a grub, or snap tiny gnats out of the air.

insect eaters and the fruit lovers who aren't tempted by even the fanciest birdseed.

What Birds Eat

If everybody in your neighborhood ate mostly vegetarian dishes, you wouldn't get many customers if you opened a steak house. It works the same way with birds: If you want a yard brimming with bird life, you need to figure out what birds like to eat.

You'll want to supply food for the three main categories of birds: seed eaters, insect eaters, and berry eaters. Though the categories often overlap (seed-eating evening grosbeaks, for instance, also like insects, berries, and fruit), it's easier to keep the customers satisfied if you know what their primary foods are.

Beaks Tell the Story

The big clue to a bird's eating habits is its beak. The beaks, or bills as they're also called, of various species are as different as night and day. Some bird beaks are smaller than your thumbnail, whereas others are as long as your arm.

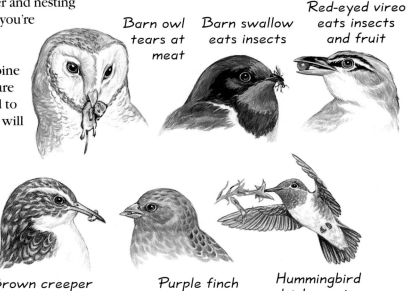

Barn owl tears at meat

Barn swallow eats insects

Red-eyed vireo eats insects and fruit

Brown creeper probes for grubs

Purple finch eats seeds

Hummingbird drinks nectar

◆ Birds, like finches, sparrows, and cardinals, that eat seeds and nuts have short, strong-looking, usually conical beaks.

◆ Sparrows, buntings, and other birds that eat small seeds, like grass and weed seeds, have small beaks.

◆ Birds, such as grosbeaks and cardinals, that seek out large seeds of maples, spruces, and pines have bigger, more powerful beaks than other seed-eating birds.

◆ Insect and fruit eaters such as vireos, orioles, and tanagers have slimmer and relatively longer beaks than seed eaters.

◆ Hummingbird beaks are long and narrow, like drinking straws, ready to suck up nectar from even the deepest flower.

◆ Birds like swallows and swifts that eat only insects have puny beaks. However, these birds often can open their mouths wide, which helps them scoop up bugs on the wing.

◆ Fish eaters, like herons, have extremely long, pointed bills.

◆ Birds, such as spoonbills and ducks, that seine the water have beaks shaped like wide, flat spoons so they can strain out the small fish, crustaceans, aquatic insects, and tiny plants and animals that they prefer.

◆ Meat eaters, such as hawks and owls, have strong, sharply curved beaks that work as well as a steak knife at carving up dinner.

Where Birds Eat

Now that you know what your backyard birds like to eat, you're halfway there. The other part of the picture is figuring out where birds prefer to dine. To do so, think of your yard as a three-story café:

The top floor is trees. It's for birds of the treetops, who spend most of their life in the leafy canopy over our heads. Their nests are usually high in trees, and they're usually insect eaters, filling their bellies with the caterpillars and insects they glean from the foliage. Tanagers, orioles, vireos, warblers, cuckoos, and grosbeaks are top-floor diners.

The middle story of your backyard café is shrubs, tall grasses, and flowers. It's for birds like cardinals, catbirds, thrashers, wrens, sparrows, and some warblers that like cover that's not too high off the ground.

The ground-level area is your lawn and garden beds. That's the dining area for birds that prefer to pull worms or grubs, scratch in the leaves for insects, or pick up seeds. Robins and grackles on the lawn are ground-level birds in action. So are the blackbirds, thrushes, sparrows, juncos, quail, pheasants, and towhees that you may have noticed hanging out below your feeders, in your meadow garden, or beneath your shrubs.

Create a bird-friendly yard. Your bird-feeding goal is to fill all three stories of your backyard café with treats for the birds. So plant trees—even when the trees are young, they'll attract the insects that birds enjoy. And it won't be long before they're producing nuts and seeds, too.

To make the birds of the brush feel at home, plant a variety of shrubs to re-create a natural hedgerow and let some areas of grass or annual flowers grow thick and undisturbed. Sparrows and other ground feeders will do fine on your lawn, in a meadow garden, or under shrub plantings in a shady garden.

Bird-Feeding Stations

Of course, there's more to bird feeding than what you plant in your garden. Some of the real fun and excitement of bird feeding is buying and making feeders for birds. To learn the details of the kinds of bird feeders available, see Bird Feeders on page 23, and to learn

In a yard designed for bird feeding, tree-dwelling birds search for insects in shade trees. Other birds flit through shrubs or annual flowers, eating berries, seeds, and insects. Ground dwellers find seeds, grubs, and earthworms in the lawn and leaf litter. A range of feeders offers birds lots of special treats, and a well-placed birdbath supplies water for drinking and bathing.

about what to fill your feeders with, check Birdseed on page 46.

Filling a feeder with seeds is just the start of the tasty treats you can offer to your backyard birds. If hummingbirds are your pleasure, you'll want to add nectar feeders. Try the fun stuff too: suet feeders for the many birds who never heard of a low-fat diet, plus fresh or dried fruit like oranges and raisins, and nutritious nuts, homemade or store-bought baked goods, molded bird treats, and peanut butter, as popular with birds as it is with kids.

It's a good idea to plan the arrangement of your bird feeders as carefully as you plan out a garden. By using a variety of feeders and placing them in the optimum locations, you can enjoy a much wider range of bird visitors. It's also important to stock and maintain feeding stations all year-round, but especially in winter. Birds really depend on your feeders in winter, when natural food sources like insects and berries are scarce or nonexistent. Once you start feeding birds, they'll make your yard a regular stop on their daily rounds. Take this commitment seriously: If your feeders sit empty in bad weather, birds may have a hard time until they find other food sources.

Keep feeders close to the house. The biggest mistake most people make is putting their bird feeders too far away from their house. The closer your feeder, the better you can see the birds, and the more pleasure you'll get out of feeding them.

Figure out which window you look out of most often, and place your feeding station there. I like to have feeders in easy view of all my favorite windows, so my feeding station is actually several places around the yard. The main batch of feeders is just off the front porch. On cold days I can stand at the door of the living room and watch the birds just 3 feet away; in milder weather I can sit on the porch and be right in the middle of the action. If you linger at your kitchen table over coffee and conversation, put a few feeders in easy view of that window, or even on the windowsill, where the birds can share breakfast time.

Mount at least one of your feeders as close to the window as you can. A few feet makes a huge difference when it comes to viewing birds. If your feeder is about 6 feet from the window, you'll have a close-up view of each

Suet Suggestions

Ask your butcher to run your suet (or beef fat) through a meat grinder. It will come out looking like hamburger, in tiny pieces that are just the size for smaller birds like juncos, wrens, bluebirds, and native sparrows that wouldn't ordinarily visit a traditional wire-cage suet feeder.

If you buy your suet in whole chunks, you can chop it yourself by hand or by blender. To chop by hand, slice the fat into half-inch-thick ribbons and freeze on a waxed paper–lined cookie sheet until it's stiff, then chop with a sharp knife. Or you can freeze fat or suet in chunks about the size of your fist, then grind the frozen chunks, one by one, in your blender. Experiment with settings and times until you find the one that works best. You'll end up with tiny crumbs of fat when you blenderize; scatter them in your tray feeder or on the ground for small birds to enjoy.

individual bird and you can easily see how they interact with each other. If your feeder is farther away, you'll miss out on a lot of the subtleties of bird behavior. When I had my feeders some distance from my window, I could see that the male cardinal was flying back and forth from the shrubs in my yard to the feeder where his mate was busily cracking sunflower seeds. He was obviously collecting tidbits for an offering to the female. But it wasn't until I moved the feeder closer that I discovered Mr. Redbird was feeding the missus the yummy caterpillars of my favorite spicebush swallowtail butterflies!

Don't stop at birdseed. Expanding the menu will bring beautiful birds to your backyard who might otherwise not visit. A nectar feeder will draw hummingbirds from your garden flowers to easy viewing range, and may attract orioles, too. Orioles may also come for oranges, and mockingbirds, thrushes, thrashers, bluebirds, and Carolina wrens will give your place the once-over when you add fruit to the selections.

Homemade treats like doughnuts and muffins (see recipe on page 35) and molded birdseed combinations will get the seal of approval from chickadees, titmice, jays, and many other birds, plus give you hours of enjoyment watching their antics as they work at getting just a bite from your offerings. Once you know the basics of bird foods, you can use your imagination to come up with new foods that suit your neighborhood birds. You'll start looking at your pantry and your refrigerator with a whole new perspective when you begin looking at foods through birds' eyes. Suddenly the last few inches of whole-grain breakfast cereal or the loose grapes in the bottom of your fruit bin take on new value as you consider them for taste tests at the feeder.

For more about these menu items, turn to Birdseed, Bread, Doughnuts, Fruit for Birds, Nuts and Nut Trees, Peanuts and Peanut Butter, and Suet. Dog Food will tell you more about what you can expect if you offer this soft food. Christmas for the Birds has more ideas for tempting, out-of-the-ordinary bird foods.

Add a dash of salt. A backyard salt block will draw birds and other wildlife to visit. House finches, indigo buntings, and native sparrows often visit the big white block in our backyard. So do common city pigeons (also called rock doves) and mourning doves.

You can buy a heavy block of salt at feed stores for a few dollars. The only problem with putting out a salt block is that rain dissolves the salt, leaching it into the soil, which can kill plants and damage the soil. It's easy to make a salt feeder for birds and other wildlife like the one shown in the illustration below.

Feed birds when they need it. Just like you and me, birds are hungry when they roll out of bed (or off the perch, as the case may be). That's why early morning is the best time for birding, whether you watch out a window or

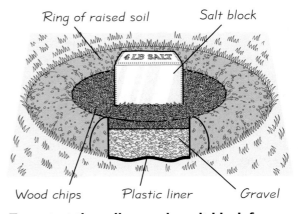

Ring of raised soil — Salt block — 4 LB SALT — Wood chips — Plastic liner — Gravel

To protect the soil around a salt block for birds, make a raised ring of soil, and spread heavy-duty plastic over the interior and the ring. Spread 4 inches of gravel on the plastic and top it with 2 inches of wood chips.

stroll your backyard with binoculars. Feeder traffic is brisk and there's a lot of activity in the trees, shrubs, and lawn areas of the backyard.

Birds may snack off and on all day long, but they come out to eat seriously again in the afternoon, to fuel their bodies for the coming night.

In winter the scene changes. Cold temperatures mean that birds have to eat much more to keep their body heat stable. In cold weather nearly all day is devoted to finding food. Many feeder watchers have noticed that birds can "predict" snowstorms. Before a blizzard hits, feeder traffic is intense.

Feeders are more than a pleasure to birds: In winter, they can be a matter of life and death. Though I admit I'm sometimes a little lax about filling feeders on a summer morning, in winter I couldn't possibly enjoy my breakfast with a clear conscience if I hadn't filled the feeders first. Before I start my own pot of coffee, I pull on a jacket, slip into boots, and step outside into the chill morning air to take care of my feathered friends.

Feeder traffic drops off dramatically in late spring, as migration ends and insects fill the stomachs of backyard birds. In winter I refill the feeders at least twice a day; in summer, once every two weeks may be enough (except for the nectar feeders).

Interestingly, while seed feeders are spurned, suet feeders have more customers than usual in late spring and summer. That's because this soft food is ideal for feeding nestlings. I never had much luck finding the cavity nests of tufted titmice and chickadees until I noticed that adult birds were visiting the suet feeders for take-out service. When I used my binoculars to follow a chickadee with a beakful of suet, I saw the bird fly to a small hole in a dead branch only a few feet off the ground. When I sat unobtrusively nearby

later in the day, I heard the unmistakable cheeps of nestlings.

I always look forward to the day when the parents bring the just-out-of-the-nest youngsters to the suet feeder. Nothing like seeing a lineup of fuzzy-headed baby chickadees to start your day!

Eating Like a Bird

The metabolism of a bird is something I can only envy—if I could burn calories as fast as they do, I'd be a fashion model in no time. Smaller birds have an especially high metabolic rate. Their bodies zip along at an internal temperature around 20 percent higher than ours, and they're often constantly in motion.

When someone claims she eats like a bird, she usually means she's a light eater. But in fact birds have to eat huge amounts to maintain their activity. Here's a comparison: Multiply your weight by 4. The result is the number of hamburgers you'd have to eat *per day* in order to truly imitate the eating habits of some species of birds.

Observations of caged birds show that food intake varies greatly from bird to bird. Some small to medium-size songbirds consume the equivalent of 80 to 100 percent of their body weight every day; for others the amount is as little as 30 percent. The bigger the bird, the less food it needs to take in; a pigeon's daily diet equals about 6 percent of its body weight.

EASY BIRD TREAT MINI-MUFFINS

Geraldine Hoehn of New Harmony, Indiana, is an experienced and imaginative cook, having raised 13 kids over the years. She dreamed up these nutritious high-fat and fruity mini-muffins as a winter feeder treat. She likes to put them on tray feeders close to her window so she can watch chickadees, mockingbirds, blue jays, and other friends enjoy her home cooking. This recipe makes about 2 dozen muffins.

⅔   cup all-purpose flour

1⅓ cups whole-wheat, buckwheat, or other whole-grain flour

2   teaspoons baking powder

1   cup sunflower seeds, raw

½   cup finely chopped raisins

½   cup finely chopped dried cherries

½   cup chopped unsalted peanuts

¼   cup finely chopped or riced dried apricots

½   cup chopped apples

6   slices bacon, cooked and crumbled

1   egg, beaten

2   tablespoons honey, molasses, or dark corn syrup

1   cup milk

3   teaspoons melted butter

1. Grease a 2-inch muffin pan.

2. Combine the flour, baking powder, sunflower seeds, raisins, dried cherries, peanuts, dried apricots, apples, and bacon.

3. In a separate bowl, beat together the egg, honey, milk, and melted butter.

4. Pour the liquid mix into the dry ingredients and stir to combine.

5. Spoon the batter into the muffin pan, filling each muffin cup two-thirds full.

6. Bake at 400°F for 20 to 25 minutes.

7. After the muffins cool, stick them on a spiked feeder, or serve whole in a tray feeder or on the ground.

BIRDHOUSES

Once you start feeding backyard birds, the next natural step is to put up a few bird-houses. Whether you buy birdhouses or build your own, you're sure to feel proud and excited when a pair of birds sets up house-keeping in your yard.

Who's the New Neighbor?

Birdhouses attract a wide variety of birds, but not all birds. Birds that use birdhouses are cavity nesters, such as bluebirds and woodpeckers. Birds like tanagers, which plaster their nest to tree limbs, or catbirds, which hide their nest in a thicket, won't be interested in your nest boxes. Neither will ground-nesting birds like thrushes, native sparrows, and towhees.

That still leaves plenty of possible bird-house tenants, from wrens to woodpeckers to owls. These are birds that chisel their own home in a dead tree limb, wooden fence post, or utility pole, or use a hole created by natural causes. Still others are birds that adopt an old woodpecker home. Robins, phoebes, and barn swallows won't nest in a closed box, but they will build a nest on a roofed shelf like the one shown on this page or in a nesting box that has one or two sides left open.

Helping Out with the Housing Shortage

Putting out birdhouses is fun for humans, but it's also very important for birds. Many cavity-nesting birds have trouble finding nesting sites these days, because wooden fence posts are outdated, replaced by metal posts. Also farmers tend to remove hedgerows between fields, meaning fewer dead trees. Putting up birdhouses in your backyard sounds like a small gesture, but it's a matter of survival for cavity-nesting birds in your neighborhood.

Adding Birdhouses to Your Yard

The best time to put up birdhouses is in late winter. Most cavity nesters are early birds when it comes to nesting. They begin house hunting as early as January or February, and most woodpeckers, chickadees, titmice, and bluebirds are sitting on their first batch of eggs by March or April.

Male house wrens, who arrive before the females in spring migration, try to make up for lost time by constructing nests that only need the stamp of approval from the female when she finally shows up on the scene (unfortunately, their efforts are often in vain—female wrens like to have the home decorating done their way).

Don't fret if you've missed the time of first nesting. Mount your bird boxes whenever you

A nesting shelf is an easy make-it-yourself project, and robins love to nest in them. You can also buy premade nesting shelves for a reasonable price.

make them (or buy them). Birds continue nesting through June, either raising second broods or replacing a failed first nesting, so a new house may still get tenants even if you put it up in May. Get a birdhouse for Christmas? Put it on a tree instead of on a shelf in your living room: Birds may use it to stay warm on wintry nights.

Choosing birdhouses. Select a birdhouse to fit the bird's needs. Plain, unpainted wood is very appealing to birds, because it looks like the real thing: a hole in a tree. But gussied-up houses are fine, too, though they take a little longer to attract tenants. Nesting holes are usually in such high demand that any kind of structure will soon have a taker.

Two or three basic sizes of birdhouse will suit the needs of most backyard birds. The diameter of the entrance hole, not the size of the box, is the main factor that determines which birds will use the birdhouse. A box with a large hole will work for a variety of birds; houses with small holes will allow only small birds access. A small entrance hole will keep out certain birds that you may not want to encourage, as shown in the illustration below. House sparrows, for example, will nest in a box with a 1½-inch entrance hole, but a 1¼-inch-wide hole will keep them out. Starlings need an opening at least 2 inches across.

Whether you go plain or fancy, make sure the birdhouse is well constructed. Joints should fit snugly, with no gaps for rain or wind to enter. A hinged side makes clean-up a snap. The roof should overhang the entrance hole, so that rain doesn't drip in on the vulnerable babies. Flimsy houses made of thin, cheap materials may crack or split under outdoor conditions, which could be fatal to any birds inside.

Mounting birdhouses. Mount your houses on a pole or tree by driving stout nails into the back board. I mount houses with the entrance hole facing east, so that cold north winds and driving rain, which usually come from the west in my area, don't blow directly into the box. An east-facing entrance collects the warm

Screech owl — 3"

Red-headed woodpecker — 2"

Chickadee — 1⅛"

Wren — ⅞" × 2½"

The size of the entrance hole is a critical feature of a birdhouse. Large birds like owls and red-headed woodpeckers can't fit into a box with a small entrance, whereas tiny wrens can squeeze through a narrow slit.

morning sun, too, but not the strong glare of southern exposure. Make sure the house is secure and can't be tipped by strong wind or climbing cats. If you mount it on a post, a predator guard is a good investment. Check bird-supply stores or the advertisements in the back of birding magazines for a metal or plastic baffle that fits over the pole below the house like an inverted funnel, blocking access from any wild things with designs on the inhabitants.

You can keep your birdhouses up all year long, to accommodate any wild friends seeking shelter, whether they're roosting birds, hibernating bats, shelter-seeking mice, or woolly bear caterpillars. If your house is a work of art, you may want to take it down in early fall and store it out of the weather to prevent damage.

It's not necessary to clean houses at the end of the season—cavity-nesting birds have gotten along just fine in the wild world without our tidying up after them—but I like to do it anyway. It's a chance to see how the nest was actually made. If a nesting fails because of raccoons or other predators destroying the nest or young, the parent birds are unlikely to ever use the box again. I take down the box, clean it thoroughly, swab it out with a 10 percent bleach solution, let it sun-dry, then mount it in a new location.

Building Birdhouses

I'm not too talented in the hammer-and-nails department, so I was a little leery about trying to build my own birdhouses. But when we moved to an old farmhouse that had not a single birdhouse in the yard, I knew I had to take action.

So I bought a small electric jigsaw and drill, a box of nails, a shiny new hammer, and two half-sheets of outdoor plywood. Following

The Wild World of Backyard Birds

One spring while I was hunting for patio slate at an old quarry site, I found a slab of slate that had a perfectly round 2-inch hole bored into it, probably from blasting.

I brought the slate home and leaned it against a cherry sapling in my garden as a decorative touch. But the very next day I noticed a parade of puzzled birds investigating the slate. Chickadees, house wrens, nuthatches, bluebirds, and downy woodpeckers would stick their heads through the hole, then wriggle through and seem mighty surprised to find themselves on the ground in the garden. They thought they'd found an entrance hole to a great nesting site, and just couldn't figure out why the hole led to nowhere. After a few days I had to move the slate indoors to end their frustration.

the diagrams and dimensions for a flicker box, I built my first birdhouse. It was a shaky effort (even hammering nails is an acquired skill, I learned), but I felt pretty proud of myself as I climbed a ladder to mount the box at the recommended height.

I felt even prouder an hour later, when a great crested flycatcher arrived to claim the new house. Within a week I had 10 new birdhouses scattered about the yard, and tenants in every one of them. The birds didn't care whether my nails were straight or my roofs crooked: As long as the houses were sturdy and securely mounted, they were quickly adopted.

Birdhouse basics. A simple wooden box will suit most birds. It's easy to make a box like this, as you'll see if you follow my directions in "A Size-to-Fit Birdhouse" on page 41. If you don't have a workshop stocked with tools, take heart: I don't either. In fact I usually ask the attendant at my local home-building supply to cut the wood I buy to the dimensions I need. The fee is quite reasonable, usually 25 to 50 cents per cut. It's also easier to tote the precut lumber home rather than fastening a long board or plywood sheet to the top of your car.

I plan out the cuts needed on paper, aiming for a minimum of waste. You can see one cutting configuration for the pieces of a basic birdhouse in the illustration below.

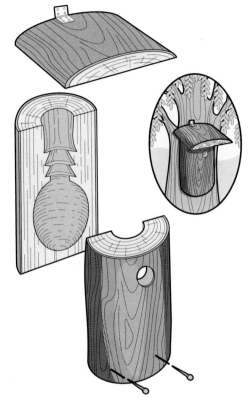

You can make a birdhouse from a natural section of dead tree limb. Saw the limb in half lengthwise, then in each half chisel out a cavity with hand tools. Then nail the halves back together and mount the branch as if it were part of a tree.

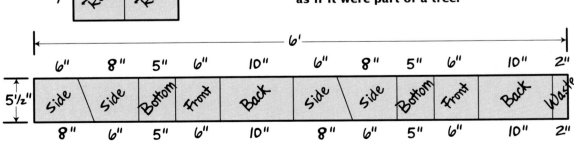

Drawing a simple cutting plan for the parts of a birdhouse is helpful whether you plan to cut wood yourself or have someone else cut it. A 6-foot-length of 1 × 6 plywood plus two pieces of 1 × 8 supply all the pieces for two medium-size birdhouses.

Special touches. There are two finishing touches I add to make my nest boxes more like the real thing. First, I put a few handfuls of soft shavings from a sack of hamster bedding in the bottom of the box to imitate the natural wood shavings that would result from a bird chiseling out a cavity in a dead tree. I also add a 4-inch length of 2-inch black rubber tubing extending from the entrance hole. This mimics the long natural entry into a cavity in a dead tree, and prevents raccoons from reaching into the box to grab eggs or baby birds.

A BIRDHOUSE FOR EVERY BIRD

A basic wooden birdhouse offers the essentials for just about any type of nesting bird from bluebirds to owls. All you need to do is make houses of the right size for the birds you're interested in hosting. Chickadees need a small house, for example, while bluebirds need a medium-size house, and barn owls need the jumbo version. Be sure you make the entrance hole the right diameter for the birds of your choice. For building instructions for a basic birdhouse, see "A Size-to-Fit Birdhouse" on the opposite page.

SIZE OF BIRDHOUSE	FLOOR DIMENSIONS	DEPTH	DISTANCE BETWEEN ROOF AND ENTRANCE HOLE	MOUNTING HEIGHT	ENTRANCE HOLE SIZE
Small	4" × 4"	6" to 8"	2"	6' to 15'	For chickadees—1⅛"; for downy woodpeckers, titmice, nuthatches, house wrens, Bewick's wrens—1¼"; for Carolina wrens—1½"
Medium	5" × 5"	6" to 8"	2"	5' to 10'	For bluebirds, tree swallows, violet-green swallows, prothonotary warblers—1½"
Large	6" × 6"	10" to 12"	2"	10' to 20'	For hairy woodpeckers—1½"; for great crested flycatchers, red-bellied woodpeckers, red-headed woodpeckers, golden-fronted woodpeckers—2"; for flickers, saw-whet owls—2½"
Extra-large	8" × 8"	12" to 15"	3"	10' to 30'	For American kestrels, screech owls—3"
Jumbo	10" × 18"	18"	4"	10' to 20'	For wood ducks—4"; for barn owls—6"

A SIZE-TO-FIT BIRDHOUSE

It doesn't take special woodworking skills to make a birdhouse. As long as you know how to use a hammer and a small electric drill, you're set! This plan works whether you're making a small birdhouse or a jumbo model.

1 × 6 or 1 × 10 knot-free pine boards (depending on the size birdhouse you want to make)

Nails

Screws

Metal hinge

1. Measure and mark lumber for cutting. (Consult "A Birdhouse for Every Bird" on the opposite page for dimensions.) NOTE: If you opt to have a building-supply store cut the lumber for you, go to Step 3.

2. Cut out the six pieces of the birdhouse—two sides, front, back, roof, and bottom.

3. Mark the entrance hole on the front piece, clamp the piece securely to a worktable, and drill out the opening using a drill bit of the appropriate size.

4. Using a ½-inch drill bit, drill four drainage holes in the bottom piece.

5. Also drill two holes at the base of the back piece (you'll use these for screws to attach the house to a post or other fixture).

6. Using one nail on each side, attach the side pieces to the bottom piece.

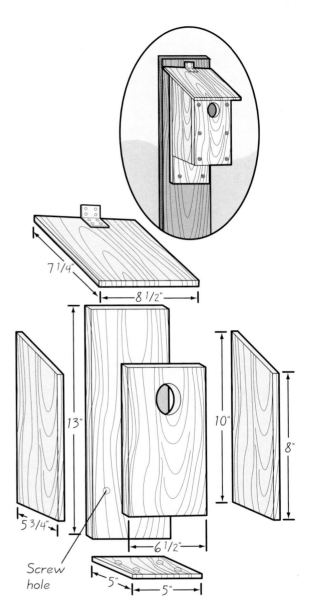

7. Nail the front to the bottom.

8. Nail the front to the sides.

9. Nail back in place.

10. Mount birdhouse on post. Use the metal hinge to attach the roof to the post.

BIRDING

Believe it or not, birding is a multibillion-dollar industry. Whether you're a backyard birdwatcher or a passionate birder who travels far and wide to spot new birds, you're supporting a diverse range of businesses. The birdhouses and feeders you buy support cottage industries, like the one in the Ozarks that makes my favorite eastern red cedar feeders. Steady sales of sunflower seeds support farmers in the Dakotas. The birding trips you take to see hawks on migration or cranes at gathering places or hummingbirds in southwestern deserts keep motels and restaurants in business. Birdwatching is an easy and enjoyable hobby to start, and it has great rewards for you and for birds! You may find that a wonderful lifetime of learning starts with a simple feeder at your kitchen window.

Backyard Birding

A bird field guide and a large wall calendar are the basic pieces of equipment you need to start watching birds in your backyard. The field guide's important for identifying birds, and the wall calendar's a handy place for jotting notes about the birds you spy at your feeders and in your garden. Some birders keep a lifelong list of the birds they've seen, and they'll chase a new species across half the continent. I'm more of a Margaret Morse Nice kind of birder: Instead of traveling, Ms. Nice decided to study one species in detail. She gained an intimate knowledge of the song sparrows in her backyard, eventually writing a two-volume set on the birds that authorities still rely on. You may never decide to publish your notes on your birding observations, but you'll find it fun and educational to compare notes of your sightings from one season and one year to another.

The Wild World of Backyard Birds

I used to live in the shadow of Hawk Mountain, a prime spot on the raptor migration route. I was a frequent visitor there, and I met my share of "serious" birders. At first I was a little intimidated in their company, but I soon found out that they enjoyed my firsthand observations of backyard birds just as much as the wildest tales of rare and exotic birds.

One afternoon on the hawk lookout, I told an older gentleman how the Baltimore orioles in my yard untied strings that I had knotted around branches. He was delighted to hear that the birds had mastered double knots, but a triple knot had them stumped. Later I found out that he had been one of the leading birders in the country, with many articles in scientific journals to his credit. Birders may come from every social stratum but they all have two things in common: They love birds and have a keen curiosity.

Some birders never travel any farther afield than their backyards, but most discover that birding becomes a passion to pursue wherever they travel. I keep a pair of binoculars with me in the car just in case. One day I happened across ducks dabbling in a shallow puddle among the stubble of a flooded cornfield. Figuring they were common mallards, I lifted the glasses to admire their green heads. Only then did I discover I was looking at a flock of vivid green-winged teals, a rare sighting for me.

Having binoculars will add enjoyment to birding both in your backyard and on field trips. If you don't already have a pair, you'll probably want to invest in some. You'll find information on types of binoculars and tips on what to buy in Binoculars on page 16. To learn how to identify birds, turn to Identifying Birds on page 143.

Finding Fellow Birders

Fellow birders are easy to shake out of the bushes. Start by getting in touch with your local branch of the National Audubon Society. Call a local nature center, sanctuary, state park, or the sports editor at the newspaper for the name and phone number of the local branch leader. You'll be invited to take part in bird counts, which you can learn about in Bird Counts on page 22, and other fun activities.

You'll bump into birdwatchers at birding hotspots, from the local reservoir to a national park. If you see somebody wearing binoculars, stop and chat. Rewarding friendships often start with the simple question, "See anything good?" If you're interested in traveling to watch birds, check out Birding Hotspots on page 44.

Use a wall calendar to keep track of the birds you see in your backyard and local travels. It's quick and practically effortless, and it's easy to pull out your old calendars to compare activity from year to year.

BIRDING HOTSPOTS

With plenty of food, shelter, and water at the ready, your backyard is sure to become a hotspot for birds in your neighborhood. Compared with the typical backyard, which may host a robin or two, a couple of doves, a blue jay, and some house sparrows, a bird haven like the one you're creating will become a great place for backyard birding. Some dedicated backyard birders have seen hundreds of species of birds in their yards over the years.

When you're ready to branch out farther afield, you can visit other hotspots across the country that draw incredible quantities and varieties of birds. The acres of wild land in national wildlife refuges and sanctuaries are prime habitat for all kinds of birds. Add the attraction of large bodies of water—lakes, rivers, or even the ocean—and birding at these hotspots becomes an event worth building a vacation around.

Famous Hotspots

The map on the opposite page shows some of the prime bird hotspots in North America. Your local branch of the National Audubon Society or Nature Conservancy can guide you to others within driving distance of your home.

A day of birdwatching at any of these nationally renowned hotspots will be the trip of a lifetime. The best times to visit vary, but spring and fall migration times are the most spectacular at many of these hotspots.

Here are some highlights of what you'll see at various refuges.

Birds of prey. To see bald eagles, head to North Cascades National Park, Washington, where the eagles hunt salmon after they've spawned in the park's rivers. You'll also spot hawks and sea ducks like Barrow's goldeneyes.

Other great hotspots for raptors include Upper Klamath Lake, Oregon; Redwood National Park, California; Grand Teton National Park, Wyoming; Cape May, New Jersey; Hawk Mountain Sanctuary, Pennsylvania (near Kempton); and Apostle Islands National Lakeshore, Wisconsin (near Ashland).

Desert birds. Head to Saguaro National Monument, Arizona (near Tucson), where you'll see cactus wrens, curve-billed thrashers, Gambel's quail, Mexican jays and yellow-eyed juncos, Steller's jays, and terrific wildflowers in April.

Hummingbirds. To see hummingbirds galore, head to the Chiricahua Mountains in Arizona, near Willcox. Also check Brownsville, Texas, where you'll see many Mexican species of birds.

Puffins. Redwood National Park in California is the place to see puffins and over 300 other species of birds.

Roadrunners. Try Big Thicket National Preserve in Texas, near Houston, where you'll also see bluebirds, cuckoos, waterthrushes, hooded warblers, and possibly the endangered red-cockaded woodpecker.

Sandhill cranes. The home of these beautiful cranes in fall and winter is in Kearney, Nebraska, where they're a spectacular sight in the air and on the ground.

Songbirds. There are several wonderful places to witness the spring and fall songbird migrations, including Point Pelee National Park, Ontario, Canada; Acadia National Park, Maine; Cape May, New Jersey; Presque Isle State Park, Pennsylvania; Mammoth Cave National Park, Kentucky; and Apostle Islands National Lakeshore, Wisconsin (near Ashland).

Trumpeter swans. These gorgeous birds breed at the Malheur National Wildlife Refuge in Oregon, where you'll also spot sandhill cranes and white pelicans. You can also see them at Grand Teton National Park in Wyoming.

Waterbirds and sea birds. There are many hotspots for waterbirds, including Upper Klamath Lake, Oregon; the Pacific Coast at San Diego, Monterey Bay, Tule Lake, and Mono Lake in California; Acadia National Park, Maine; Fire Island National Seashore, New York; Sanibel Island and Everglades National Park, Florida; and Long Lake National Wildlife Refuge in North Dakota.

Whooping cranes. Whooping cranes are at home in Aransas National Wildlife Refuge in Texas from late October through early April; also look for roseate spoonbills, white-faced ibises, white pelicans, and sandhill cranes. You can also see whooping cranes during migration at Long Lake National Wildlife Refuge in North Dakota.

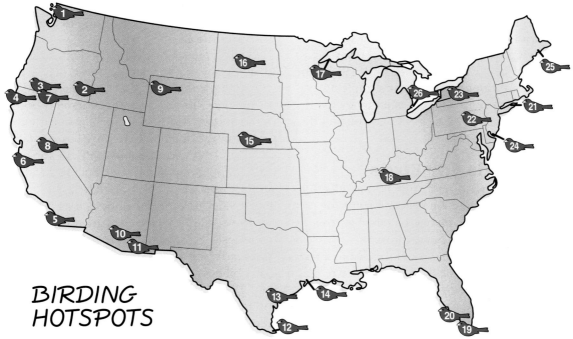

BIRDING HOTSPOTS

1. North Cascades National Park, WA
2. Malheur National Wildlife Refuge, OR (near Burns)
3. Upper Klamath Lake, OR (near Klamath Falls)
4. Redwood National Park, CA (near Orick)
5. coast at San Diego, CA
6. Monterey Bay, CA
7. Tule Lake, CA
8. Mono Lake, CA (near Lee Vining)
9. Grand Teton National Park, WY
10. Saguaro National Monument, AZ (near Tucson)
11. Chiricahua Mountains, AZ (near Willcox)
12. Brownsville, TX
13. Aransas National Wildlife Refuge, TX
14. Big Thicket National Preserve, TX
15. Kearney, NE
16. Long Lake National Wildlife Refuge, ND
17. Apostle Islands National Lakeshore, WI (near Ashland)
18. Mammoth Cave National Park, KY
19. Everglades National Park, FL
20. Sanibel Island, FL
21. Fire Island National Seashore, NY
22. Hawk Mountain Sanctuary, PA (near Kempton)
23. Presque Isle State Park, PA
24. Cape May, NJ
25. Acadia National Park, ME (near Bar Harbor)
26. Point Pelee National Park, Ontario, Canada

BIRDSEED

If you live in a neighborhood full of people who like to feed birds, knowing a few birdseed secrets will make your bird feeders the busiest on the block. Sunflowers and small millet seed are the basic seeds for bird feeders, but it's the little treat seeds that can draw those extra-special birds. If cardinals have been spurning your place in favor of the feeder up the street, you can tempt them with safflower seed; if you love goldfinches, you can add a tube feeder brimming with niger, their number-one favorite.

Buying wisely—good quality seed at a reasonable price—will make your birdseed dollar go further. Proper storage means you'll always have a ready supply of seed, even when a sudden blizzard or ice storm takes you and the birds by surprise.

Best Seeds for Birds

Bird supply stores offer a stupendous selection of seed mixes. There are special blends for finches or cardinals, mixes that are supposed to be "no waste," and many more.

For simplicity's sake—and to stick to a reasonable budget—I usually depend on two seeds to fill my feeders: black oil sunflower and white millet. Cardinals, blue jays, chickadees, titmice, nuthatches, and some woodpeckers love the sunflower seeds, and just about everything else eats the millet.

When you're feeding a crowd, you want seed that appeals to a lot of different birds. Sunflower and millet will do the trick for nearly all areas of the country. They're nutritious and evidently they taste pretty good, too.

But do I stop there? Of course not. What fun would feeding birds be if you didn't put out some treats? I supplement my basic menu with niger seed (often incorrectly called thistle seed), peanut pieces and other nuts, canary seed, flaxseed, safflower seed, and homemade molded treats. I figure birds appreciate a little variety in their diet as much as I do in mine. Here's a rundown of the best seeds for backyard bird feeding.

Sunflower seed. Sunflower seeds come in two varieties, black oil and striped, plus a hulled, shell-less version that offers waste-free feeding. Striped sunflower seed is bigger and plumper, with larger meats inside the shells. Black oil sunflower is smaller and flatter, but just as nutritious.

I fill my feeders with black oil sunflower seeds for two simple reasons: They cost less than striped sunflower seeds, and more birds eat them. There's no difference in palatability between the two seeds—taste them yourself and you'll see. The difference is in their size. Birds with large beaks, like cardinals and jays, can easily crack a striped sunflower seed. But birds with smaller beaks, like chickadees, have a harder time, so they'll head for the black oil seeds.

Hulled sunflower seed is great if you want to eliminate waste and keep the area beneath your feeders tidy. With no shells to crack, every bit gets eaten. The downside to this seed is that mobs of starlings, house finches, and house sparrows may descend on your feeders and empty them faster than you can say "Shoo!"

Niger. Niger is the tiny, skinny black seed of the niger plant (*Guizotica abyssinica*), a golden-flowered sunflower relative. Add it to your feeder menu and you're likely to attract every finch in your area, from goldfinches to purple finches to hordes of house finches. Offer your niger in a tube feeder, and watch for ground-feeding birds to pick up any leftovers that fall to the ground. You may see song sparrows, chipping sparrows, and other native sparrows, pine siskins, towhees, juncos, and mourning doves arriving to nibble the niger. To learn more, turn to Niger on page 179.

Millet. Millet is a small, shiny, roundish golden tan or reddish brown seed. Small seed eaters like buntings, juncos, sparrows, finches, goldfinches, plus larger towhees, doves, starlings, and blackbirds all welcome a meal of millet. Carolina wrens may also drop in to sample the fare. For more details, see Millet on page 167.

Safflower seed. Safflower seeds are white, pointed, plump seeds of a farm plant raised for oil production. The flowers that produce the seeds are an eye-catching bright orange, and often turn up in dried arrangements. They're easy to grow as annuals in a sunny garden.

If you love cardinals, you'll want to add safflower to your shopping list. Once the word gets out, you may find the number of cardinals at your diner increases daily, as long as you continue the handouts of oil-rich seeds. Other birds with strong seed-cracking beaks, particularly grosbeaks, may occasionally nibble at the seeds.

Grass seed. Small, narrow, bleached-tan grass seed is a great favorite of small seed-eating birds. Native sparrows and juncos—the same birds that eat most grass seeds in the wild— are the main customers for grass seed at the feeder. You may not be able to find grass seed in the birdseed aisle of your local discount store, but step across a few aisles to the lawn and garden department and you'll find all the 50-pound sacks you can carry. Smaller bags are easier to transport and will work as an occasional treat. Just remember to stock up on grass seed at the end of summer, before lawncare products yield to Halloween candy and costumes. Be sure to check the label of the seed you're buying, and don't buy seed that's been chemically treated.

Flaxseed. Birds know what's good for them, and oil-rich seeds are always tops on the menu. Flax certainly fills the bill: The shiny brown, flat oval seeds are so high in oil, you can squeeze it out of them with a strong fingernail. This seed can be expensive, so dole it out during rainy weather, when birds need extra energy. Nesting season, when birds are running themselves ragged bearing food to the young, is another good time to offer flaxseed. Pine siskins, native sparrows, juncos, buntings, purple finches, house finches, goldfinches, and other finches are the main fans of flaxseed.

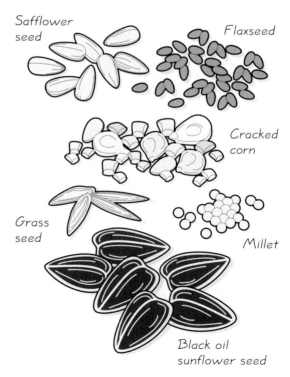

To attract the widest range of birds, select several kinds of seeds to suit different tastes and beak sizes.

Homegrown WISDOM

SAVE THOSE WEED SEEDS

Millet is one of the most popular seeds for the small birds that visit my feeders. But there's something they like even better: ragweed and lamb's-quarters seeds. When these weeds go to seed around my yard, the song sparrows, tree sparrows, juncos, and other small birds turn their back on the feeder in favor of these natural goodies.

My seasonal sniffles are bad enough, so I try to pull out allergy-inducing ragweed before it flowers. I'm less diligent about pulling nonallergenic lamb's-quarters, and now I make the most of the crop. I cut off almost-ripe seedheads and hang them in my garage to mature, then I save the seed clusters for winter feeding. The word spreads quickly among the dining patrons when I stock the feeder tray with tiny lamb's-quarters seed!

Cracked corn. In deep winter, when every cardinal for miles comes to dine, I lay in 100-pound sacks of cracked corn, which they love. Sometimes I play host to more than 70 cardinals at a time. I simply spread the corn generously on the ground. In spring I rake the remains of the corn pile into the flowerbeds, where it acts as a slow-release natural fertilizer. House sparrows, blackbirds, and starlings also favor the corn, which keeps them away from my other feeders.

Unusual seeds. Your feeder birds will also enjoy occasional treats of other seeds that you can find in bird supply stores or in the caged-bird department. You may also be able to find these seeds in bulk at local feed mills, or through garden seed suppliers.

Lettuce seed is tops with goldfinches and other finches, as well as indigo buntings and native sparrows. Shiny brown canary seed, which has made a pest of itself in some areas, is relished by the same crowd.

Rapeseed, grown for oil production and farm-animal feed, is appreciated by the same small seed-eating birds, as well as blackbirds. If your pet-supply store sells canary seed mixes, consider them like candy for finches and sparrows. Many of the seeds in parrot mixtures are welcomed by larger seed-cracking birds, like cardinals and grosbeaks (and the fruit pieces in such mixes are a treat, too).

Custom-Blended Birdseed

It's fun to mix up your own birdseed mixes, tailor-made to the birds in your garden. Here's a good general recipe that appeals to many kinds of birds. I use a coffee can as my measuring cup when I make this mix. Just combine:

◆ 10 scoops black oil sunflower seed
◆ 5 scoops millet
◆ 3 scoops cracked corn
◆ 2 scoops safflower seed
◆ 1 scoop flaxseed
◆ 1 scoop untreated grass seed

You can tinker with the proportions in this mix depending on your feeder clientele. When more cardinals show up at my feeder, I increase the safflower seed; if pine siskins arrive, I add niger to the mix too.

Once you get started playing around with birdseed, you'll probably enjoy making birdseed treats. For one recipe, see "Cookie Cutter Treats" on the opposite page.

COOKIE CUTTER TREATS

It's loads of fun to watch the way birds work at molded birdseed treats. Make them as decorative as you want them. You can either pour the mixture into cake pans and then crack it into pieces once it has hardened, or use cookie cutters as molds. I use star-shaped cookie cutters and decorate a sturdy bare-branched witch hazel with the star treats in wintertime.

6 cups millet, 1 cup flaxseed, and 1 cup black oil sunflower seed

or

4 cups chopped unsalted peanuts and 2 cups black oil sunflower seed

1 tablespoon butter

½ cup sorghum or molasses

¼ cup sugar

1. Spray cake pans or waxed paper (under molds) liberally with nonstick cooking spray.

2. Combine one of the seed mixes in a large bowl.

3. Melt the butter in a large saucepan; add the molasses and sugar.

4. Stir until the sugar is dissolved.

5. Bring to a boil; cover and cook for about 3 minutes without stirring.

6. Uncover and continue to boil without stirring until syrup reaches 290°F on a candy thermometer. IMMEDIATELY pour over the seed mix.

7. Stir the mixture with a strong, long-handled wooden spoon until syrup is distributed evenly.

8. Spoon birdseed mix into cake pans or cookie cutters.

9. Grease fingers and press very firmly into pans or molds until seed mixture is at least ½ inch thick, or to depth of cookie cutter (work quickly but carefully: molasses will be HOT!).

10. Thread a large upholstery needle with string and poke through treat to hang; if treats are too hard to insert needle, heat the tip of the needle in a flame before inserting.

Star-shaped birdseed treat

Buying and Storing Birdseed

Plastic bags and paper sacks of sunflower seed and birdseed mixes are a common sight in any discount store, hardware store, or supermarket. Even convenience stores keep a few bags on the shelf for people like me, who run out of seed at the worst times. You can also buy birdseed through the mail and have it delivered right to your door.

Prices vary widely. The best buys are usually at feed mills or stores that deal with big quantities, where they can afford to buy in bulk and pass the savings on to you. It pays to shop around. Small bags of seed cost more per pound than 50-pound monsters. If you can manage a big sack, you'll save a lot of pennies that can go to treat foods. You may want to join your neighbors in splitting a big sack if you can't use it all yourself.

Wherever you buy your seed, make sure it's fresh. Birds won't touch bad seed that's moldy, rancid, or insect infested. Because of the high oil content in the seed, it can spoil if not stored in a cool, dry place, or if it has sat on the shelf too long. Seed packaged in plastic or heavy paper stays fresh much longer than open bins of seed, which are especially vulnerable to insect infestation.

Birdseed mixes. When you buy mixed birdseed, read the label carefully to make sure the mix contains a high percentage of desirable seeds like sunflower, safflower, millet, canary, and flax, and a very low percent of fillers, like cracked corn, wheat kernels, and milo (also called sorghum).

If the birdseed you're buying is in a brown paper bag or some other wrapper you can't see through, make sure you read the list of ingredients. They're listed in order by quantity. So if fillers are near the beginning of the list, choose another brand if possible. Don't be misled by appealing names like "Best Bird Seed"; it pays to be suspicious. You may want to ask to have a sample bag opened so you can see for yourself what's in it.

Buying by the season. During the busy fall and winter feeding times, I like to keep lots of extra birdseed on hand. If the cans on the porch are almost full, and there's an extra sack in the trunk of the car, I know I'm set if a sudden winter storm hits and brings birds flocking for precious food.

Metal trash cans or other containers work well for storing birdseed, as will large pretzel and popcorn tins. To tote seed outside, use a plastic bucket with a handle, and keep a broom and dustpan nearby so you can clean up any spilled seed immediately.

Fifty-pound sacks are the size I need for the prime feeding season. They'll last me about one week. My storage space can handle only a couple of trash cans of seed. Otherwise I'd stock up with three months' supply so I wouldn't have to shop for seed so often. Seed stays fresh for months in winter if you store it in an unheated garage or porch area.

In spring and summer, feeder traffic slacks off dramatically. It's wise to buy smaller quantities, because seed stored for longer than two to three months in warm, moist weather can turn rancid, or become infested with insects, including weevils, click beetle larvae, and Indian meal moth larvae. I like to check oil-rich seeds like sunflower, flax, niger, and peanut hearts for freshness in the store before I buy. A simple taste test tells me whether the seed is still good, though I do get some funny looks from clerks when I crack a few kernels between my teeth.

Storing birdseed. Mice and their kin are the biggest problem you'll face when it comes to storing seed. Mice can ruin a sack of birdseed in short order. To keep your stored seed out of the clutches of rodents, invest in metal storage cans. If you feed only a few birds, a pretzel can or similar container will work; if you buy seed in bigger sacks, invest in a couple of metal trash cans with tight-fitting lids. Keep a dustpan and broom handy for cleaning up spills in your storage area.

Heavy-duty plastic containers will usually keep mice out, but I have known a deer mouse to chew a hole through the base of a 30-gallon plastic trash can. But if you refill your feeders daily and store 50 pounds of seed or less, a heavy-duty plastic container should work well.

Save extra sunflower heads and tie them together to make an outdoor decoration that will bring birds flocking.

Growing Your Own Birdseed

Growing enough birdseed to sustain your birds for weeks isn't a reasonable plan. Planting isn't the problem—broadcasting the seeds by casting handfuls on prepared soil works great. It's harvesting and cleaning the seed that calls for either lots of time doing old-fashioned winnowing, or else a newfangled farm machine.

But it is fun to grow small quantities of birdseed, especially those that are hard to come by. I buy ½ pound of lettuce seed and plant several crops in a big patch. I let it grow and go to seed, then lay the stalks of ripe seeds in an open tray feeder for finch treats. Several rows of giant sunflowers will give you armloads of seedheads that you can tie to a post and let the birds pick off.

If you'd like to know how to plant a garden full of birdseed, see Birdseed Gardens on page 52.

BIRDSEED GARDENS

Watching birds at a feeder is great for a close-up view, but watching birds eating natural foods growing in a garden is even more fun. One of my favorite sights in a birdseed garden is watching goldfinches eat cosmos seeds. I love watching their antics as they quarrel over the ripest seedheads and skirmish for space on the bending stems. Goldfinches are little acrobats—they stretch their bodies to reach the seedheads at the tips of the swaying stems, even turning upside down.

A garden filled with plants that produce delectable seeds will last longer than any tray of offerings you put out. Seeds of annual flowers like zinnias mature for months, as new flowers keep opening, so there's a bounty of food. And in winter, when pickings are slimmer, birds will still visit the garden to glean overlooked seeds from the ground and from almost-empty seedheads.

All the native sparrows in your area will feed in your birdseed garden, plus buntings, jays, cardinals, titmice, and chickadees. During fall migration, a birdseed garden can also draw unusual birds like rose-breasted grosbeaks (in streaky brown fall plumage) and tree sparrows.

Fast Results

Most birdseed plants are annuals, so planting a birdseed garden offers quick gratification. If you start a birdseed garden in the spring, by summer the birds will be reaping the rewards. Some of the brightest, cheeriest annuals produce seeds for birds, including my favorite red cactus-flowered zinnias and vivid orange-red Mexican sunflowers.

Many of the best perennials for birds are pushy ones that spread quickly by roots or by dropped seeds. For example, the native American perennial sunflower called Maximilian sunflower (*Helianthus maximilianii*) is much too invasive for a traditional ornamental border, but it's ideal for a bird garden, where more is better. When Maximilian sunflower spreads beyond its boundaries, I pull out the extras or strip more sod so I have more room to plant.

If you'd like a birdseed garden that's easy to keep under control, stick to annuals exclusively. Naturally, annuals for birds are plants that produce lots of seeds, so after the first year the garden will resprout of its own accord. Of course it won't follow your design exactly, but birds will still love it.

For ideas on plants to include, check the list on the opposite page, and also refer to Annuals, Ornamental Grasses, and Perennials.

Planting the Garden

I often mix bird-favorite plants among my usual perennial beds, but I also plant a sunny patch just for my birds. You can plant a special birdseed garden like the one shown on the opposite page in a single afternoon. Choose a site in full sun with well-drained soil. If you have poorly drained soil, loosen it and build up a raised bed of compost and other organic materials—most birdseed plants don't grow well without good drainage.

I start perennials and grasses from small container plants, spacing the plants about a foot apart. I start annuals from seed. It's important to water the garden to keep the soil constantly moist, especially until the seedlings sprout. Once the garden is established, it may need watering only in case of severe drought. And because a birdseed garden is densely planted (birds like the cover of a thick garden), you'll have few problems with weeds—and the birds will eat weed seeds too!

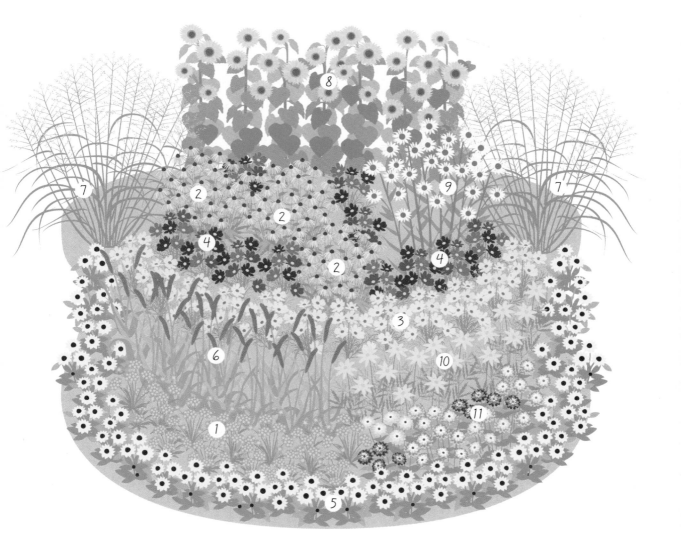

A Garden Full of Birdseed

1. Bachelor's-buttons (*Centaurea cyanus*)
2. Purple coneflower (*Echinacea purpurea*)
3. Yellow cosmos (*Cosmos sulphureus*)
4. 'Sensation Mix' cosmos
   (*Cosmos bipinnatus 'Sensation Mix'*)
5. Creeping zinnias (*Sanvitalia procumbens*)
6. Foxtail millet (*Setaria italica*)
7. Switch grass (*Panicum virgatum*)

8. 'Autumn Beauty' common sunflower
   (*Helianthus annuus 'Autumn Beauty'*)
9. Saw-toothed sunflower (*Helianthus grosseserratus*)
10. 'Golden Goddess' tickseed sunflower
    (*Bidens aristosa 'Golden Goddess'*)
11. 'Persian Carpet' zinnias (*Zinnia haageana 'Persian Carpet'*)

BIRD SONGS AND CALLS

Birds don't speak English, but their songs and calls allow them to communicate about all the vital matters that arise in bird life. For example, when robins call *tuk-tuk-tuk-tuk,* I know they're saying "look alert." And if they start shrieking *teek! teek!* danger is near at hand. Besides the sharp, short warnings of danger, birds have a repertoire that includes:

◆ Love songs: sung by males during courtship in full view of an adoring female
◆ Territory songs: sung from high perches around the edges of the breeding territory
◆ Whisper songs: sung from concealment, usually after breeding season, and seemingly for the bird's own pleasure
◆ Flock communication calls: whistled or chipped back and forth from bird to bird as a group is foraging or flying
◆ Scolding calls: usually a rattle or *chirr,* given as a warning to another bird who may have horned in on a food supply or a nesting area

You can buy books that describe and translate call notes for dozens of birds (like the ones in "Bird Song Translations" at right).

Seasonal Songs

May and June are prime times for bird songs. The best concert is in the morning, starting even before the sun breaks the horizon.

I'm not a morning person, but in spring I change my habits because I simply can't sleep through bird songs. As soon as the first notes of a sparrow seep through the gloom, I'm awake. As the dawn chorus continues, I hear a robin take up the song, then a cardinal joins in, followed by a wren. I can pick out the

Bird Song Translations

The best way to learn bird songs is to go outside and listen. You can also try listening to tapes and videos of bird songs. English translations of bird songs, like the ones below, are great aids for remembering the rhythm of a song, and enjoyable to learn just for fun.

Barred owl: *Who cooks for you? Who cooks for you aaaalllll?*
Carolina wren: *Teakettle, teakettle*
Common yellowthroat: *Get a penny, get a penny*
Eastern bluebird: *Purity... Purity*
Eastern or spotted towhee: *Drink your teeeeeeea!*
Northern cardinal: *What cheer! What cheer!*
Olive-sided flycatcher: *Quick, three beers! Quick, three beers!*
Red-winged blackbird: *Okalee, conkaree, Youchoo tea, Oolong tea!*
Tufted titmouse: *Peter, Peter*
White-throated sparrow: *Old Sam Peabiddy, Peabiddy, Peabiddy*

voices of catbirds and vireos, meadowlarks and red-winged blackbirds, and a few white-throated sparrows, who haven't left yet for their northern breeding grounds.

I know these spring songs are territorial—a way of warning off other birds of the same species, a "No Trespassing" sign set to music. Male birds also sing to impress the female, who supposedly looks for good singing genes to pass on to her offspring. (Only a few female birds sing, including the house finch, who often sings on the nest.) But I also believe that birds sing for the pure joy of it.

Bird Calls

Birds have other sounds in their repertoire that they use at any time of year. These include a variety of chips, twitters, and squeaks that they use to signal danger or stay in touch with companions. Stand outside on a moonlit night during spring or fall migration and you may be able to hear soft chipping calls from high overhead as bands of song-birds travel through.

Getting to know what your backyard birds are saying is a great way to study backyard wildlife in general. When a titmouse chips a sudden warning at the feeder, notice how the birds take cover in a flash. Look around and you may spot a hawk overhead.

I've watched birds contending with attacks by snakes, owls, and cats after being called to the scene by the sharp alarm calls of the birds. Those alarms also raise other helpers: Every nesting bird in the area will fly to the aid of others when it hears the call that says a nest is threatened.

Whisper Song

Among the most beautiful bird songs is a very private performance known as the whisper song. Singing from a perch hidden in shrubbery or vines, the bird softly twitters its usual proud song so quietly that you'll miss it unless you happen to be standing close by.

Mockingbirds, catbirds, brown thrashers, blue jays, gray jays, scrub jays, evening grosbeaks, and a few other birds sing a whisper song. Nobody knows exactly why. It appears to be a song sung purely for the pleasure of the singer.

Calling the Birds

Birders know that they can draw out birds from dense thickets by making squeaking, "shushing," or "pishing" noises. The little wooden Audubon bird call (see Sources) produces a creaky shriek that apparently sounds like a bird in distress, and tapes of owls that will raise alarm among nesting songbirds are widely available.

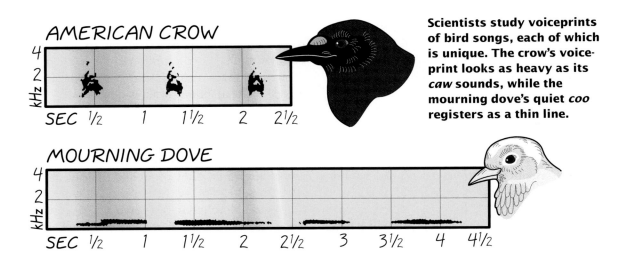

Scientists study voiceprints of bird songs, each of which is unique. The crow's voiceprint looks as heavy as its *caw* sounds, while the mourning dove's quiet *coo* registers as a thin line.

BLACKBIRDS

When a pleasant early spring evening lures you out for a walk, turn your attention to the sky. You'll often see long lines of migrating blackbirds heading north. Sometimes they're so close you can hear the whir of a million wings, but often they're just a distant black smudge across the sky.

Getting to Know Them

After the nesting season, blackbirds gather in spectacular flocks that may number in the millions. Different kinds of blackbirds—redwings, grackles, cowbirds, and others—join to forage, roost, and eventually migrate. When they fly south at the end of summer, it's quite a sight.

Blackbirds are medium to large birds, ranging from just under robin size to as big as a blue jay, with fairly long, sharp beaks and a loudmouth habit. Many are good—or at least enthusiastic—singers. (Unfortunately some of their tones sound as sweet as a car door that needs oiling!) Some members of the blackbird family aren't black at all. This large family of birds also includes bright-hued orioles and meadowlarks.

Unlike most songbirds, which make their homes in wooded areas, blackbirds flourish in open farm country. Most blackbirds spend much of their time close to the ground, strutting about your lawn or foraging in farm fields and meadows, or along the edges of ponds. And although I love to see a few pairs of red-winged blackbirds nesting in my shrub border, I'm sure farmers are dismayed when thousands of blackbirds descend on a freshly planted cornfield like it's an all-you-can-eat buffet. In their defense, blackbirds also eat millions of pesky insects, plus assorted weed seeds and berries.

Blackbirds often nest near water. Their nests are deep, well-constructed bowls of grasses, twigs, and weed stalks, usually with a mud foundation and a soft lining of feathers, moss, paper, rags, or grass. Blackbirds may attach their nests to shrubs, cattails, or rushes near the water's edge, but they also nest in fields and in backyard shrubs where there's plenty of cover.

Attracting Blackbirds

Cracked corn and millet will attract blackbirds to your feeders, and the birds will also feast on weed seeds like smartweed and ragweed around your yard. If you have a backyard pond or a nearby marshy area where they can nest, you may see them search through your trees and shrubs or your lawn grass in early spring through midsummer.

Blackbird Checklist

Because blackbirds often spend time in mixed flocks, it can be tough to identify individual birds. Birds like rusty blackbirds blend in with the starlings, cowbirds, and grackles. The distinctively marked red-winged and yellow-headed blackbirds stand out in a crowd. Most female blackbirds are brown or brown streaked.

Brewer's blackbird. Look for this plain black, light-eyed blackbird on your open lawn, in the company of his gray-feathered, dark-eyed lady friend. Brewer's blackbird is found in open country and is more common in the West, although it ranges through the central United States. Its head-jerking walk is distinctive. Watch for big migrating flocks of Brewer's blackbirds in spring and fall, and listen for their creaking *ksh-eee* song in spring. Brewer's blackbirds nest in hedgerows and in marshes and along water. They often line their nests with horsehair and lay five or six pale greenish gray eggs splotched with brown.

Red-winged blackbird. Red-winged blackbirds have a range that extends from southeastern

You'll often find red-winged blackbirds perching on the cattails of a marshy area or hear the showy males (top) singing in the fence row next to a newly planted field.

Alaska to the southern tip of Florida, although they winter mostly in the South. The gorgeous black males have a vivid red shoulder patch trimmed with yellow; females are streaky brown. Red-winged blackbirds build well-camouflaged nests near the ground, but they often betray the location by calling *check!* repeatedly when you get near. The three to five pale bluish green eggs are spotted or scribbled with dark lines.

Rusty blackbird. Rusty blackbirds summer in Canada and winter in the United States. I've seen migrating flocks so dense they cast a shadow over roads and fields. Rusty blackbirds resemble Brewer's blackbirds, but the female rusty has light eyes and lighter brown feathers. Watch the edges of your backyard pond in spring; if there's a blackbird strolling in the shallow edges, it's most likely a rusty. The

male's song is a squeaky *totalee–eek, totalee-eek.* Rusty blackbirds make their bowl-shaped nests in conifers or over water, laying four or five pale blue-green eggs blotched with browns and grays.

Yellow-headed blackbird. Yellow-headed blackbirds nest in wetlands from the midwestern prairies to the Pacific Coast, but frequently show up on lawns in towns and suburbs. The striking male is a big black bird who looks like he's wearing a bright yellow hood that extends onto his chest. The female is dull brown with a yellow throat. The male sings *klee klee klee ko-kow-w-w* and, like other blackbirds, has a hoarse single-syllable alarm call. They often build nests in willow trees above water. The nest holds three to five pale gray to pale green eggs splotched with browns or grays.

Yellow-headed blackbirds range across the western half of the country, and gardeners may spot the brightly hooded male bird in Japanese maples or other trees and shrubs planted by backyard water gardens.

BLUEBIRDS

Pretty and pleasant, bluebirds are more than just decorative backyard visitors. They're also extremely helpful birds that eat thousands of insect pests, including beetles, grasshoppers, caterpillars, and other delectable critters. Entice a bluebird to nest near your vegetable garden and you'll have chemical-free pest control of the most delightful kind.

Getting to Know Them

One of the best-known and best-loved birds, bluebirds are such an intense blue that the sight of the handsome male bird practically takes your breath away. Their color alone would be reason enough for bluebirds' immense popularity, but these gentle songbirds have a warbling musical song that is as welcome as their beauty.

Bluebirds have little fear of people and will happily move into a relatively undisturbed part of your garden or backyard. As long as they have some open grassy space nearby—a park, a golf course, a meadow, even a cemetery—bluebirds will quickly take up residence in a birdhouse built just for them.

With their straight, pointed bills, bluebirds are well equipped for nabbing insects. Both males and females are blue, but the male birds wear the brilliant blue feathers, whereas the females dress in duller, blue-gray shades. Bluebirds are about 7 inches long, a little smaller than their cousin, the robin.

Bluebirds nest in cavities such as holes in trees or wooden posts, or in nest boxes. The female builds the nest and sits on the clutch of four to six—or as many as eight—pale blue eggs. Inside a nest box or in a natural cavity (often an old woodpecker hole), bluebirds build a nest of dead grass, weed stems, rootlets, and fine twigs.

Attracting Bluebirds

When it comes to welcoming bluebirds to your yard, housing is the key. Bluebirds have trouble finding natural homes these days because we don't tend to leave dead trees standing and we've stopped using wooden fence posts in favor of metal or plastic.

This reduction in prime bluebird real estate, along with competition from other species of cavity nesters, has led to a serious decline in bluebird populations. Fortunately organized efforts to provide nest boxes have helped bluebirds make a comeback. And housing isn't the only way to invite bluebirds to stay—you can also tempt them to visit your yard by planting berry bushes, by putting up a birdbath, and by offering special bluebird treats at your feeders in winter.

A place to bathe adds "bluebird appeal" to your yard. When a pair of eastern bluebirds drops by, the richly colored male bird (right) steals the show. The female's feathers are a pale imitation of her handsome mate's.

Hang out the "vacancy" sign. "Build it and they will come" is a good motto for attracting bluebirds. Bluebirds appreciate a nice nest box to replace the holes in dead trees and wooden fence posts that were once their homes of choice. That's where we bluebird lovers can help: by putting up nest boxes individually or in bluebird "trails." These houses help ease the housing crunch, although bluebirds still have to compete with birds like tree swallows and house sparrows for these houses.

Bluebirds nest as early as March, but they start apartment hunting weeks before they're ready to lay eggs, so it's helpful to get your nest boxes up by the beginning of February. Build your boxes with a hinged side or front (see Birdhouses on page 36). That way, if house sparrows start building a nest in the box, you have the option of cleaning out the beginnings of their nest in the hope that they'll get discouraged and move elsewhere.

Mount the box on a post or on a tree, from 3 to 20 feet above the ground. If house sparrows are troublesome, experiment with boxes mounted at different heights. If you mount a box on a post, wrap the post with a sheet of aluminum at least 18 inches high or attach a metal squirrel guard (available at bird supply stores) beneath the box to keep raccoons from reaching the nest.

Don't forget about food. Once you have your bluebird houses up, you can turn your attention to other ways to attract these wonderful birds. A backyard that features natural populations of insects is an excellent offering all by itself. Bluebirds have an interesting technique for catching bugs that seems designed to show off the birds' colorful feathers: They often perch on a branch or post or rock, then

JUST FOR BLUEBIRDS

■ Bluebirds appreciate a bath—and a nearby perch for preening afterward. Place a birdbath where a fence or the branches of shrubs or trees give bluebirds a spot for fluffing up their feathers after bathing. A backyard pond with nearby perches also appeals to bluebirds.

■ Bluebirds like to have open space around their nests. Position nest boxes near the edge of a wooded area, but in a site that's open on all sides.

■ Wild grapes and sumac are practically guaranteed to attract bluebirds. Other bluebird favorites include the fruits of elderberries, currants, bayberries, deciduous hollies, blackberries, raspberries, Virginia creeper, juniper, pokeweed, and all species of euonymus, particularly burning bush (*Euonymus alata*) and wahoo (*E. atropurpurea*).

■ Use an open tray feeder to offer bluebirds food in the winter. They'll appreciate a handout of peanut-butter dough—peanut butter mixed with cornmeal to a crumbly cookie-dough consistency (see Peanuts and Peanut Butter on page 191 for mixing directions).

■ For a special bluebird treat—in winter or during the breeding season—stock a tray feeder with live mealworms (available at bait shops and pet supply stores).

flutter to the ground after a tasty grasshopper, cricket, or beetle.

While bluebirds get most of their nourishment from insects, they also feed year-round on berries and other small fruits. In areas where mistletoe grows, bluebirds are one of the natural factors that help the plant spread, as they "deposit" the seeds from previous meals on branches of other trees.

When western gardeners see fruit forming on their burning bushes (*Euonymus alata*), they should watch for visiting mountain bluebirds—these berries are one of the birds' favorite noninsect foods.

Bluebird Checklist

Three species of bluebirds occupy overlapping ranges across the United States and into Canada, ensuring that gardeners everywhere can enjoy the company of these handsome songbirds.

Eastern bluebird. The male eastern bluebird sports a rich blue back that contrasts beautifully with his rusty red breast and throat and white belly. The female's back is a grayer blue and her rusty breast is somewhat paler. They sing a lilting *tru-a-ly, tru-a-ly!* in a quiet warbling voice that carries quite a distance. These bluebirds line the nest with a soft inner circle of feathers, hair, and fine grasses.

"Eastern" is a bit of a misnomer, because this bird's range covers almost two-thirds of the country, from the Great Plains and eastern foothills of the Rockies to southeastern Arizona and eastward in a solid sweep to the Gulf Coast and Atlantic seaboard. Eastern bluebirds live in open woods or woods' edges as well as more open spaces. They're often found in farming country, but also show up in city parks, orchards, roadsides, and suburban backyards—anyplace where there's a good-size stretch of grass or hedgerow. They nest throughout their range, but spend their winters south of the Great Lakes.

Western bluebird. Western bluebirds take over where the eastern bluebird leaves off, with a bit of overlap in some areas. The same vivid rich blue decorates this beauty, but it has a blue throat and a wash of chestnut where its wings join its body. Female western bluebirds are grayer and paler, appearing faded like a pair of jeans that's been through the wash several times.

Western bluebirds prefer open woodlands or backyards with big trees; they also show up around farms, orchards, and in meadows and gardens. Their song sounds like *f-few, f-few, f-few*. Western bluebirds use soft, fine grasses to line their nests.

Mountain bluebird. Mountain bluebirds are birds of a different color: an unusual shade of blue that's a blend of turquoise and sky blue on the back, paler sky blue on the breast, with white lower underparts. They lack any rusty color at all. Females are dull brownish gray with a cast of blue on the rump.

Mountain bluebirds are well named—they nest in the mountains, from just below the timberline to the foothills. Their nesting range extends from the Rockies west to the Pacific, and their nests often include the outer bark of fragrant sagebrush. In winter they may move down to elevations as low as sea level. A two- or three-note, clear, short warbling song is the mountain bluebird's trademark.

BRAMBLES

Birdwatching is even more fun when you have refreshments like sweet, sun-ripened blackberries and raspberries at hand. A patch of blackberries, raspberries, or other "bramble" fruits in your yard attracts fruit-loving birds like thrushes and wrens, and many birds will nest in brambles.

Growing Brambles

If you're planting red or yellow raspberries, blackberries, or black raspberries, start with certified virus-free, bareroot plants from a garden center or catalog. Look for unusual species at native-plant nurseries, or in specialty mail-order catalogs. Most brambles are hardy enough to grow in Zones 5 to 9.

Plant bramble plants 3 feet or more apart in a moist, sunny spot. Wineberries, salmonberries, and thimbleberries grow better in shade or partial shade. Bramble canes won't fruit the first year. In the second year they'll flower, fruit, and die. However, new canes sprout from the crowns each year. The varieties called everbearing, like 'Heritage' or 'Fall Red' red raspberry, will produce a few berries in their first year of growth.

My brambles grow in an informal hedge. When my hedge dies out in the center, I simply cut it to within a few inches of the ground with a trimmer. The crowns then send up a bounty of fruitful new canes.

Best of the Brambles

Most bramble fruits will attract birds, so choose brambles whose fruit you like to eat yourself (you can cover some of the plants with netting to preserve some berries for yourself if you need to). To avoid disease problems, choose disease-resistant cultivars if they're avail-

The Wild World of Backyard Birds

In June I like to harvest just-ripened black raspberries to top my breakfast cornflakes. I often scare the local catbird couple or a mockingbird as I walk toward the bramble bushes.

One morning I popped my hand into the bush to grab some big berries and something sharp jabbed the tender skin between my thumb and forefinger. As I pulled my hand back, an irate brown thrasher flew out of the tangled canes. I looked in and saw that I'd reached in just an inch from a mother bird sitting on her nest. I retreated with a few berries and as much dignity as I could muster.

able, and plant the brambles on a site with the soil and light conditions that suit them best.

Blackberries. Moving to Oregon several years ago introduced me to the wonders of blackberries (*Rubus* spp.), which grow so vigorously in the Pacific Northwest that they're considered a weed. Blackberries range from erect cultivars like 'Comanche', to trailing ones like 'Olallie' and 'Cascade', to American dewberry (*R. flagellaris*), which makes a perfect groundcover. Blackberries have vicious thorns, but the thorns protect roosting and nesting birds. Thornless cultivars, such as 'Black Satin Thornless', 'Chester', and 'Navaho', attract birds with their bounty of delectable fruit.

Blackberry hybrids also produce solid berries with firm cores. The hybrids are less hardy than regular blackberries, most growing only in Zones 8 and 9. Loganberries have big, light red berries with a slightly tart taste. Marionberries have a mild flavor. Boysenberries bear huge, maroon berries brimming with juice. Tayberries (a cross between blackberries and black raspberries) have a strong, complex flavor.

Raspberries. Black raspberries (*Rubus occidentalis*) are so delicious that no backyard should be without them. As with blackberries, some cultivars are thornless. 'Cumberland' has very large, round berries. 'Bristol', 'Black Hawk', and 'Jewel' are good choices, too.

The hollow, elongated caps of red raspberries (*R. idaeus*) have a milder, sweeter flavor than black raspberries. Summerbearing and everbearing cultivars are available. 'Latham' is a summerbearer; 'Heritage' is an everbearer that gives a summer crop and a heavier fall crop; 'Fall Red' and 'Fall Gold', which has yellow fruits, also produce berries in summer and fall.

Wineberries. The fuzzy red canes of wineberries (*Rubus phoenicolasius*) bear tangy-sweet red fruits. The trouble-free mounded plants with arching canes flourish in moist soils and partial shade. Though the canes are prickly to touch, they're beautiful to look at in the garden in winter, especially when you grow the plants next to ornamental grasses.

Other brambles. Thimbleberries (*R. parviflorus*) and salmonberries (*R. spectabilis*), both native to the Northwest, don't bear heavily, but thrushes and other birds like the fruits. Thimbleberries have nonjuicy berries. The bushes, which are hardy to Zone 3, have nearly thornless stems to 5 feet long, fuzzy maplelike leaves, and white flowers in spring. Salmonberry, which is hardy to Zone 7, has deep pink flowers and fuzzy orange berries.

An unruly patch of unpruned brambles (left) offers birds tasty berries to eat and a safe haven for building nests. Training brambles like raspberries on a trellis (right) is more work, but increases yields and makes it easier for you to harvest berries for yourself.

BREAD

In the "good old days," bread was the mainstay of the backyard bird feeder. One of my earliest memories is of helping my mother on a treasure hunt through the cupboards on a cold, snowy morning, gathering up stale bread for the hungry birds outside.

Feeding bread to birds. Bread is still an acceptable bird food, but birdseed is much more nutritious and much less expensive to feed. Still, if you find yourself with a few stray slices of stale bread, there's no sense letting it go to waste. Tear the slices into small pieces and toss them out where birds can easily see them. If you're feeding more than a handful of bread, put it in an open tray feeder so undesirable critters like mice aren't attracted by leftovers.

Birds that scavenge for a living, like starlings and house sparrows, may be the first ones to head for the bread. Jays are curious and quick to investigate, so they'll probably be the next customers. Cardinals, juncos, native sparrows, and other birds won't eat bread unless they're very hungry. Crumble the bread into medium to fine crumbs to entice these reluctant birds. If there's a spring ice storm or cold snap in your area, birds like robins that normally eat insects may feed on bread too.

Birds can't live by bread alone—it doesn't contain enough nutrients or fat to sustain them, but it's a fine supplement. Ducks and geese at public ponds are usually quick to grab bread from your fingers, but they'd be better served if you lugged along a sack of shelled corn instead. Wild ducks and geese have little interest in bread, because they're not accustomed to getting such handouts.

Making bread for the birds. If you like to bake, you can try making special bread or other baked treats just for birds. Add liberal doses of nuts, raisins, hulled sunflower seeds, and other high-fat or fruit goodies to your dough before baking. These special breads attract more takers than a standard loaf of white bread. For one recipe, see "Easy Bird Treat Mini-Muffins" on page 35.

BUNTINGS

Buntings win first prize when it comes to colorful plumage. Their feathers are vivid sapphire blue, stunning turquoise, and chestnut, or a rainbow of blue, red, yellow, and green. You might think that such gorgeous creatures must be a rare sight, but buntings are as common as song sparrows and as easy as sparrows to attract to your own backyard.

Getting to Know Them

Just 4½ inches from beak to tail, buntings deliver a lot of birdwatching pleasure in a small package. They're active birds, at home in hedgerows, along roadsides and woods' edges, and in weedy patches in the wild. In backyard gardens, you'll spot them in meadow gardens, in flower borders, and flitting among shrubs.

On hot summer days when other birds are still and quiet, the voice of the indigo bunting rings out, usually from a high perch atop a tree or a utility pole. Buntings have long, varied songs that often contain repeated melodies.

Buntings like to nest in weedy patches, amid curtains of Spanish moss, or in dense, multistemmed plants. They usually build their nests about 3 feet off the ground and rarely nest higher than about 6 feet up. Like sparrows, buntings weave well-constructed cups of grasses and weed stems, with a lining of fine grasses and sometimes hair and feathers. They lay three to five skim-milk white to pale blue eggs. If you find a grassy nest with a bit of snakeskin woven into the foundation, you've found an indigo bunting home.

Attracting Buntings

Buntings are finches, which means seeds are their primary food. The seeds of dandelion, lamb's-quarters, smartweed, goldenrod, and asters are bunting favorites. During the summer their diet also includes grasshoppers, crickets, flies, wasps, ants, aphids, beetles, and caterpillars, and small fruits like elderberries and raspberries. Buntings will grace your feeders with their beautiful plumage while they dine on millet. They also like grass seed, which they'll eagerly pick up from a feeder or gather from the grasses in your yard.

To encourage buntings to nest and sing in your yard, be sure it includes shrubs, hedges, and the brushy, weedy areas they prefer. A

If your lettuce plants send up seedstalks, don't pull the plants out. Indigo buntings will gladly dine on the seeds. Like other buntings, the male indigo (top) is brilliantly colored, whereas the female is mainly brown.

planting of blackberries, a group of garden phlox plants (*Phlox paniculata*), or a colony of perennial sunflowers is just the kind of protected place they like.

Bunting Checklist

No matter where you live, you're likely to find at least one type of bright-colored bunting visiting your feeders if your yard has suitable habitat. Three species cover most of the lower 48 states, with ranges that overlap in the central and southwestern states.

Indigo bunting. When you hear an indigo bunting song (*sweet-sweet, where-where, here-here, see it, see it*), look for the highest perch in the area and you'll probably spot the brilliant sapphire blue male bird. You're less likely to see the rather shy, brown female. Indigo buntings are common across the entire eastern half of North America, from Canada to Texas and Florida. They spend the winter in Mexico, Panama, and the West Indies.

Lazuli bunting. This western bunting takes up where indigo buntings leave off, covering the West from British Columbia to Baja, and east to the plains. The lovely male with his high, lively voice is turquoise blue on top, with a rusty breast and white belly. The female is dull brown.

Painted bunting. The showiest of the colorful buntings, the male painted bunting's head is a rich blue-purple; its back is bright frog green, and its underside is bright red from its chin to its tail. Female painted buntings are bright green; young birds are drab green. The male bird sings a sweet high-pitched, tinkling musical song. Painted buntings nest in the south-central United States and along a strip of the southern Atlantic coast. They spend the winters from Louisiana and Florida to Central America and the Caribbean. Painted buntings' pale blue-white eggs are sometimes speckled with brown.

BUTTERFLIES

Once you've planted a bird garden, you'll be pleasantly surprised to find that butterflies like it, too. Many plants that produce seeds for birds also have flowers that attract swarms of colorful butterflies. Most of these plants are summer bloomers that are at their best just when butterfly populations peak. I often see swallowtail and monarch butterflies sipping from the flowers of cosmos, zinnias, and coneflowers just inches away from finches nibbling on seeds.

Butterflies are connected to birds in another way, too—many insect-eating birds enjoy a meal of butterflies. Butterflies also feed birds by laying eggs that hatch into tasty caterpillars, which bird parents nab to fill the gullets of their nestlings. You may think it's sad to see fragile, beautiful butterflies snapped up by hungry birds, but remember: The birds certainly won't catch every butterfly and caterpillar in your garden, so you'll get the enjoyment of watching both birds and butterflies on the wing.

Host Plants for Butterflies

Butterfly caterpillars have specialized food needs, so if you want to encourage butterflies to lay eggs in your garden, you need to plant the caterpillar "host plants." For example, monarch butterflies lay their eggs only on milkweeds, including butterfly weed (*Asclepias tuberosa*). Zebra swallowtails must have pawpaw trees for their nursery; caterpillars of the small, golden hackberry butterfly eat only elm leaves.

Sometimes you'll discover that you've planted a butterfly host plant without knowing it. I planted spicebushes in my front yard for birds, which love their appealing red berries. The bushes became a living feeder in more ways than one. Gorgeous black-and-green spicebush swallowtail butterflies lay eggs on the spicebush leaves, and when the tiny caterpillars hatch, the bushes become a favorite feeding stop for the tanagers and orioles nesting in the garden.

Purple coneflower   Monarch   Zinnia   Common sulphur   Mexican sunflower   Verbena   Tiger swallowtail   Tickseed daisy

Colorful flowers like purple coneflowers, zinnias, and Mexican sunflowers attract both birds and butterflies. Butterflies visit to drink the nectar, and birds follow later in the season to pick seeds from the seedheads.

CARDINALS

Cardinals are the perfect backyard bird: They are beautiful, have a lovely song, and nest close to homes in both towns and rural areas, often returning to the same bush season after season. When I was a kid, a pair of cardinals returned each spring to nest in the climbing red 'Blaze' rose that grew up to the second-story windows of our house. My bedroom was just over the bush, giving me a perfect "catbird" seat for watching the activity of the parents and nestlings. In my current yard, our resident cardinals build their summer home every year in the tangle of fox grape vines that swarms over an old redbud tree where lawn meets woods.

Getting to Know Them

Male cardinals, with their rich red feathers and snazzy black mask, are beautiful indeed, but I also love the coloring of the female bird; her buffy brown feathers have splashes of orange-red on crest, wings, and tail. Both birds have a crest on their heads. Usually carried at half-mast, that pointy crown goes up in a flash when the bird is alarmed or threatened. During courtship, when the female crouches before the male and begs for food like a nestling, she flattens her crest.

Evidently cardinals are everybody's favorite bird, at least in the eastern half of the continent. This beautiful red bird is the official state bird in seven states: Ohio, Indiana, Illinois, Kentucky, Virginia, West Virginia, and North Carolina. (Cardinals also live in parts of Arizona, New Mexico, and Baja California south into Mexico.)

Cardinals in winter. Cardinals don't migrate like most other songbirds. In winter some birds remain near their nesting territory, while others draw together into flocks that can include 50 or more birds. It's always a treat to flush out cardinals on a winter walk, especially on a gray day when the bright color of the birds adds a wonderful splash of color to the landscape. Thick stands of dried giant ragweed will lure cardinals in fall and winter—the weeds will be full of cardinals seeking the oil-rich seeds.

The clear, whistled *What cheer! What cheer!* of this large member of the finch family is one of the first bird songs to drift through the window in early spring. It's an easy song to imitate with a human whistle

In winter, cardinals may seek shelter in backyard conifers. Also watch for the bright red males along streams, in brushy fields, or in thickets of honeysuckle, privet, or other dense vines and shrubs.

(except for the introductory *whoit! whoit! whoit!* which my lips just can't do). When the birds are feeling territorial in early spring, you can often entice a male singer to come close by challenging him with your version of his song. (Cardinals are, by the way, one of the most aggressive birds during the flush of spring mating: Fights between males are common.)

Nesting cardinals. A cardinal's nest is a bowl woven of whatever's handy, it seems: twigs, plant stems, paper, strips of bark, grasses, and usually a few leaves. The birds fasten the nest securely in a forked branch, usually hidden deep in a dense shrub or tree, often surprisingly low to the ground. I've found many nests that were only about 4 feet off the ground. Garden roses and bramble patches are good spots to look for cardinal nests.

Cardinals lay only three or four eggs, but they nest at least twice a season—often three times, and sometimes even four. They start nesting in March, and build a final nest in August. Both parents build the nest, but it's almost always the female's job to sit on the eggs, which are grayish tan to greenish white, with dark spots and speckles. The male tenderly feeds the female while she incubates the eggs. Cowbirds may parasitize the nest, leaving the cardinal to raise the loudmouthed cowbird baby.

Attracting Cardinals

The heavy-duty beak of a cardinal marks it as a seed eater. (That heavy beak also gives cardinals a comical look when you see them head-on.) At feeders, cardinal favorites include sunflower and safflower seeds, and cracked corn. Here in the Corn Belt, I often see cardinals gleaning farm fields in winter for bits of corn.

Cardinals often build nests in bushes with thorns: You may spy a female on the nest in a big mound of multiflora rose in a pasture or along roadsides.

Cardinals also relish weed seeds, fruit, and elm buds, along with a wide variety of insects. When yellow-bellied sapsuckers have been boring holes in our trees, I sometimes see a cardinal visiting the holes a couple of days later, drinking the oozing sap and picking off beetles and moths that were also attracted to the liquid. Cardinals like a yard with lots of shrubs for cover, where they can safely move through corridors of hedges or shrubbery. Tangled curtains of vines are favorite hiding places, especially in fall and winter, so add a sweet autumn clematis (*Clematis terniflora*) or Concord grape to a trellis beside your porch, or let vines scramble over a fence. Dense old shrub roses and climbing roses are cardinal favorites for nesting sites. Cardinals will roost in pines, spruces, hemlocks, and other dense evergreens.

CATBIRDS

If there's a bird singing in your yard on a mellow summer night, it could very well be a catbird. You'll hear catbirds much more often than you'll see them because they're shy types who prefer to sing from a hidden perch.

Getting to Know Them

Officially known as the gray catbird (to distinguish it from the black catbird, a Mexican species), both males and females are dark gray with a black cap and a patch of rich deep chestnut beneath the base of the tail. Adult birds are about 8½ inches long. During the summer, catbirds range throughout the northern United States and Canada. When winter arrives, they withdraw to the unfrozen South and to Mexico, although a few birds stay north in winter—especially where berries are abundant.

A catbird's distinctive *mew* sounds just like a complaining cat, and I sometimes mistake it for a stray tom in the bushes, at least until the bird begins the rest of its song. Catbirds belong to the family of mimic thrushes, which means they imitate other sounds. The catbird that returns each spring to the jungle of Japanese honeysuckle along our fence row usually punctuates his concerts with a tree-frog's guttural *creeeeeak* and short bursts of a song he stole from Mr. Robin. The catbird's voice is sweet, but its song often is disjointed, and it may slip in a grating *tcheck-tcheck* or other harsh notes here and there.

If your backyard includes deutzia, honeysuckle, weigela, lilacs, or other shrubs, look there for a catbird nest. Catbirds don't get an "A" in nest building—at least not for the rough collection of twigs, weeds, grasses, and leaves that makes up the outside layer of the nest. Inside, though, a soft cup of horsehair, fine roots, or pine needles cradles four shiny, dark greenish blue eggs.

Attracting Catbirds

Catbirds may eat fruit and bread at feeders, but they're more likely to forage in your yard for beetles, grasshoppers, and other insects. They like berries, too, and will visit your yard if it includes elderberries or other backyard fruits. The Concord grapes growing on my fence are a favorite, as are the wild fox grapes that clamber into my trees. Catbirds seem to find the wild grapes especially appealing when they're migrating in fall.

If you hear a cat meowing from your lilacs, take a look among the branches, and you may find a catbird's nest. These shy gray birds with the catlike call nest in leafy shrubs, usually raising two families each summer.

CATERPILLARS

To gardeners, caterpillars are both friend and foe, but to birds, caterpillars are a perfectly timed, high-protein meal. Early hatchings of caterpillars coincide with spring migrations, so in April, for example, you'll find tiny, bright-colored wood warblers flitting through young oak leaves, picking off bite-size caterpillars. Caterpillar populations continue to swell right through the nesting season.

Some caterpillars have special defenses against hungry birds. The spikes on giant cecropia caterpillars and the fearsome eye-spots on spicebush swallowtail caterpillars do certainly deter birds. So do the protective bristles and hairs that cover tent caterpillars, gypsy moth larvae, and woolly bears. But a few types of birds don't seem to mind a hairy meal. Both yellow-billed and black-billed cuckoos can eat hundreds of gypsy moth caterpillars each day.

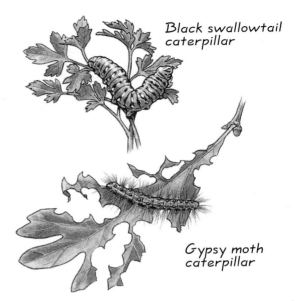

Black swallowtail caterpillar

Gypsy moth caterpillar

Many birds enjoy a tasty meal of caterpillars, including pests like gypsy moth caterpillars and mild garden nuisances like black swallowtail caterpillars, which chew on dill, fennel, and parsley, but then turn into beautiful butterflies.

CATS

House cats are great birdwatchers. They sit for hours at the window overlooking the feeders observing the sparrows and cardinals. Only their twitching tails betray their true intentions. At my house, when a chickadee visits the suction-cup feeder attached to the window, the cats' instincts occasionally get the better of them and they spring for the bird, crashing into the glass. Then the guilty kitties retreat under the dining room table where they lick their paws and pretend that nothing happened.

Cats that aren't kept strictly indoors may be one reason songbirds are in decline. Some sources estimate that cats catch as many as a million songbirds each year. Cats, whether they're free-roaming feral cats or pet cats, are major bird predators in the United States.

If you invite birds to your yard, you owe it to your feathered guests to try to keep cat predators away. Putting a bell around Kitty's neck isn't good enough; cats soon learn to stalk without making the bell ring. The best approach is to keep your cat in the house. Your cat may complain at first, but it'll get used to its leisure life soon enough. It's especially important to keep cats inside during the spring nesting season, because fledgling birds don't fly well and are especially vulnerable to cats.

What to do about neighbors' cats that stray into your yard? I shoo cats the old-fashioned way, by clapping my hands and rushing toward them yelling at the top of my lungs. It works.

CHERRIES

On the tree or off, ripe cherries make a great treat for birds. More than 20 species will flock to share the bounty from a backyard cherry tree. And such birds! Cedar waxwings and vireos will spend all day eating cherries—and so will catbirds, thrushes, thrashers, grosbeaks, robins, bluebirds, and wrens. When cherries drop off the tree, they'll attract pheasants and grouse, as well as small wildlife like rabbits and raccoons.

Cherry trees make handsome additions to any yard. In the spring they're covered with filmy masses of white or pink flowers, followed by colorful fruit in summer. In the winter their satiny smooth bark brightens dull landscapes. Cherry trees range in size from 10 foot-tall species like chokecherries (*Prunus virginiana*) to huge black cherry trees (*P. serotina*) that tower 70 feet. Species that bear sour fruit are generally hardier than sweet-fruited types. Some sour types will even withstand winters in Zone 2. Cherry trees grow best in full sun, but some species tolerate light shade, and all grow well in average soil.

Cherry Choices

If you have a small yard, try planting common chokecherries or tart cherries. Chokecherry (Zones 2 to 8) is a shrub or small tree that reaches 10 feet tall. In the spring it's covered with creamy, fragrant flowers, and in summer with tart red or yellow fruits. Tart cherry (*P. cerasus*), which is also called sour cherry, grows to 20 feet and sets tangy red fruits.

For a moderate-size tree that will also provide some shade, try sweet cherry (*P. avium*) or pin cherry (*P. pensylvanica*). Sweet cherry (Zones 3 to 9) grows to 35 feet tall and has large, sweet fruits that can be red, purple, or yellow. Unlike other types of cherries, sweet cherries require cross-pollination, so ask your supplier which cultivars to plant to ensure good fruiting. Pin cherry grows to 40 feet, and it produces clusters of sour red fruits.

If you have an open spot in your yard big enough for a tree that will eventually top 100 feet, you can try planting a black cherry (Zones 3 to 8). This impressive tree bears sweet black fruits along its short drooping stems.

A backyard cherry tree will draw dozens of birds, including flocks of elegant cedar waxwings. If you want to save cherries for yourself, you'll have to cover the trees with netting, as shown on page 120.

CHICKADEES

Everyone's favorite at the feeder, active little chickadees are endearingly friendly and undeniably cute. They quickly become accustomed to human comings and goings and can be easily hand-tamed, especially with the incentive of nuts held in your open palm.

Getting to Know Them

All chickadees are about 4 to 5 inches long and have a snazzy dark cap and black bib with white cheek patches. Males and females look alike. They're in motion nonstop, so they appreciate lots of high-energy foods at the feeder. Jaunty acrobats, they often turn upside down to nab insects from leaves or peck at pinecones. Chickadees nest in decaying branch stubs, old woodpecker holes, or other cavities in wood, often surprisingly low to the ground—from 1 to 10 feet high. They're gratifyingly quick to move into a nest box. Their soft nest is made of moss, feathers, silken cocoons, plant fibers and down, and hair. Their eggs are white with brown dots, and most species lay six or more eggs.

Each chickadee species has its own style of announcing itself, but they all say their name. Some say *chick-a-dee* in a fast, high voice, whereas others have a slower, hoarser call. Most also have an easy-to-imitate whistled call and will "talk" back and forth if you respond.

Attracting Chickadees

Chickadees are attracted to gardens with trees where they can glean insects, larvae, and insect eggs. They'll also eat tree seeds. Bayberry bushes (*Myrica pensylvanica*) are a draw, too. At the feeder, offer chickadees sunflower seed, chick scratch, peanut butter, doughnuts, and suet.

Chickadee Checklist

You can spot chickadees year-round almost everywhere across the United States. They visit feeders and gardens in all seasons. In winter, look for them ranging through the trees with titmice, downy woodpeckers, brown creepers, nuthatches, and kinglets, chattering companionably.

Black-capped chickadee. You can spot the black-capped chickadee in the woods, in town, and in the countryside throughout its wide range from Alaska and Canada through mid-America. It's a year-round resident except in the southern part of its range, where it's a winter bird. You'll know black-capped chickadees by their black cap and bib with light gray back and paler belly and breast. In winter, watch the buffy color below the wings deepen in hue.

Friendly black-capped chickadees are voracious insect eaters. They'll even tackle bagworm cocoons to get at the larvae inside. The Carolina chickadee is virtually identical to the black-capped, but is a resident of southern states.

Black-capped chickadees forage on bark, twigs, and leaves for insects. Their call is a familiar *chick-a-dee-dee* call plus a melancholy two- or three-note whistle.

Carolina chickadee. A black-capped chickadee look-alike, the Carolina chickadee lives in the Southeast and northward to New Jersey, Ohio, and west to Missouri and Texas. Other than geography (which overlaps), the best way to identify a Carolina is by its voice. Listen for its higher, faster *chick-a-dee-dee-dee-dee* call and its often ear-piercing whistled *see-dee see-dee* song. Carolina chickadees may line their nest with thistledown or milkweed fluff.

Mountain chickadee. Variation on a theme, this bird of the western mountains sports a black stripe through its white cheek patch, giving its head an eye-catching striped look from a distance. It has a grayish body with white breast. The mountain chickadee's call is *chick-a-dee-a-dee-a-dee,* and it also sings a

You can tell a mountain chickadee from a black-capped by the stripe down its cheek. In winter all chickadees will scour the branches of willows and many other trees searching for insects.

JUST FOR CHICKADEES

■ If you're trying to hand-tame a chickadee, tempt it with hard-to-resist walnut kernels.

■ Plant common mullein (*Verbascum thapsus*) to attract chickadees in winter. The tall spires of seedheads often shelter insect larvae, which chickadees will peck out.

■ Chick scratch, sold at feed stores for baby chicks, is an inexpensive feeder favorite.

■ Shelled sunflowers are a special treat, and so are any kind of nuts. Chop nuts into small pieces so bigger birds like jays don't carry off these costly treats whole.

■ Wait until spring to clean out chickadee nest boxes. They seek shelter in the boxes on cold winter nights, and the cozy nest will help keep things warm.

three-note whistled song that sounds just like "Three Blind Mice."

Boreal chickadee. Sometimes called the "brown-capped chickadee," this bird of the Far North has a deep brown cap and grayish body with a white breast and buffy rust sides. Its call is a slow, hoarse *chick-a-deer-deer*, and it doesn't whistle.

Chestnut-backed chickadee. Resident of the Pacific Northwest, chestnut-backed chickadees are a tiny, bright russet bird with a snowy breast and striking black cap and bib to accent its rich rusty back and sides.

Chestnut-backed chickadees prefer the deep, dark forests of their native Northwest and coastal Northern California range. The call is a fast, hoarse *seek-a-dee-dee* or *kiss-a-dee* call, plus a repeated *chick-chick-chick* "song." Their white eggs have reddish brown dots rather than the usual brown dots.

CHICKADEE DOUGHNUT DELIGHTS

Chickadees are a favorite of Geraldine Hoehn of New Harmony, Indiana. She developed these peanut doughnuts just for them—but many other backyard birds like them, too!

2 eggs

1 cup sugar

1 cup milk

5 tablespoons melted shortening

4 cups all-purpose flour

4 teaspoons baking powder

1 cup unsalted peanuts, finely chopped

Lard or oil for frying

Peanuts, finely crushed, or cornmeal

1. Mix eggs, sugar, milk, shortening, flour, baking powder, and chopped peanuts. Put the dough in the refrigerator for 30 minutes to make handling it easier.

2. Heat lard or oil to 375°F in a deep pan. Roll or press the dough out to ½-inch thickness.

3. Use a doughnut cutter to cut doughnuts from the rolled dough.

4. Immediately put doughnuts in heated lard or oil, sliding them in one at a time with a spatula (dip the spatula in oil before using it for doughnuts so they slide off easily).

5. Let the doughnuts fry 2 to 3 minutes, then turn them over and fry the other side. Meanwhile, sprinkle a triple thickness of paper towels with the crushed peanuts or cornmeal.

6. Lift the fried doughnuts out of the fat and place them on the crushed peanuts or cornmeal on the paper towels. Turn them to coat both sides. If the crushed peanuts don't stick to the doughnuts, "glaze" the doughnuts first by spreading a thin coating of peanut butter on them, then press them against the crushed peanuts.

7. When cool enough to handle, stick them on large nails on a vertical board mounted at your bird-feeding station (see page 95 for one example of a doughnut feeder).

8. Store extras in a waxed paper–lined tin with a tight-fitting lid.

CHRISTMAS FOR THE BIRDS

After you cross your family and friends off your holiday gift list, turn your attention to your backyard bird friends. Making Christmas treats for the birds can become a wonderful tradition. It's an afternoon of activity and fun that has nothing to do with spending money or fighting crowds at the mall, and kids love to help. (They also like watching the birds eating the goodies they made.)

High-fat, high-calorie bird treats and a smorgasbord of other delights help birds conserve precious energy in winter. They can fill their bellies on your homemade gifts without expending calories searching the woods and fields for sustenance.

Kitchen Cupboards Concoction

Nuts fill the bill for bird treats perfectly, but pouring a pound of walnuts in the feeder would be too easy! Look on making Christmas bird treats as the perfect reason for cleaning your kitchen cupboards. Start by ransacking the pantry shelves—perhaps you'll find a half-empty box of raisins petrified to break-your-tooth dryness. If so, dump them into a bowl along with the nuts, then add the last couple of inches from an old bottle of molasses and the remains of a couple of boxes of cornmeal. To give the treats a little more substance, add a few handfuls of fine-chopped suet.

With all those ingredients in the bowl, the challenge is how to mix them together. I recommend rolling up your sleeves and mixing the ingredients with your hands. Grease your hands so they don't stick to the gluey mess. Then just plunge them into the bowl and start

Homegrown WISDOM

CHRISTMAS TREES FOR BIRDS

"For years, I've been putting the Christmas tree out for the birds after we're done with it in the house," says Pauline Gerard of Henderson, Kentucky. "I prop it near the feeder, and it's always full of birds, especially when the weather's bad."

Pauline used to string chains of popcorn and cranberries and put them on the tree. Although they looked pretty, the birds didn't eat them.

"Then one year, a friend gave me some dried persimmon slices. They were a pretty orange color and had a neat pattern of seeds. I hung some of them on the bird tree, and the woodpeckers came for them. Then I had a brilliant idea and decided to string peanuts—which I knew the birds loved—instead of popcorn." Pauline found she had to push with a thimble to get the needle through the peanut shells. The results were wonderful. Chickadees, titmice, and blue jays pecked at the peanuts for weeks. Pauline also hangs apple and orange slices and other treats.

kneading—children usually love this part of the job.

Once the mix is thoroughly mixed, mold it into small balls (don't worry if they're lopsided—the birds won't notice). Wrap each ball

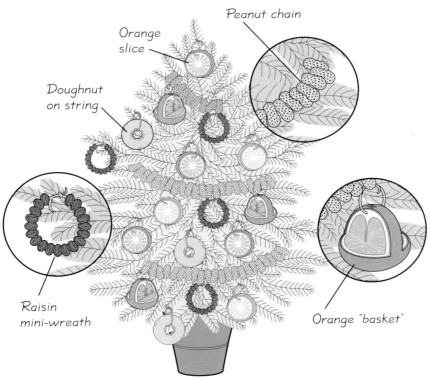

Peanut chain

Orange slice

Doughnut on string

Raisin mini-wreath

Orange "basket"

When you're finished with your Christmas tree, move it outside for the birds. Stick it in a 5-gallon bucket filled with sand and decorate it with peanut strings, doughnuts, fruits, and other bird treats.

a few times around with light-gauge wire for hanging, then store the balls in the freezer until you need them. These suet balls are perfect for decorating young hemlocks or bare-branched shrubs.

Decorations for Birds

There are plenty of wonderful bird-pleasing ways to decorate your yard. Here are some of my favorites.

◆ Include some branches of berries when you fill your window boxes with fresh greenery for Christmas. Birds will soon find branches of holly, both the traditional evergreen type and the interesting deciduous varieties. Birds also like bayberries or juniper berries. The berries may attract robins, mockingbirds, waxwings, yellow-rumped warblers, and other berry lovers.

◆ Hang a wreath (or two or three) for the birds. A giant sunflower head, like the one shown in the illustration on page 76, makes a great instant wreath. Remove the center and add a decorative touch with a cluster of millet sprays or peanuts wired together. You may be able to find sunflower heads at craft shops or bird supply stores. Plan ahead for next year: Make a note on the August page of your calendar to set aside some of your own garden sunflower heads for making Christmas bird wreaths.

◆ Prepare for a bird Christmas by planting a spruce, fir, hemlock, pine, or other evergreen in fall, so it's ready for embellishment at holiday time.

◆ Ask your grocer for old grapes that are past their prime. You can often collect pounds of grapes for free or only a dollar or two. (While you're asking, you might mention that you'd also be happy to take old blueberries, cherries, and raspberries off your grocer's hands. Birds adore them.) Hang or wire the bunches of grapes to trees and shrubs around your yard and you may attract mockingbirds, robins, cedar waxwings, and bluebirds.

◆ Slice oranges into ¼-inch rounds and hang from strings sewn through the rind.

◆ Save red plastic mesh onion bags when they're empty. Cut the mesh into 4- or 5-inch squares and wrap around small chunks of suet or beef fat. Fasten tightly with a twist tie and hang from trees for colorful decorations.

◆ Day-old doughnuts are a favorite with chickadees, and even stale bread has appeal for lots of birds. Hang from short strings or poke onto branches.

◆ Make mini-wreaths of raisins by threading them onto a circle of wire.

◆ Save cat food or tuna cans. Punch a hole in each can and insert a loop of wire for hanging. Fill with melted suet. When the suet is almost hard, insert a 3-inch piece of ¼-inch dowel for a perch. Hang when the suet is firm.

◆ Peanut butter–stuffed pinecones are a classic. Using a spoon, spread extra-chunky peanut butter onto the cone, then loop a piece of wire or string beneath the first row of scales for hanging. You can stretch that expensive peanut butter by mixing it with ground suet or cornmeal, but don't roll the cone in birdseed; not all peanut-butter eaters eat birdseed mix.

To make edible wreaths for birds, decorate a metal wreath frame with mini-sunflower heads and mini-corn ears (left). Or cut the center out of a giant sunflower head and decorate it with clusters of peanuts in their shells and sprigs of millet (right).

ORANGE-RIND FEEDERS FOR BIRDS

You can turn an orange rind into a small bird feeder. Fill it with a special suet-and-fruit combination as a winter treat for the birds.

Several large oranges, any kind
Strong thread or twine
Gold and black raisins
Dried cherries (optional)
Chopped suet

1. Cut the oranges in half and scoop out the flesh.

2. Coarsely chop the orange flesh and set it aside.

3. Thread a carpet or tapestry needle with the thread or twine, and sew through the orange rind on one side, about ¼ inch from the top of the rind. Pull the thread most of the way through the rind.

4. Tie a knot in the twine so it's securely fastened to the rind. Then sew through the opposite side of the rind in the same position. Leave enough slack in the thread to create a short handle. Then tie off the thread as you did on the first side, and clip off the extra thread above the knot.

5. Combine the orange pulp with the raisins (and cherries, if used).

6. Fill half of the orange rind with the fruit mixture. Fill the other half with chopped suet.

7. Hang the filled feeder from a tree branch.

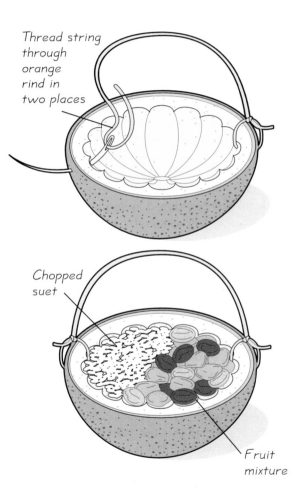

Thread string through orange rind in two places

Chopped suet

Fruit mixture

COLOR OF BIRDS

In spite of their diverse colors and their array of streaks, stripes, and spots, most birds are dressed for camouflage. A bird's survival often depends on concealment, especially for females sitting on the nest. So while male tanagers are fire-engine red and male orioles flash their brilliant orange or yellow in the sun, their mates are low-key olive green, all the better to blend in with the foliage around the nest.

Many male birds are brightly hued, possibly to advertise their presence not only to adoring females but also to rivals, who can easily spot a competing bird and either stay out of its territory or challenge it. But not all males sport flashy feathers. Many are as well concealed as females, especially birds that spend most of their lives close to ground level, where they're especially vulnerable to predators.

Concealing Colors

Many birds wear mottled, streaked, or greenish feathers that make them hard to see in their natural surroundings. When the bird sits still, this protective, or cryptic, coloration makes them almost disappear. It's a neat trick that birds use when danger threatens or when they're waiting for unsuspecting prey to come near. Cryptic colors come in several variations.

◆ When you see a bird with streaked or striped feathers, you can bet that it lives in grassy areas. The streaky white-and-brown belly of a song sparrow, for instance, makes it hard to separate bird from field grasses when it's sitting still.
◆ Birds with green feathers are birds of the treetops. If they didn't have such a herky-jerky habit of nervous motion, you'd probably never spot a warbler or a kinglet in the trees over your head. When the birds pause for a moment, they seem to disappear. Female scarlet tanagers and crossbills, which nest in the canopy, are green to match the leaves.
◆ Birds with dark backs and light bellies, like juncos, sparrows, sandpipers, and plovers, usually spend a lot of time on the ground. The light underside breaks up the shape of the bird and separates it from its shadow. It's much less noticeable than an all-dark bird would be.
◆ The mottled gray or brown feathers of an owl look just like the bark on the branch on which it's perched, making it easy to overlook the bird even in broad daylight.

Golden feathers and a streaky breast make a male yellow warbler blend in like a splash of sunlight on foliage. Finding well-camouflaged birds like this is a challenge for birdwatchers, and for bird predators.

Changing Colors

The color of a bird's feathers changes with the seasons and with its age. Young songbirds wear juvenile plumage that's usually more like Mom's than Dad's for their first year. When a male bird is ready to take a mate, he switches to fancy-dress breeding plumage, often with bright colors to show off to the female. It makes sense for juvenile males to look different from adult males. It helps the females avoid wasting time responding to an underage male. You can learn more about which birds change color in breeding season by reading Molting on page 168.

Unusual Coloring

Albino birds, which lack pigment in eyes and skin as well as feathers, are rare, but partial albinos are not all that unusual. Age, injury, ill health, or poor nutrition can make feathers turn white. I frequently notice birds sporting a few white feathers on their heads or elsewhere, and sometimes I see a white blackbird or robin among a migrating flock.

Albinos and albinistic birds are eye-catching, and not just to us human observers. They're quick to be picked off by hawks because they stand out from the flock.

At the other end of the scale is melanism, an excess of dark pigment in the feathers. Unlike albinism, this is no freak accident but rather a genetically determined color form that is passed down through the generations. In some hawks the melanistic color phase is so pronounced that the bird is known by another name: Harlan's hawk, for instance, is a dark variation of the red-tailed hawk, lacking the usual white belly and chestnut tail.

The elusive color blue. Is an indigo bunting really blue? Well, that depends. Blue pigment doesn't exist in bird feathers: It's all an optical illusion. Only when light strikes

"blue" feathers do they show that delightful hue. In dim places, a "blue" bird shows up as dark brown or black. The $10 word for this is "schemochrome color." Blue birds apparently have a layer of reflecting cells over the dark brown pigment of their feathers. These reflecting cells shine blue when light hits them. Watch a goldfinch when it flies from shade to sun and you'll see it's yellow all the way; watch a bluebird follow the same route and its color will change suddenly when it hits the light.

Normal male house finch

Partial albino house finch

Normal female house finch

Watch for birds with unusual coloring at your feeders. Some birds are almost black; others are pale or have striking white patches. Other birds are true albinos, born lacking pigment in feathers, eyes, feet, and beaks.

COLUMBINES

Hummingbirds relish columbines. The jewel-toned birds hover above columbine flowers like helicopters as they slip their slender beaks into the long "spurs" of each blossom to reach its sweet nectar. If you haven't attracted hummers to your yard yet, put out the welcome sign by planting red-and-yellow-flowered wild columbine (*Aquilegia canadensis*) and its cousin, crimson columbine (*A. formosa*). Once the birds find your garden, any color of columbine will keep them coming back.

Columbine Basics

Plant columbine seeds in full sun to light or part shade in average to fertile, well-drained soil. For best flowering, dig in a generous helping of compost or other organic matter before you plant. I like to sow a seed mix that will produce flowers in many colors, such as the large-flowered 'McKana' hybrid columbines.

Columbines are long blooming, but not long-lived. The parent plants peter out after a few years, but volunteer seedlings usually spring up to take their place. When we moved into a century-old Pennsylvania farmhouse, I was delighted to find a bed of old-fashioned columbines. Left to their own devices, they'd seeded themselves for years into a dozen different colors and a beautiful variety of plant

Hummingbirds find columbines irresistible. Gardeners in the Southwest and Far West may spot black-chinned hummingbirds sipping nectar from blue-flowered Rocky Mountain columbine.

forms and flower shapes. That's one of the many pleasures of columbines: They hybridize freely and seedlings, which bloom in their second year, are always a delightful surprise.

Columbines look best planted in drifts. The flowers open from spring through early summer, and the ground-hugging fernlike foliage forms a beautiful dense blue-green carpet, flourishing even in dry shade beneath trees or in rocky areas.

Choosing columbines. You can choose from species and cultivars ranging in size from 6-inch mounds to plants that grow 3 feet tall and wide. My favorites are some of the medium-size columbines such as golden columbine (*A. chrysantha*), which has big, long-spurred, sulfur yellow flowers. Other good choices are Rocky Mountain columbine (*A. caerulea*) with its airy blue flowers, and the short-spurred cottage garden columbine (*A. vulgaris*) and its hybrids, which seed themselves in a wonderful mix of colors and flower types. Most species thrive in Zones 3 to 10. Grow the hybrids in Zones 5 to 10.

COMPOSTING

Compost changes garden trash to garden treasure. When you make compost, you turn garden wastes like pulled weeds, veggie scraps, and dead leaves into a rich organic soil improver and fertilizer.

One bonus for backyard birdwatchers of keeping a simple compost pile is the great birdwatching opportunities it provides. A compost pile is always full of food for the birds: earthworms and assorted bugs, from sow bugs to millipedes to beetles of every persuasion. Robins visit compost piles to grub around in the finished compost at the bottom of the pile. Wood thrushes, towhees, and thrashers flip over leaves in the pile to snatch up tasty insect morsels. One summer I tossed several pounds of over-the-hill bananas, swarming with fruit flies, atop the compost heap. In minutes, a phoebe showed up to do some serious fly catching.

My compost pile also serves the birds in another way. Judging by the traffic it draws from late spring to early summer, it's a great source of material for nests. Everybody from blue jays to house wrens visits the pile to select just-right twigs, leaves, plant stems, and grasses.

Easy Composting

I like the get-it-for-free aspect of compost. It really doesn't take much energy to cart a load of clippings and snippings to the compost heap behind my shed, and it certainly doesn't cost me anything but my time. I'm an easygoing composter—I just shovel material onto the pile and leave it to rot.

To build a lazy compost pile, all you need is a low pile of twigs on well-drained ground.

On the brush, pile up layers several inches thick of dry brown material, such as straw, dead grass, or leaves. Cover each brown layer with a thin layer of fresh green material, such as fresh clippings, weeds, and vegetable scraps. Water each layer enough to keep the pile slightly damp. When the pile is 3 feet square by 3 feet tall, cover it with a brown layer and let it decompose for at least six months. Sift the finished compost before you use it, pulling out the undecomposed ingredients for starting a new pile.

If you want to speed up the composting process, use a garden fork to turn and fluff the materials in the pile every week or two. This will increase the biological activity in the pile and give you more compost sooner.

A healthy compost pile full of bugs and earthworms is an all-you-can-eat buffet for backyard birds. In the spring, birds also raid compost piles looking for twigs and grasses to build nests.

CONEFLOWERS

No self-respecting bird garden should be without coneflowers. These long-blooming perennials have daisylike flowers with centers that stick up like the crowns of Mexican sombreros. And those high-hat centers are packed with nutritious seeds for backyard birds like finches, sparrows, and buntings.

These easy-to-grow perennials flourish in poor soil or rich loam. They're hardy over a wide range, most types at least from Zones 4 to 9. Coneflowers are usually untroubled by pests and diseases, take the worst droughts in stride, and rarely need dividing. Best of all, they bloom their heads off for most of the summer, year after year.

Carefree Wonders

Coneflowers are easy to grow from seeds. Sow the seeds in a sunny spot in well-drained average garden soil, and keep the soil evenly moist until the young plants have several sets of leaves. After that they need watering only when the soil dries out. These knee-high to waist-high flowers are also beautiful combined with other meadow flowers or with ornamental grasses like feather reed grass (*Calamagrostis acutiflora*) and maiden grass (*Miscanthus sinensis*). And any coneflower seeds the birds don't eat will self-sow to spread the beauty.

Choice Coneflowers

You probably know one of the most common coneflowers by another name: black-eyed Susan (*Rudbeckia fulgida*). Ol' Susie is so named because of the big black centers in her yellow flowers. She has several garden-worthy sisters who share her looks: shining coneflower (*R. nitida*), brown-eyed Susan (*R. triloba*), and cut-leaved coneflower (*R. laciniata*).

Prairie coneflowers (*Ratibida* spp.) have "wilder"-looking flowers than black-eyed Susans—their petals droop and are often widely spaced around the raised center like a gaptoothed smile. My favorite is the gray-headed coneflower (*Ratibida pinnata*), partly because it's also a favorite with goldfinches.

Beautiful purple coneflowers (*Echinacea purpurea*) are one of the longest-blooming perennials in my garden. They start in early summer and don't stop until frost. I don't deadhead the spent blooms, because the birds arrive to dine as soon as each seedhead ripens.

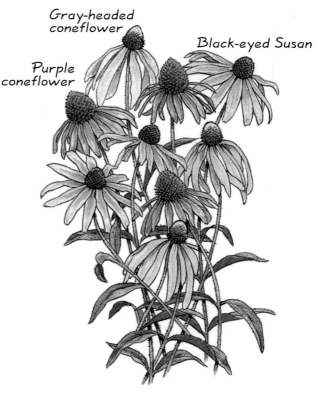

Coneflowers and black-eyed Susans are easy to grow, and they'll bring winged wildlife flocking. The flowers attract butterflies, and the seedheads are a great draw for birds.

CORAL BELLS

Coral bells flowers are delicate, but they pack a big punch with hummingbirds. Coral bells (*Heuchera sanguinea* and *H. × brizoides*) sport tiny red, pink, white, or salmon blossoms that dangle above the foliage like fringed bells in late spring. If you clip off old flowerstalks when the blossoms fade, the plants will continue pushing up new flowering stems for months. But even when they're not in bloom, the 1- to 2½-foot-tall mounds of foliage add an air of tidiness to the garden (even one as unmanicured as mine). Some types have fancy leaves ranging from bright green to nearly black, with splotches of silver and pink, or red veining.

Plant coral bells at the fronts of your borders and along the edges of paths in rich, loose, well-drained, moist soil. If you're cursed with clay soil, lighten it up with plenty of leaf mold and compost to make your coral bells happy. These hardy perennials (Zones 3 to 8) do best in full sun in the North, but in the South they'll live longer in sites with partial or afternoon shade.

Coral bells have beautiful scalloped leaves, and ruby-throated hummingbirds and other hummers love their dainty flowers, particularly when the blossoms are red.

CORN

Corn is great bird food for birdwatchers on a budget. When I lived on a shoestring, I looked forward each fall to gathering corn left behind after the farmer had harvested the neighboring fields. I'd come home dragging burlap sacks full of corncobs, feeling like a wealthy woman. It was easy to collect enough to keep my cardinals happy all winter.

Since those days I've learned that the stray ears of corn in farm fields are an important resource for birds in winter, so now I buy corn for my feeders at the store. I still enjoy birdwatching in nearby cornfields in the winter. It's easy to spot cardinals, jays, blackbirds, sparrows, crows, pheasants, and woodpeckers industriously pecking at corncobs and kernels.

Cracked corn for the birds. At the home feeder, cardinals often prefer cracked corn to sunflower seeds. That's good news, because corn is a great bargain. It's available from bird supply stores, but you may find the best prices if you buy it at hardware and farm-supply stores, where it's sold as chicken feed.

Corn in a hedge. For a long-lasting, help-yourself bird feeder, try planting a corn "hedge." I like to plant unusual corn, such as red-leaved 'Stalker' or 'Santo Domingo Blue', which produces huge ears. The hedge will be lovely and green during the growing season, and will draw birds to feed all through the fall and winter.

Corn for squirrels. If you like to feed squirrels in your backyard, you'll find that dried ear corn is the food of choice for squirrel feeders. It's easy to build a simple corncob feeder; for directions, see the illustration on page 228. The feeders may draw birds as well as squirrels. Many a time, I've seen squirrels driven away from feeders by a determined red-bellied or red-headed woodpecker. Both of them are big fans of corn, and when they're eating, they don't like to share. The scene on the ground below feeders is a different story. That's where juncos, cardinals, sparrows, and towhees gather to snap up bits of corn that drop from above.

Cosmos

"Cosmos" comes from the Greek word for beauty, and this plant certainly is. Its 4-inch flowers have bright yellow centers, and the petals can be white or eye-popping shades of hot pink, mauve, or red. Individual flowers fade quickly, but as the seedheads ripen, finches, buntings, and sparrows will find them. The birds in my garden nibble on cosmos seeds from summer all the way through winter, when the ground beneath the plants looks stitched together by the prints of bird feet after every dusting of snow.

Cosmos (*Cosmos bipinnatus*) is a long-blooming annual that produces new blossoms from midsummer until fall. It has lacy foliage on branching stems up to 4 feet tall. Yellow or Klondike cosmos (*C. sulphureus*) plants are shorter and stiffer.

Sow cosmos seeds in moist, well-drained garden soil after all danger of frost is past in spring. The seeds germinate in less than a week. Cosmos plants are practically carefree, and the seeds that the birds drop will self-sow, no matter where you live, guaranteeing flowers for next year. For a colorful, easy-care planting, try mixing regular cosmos and yellow cosmos together. Over the years, as the plants self-sow, the flowers may revert to other colors like purple-rose and deep orange. Believe it or not, the colors will look great together!

Goldfinches love to nibble cosmos seeds. You may spot these gorgeous yellow birds hanging nearly upside down from delicate stems as they pluck the seeds.

COURTSHIP

"Friendship, courtship, love, marriage": Adapt that old jump-rope rhyme to birdlife and the same steps apply. Birds pal around as "just friends" until lengthening spring days cause hormonal changes that trigger the instinct to mate. Then, like teenagers at the mall, they start showing off to attract the attention of a potential mate with whom they can share the duties of building a nest and raising a family.

The courtship stage may be serious business for birds, but it's great fun to watch. Birds will play out their love scenes right under our noses. From the first billing and cooing of mourning doves at crocus-blooming time, to the heartbreaking aerial love song of the indigo bunting during those mild May days that put everyone in the mood for love, your bird-friendly backyard will be full of courtship displays and song during dating season for birds.

Competing for Females

Male birds are at the mercy of their pituitary gland, which reacts to the longer days of spring by pouring out a dose of sex hormones that trigger the urge to mate. In spring, migratory male songbirds arrive in their breeding territories before the females. By the time the girls roll in, the male is in fine fettle, his feathers bright, his singing voice tuned up, and his boundaries defined and defended. Now it's time to find a date.

A male bird's best pickup line is his song, which he repeats over and over. Like girls at a junior high dance, when female birds first move into a male's territory, they pretend not to care much about silly boys. So the male bird becomes an ardent pursuer, pulling out

Male house wrens work industriously to please their mates. The male bird builds several trial nests for the female's inspection. If she approves of one, she'll line it with soft material and lay her eggs there.

all the tricks in his book: courtship flights, head bobbing, and other bizarre body movements, food offerings, and other rituals. Who could resist? Though she may be blasé for a day or two or three, the female soon accepts the male.

Billing and Cooing

"Billing and cooing" isn't a phrase made up by the lyricists of mushy love songs—it's a literal description of the courtship behavior of birds in the pigeon family.

Listen for the low, mournful, "cooing" love song of mourning doves in your backyard and you'll know that the pair is about to embark on another round of nesting. (These prolific birds raise a new brood every few weeks; in mild climates, they may start a new nest every month of the year!)

If you happen to intrude upon a more private moment of dove courtship, you may get to see "billing" in action. Just like passionate human kissing, this behavior is often performed prior to mating. The female begins the ritual by putting her beak into the male's open mouth. Together, with beaks joined, the two bob their heads up and down.

Long-Lasting Pairs

Many songbirds pair up for life. For example, that pair of cardinals in your rosebush may be the same Mom and Pop returning each spring. Keep in mind though that wild birds usually live only a few years, so "till death do us part" isn't as long-term a commitment as it is for longer-lived animals. And DNA testing of offspring and their parents shows that the female may breed with more than one male, even though she bonds with one particular male. Songbird pairs still go through a courtship phase each spring—call it a second honeymoon.

Other birds, including house wrens and bank swallows, may join together for only a single season or even a single brood (many birds raise more than one batch of nestlings a season). But whether they're mated for life or just for the moment, both birds usually share parental duties—they take turns incubating the eggs, bringing food to the nestlings, and helping the fledglings get off on their own.

Love Hummingbird-Style

Some birds, including hummingbirds, may mate with any other bird of their species that comes along. Hummingbird life moves at such a fast pace that the pair bond may last only a couple of hours. The female hummingbird builds her nest single-handedly and then looks for the closest available male. There's still a brief courtship, including dazzling aerial courtship flights by the male, which is quickly followed by mating.

The first time I saw a pair of ruby-throated hummingbirds mating, I couldn't believe my eyes. The birds were locked together in what I took to be a death grip, and were spinning just above the ground like Fourth of July fireworks. Whizzing in circles, they were oblivious to my approach, and when I bent down to separate them, I realized why. Oops!

As the birds spun with loudly buzzing wings, the male tilted his head back so that the sun could strike his brilliant throat feathers, lighting them like fire. The wind this little duo created was strong enough to bend and flatten the plants in the garden beneath them. After a few minutes the fire-

While a male red-winged blackbird sings to establish his breeding territory, he also spreads his tail and displays his bright wing patches.

COURT AND SPARK

Birds don't seem to be shy about performing their loving gestures in front of a human audience, so if you keep an alert eye on your backyard, you may get to witness many of the odd and endearing rites that birds use during courtship, like head bobbing, bowing, and drumming.

BEHAVIOR	DESCRIPTION	BIRDS THAT INDULGE
Bowing	Male tilts its head and body as if bowing to the queen	Jays, house sparrows, grackles
Courtship flight	Male flies over open space, often rising extremely high into the air, and sings an accompanying song	Larks, buntings, woodcocks, hummingbirds
Crown display	Male raises head feathers to display a bright-colored patch	Kinglets, ovenbirds, eastern kingbirds
Drumming with beak	Male drums with his beak on tree limbs, roofs, barrels, and other objects	Woodpeckers
Head bobbing	Male and female face each other and dip their heads quickly and repeatedly	Pigeons, doves, flickers, crows
Parading	Male struts or postures before female to show off colorful feathers on head, breast, or body	Robins, tanagers, orioles
Wing flashing	Male opens and closes wings and tail to show off bright patterns	Wood warblers, woodpeckers

works were over and the birds went their separate ways.

Once mating is finished, the female hummingbird goes off to lay her eggs and rear her young by herself. She's so intent on her role as female head of household that she'll drive off the male if he happens to wander into her nesting territory.

Male birds of some species, including the red-winged blackbird and the house wren, don't stop with one mate: They often court and mate with several females. With so many nests and so little time, the male doesn't get involved in caring for the baby birds. Instead, it's the females of these species that raise the young. They get little or no help from the males, who are usually busy strutting their stuff for some other admiring female.

You may find yourself feeling fonder of bonded bird pairs that share the chores of raising youngsters, but remember, birds and other wildlife follow nature's rules, not human rules. No matter what kind of courtship techniques your backyard birds indulge in, the courtship season is always a great time to learn more about bird behavior.

COWBIRDS

When it comes to no-work parenting, cow-birds have things all figured out. Instead of providing for their nestlings, they let other birds do all the work. Cowbirds lay their eggs—usually one at a time—in other birds' nests, and never look back. The unsuspecting "babysitters" raise the cowbird nestling as if it were their own. When a cardinal in your back-yard shows up with a squalling, plump gray youngster in tow, you're seeing the results of cowbird behavior in action.

Handsome Home Wreckers

You'll often find cowbirds among a flock of blackbirds, and it's difficult to tell them apart. The attractive male brown-headed cowbird is 7 inches long—slightly smaller than most blackbirds—and has a shorter, wider bill. It has a lustrous black body and a contrasting rich brown head, and a pretty, gurgling song. The female brown-headed cowbird is a dowdy gray. They range across most of the country.

In the Southwest and Texas, bronzed cow-birds are the common species. They're larger than brown-headed cowbirds and the males have stunning metallic glints of green, bronze, and sometimes blue on their midnight black feathers. Female bronzed cowbirds are paler. Both males and females have red eyes.

Cowbirds' habit of leaving their eggs for other birds to care for poses some serious problems for songbirds: The cowbird's egg often hatches earlier than the songbird eggs it shares a nest with, and the young cowbird is often larger and more aggressive than its fellow nestlings. As a result the cowbird nestling gets more food than its nest mates, and may crowd them out completely.

At Home amid Housing

Cowbirds are birds of the backyard or open country and woods' edges. They don't usually venture deep into woods or other under-growth where many songbirds nest. Cowbirds benefit—and songbirds suffer—when housing developments and other human activities re-duce the size of wooded and brushy areas. These smaller "wild" sites no longer give song-birds' nests the protection they need against the parasitic cowbirds. For example, the black-capped vireo of the south-central United States was rarely bothered by cowbirds until clearing brush became common in its Texas habitat. Now black-capped vireo nests often hold a brown-flecked white cowbird egg.

Because they lay their eggs in songbird nests, cowbirds aren't always a welcome sight, but they're not all bad. Cowbirds eat grasshoppers and other pests, as well as the seeds of many common garden weeds. Dandelions are among their favorites!

A few birds have learned to outwit cowbirds. Some push the cowbird's egg out of the nest. Others, like the common yellowthroat, may build a second nest on top of the first one, burying the cowbird egg.

If you keep an eye out for cowbirds during nesting season, they'll often show you where songbirds are nesting in your neighborhood. They have a much better eye for spotting nests than most of us do.

CRABAPPLES

Fruit isn't the only attraction that crabapples have for birds—or for gardeners. When you plant crabapples, you'll also enjoy the cloud of flowers that cover the trees in spring. You may not notice the insects on those flowers, but vireos, warblers, orioles, and other insect-eating birds certainly will. Later in the season, crabapple fruits attract waxwings, robins, bluebirds, and other thrushes, along with blue jays, Carolina wrens, mockingbirds, and more. Birds seem to like crabapples best in late fall after a few hard frosts, when the fruits are shriveled and soft.

Because most crabapples (*Malus* spp.) are small to midsize trees (under 20 feet tall),

'Prairifire'

'Hopa'

'Dolgo'

'Centennial'

'Chestnut Crab'

Crabapples are eye-catching to birds and gardeners alike. The reddish bronze, purplish red, or crimson fruits will brighten up your fall and winter garden—but only for as long as it takes hungry birds to discover and devour them.

they're easy to fit into a backyard. Crabapple trees grow best in moist but well-drained, acid soil, but they'll adapt to less perfect conditions. Grow crabapples in full sun in Zones 3 to 9.

Crabapples are vulnerable to diseases including fire blight, scab, and cedar apple rust. Most of these diseases result in discolored foliage or early leaf drop, but aren't fatal. When you buy crabapples, choose cultivars labeled as disease-resistant. If you already have crabapple trees in your yard, appreciate them despite their disease problems—the birds won't mind if the fruit isn't picture-perfect.

Crabapple Choices

To get a winning crabapple for your bird garden, find a local nursery that grows its plants in the ground (rather than in containers), and ask the staff which cultivars attract lots of birds during the winter. Tried-and-true cultivars include 'Cardinal', which has few disease problems and is loaded with sweet fruits that have dark red skin and red flesh.

Disease-resistant 'Prairifire' is hardy to Zone 4, has foliage that's tinged reddish purple, and produces small fruits of the same color. 'Dolgo' also shrugs off common diseases. Its olive-shaped fruits are a rich crimson. Hardy to Zone 2, 'Dolgo' laughs off winter cold, and so does 'Chestnut Crab', which can survive Zone 1 winters. 'Chestnut Crab' is resistant to cedar apple rust, and robins love its reddish bronze fruits.

If you have a very small yard, try the compact 'Centennial', which tops out at only 12 feet. Its bright red-and-yellow fruits are tops with birds.

Old-fashioned 'Hopa' is more disease prone than most modern, disease-resistant cultivars, but it will grow well in dry climates, like that of the Rocky Mountains. In humid climates, 'Hopa' will probably suffer from apple scab, but birds are so fond of its red-orange fruits that you may decide it's worth planting this tree in a discreet garden corner. That way you won't notice the diseased leaves as much, but you can still enjoy the tree's bird-drawing power in winter.

In my experience, crabapples from older cultivars like 'Hopa' as well as those from prairie crabapple (*M. ioensis*), wild crabapple (*M. sylvestris*), and Siberian crabapple (*M. baccata*) attract birds the best. These crabapple trees are less showy than most new cultivars, but apparently their fruits taste better to the birds!

CROSSBILLS

It's easy to see how crossbills get their name: the upper and lower parts of their beak overlap at an angle. Although the crossed beak looks extremely awkward, it's actually the perfect tool for extricating seeds from a pinecone, one of their favorite foods.

It's fascinating to watch crossbills eat. These slow-moving, almost tame birds contort themselves like parrots as they reach for cones. Train your binoculars on a dining crossbill and you'll see that the bird uses its beak to force open the scales of a cone, then wraps its tongue around the seed to extract it.

Getting to Know Them

Red crossbills and the very similar white-winged crossbills belong to the finch family. The males are reddish birds about 5 to 6½

Like all crossbills, red crossbills have specialized beaks that are perfect for picking seeds out of pinecones. It's tricky for crossbills to eat other foods, but they do manage to take their share of sunflower seeds at backyard feeders.

inches long. The females are dusky yellowish green, just the right coloring for hiding at their nests in evergreens.

Crossbills build nests of twigs, fine roots, and strips of bark and fasten them to branches of conifers like pines or spruces, usually near the tip of a branch. Females lay three or four pale blue or pale green eggs. To keep the eggs cozy, crossbills line their nests with soft mosses or springy lichens, fine grasses, feathers, and fur.

Red crossbills and white-winged crossbills may look and act alike, but their songs are very different. The red bird is the more accomplished songster. Its warbled phrases have a

beautiful tone, but they're impossible for humans to "translate." White-winged crossbills have a song like the tweets of a goldfinch or pet canary. The males of both species have the utterly charming habit of serenading their mate while in flight, circling her as she sits perched. Who could resist?

Both red crossbills and white-winged crossbills live year-round in evergreen forests ranging from the Atlantic Ocean to the Pacific. Red crossbills are the species you'll usually see, because white-winged crossbills are birds of the frigid North. When food is short or populations build, both species may leave their usual haunts and invade other territory in search of food.

Attracting Crossbills

Planting conifers is the surest way to attract crossbills to your yard. Pines, spruces, hemlocks, firs, and larches are all good choices.

Crossbills also enjoy the seeds of deciduous trees, like maples, birches, and alders. Alders are widespread across the United States in mixed hedgerows and streamside thickets. They usually take the form of multistemmed shrubs. If you have alders in your yard, let your crossbills enjoy them. If you don't, take care before you decide to plant them: They spread fast, especially in moist soil.

Sunflower seeds are also a favorite crossbill food, either gleaned from plants in the garden or taken from a feeder. Another good way to lure crossbills is by offering a salt block, as shown on page 33. Both species have a craving for salt. If you live in a brick house, take note: Red crossbills have also been known to eat the mortar between bricks!

CROWS AND RAVENS

Crows and ravens are mighty smart birds, as you know if you've ever tried to keep them out of your vegetable garden: A scarecrow doesn't fool them for long at all. These clever birds are fascinated by shiny objects and can even invent their own games.

Ornithologists agree that crows and ravens are most intelligent kinds of birds. In experiments, they've been taught to count (up to four, but it's a start), plus they're fast and skillful at solving puzzles.

Big and Bold

Big, bold, and glossy black, crows and ravens are closely related birds that are common across much of North America. Male and female look alike.

These big, fearless birds are aggressive attackers when a predator invades their turf. They can drive off a hawk, owl, or prowling pussycat. They can be great mimics, imitating humans as well as other birds and animals.

Crows and ravens are well known for their cast-iron stomachs, eating just about anything from bird eggs to insects to shellfish to roadkill, plus plenty of corn and berries. They build huge, bulky nests often high up in large trees, with an outer layer of sticks and a soft lining of fur, grasses, and seaweed if it's handy, for their four to seven greenish or blue-green, brown-splotched eggs.

American crow. The American crow is about 18 inches long and ranges across the United States. Usually solitary or in pairs during most of the year, they roost in huge flocks in winter. American crows are usually solitary nesters, but they may occasionally nest in colonies, especially in the West.

The Wild World of Backyard Birds

When you hear a bunch of crows making a commotion, check it out. Chances are you'll find something interesting going on. Often an outbreak of harsh caws leads me to an owl perched motionless in a tree, or to a hawk in the yard, or to a threatening cat or other predator.

One morning I hung my black sweater on a handy shrub while I worked in the garden. Minutes later I heard crows causing a fuss nearby. It took me several minutes to realize they were yapping about my sweater. I think maybe they thought it was a member of their tribe in trouble.

Fish crow. The fish crow is about 15 inches long and is found along the Atlantic and Gulf Coasts, usually near water. Fish crows hang out in groups and, like the American crow, roost in winter in large flocks. They often use small evergreen trees like hollies and cedars for their nests. If you live in fish-crow range, one way to draw them to your yard is to plant hollies and dogwoods—these birds love the fruits.

Common raven. The common raven looks a lot like a crow that's been working out. At about 24 inches long, it's bigger and chunkier, with a heavy beak and shaggy throat feathers. Ravens are common in northern forests, in the West, and also occur in the Appalachians and along the Pacific and Atlantic Coasts. The raven uses its hoarse voice to create a variety of unearthly croaking sounds.

If you want to lure these statuesque birds to your yard, try putting out tufts of undyed sheep wool (you can get them at a weaving supplies or craft shop) during nesting season, which lasts from March to June.

Savvy Scavengers

Crows and ravens eat just about anything—dead or alive—that they can get their beaks on. Both are scavengers, which helps keep our roadsides tidy. They also dine on insects, frogs, snakes, shellfish (which they drop from the air to crack on rocks), crayfish, mice, grain, fruit, and other goodies. Adapting to human ways, they've become expert at raiding the trash and begging for handouts at picnic grounds, campsites, and fast-food parking lots.

Crows and ravens also feed on bird eggs and young birds. Songbirds treat them as predators, and rightly so. Watch a crow fly over your yard and you'll see every nesting bird go on the alert, with a few brave souls, usually blue jays, mockingbirds, or blackbirds and grackles, mounting an aerial attack.

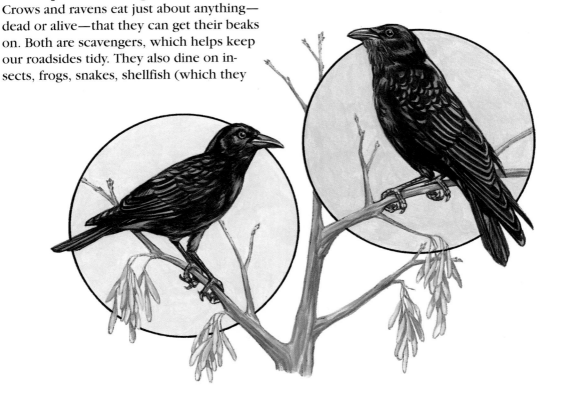

If you spot a large black bird perched high in the top of a tall tree, you may have trouble deciding whether it's a crow (left) or a raven (right). Watching these birds in flight offers useful clues: Crows fly "straight as the crow flies," while the raven often soars in wide circles like a hawk.

CUCKOOS

If you hear a low-pitched *cooo-cooo-cooo* on a humid summer afternoon, you're listening to a real cuckoo, also called a "rain crow" by folks who say this bird can predict the weather. It's true that cuckoos do seem to be more vocal when the air is thick with humidity, but it's also true that they're rather talkative birds whatever the weather.

Getting to Know Them

Cuckoos are slim, streamlined birds, almost a foot long from the tip of their down-curved beak to the end of their long tail. They hold their heads low, with hunched shoulders, and slip between the foliage of the trees with almost snaky movements.

Cuckoos have brown backs and snowy white bellies, and the male and female birds look alike. Two species—the yellow-billed cuckoo and the black-billed cuckoo—are common across most of the United States. The yellow-billed cuckoo nests across the entire country except for a skinny strip along the coasts, whereas the very similar black-billed cuckoo nests in the eastern two-thirds of the continent. Both species retire to South America for the winter.

Black-billed cuckoos have black beaks; the yellow-billed cuckoo's beak has a yellow lower half. In flight the yellow-billed cuckoo flashes beautiful rusty wing patches. The yellow-billed cuckoo sports distinct, wide, bright white spots on the black underside of its tail. The black-billed cuckoo's tail has narrower white patches that don't show up as well against its grayish brown underside.

Black-billed cuckoos prefer woodlands, though they'll visit your yard if it features trees and adjoins a nearby patch of woods. Yellow-billed cuckoos stay clear of dense woods and prefer thickets and brush and well-shrubbed yards. Both nest surprisingly low to the ground, from 2 to 12 feet high, laying two to four blue-green eggs in a flattish nest built of twigs and grasses and lined with ferns or moss.

Attracting Cuckoos

World-class caterpillar eaters, cuckoos keep trees healthy by cleaning their foliage of all kinds of leaf-eating caterpillars, including tent caterpillars and gypsy moth caterpillars. They also eat other insects and fruit.

Planting plenty of shrubs and trees will invite cuckoos to your yard. You can also plant mulberries, raspberries, and grapes to attract them. If open space separates your yard from a nearby brushy or wooded area, watch for cuckoos flying across the open space. They have a distinctive look in flight, flying swiftly with their long tail gracefully streaming out behind.

Even though other birds turn up their beaks at such fuzzy fare, yellow-billed cuckoos consider gypsy moth caterpillars a real treat!

DOG FOOD

A 50-pound sack of kibble can go a long way toward keeping your backyard birds well fed. In winter, dry dog food makes an excellent high-protein food for insect-eating birds like wrens and bluebirds. And mockingbirds, starlings, grackles, crows, jays, and other birds who like a little meat in their diet will appreciate an offering of dog chow at any time of year.

Soft dog food is easier for birds to swallow than whole dry pieces, which can get lodged in their throats. To moisten dry kibble, just pour enough hot water over the dog food to give it the consistency of a moist sponge, and set a container of it near a bird-feeding station in your yard. An old lasagna pan or cookie sheet (check thrift shops for a bargain-priced selection) makes a good serving container.

When you first start offering dog food, put it out in small amounts—a cup at a time. After you get a feel for how much the birds are eating, you can increase the amount. Dog food that's still in the pan at the end of the day will attract other wildlife to your feeding area: opossums, raccoons, and possibly stray cats, dogs, foxes, or coyotes. If they're not on your list of invited guests, reduce the amount of dog food you offer so that the birds empty the pan during the daytime.

DOUGHNUTS

Become a regular at the day-old counter of your local doughnut shop and your chickadees will thank you for it. These high-fat, high-calorie treats are a good source of energy for birds. Chickadees, titmice, mockingbirds, jays, robins, sparrows, starlings, and even bluebirds all enjoy an occasional nibble of doughnut. Feed birds store-bought doughnuts of the plain cake type or use your favorite recipe to make your own cake doughnuts. If you don't have a doughnut recipe, turn to page 73 for a recipe for "Chickadee Doughnut Delights."

You can serve birds doughnuts one of two ways. Break the stale doughnuts into pieces and place them on a tray feeder, or hang a whole doughnut on an easy-to-make doughnut feeder like the one shown on this page. If you're feeding small birds like chickadees, who nibble politely at their food, just hang the doughnut from the nail. But if larger birds such as jays frequent the feeder, impale the doughnut on the nail—otherwise the big birds may knock the treat off and fly away with it wholesale.

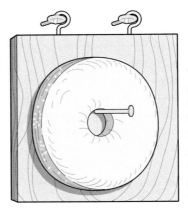

To make a simple doughnut feeder, hammer a long, stout nail into a 1 × 4 or 2 × 4 board and hang it from a post.

DOVES

Doves live up to their reputation as the symbol of love. The birds mate for life, although if either spouse dies, the survivor doesn't stay a widow or widower for long. They're definitely the right subjects for Valentine's Day cards—when mating season begins, the male is constantly in pursuit of his lady love.

Getting to Know Them

Doves are large birds, about 12 to 14 inches long, with a small head atop a plump-breasted body. Male doves are decorated with iridescent color on their necks that glows with metallic green, purple, or pink in the sun.

You won't often see a lone dove; they're usually in pairs or in groups. They raise several broods each year, nesting year-round in mild-winter areas. Their construction skills aren't as fine as most birds: The nest is a crude, flimsy-looking shallow platform of sticks so thin you can often look right through the twigs from below and see the white egg or eggs—only one or two babies are usually raised at each nesting.

Attracting Doves

It's easy to attract doves to your backyard. They frequently make their homes near houses and are quick to come to a handout of millet, grass seed, corn, or other grains and seeds. Bread crumbs are also a favorite.

In the garden, doves devour grass and clover seeds, along with weed seeds like ragweed, lamb's-quarters, and wood sorrel, and they enjoy the fruits of elderberry and pokeberry. Water is a big draw for doves. They like a ground-level pool or shallow basin for drinking and bathing. Put out grit for these birds, and add a salt block to your garden.

Dove Checklist

Doves are marvelous in flight. They have large breast muscles and streamlined wings, making them among the fastest fliers in the bird world.

Mourning dove. Mourning doves, the soft gray-brown birds that nest in every mainland state, are a common sight in the backyard or open country. The sweet, sad, familiar *coooah, cooo, cooo, cooo* gives the bird its name. They usually lay only two eggs, but they nest several times a year—year-round in warm regions and from late winter through fall in colder places.

Rock dove. Another widespread dove is the ubiquitous rock dove, or pigeon. Long ago these gray, brown, or occasionally white birds were most common on rocky cliffs, but nowadays rock doves nest in cities on buildings and under bridges. If you're a city dweller or if you

Both mourning dove parents take turns sitting on their crude stick nests. Mourning dove nests are easy to find because these big birds are so noticeable as they come and go.

live in the range of a countryside flock, you may host these large, pretty birds in your garden, where they eat seeds of weeds, grass, and clover, or at your feeder, where they enjoy bread crumbs and cracked corn.

Band-tailed pigeon. Band-tailed pigeons, which nest in the Northwest and winter in the Southwest, look like blue-gray rock doves but live in the woods and mountains. Their call sounds like an owl's hoots, and they eat mostly berries and acorns instead of seeds. Plant elderberries, blueberries, or dogwoods to attract them to your garden; they may also come for corn at the feeder.

DUSTBATHS

Most birds prefer to clean their feathers in water, but some like to get down and dirty in soft dust. Watching a bird at a dustbath is as entertaining as watching one splash in a puddle. They lie belly-down in a soft spot of dust, then ruffle their wings and waggle their tails to flick the silt through their feathers. When they're finished, they rise, give a great shake that raises a dusty cloud, and retreat to a perch to preen.

Most of the birds that dust bathe are birds of open country, like larks and quail, but even some birds that live in very humid regions prefer never to splash in the wet stuff. Once a dust bather always a dust bather is the rule for most birds that engage in this behavior. And vice versa—birds that happily splatter about in the birdbath can't seem to see the point of wallowing in dust.

House sparrows are great dust bathers. They often squabble over who gets rights to the best spot. You may also see quail, pheasants, and wrens lolling in your backyard dustbath.

Dust bathing keeps feathers in shape just like water bathing: It realigns the tiny interlocking barbs of the feathers and fluffs up the small body feathers. It also reduces dandruff and removes excess oil. Another purpose of sifting dust through feathers may be to help control mites, lice, and other parasites.

Making a Dustbath

Just as you put out a birdbath for water-loving songbirds, you can make a convenient dust bowl for the dry-bathing birds that visit your backyard. Choose a sunny place away from pathways and other active areas of your yard. Strip the sod or other vegetation from an area about 3 feet square. Rake and crumble the soil to fine particles, and scoop out a couple of inviting shallow depressions. The birds will do the rest!

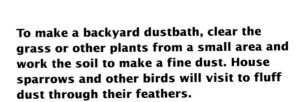

To make a backyard dustbath, clear the grass or other plants from a small area and work the soil to make a fine dust. House sparrows and other birds will visit to fluff dust through their feathers.

EARTHWORMS

If it weren't for earthworms, some of our favorite birds would have a hard time filling their bellies. Robins are the best-known worm eaters (for good reason—one estimate puts the figure at 43 percent of a robin's diet), but other birds enjoy these slimy treats, too. Most birds that eat earthworms spend much of their time on the ground or the forest floor eating insects and fruit rather than seeds. Wood thrushes, grackles, varied thrushes, magpies, and ovenbirds all devour earthworms, but they're not as dependent on them as robins. Eastern bluebirds also occasionally eat earthworms. Despite its name, the worm-eating warbler seldom indulges. What it eats are caterpillars, once commonly called "worms" (such as "woolly worms" and "oakworms").

Earthworms are welcome inhabitants of the backyard for other reasons, too. The tunnels that worms create to move through the soil help keep the soil light and fluffy. Roots can penetrate fluffy soil more easily, so plants grow better. Worms also work nutrients throughout the soil.

To encourage the presence of worms in your garden, use organic mulch such as grass clippings, aged manure, compost, or shredded leaves around your plants. These wigglers like moist soil, and the mulch preserves the dampness even in hot summer. They also will feed on the mulch and work it into the soil as they travel. Lift a layer of decomposing grass clippings or shredded leaf mulch and you'll see earthworms quickly withdrawing into their burrows.

EGGS

Bird eggs are beautiful. Unlike the bleached white chicken eggs we buy at the store, songbird eggs are often soft green, blue, or buff. Many have dark speckles or splotches that make each one a unique work of art. But although bird eggs can be wonderfully artistic, they're not for collecting. Songbirds are under federal protection, and it's against the law to collect nests or eggs. So if you spot a nest in your yard, take a discreet peek at the eggs, but don't touch.

When you're out working in your garden or walking in your yard in early summer, chances are you'll come across a bird eggshell, or part of one, on the ground. That's when you have the opportunity to take a close look at the size and markings. It's always fun to try to figure out what kind of bird laid the egg.

Egg Size

The first step in identifying the owner of a songbird egg is noticing the egg's size. Robin-size birds lay robin-egg-size eggs; sparrows lay small eggs; hummingbird eggs are tiniest of all, about the size of a big pea. After that, the egg's background color and any patterning on the shell can help you figure out who the parents might be.

Protective Coloring

Bird eggs aren't colored just to be pretty. Their coloring helps them blend in with the nest. Given that, you might think that white eggs belong to cavity-nesting birds, where protective coloration isn't necessary. Many birds that nest in holes, such as woodpeckers, swifts, and kingfishers, do lay white eggs. But the white-egg theory has several cracks: Some birds that nest in cavities—chickadees, nuthatches, wrens, and bluebirds, for instance—lay colored eggs, and doves, hummingbirds, owls, and some other birds that nest in the open lay white eggs. Check "Whose Egg Is It?" on page 100 for descriptions of some common songbird eggs.

Egg Predators

When you find eggshells in your yard, chances are it's a sign that predators have been at work. Jays and crows relish bird eggs, as do raccoons and even black bears. If the egg you find has yolk inside, it was probably dropped by a predator. If the eggshell is clean inside, it may be a leftover after hatching. Some parent birds tidy the house and carry eggshells away from the nest once the babies hatch.

Egg Laying

Backyard birds start nesting in your yard in early spring and continue into late summer. Birds like hawks and owls start nesting and egg laying in winter. To learn more about the whole nesting cycle, turn to Nesting on page 176.

Most songbirds lay an egg a day until they reach the appointed number, which is usually between three and six. Some birds are well known for their habit of laying eggs in other birds' nests. The cowbird is the most notorious example. Despite the difference in color and size, many birds apparently don't recognize a cowbird's egg as a foreign member of the family. Catbirds and robins, however, seem to see through the cowbird's ploy and will usually push cowbird eggs out of their nests.

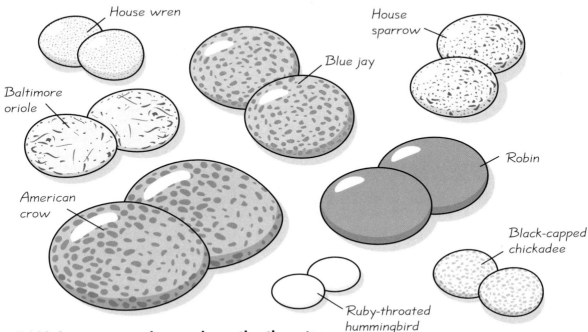

House wren

Baltimore oriole

American crow

Blue jay

House sparrow

Robin

Black-capped chickadee

Ruby-throated hummingbird

Wild bird eggs are much more decorative than standard hen eggs, and range in size from thumbnail-size hummingbird eggs to 2-inch-long crow eggs.

WHOSE EGG IS IT?

Bird eggs are delicate wonders. Here's a guide to the variety of eggs laid by some common backyard birds.

BIRD	USUAL NUMBER OF EGGS	EGG SIZE	EGG COLORING
Black-capped chickadee, Carolina chickadee	6 to 8	$\frac{9}{16}$" × $\frac{7}{16}$"	White with fine dots of reddish brown
Blue jay	4 or 5	$1\frac{1}{8}$" × $\frac{13}{16}$"	Pale olive to buff with some dark spots
Eastern bluebird	4 or 5	$\frac{13}{16}$" × $\frac{5}{8}$"	Pale blue
House sparrow	5	$\frac{7}{8}$" × $\frac{5}{8}$"	White, pale blue, or pale green with a few sparse brown or gray dots
House wren	6 to 8	$\frac{5}{8}$" × $\frac{1}{2}$"	White with brown speckles
Robin	4	$1\frac{1}{8}$" × $\frac{3}{4}$"	Clear pastel blue ("robin's-egg blue")
Song sparrow	3 to 6	$\frac{3}{4}$" × $\frac{5}{8}$"	Pale green to whitish green with heavy reddish brown splotches and spots
Starling	4 to 6	$1\frac{1}{8}$" × $\frac{13}{16}$"	White, pale blue, palest green
Tufted titmouse	5 or 6	$\frac{3}{4}$" × $\frac{9}{16}$"	White or creamy white with tiny reddish brown speckles

EGGSHELLS

Leftover shells from your breakfast sunny-side-ups are a good source of calcium for birds. Calcium is an important mineral supplement for egg-laying female birds in late winter and early spring. They need the calcium to strengthen the shells of their own eggs and the developing bones of the chicks within.

Small pieces of eggshell are the easiest for birds to eat. You can crush eggshells into small pieces by putting them between two sheets of waxed paper and running a rolling pin over the top sheet. Sprinkle the crushed shells in a tray feeder, in a spot that's separate from birdseed, so that birds who want the crushed shells won't have to compete with a crowd of seed eaters.

If you live in the North, where crossbills and evening grosbeaks make their home year-round, add crushed eggshells to the regular menu at your feeder. Crossbills and evening grosbeaks seem to crave calcium more than most other kinds of birds, so they especially will welcome an offering of crushed eggshells at your feeders.

Eggshells are also good for your garden, because your plants need calcium, too. You can add eggshells to your compost pile or sprinkle crushed eggshells directly on the soil in your garden beds.

EVERGREENS

Evergreens serve double-duty in bird-friendly yards. They provide year-round shelter for birds, and their cones and berries are a great food source.

When you think of evergreens, you probably picture familiar needled shrubs and trees like junipers and pines, but evergreens also include broad-leaved plants that keep their leaves in winter, like hollies and rhododendrons, and even groundcovers like some cotoneasters. When birds roost or nest in the dense heart of evergreens like these, they're protected from wind, rain, and snow. Raccoons and other night stalkers will think twice before they go after sleeping birds surrounded by the prickly evergreen branches.

Choosing Evergreens

Broad-leaved and needled evergreens provide all-season bird foods. In spring, rhododendrons and azaleas are smothered in pink, orange, or white nectar-filled flowers that attract hummingbirds. The sugary blossoms draw thousands of small insects, which in turn attract wood warblers, phoebes, and other insect-eating birds. In late summer and fall, the blue berries of junipers are popular with cedar waxwings and other fruit eaters. Robins and bluebirds can't resist holly berries, and neither can mockingbirds, thrushes, and starlings. Pinecones and the cones of spruce, fir, hemlock, and other conifers are packed with nutritious seeds that draw grosbeaks, crossbills, titmice, and pine siskins. The petite, seed-filled cones of hemlocks attract small seed eaters like chickadees, juncos, and goldfinches.

When you choose evergreens for your garden, remember that they're not all green, and they're not all the same shape or size.

Take advantage of the diversity of evergreens—try combining tall, columnar plants like cedars with rounded shrubs like yews, and then carpet the ground around them with spreading junipers. For added interest, combine needled evergreens in a variety of colors, such as gold, burgundy, and blue-green, with broad-leaved evergreens, such as hollies and rhododendrons. See "Best Evergreens for Birds" on page 102 for more ideas. For tips on planting and care of evergreens, turn to Trees on page 246.

Hemlock

Leatherleaf mahonia

Creeping juniper

American holly

To beautify your garden and provide first-class accommodations for birds, plant a grouping of evergreens, including shrubs, trees, and groundcovers.

BEST EVERGREENS FOR BIRDS

Here are eight of my favorite bird-attracting evergreens. Hemlocks, hollies, junipers, and pines are also fabulous evergreens for birds. To learn more about them, turn to their individual entries.

PLANT NAMES	BIRDS ATTRACTED	PLANT DESCRIPTION	CULTURE
Balsam fir (*Abies balsamea*)	Nesting and roosting birds, including grosbeaks and robins; chickadees, juncos, jays, nuthatches, and other birds eat seeds	Narrow, upright trees, 40' to 60' tall, with rounded fragrant needles	Grows best in moist, acidic soil in cool conditions. In warm areas, try Fraser fir (*A. fraseri*), which tolerates some heat. Zones 2 to 5
Blue spruce (*Picea pungens*)	Nesting and roosting birds, especially grackles, house finches	150'-tall, cone-shaped tree with short, blue-gray needles	Plant in average, well-drained soil, in sun or light shade. Zones 2 to 7
Box huckleberry (*Gaylussacia brachycera*)	Nesting and roosting birds, especially sparrows, towhees, and thrushes; catbirds, jays, thrushes, and waxwings eat fruits	Fine-textured, low-growing shrub that spreads slowly to form a large mat 6" to 18" high, with glossy leaves and blue-black berrylike fruits in late summer	Plant in fertile, moist, well-drained, acidic soil, in partial shade. Zones 5 to 8
Buckthorn (*Rhamnus cathartica, R. crocea,* and other spp.)	Nesting and roosting birds; catbirds, mockingbirds, and thrushes eat fruits	Spiny, dense shrub 3' to 10' tall, with dark, glossy green leaves and black or red berries	Grows in sun or shade, and can become invasive due to birds spreading seeds. Zones 2 to 9
Douglas fir (*Pseudotsuga menziesii*)	Nesting and roosting birds	200'-tall, cone-shaped tree with soft needles and dangling, shaggy cones	Plant in sun to shade, in average, well-drained soil. Zones 4 to 6
Japanese yew (*Taxus cuspidata*)	Nesting and roosting birds, especially doves and chipping sparrows; fruits eaten by mockingbirds, robins, and sparrows	15'-tall evergreen shrub with dense, soft-needled, green foliage in summer and green-black foliage and red fruits in winter	Plant in well-drained soil, in sun to shade. Zones 4 to 7
Norway spruce (*Picea abies*)	Nesting and roosting birds, especially grackles and house finches	Tree tops out at 150' tall, with short, sharp-tipped needles and long dangling cones	Plant in average, well-drained soil, in sun or shade. Zones 2 to 7
Rhododendrons (*Rhododendron* spp.)	Nesting and roosting birds, and hummingbirds when flowering	Shrubs of 15' or more in height, with long, smooth leaves and clusters of showy flowers in spring	Plant in well-drained, acidic soil, in sun or shade. Zones 4 to 7

Fall ALMANAC

Fall brings big changes in the cast of characters you'll see at your bird feeders and in your yard. Songbirds began migrating south as early as August, so by early October winter birds have settled in while your summer birds are long gone. In the meantime, though, there are plenty of surprises in the garden, as migrating birds stop over for a rest or for refueling.

Watch for changes in plumage among your backyard birds in the fall. Male goldfinches, grosbeaks, tanagers, orioles, and others lose their brilliant colors and switch to winter drab, mostly olive green. Starlings show a scattering of light-colored "stars" at the tips of their feathers.

At the Feeder

There will be heavy traffic at your feeding stations as cold weather sets in, so fall is the time to clean and stock feeders and to stock up on birdseed. Here are some tips to keep in mind.

◆ Repair any feeders that need a makeover. You may need to pound in a loose nail or replace a cracked bottom piece.

◆ A single woodpecker can monopolize a suet feeder for most of the day. Put out several suet feeders so all your resident birds get a turn.
◆ Stock a very low tray feeder (1 foot or less above the ground) with cracked corn for mourning doves, who gather in flocks to feed in fall.
◆ Keep the hummingbird and other nectar feeders up as long as you dare, until freezing temperatures threaten; more than one late migrant has been saved by a forgotten feeder.
◆ Fresh water is vital year-round. Keep the birdbath brimming.

In the Garden

Fall is perfect planting and transplanting time for trees and shrubs. The soil stays warmer than the air for weeks or months, giving roots time to establish. Planting container shrubs and trees is a simple process; see the illustration below to learn how. If you're planting a balled-and-burlapped plant, turn to Trees on page 246 for planting instructions.

There are plenty of ways to provide bird treats in your garden in the fall. Try some of these ideas.

To plant a potted shrub, dig a hole that's as deep as the pot and twice as wide. Pull the shrub out of the container, set it in the hole, backfill with soil, and water deeply. Shrubs with berries on them, like holly, may attract birds the same day you plant them.

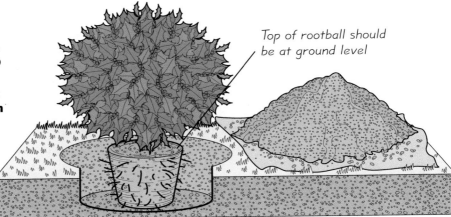

Top of rootball should be at ground level

◆ Keep an eye on any berries or fruits in your yard. They're prime foods for birds that may alight during migration. The Virginia creeper that sprawls through my garden as a ground-cover offers its midnight blue berries in early fall, right when vireos and orioles are passing through. The vines of fox grapes winding among the treetops attract later migrants like rose-breasted grosbeaks and tanagers.

◆ Listen for the quiet twitters and sharp *chip!* notes that betray the presence of song sparrows, white-throats, and other hard-to-see native sparrows around your yard. In the fall, a bounty of ripening seeds on garden plants, grasses, and weeds brings flocks of these LBBs (that's "little brown bird" in birder talk) to backyards. They may stop at abundant seed patches for a morning or a whole week, but they're small, quick moving, and wary of people, so you'll hear them more often than you'll see them.

◆ Check garden centers and nurseries for viburnums, bayberries, and other shrubs that are already full of berries. Cart them home carefully so as not to dislodge the fruit, pop them into the garden, and the birds will reap the benefits immediately. One September I brought home three deciduous hollies; while I was planting the first one, cedar waxwings descended on the shrubs that were still in the pickup truck.

◆ If you love a bargain, check the end-of-season sales at nurseries and garden centers. Trees and shrubs—usually the biggest investment you'll make when creating a bird-friendly yard—are often available at half price. Although the selection may not be as big as it is during the spring, the savings are hard to beat!

Migration Notes

Fall is one of my favorite times to watch birds. The scene at my bird feeders changes nearly every day, as birds pass through on their way south, and birds that call my yard home for the winter arrive on the scene.

Say goodbye to old friends. In the fall, birds like warblers, swifts, flycatchers, and swallows that eat mostly insects are the first to depart from colder areas. They head for warm-winter regions where their food supply will keep on flying, creeping, or crawling all winter long.

It's much easier to keep track of new birds arriving than to notice the departures among backyard birds. For example, by the time it dawns on you that you haven't seen a chipping sparrow lately, the birds may have been gone for a week or more. To keep track, jot down on your wall calendar a twice-a-week census of who's around, both at feeders and in the yard. Be sure to note how many birds of each species you see. Looking back over your fall calendar, you can see at a glance when populations swell during migration or with the arrival of winter residents. Next fall, hang last year's calendar next to the current one and you'll have a good idea when to expect the first junco or when to wave goodbye to the orioles.

Keep an eye on the sky. Remember to look up during fall. Many migrating birds won't land in your yard, but you'll spot some exciting birds in flight. I've added some wonderful entries to my list of "Birds Seen from My Back-yard" during the fall: bald eagles, sandhill cranes, and snow geese, just to name a few.

Watch the weather report. Your local forecast contains clues that can help you figure out when migrating birds will arrive. Birds like to fly ahead of cold fronts because they can take advantage of the tailwind to make their journey faster and easier. When the weather report says "cold front coming in," chances are your yard will be teeming with birds the next day.

FEATHERS

Feathers are one feature that makes birds unique—no other creatures have them. Without their feathers, birds couldn't survive. Feathers are both a bird's source of natural insulation and a critical part of its flight gear.

Kinds of Feathers

Feathers are made of the same stuff as your fingernails—keratin, a mostly protein substance that's as versatile as plastic. Keratin can take many forms, from the hard, horny material of beaks to the scaly coating of feet and legs and the soft fluff of feathers. You can see that variety at work by taking a close look at a feather.

Running up the middle is the central shaft, or *rachis*. The rachis attaches to the bird's skin, where it can be moved by muscles (to fluff out when the bird is cold, for example, or to ruffle away drops of rain). The *vane*, which is attached to the rachis, consists of the filaments of the feather. In wing feathers, the filaments are bound together in a sleek, stiff fashion. Down feathers have unconnected, billowy filaments. Other feathers have filaments that are interlocked in one part and downy in another, as in an outer breast feather.

Feathers are held in shape by an ingenious system of interlocking barbed hooks, so tiny you'll need a magnifying glass to get a good look at them, as shown in the illustration on page 106. When you see a bird running a feather through its beak after a bath, it's realigning these

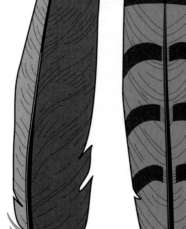

Down feathers

Wing feather

Tail feather

Birds have several kinds of feathers. Soft, light feathers are down feathers or semiplumes. Flight feathers are large and stiff. If one side is narrower than the other, it's a wing feather. If both sides of the feather are equally wide, it's probably a tail feather.

barbs and even tinier structures called barbules to make a perfect, smooth-surfaced web.

What we think of as typical bird feathers are called *contour* feathers. These feathers cover the outer body of the bird and form the wings and tail. Some contour feathers are specialized flight feathers—the big, stiff feathers in a bird's wings and tail. They may be straight or slightly curved.

Under these feathers are *semiplumes,* which have a large central shaft and downy sides. There are also *down* feathers, which are small, fluffy feathers that may have a thin shaft or none at all. Like a down comforter, semiplumes and down feathers keep the bird's body well insulated and warm.

How Feathers Grow

Feathers grow rather like human hair does: They sprout out of the bird's skin. But feathers do reach a maximum size and then stop growing. It takes about two to four weeks for a feather to grow.

Scientists have discovered that the width of colored wing bars on a feather are a sign of how well a bird is eating. When birds are well fed, the feathers they produce have wide wing bands. But if the bird has been stressed by lack of food, the wing bars will be narrow.

Drop That Feather!

Once you start watching birds in your backyard, you're bound to start noticing feathers on the ground now and then. Sometimes birds just naturally lose a feather, to make room for a new one growing in. Or, you may find a whole pile of feathers, which is probably a sign that a bird fell victim of a cat or other predator.

When you find feathers, feel free to admire them, but let them remain as part of the natural scene. It's actually illegal to collect feathers— provisions of the Migratory Bird Treaty prohibit

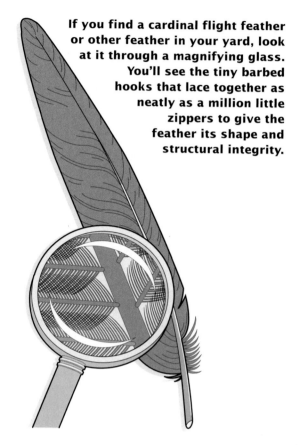

If you find a cardinal flight feather or other feather in your yard, look at it through a magnifying glass. You'll see the tiny barbed hooks that lace together as neatly as a million little zippers to give the feather its shape and structural integrity.

the sale, purchase, taking, or possession of birds, eggs, nests, and feathers. While these rules may seem very strict, keep in mind that they help protect many threatened species that might otherwise be killed for their feathers.

More Feather Facts

Feathers have lots of fascinating features. They can be wildly colored or have no color at all, as explained in Color of Birds on page 78. Feathers play a critical role in flight; you'll find an explanation in Flight on page 115. And birds lose their feathers and grow new ones in seasonal patterns; for details, turn to Molting on page 168.

FINCHES

Bright, energetic finches might easily become some of your favorite backyard birds. These small birds aren't shy around people, so it's easy to spot them when they visit the feeder or gather in your garden. And gather they do—most finches are sociable birds that enjoy their friends. There's no such thing as one house finch at the feeder: If you have one, you most likely have a dozen, or a hundred, depending on how well established these birds are in your area.

Getting to Know Them

To ornithologists, the finch family is a big one that includes sparrows, grosbeaks, and other seed eaters. But most backyard birdwatchers think of purple finches, house finches, and goldfinches when they picture a finch. You can learn more about goldfinches by turning to Goldfinches on page 122. Leaving these brightly colored birds aside, it's tricky to tell the difference between the other common finches.

Most of the finches that frequent backyard feeders are streaky brown, sparrow-size birds that are about 6 inches long. The males of different species display varying amounts and shades of reddish purple coloring on their heads, backs, wings, and breasts. Female finches are streaky brown or grayish brown.

Attracting Finches

While most birds eat insects at least some of the time, finches feed almost exclusively on seeds year-round. If your yard features well-stocked feeders filled with finch favorites—sunflower seed, millet, and niger seed—you can count on seeing plenty of finches. They also enjoy berries and other small fruits, and will feast in fruiting trees and bushes growing around your home. A yard full of dandelions is heaven to finches, who devour the little seeds at the ends of the silky "parachutes."

Finch Checklist

Whereas house finches, purple finches, and Cassin's finches look quite similar, you can learn to tell them apart. To fine-tune your finch identification skills, look closely at color and markings. When the birds are side by side—as they might be at your feeders—the differences are obvious.

Location can be a good clue when it comes to identifying finches. Cassin's finches live in western coniferous areas, either in the treetops or on the ground. Purple finches, which share some of their western range with Cassin's finches, prefer oak woods in the West, but coniferous forests in the North. In other parts of their range, purple finches appear

The seeds of small-headed sunflowers spell fine dining for hungry purple finches. The brown—not purple!—female (top) has a distinctive white stripe next to each eye.

in deciduous trees or in backyard Norway spruces and other conifers. House finches are well adapted to human habitats: They show up around our houses and farms, in cities and countrysides, as well as in suburbs.

Purple finch. The male purple finch wears a deep, rich shade of raspberry red that covers his head, back, breast, and dark brown–marked wings; his belly is whitish. Look for a distinctive wide, light-colored stripe above the eye. In addition, purple finch males often hold their head feathers somewhat erect to create an alert, almost crested effect.

Female purple finches aren't purple at all—like most female finches, they're rather sparrowlike in appearance with streaky brown-and-white plumage. A well-defined white "eyebrow" and brown cheek patch distinguish this female from the females of other species.

Purple finches nest in the northern part of their range. They like to hide their nests in dense foliage, often amid the needled branches of evergreens, from 6 to 50 feet above the ground. The cupped nest of twigs, grasses, moss, and string is lined with horsehair and bits of wool, and holds four or five black- or brown-speckled green-blue eggs.

Beautiful purple finches stop in my yard during their spring and fall moves between nesting grounds in the North and winter vacation in the South and West.

Many kinds of deciduous tree buds and seeds are on the purple finch's menu. When the tightly packed brown seed balls of sycamores shatter into fluff along the streets, I sometimes see purple finches at the roadsides, gleaning seeds from amid the fuzzy remains. They also love sunflowers, grass seed, many weed seeds, and an occasional helping of berries. In the garden they like to forage among homegrown stalks of millet, but at the feeder they prefer sunflower seed.

House finch. Even when he's dressed in his brightest spring plumage, the male house finch can't compare to his colorful and slightly larger purple finch cousin. Male house finches show most of their lighter, strawberry red color on their head and upper breast, but the rest of their body is a streaky brown. Occasionally you may spot an orange house finch among the visitors at your feeder. Female house finches are evenly streaked in brown over their entire bodies.

Watch out when watering your hanging planters—you may find a house-finch nest hidden among the geranium leaves and flowers. The brown-streaked female bird (right) builds the nest and sits on the eggs.

House finches were originally native to the West, but today they range across the continental United States. They were once sold as pets, and in the 1940s, some were released in New York City. The freed finches took wing and quickly made themselves at home on Long Island.

Thirty years later, house finches were well established in New York and gaining territory along the East Coast and inland. By 1980 I was hosting hordes of house finches at my Pennsylvania feeders. Today they're a little too common in many areas, but still enjoyable to watch and listen to.

Like other finches, house finches have a melodious, warbling voice. They have a charming habit of singing while they're on the nest. Hanging baskets and other potted plants on porches and windowsills are favorite house finch nesting sites, along with blue spruces and other evergreens. In the West, house finches may nest in cavities, too. They lay four or five speckled blue-white eggs in a well-built nest of stems, grasses, leaves, twigs, string, hair, wool, and other materials.

If you watch house finches at your feeders, you may think that they live on seeds alone. That's not entirely true. They also eat tree buds, and they have a definite fondness for sweets. Fruit juice is a favorite treat, and house finches can be orchard pests, pecking at ripe fruit to drink the sweet juice. These creative birds have even learned how to tap nectar feeders. Don't be surprised to see them swinging from your hummingbird feeder.

Cassin's finch. Cassin's finch is a western species that looks very much like a larger version of the house finch. The male Cassin's finch has a striking red patch on the top of his head, and a streaky brown back, with rosy red throat, belly, and rump. Its nesting

JUST FOR FINCHES

■ Plant mulberries, blackberries, cherries, and cotoneaster to supply fruit for finches.

■ Leave a few weeds for seeds: Finches feed on many types of weed seeds, especially dandelions.

■ A salt block is also a big draw for finches, who congregate in groups to peck at the mineral.

■ Plant a cheery finch garden where they can dine on the seeds of their favorite flowers: sunflowers of all descriptions and zinnias.

■ If you can't afford to keep your house finches supplied with all the niger seed they can eat, offer them a feeder filled with millet or sunflower seeds. Turn your tube feeders for goldfinches upside down to put the perches above the holes, and house finches will be unable to gobble up your pricey niger.

■ Finches like soft materials for lining their nests. As a treat, buy a bit of raw, unspun wool (check your Yellow Pages to find a shop that sells weavers' supplies). Gently fluff it apart with your fingers, then snag tufts of it on twigs and watch the birds gather it gleefully at nesting time.

range in the western mountains may overlap with those of house finches and purple finches. If you hear a finch singing from the very top of a tall conifer, it's most likely a Cassin's, which eats mostly buds and seeds of these trees. You may also see this finch on the ground, where it forages for dropped morsels. The Cassin's finch nests low or high in big conifers, laying its four or five brown- or black-speckled, pale green or blue eggs in a well-built cup of fine twigs, stems, and rootlets, lined with soft shredded bark, fine rootlets, and hair.

FIRST AID FOR BIRDS

Knowing a few basics of first aid for birds can make a big difference in the small world of your backyard birds. Injured birds and abandoned babies are easy prey for cats and other hungry hunters. By learning a few tricks and having supplies ready just in case, you can spring into action when a bird needs rescuing.

Keep in mind that unless you're a licensed rehabilitator, it's against federal law to keep songbirds, even though you have the best of intentions. Your aim should be to stabilize the bird and then turn it over to a rehabber if it needs extended care.

To locate a bird rehabilitation specialist, ask your vet or the local chapter of the Humane Society for a referral, or call the Department of Natural Resources office listed in the blue pages of your phone book.

Collision Course

If your yard is full of birds, chances are sooner or later you're going to hear the "thump!" that means a bird has hit a window. Collisions are more likely if the window is large and unbroken by panes, but even a small window can be a tragic trap.

The problem is that birds don't even see the glass—they see the reflection in it. When a hawk or cat panics the birds in your yard, they'll fly desperately in all directions. Sadly the reflections in a window can look like a safe escape route.

If you hear that surprisingly loud thump of a few feathered ounces hitting the window, go find the bird immediately. A bird that's just whacked its head is easy prey for any passing cat or dog. If you leave it outside, chances are

you'll find nothing but a pile of feathers in the morning. Birds can bounce or flop around a long distance after hitting a window, so look around within 20 feet or so.

If the bird is still alive, it may recover if you give it shelter for a few hours in a dark, safe place to restore its equilibrium after that head-banging experience. I've saved dozens of window victims—and even birds that tangled with cars—this way. As long as the bird shows any signs of life, don't give up.

Helping a bird recover. If you want to treat a bird that's had a head-on collision, start by making a nest of lightly crumpled tissues in a small deep box with a lid. A shoe box is perfect. Gently place the bird on the tissues. It may immediately fall over onto its side, but don't give up hope. Collision victims can seem to be almost dead and yet, amazingly, recover fully.

Punch several air holes in the lid (not too many—you want the interior to stay comfortingly dark) and cover the box. Put the box in a safe indoor place, away from cats, dogs, kids, and noise. If the bird is bigger than a sparrow, put a weight on the lid so it can't get out when it gets its strength back.

After an hour, carry the box outside, far away from windows, and lift the lid slowly, just enough to peek inside. If the bird begins to flutter wildly as soon as you lift the box or crack the lid, it may be ready to go. Remove the lid and it should gather itself in a few seconds and fly off.

If the bird is struggling to get up or still very weak, put the lid back on and try again in another hour or two. Some birds need a good night's rest before they're recovered. If the bird is still weak when nightfall approaches, try again at break of day. In my experience, the bird will be either all well or belly-up in the morning.

If the bird seems to have recovered its strength, but can't fly, it may have an injured leg or wing. Splinting legs and wings is advanced first aid best left to a licensed rehabber. Don't try to splint the injured limb yourself.

To prevent any future window collisions, try covering your windows with a lightweight trellis, or stick hawk or owl decoys on the glass, as explained in Windows on page 278.

Saving Baby Birds

Sooner or later, most backyard bird lovers find an abandoned baby bird in their yard. The first question to answer is, Does the baby really need your help? If you're not sure, turn to Baby Birds on page 5 for some guidelines. Chances are the bird's parents will still care for it if you can get it back up near its nest. Try getting out a ladder and putting the bird back in the nest. Don't worry, the parents won't reject it because it smells like a human—that's a myth.

If you can't reach the nest, try settling the bird into a nearby surrogate nest as shown in the illustration on this page. If the parents don't go to it within an hour, you inherit the nestling by default, and you'll have to prepare to feed it until you can get it to a rehabilitator.

If you find yourself playing Ma or Pa to a baby bird, the most important things are to keep it warm and keep it fed. Sounds like a cinch, right? Not when you consider that parent birds may make more than a thousand food-delivery visits to the nest in a single day! If you're tending a single nestling, figure on feeding at least every half-hour (every 15 minutes for birds whose eyes haven't opened yet), from before sunup to after sundown.

Keeping baby birds warm is a lot easier. You can use a heating pad, a hot water bottle, or an improvised setup like the one shown in the illustration on page 112.

Be prepared for the worst. Although nestlings can survive with substitute parenting, it's not a guaranteed proposition.

To reunite a lost baby bird with its parents, line a plastic strawberry pint box with cotton and wire it to a branch as close to the family nest as you can get. Then settle the baby in it, withdraw, and watch what happens.

Feeding baby birds. You probably aren't prepared to hunt insects to feed your baby birds, so you'll need to prepare a substitute. For the first meal, stir 2 tablespoons of Karo syrup into 4 tablespoons of warm water until it's thoroughly dissolved. Let the solution cool until it's comfortably warm, not hot, when you drip a few drops on your wrist (just like testing the temperature of a human baby bottle).

Feed with an eyedropper (you may be able to get a specially designed, very narrow eyedropper at veterinary supply stores or from your vet). Most baby birds will quickly open their beaks if you make a slight disturbance near them. Be prepared with food at the ready; you'll need to be quick to shove in the eyedropper.

If the nestling refuses to open its beak, tap the top or side of the beak lightly with a broom straw or lightly touch the top of the bird's head. Some babies are stubborn. If yours keeps its beak clamped shut, hold the bird in one hand and very gently pry its beak open at the back end. After the first feeding, switch to the "All-Purpose Nestling Food" recipe on the opposite page.

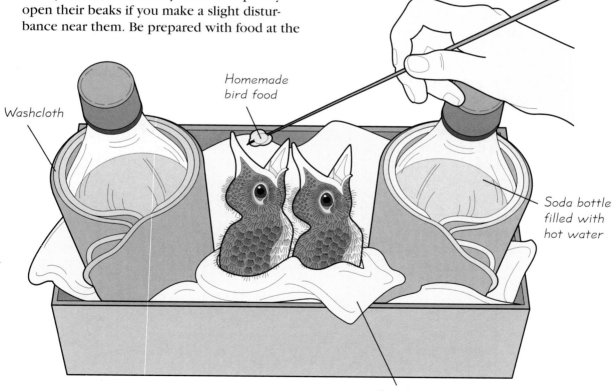

Washcloth

Homemade bird food

Soda bottle filled with hot water

Facial tissues

To keep baby birds warm, settle them in a shoe box lined with facial tissues. Fill two 20-ounce soda bottles with warm water, wrap them in washcloths, and put them in the box. Refill the bottles when the water cools.

ALL-PURPOSE NESTLING FOOD

This mixture provides the protein and moisture that baby birds need in a form they can swallow. For older nestlings, try adding good-quality canned dog food to the mixture, or offer them some cooked hamburger in addition to the basic soft food. You can also feed older nestlings natural food—green, nonhairy caterpillars are an excellent choice. Baby robins love chopped worms. (You'll soon appreciate a parent bird's food-gathering skills!)

1   hard-boiled egg

2   tablespoons unmedicated chick scratch, baby cereal, or crushed cornflakes

1   tablespoon canned dog food (optional)

1. Peel the hard-boiled egg, remove the yolk, and mash it.

2. Mix the mashed egg yolk with the chick scratch, baby cereal, or crushed cornflakes. For older nestlings, also add canned dog food to the mixture.

3. Add warm water, a few drops at a time, until mixture is soft but not runny.

4. Break off the sharp end of a wooden skewer (the type you'd use for making shish kabob). Pick up a small dab of the mixture on the skewer and feed it to the baby bird.

5. Continue feeding the bird small dabs of food until it doesn't want any more.

6. Repeat feedings every half-hour. Once the babies learn you're their food source, they'll greet your appearance with gaping beaks. Feed each nestling all it will eat each time you feed them.

FLICKERS

Active, noisy, and beautiful, flickers are fun to watch and easy to see as they feed in your yard. In addition to amusing you with their antics, flickers help to keep your trees healthy by eating insects such as wood-boring beetles and carpenter ants that threaten their bark and wood.

Getting to Know Them

Flickers are big brown woodpeckers—about 12 inches long—with a dashing black crescent across their chest and vividly colored underwings. When the bird takes wing, you'll spot a white patch above its tail flash as it flies—the trait that gives the flicker its name.

Depending on where you live, the flickers you see may be one of three closely related

Wintercreeper berries make a fine treat for flickers. The yellow-shafted flicker (shown) and other flickers are fond of all kinds of berries, even those of poison ivy!

birds, each type named for the striking color of their underwings. The yellow-shafted flicker covers the eastern part of North America; the red-shafted overlaps with it in the Plains and ranges westward. The gilded flicker—another golden-winged bird—lives in the desert Southwest. The birds generally don't move far in migration, and some are resident year-round.

When you hear a loud *whicka! whicka! whicka!* ringing emphatically through your backyard, scan the trees or look on the ground to spot the flicker, which may be digging into bark or nipping up ants one by one. Whether they're huge black carpenter ants or tiny brown everyday ants, these insects are a favorite flicker delicacy.

Attracting Flickers

Flickers are cavity nesters, and they appreciate a helping hand when it comes to finding a home; put up woodpecker nest boxes and they'll quickly take advantage of the new housing opportunities. See Birdhouses on page 36 for directions and dimensions for a woodpecker house.

Like bluebirds, flickers have been displaced from many of their chosen homes by starlings. Even after working for days to excavate a new penthouse, flickers will hand it over without much of a fuss to starlings who challenge them.

At feeders, flickers go for suet, bread, raisins, and peanut butter–cornmeal dough (see the recipe in Peanuts and Peanut Butter on page 191). In addition to being big on bugs like ants, lawn grubs, grasshoppers, and crickets, flickers enjoy berries of all descriptions. Planting berry bushes or other fruiting shrubs is a good way to attract these showy birds to your yard.

FLIGHT

"As the crow flies" is a fitting phrase—crows have a purposeful, shortest-distance-between-two-points flight style. Most birds are distinctive in flight, and learning to recognize their flight patterns and silhouettes will help you recognize birds from a distance.

"As the hummingbird flies" is a different case entirely: Unless they're migrating, hummers never travel in a straight line for longer than a few feet. They zig and zag, making detours to sip at every flower along the way.

What other birds can you recognize from their flight pattern? Check the illustration below to find out.

Flight Speed

Among backyard birds, doves are one of the fastest fliers. Hummingbirds, swifts, and swallows fly even faster than doves. Falcons are champs when it comes to speed; they can dive through the air at up to 200 miles per hour.

On the other end of the scale, house sparrows are one of the slowest birds, reaching only about 16 miles per hour.

How Birds Fly

Wings are only part of the miracle of flight. It's also the huge breast muscles and their hollow air-filled bones that give birds the incredible lightness of being they need to stay aloft.

A bird's wing has the same joints as our arm, but not where you'd expect them. The shoulder joint is easy—that's where the front part of the wing connects to the bird's back. The elbow joint is at the back of the wing, fairly close to the body. The wrist is the bend in the wing, where the large, stiff feathers of a bird's wing (the "primaries") begin.

The forward movement in flight starts at the wrist. Think of the primaries as its propellers. Powered by the bird's heavy-duty breast

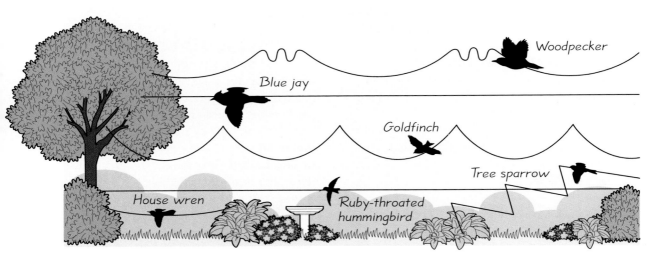

Study birds as they fly across your yard, and you can learn to recognize them by their flight patterns alone. Note how high above the ground the bird flies, whether its flight is fast or slow, and whether it flies straight or dips or zigzags as it goes.

muscles, these strong flexible feathers give the bird speed when it flaps. The bird can move its primaries to any position. These subtle adjustments are poetry in motion in birds with slow, soaring flight, like eagles, hawks, and vultures.

The bladelike part of the wing, like an airplane's wings, gives the bird lift. In flight this inner part of the wing is held stiff, but the bird constantly makes slight tilting adjustments according to the force of the air.

Hummingbirds are the only birds that can fly backward at will. But they're not the only birds that can hover in one place. Some hawks, the small falcons known as kestrels, and kingfishers are also adept at staying in one place.

FLYCATCHERS

"No wasted motion" must be the motto of the flycatcher clan. These alert but restrained birds sit tight on a perch, waiting for insects to fly by within easy reach. A few wingbeats off the perch, a graceful loop in the air, a snap of the beak, and the flycatcher returns to its post to wait for the next bite to come along.

Getting to Know Them

Flycatchers are easy to recognize by their erect posture and their typical perch-and-fly feeding behavior. They sit almost vertically with their head held high and straight. And they're quiet birds, not fidgety like sparrows or finches. They're always ready to zip out from a branch or other perch and nab their own brand of fast food.

The appearance of individual species varies quite a bit, but males and females of each species look alike. Nesting habits also vary with species.

Attracting Flycatchers

Many kinds of flycatchers adore fruits and berries as well as insects. Planting fruits such as brambles, grapes, cherries, and mulberries will help bring these birds to your yard. A large garden pool or pond is a great attraction because the water provides a hatchery for mayflies and other winged insects.

Flycatchers prefer wooded or shady backyards near natural woodlands or other large areas with old trees, like parks and golf courses. Flycatchers also like shade trees and shrubs, and even utility poles, as lookout posts where they can perch at mealtime. A garden full of butterflies, especially smaller sorts like white cabbage butterflies, is another attraction for flycatchers. Bees and wasps are favorite foods, too, along with moths, dragonflies, houseflies, mosquitoes, cicadas, spiders, and many others.

Flycatcher Checklist

Although it's easy to recognize a flycatcher, many dedicated birdwatchers have lost all pride trying to figure out exactly which flycatcher it is. There are many look-alike members that can only be identified by their slightly different calls.

Great crested flycatcher. The great crested flycatcher is an unmistakable bird of the eastern half of the country to the Plains. This robin-size greenish bird has a distinctive crest on its head, a yellow belly, and beautiful cinnamon-splashed wings and tail. They're loudmouths, yelling their raucous *wheeeep!* on and off all day in spring. Despite their size and call, they're tricky to spot until they dart out after an insect. When you hear that distinctive voice, follow it to find the bird, who's often perched in the shade.

Great crested flycatchers are quick to take to nest boxes mounted 6 to 15 feet high. Their five or six whitish eggs, splotched and streaked with brown and purple, are protected in a cupped nest made of grasses, leaves, moss, bark strips, pine needles, and feathers, with a finishing touch of snakeskin or anything similar—even strips of cellophane or onion skin.

Empidonax flycatchers. This group of flycatchers includes yellow-bellied flycatchers, Acadian flycatchers, willow flycatchers, and least flycatchers. All of these birds are small— less than 5 inches long—and dressed in drab olive green with yellowish bellies and light wing bars and eye rings. Their nests are soft and cottony, with feathers, tufts of cattails, and silky catkin fluff of willows and alders making a fine cradle for the black-spotted whitish eggs.

Yellow-bellied flycatchers live in spruce-fir forest areas; Acadians stay in places where there are patches of deciduous woods; willow flycatchers are found on brushy slopes; and least flycatchers live at woods' edges or backyards adjoining woods.

Scissor-tailed flycatcher. Scissor-tailed flycatchers are exotic-looking pearl gray birds of the south-central states, with fabulous 9-inch-long tail plumes that they can open and shut like a pair of scissors. During the male's courtship flight, he rises 100 feet in the air, then zigzags down in plunges and somersaults accompanied by a loud, rapid cackle.

The scissor-tailed's big cupped nest is usually saddled to a shade tree or mesquite bush, and is made of weeds, rootlets, and cotton tufts, with a lining of small rootlets and horsehair to hold the four to six creamy, brown-spotted eggs.

Vermilion flycatcher. The vermilion flycatcher, a small southwestern bird that occasionally strays to the East or South, is noteworthy for the flaming red color of its head and underparts. It's as bright as a tanager or cardinal, but easy to identify because of its flycatcher-style of sit-and-swoop hunting. Water—especially a stream—may bring this bird to your yard. The small, flat nest of weeds, grasses, and rootlets is held together with spider silk and lined with feathers and other soft materials to hold three whitish, brown-splotched eggs.

A mulberry tree makes an irresistible perch for great crested flycatchers, who will swoop in with loud *wheeeep!* calls and spend the day gorging on the juicy berries. Like other flycatchers, this bird is also an efficient insect eater.

FRUIT FOR BIRDS

Fruit is such a treat for birds that they'll travel long distances to reach a ripe cherry tree or raspberry patch. Like kids in a candy store, birds feast on the fruit until they've stripped a tree or bush. A flock of cedar waxwings can clean off a serviceberry tree in a single day; a big old mulberry tree will attract scores of vireos, tanagers, orioles, robins, bluebirds, and other fruit-eating birds every day for weeks, until the last delectable fruit is gone.

Filling your yard with fruit trees and berry bushes is probably the single best way to get unusual birds to visit. Scarlet tanagers usually scorn backyards in favor of woods, but add a dogwood tree to your landscape and you can bet they'll stop by when the berries are ripe (which happens to be right at their migration time). If you yearn to see a rose-breasted grosbeak, plant a Concord grape vine or a Virginia creeper vine and you just may get your wish.

Growing Backyard Fruits

It's easy to create an edible landscape—for you and for the birds. Try blueberries as foundation shrubs, and use serviceberries as small trees. Plant strawberries or creeping varieties of blueberries as groundcovers. Dwarf cherry trees, with their cloud of fragrant white blossoms in early spring, are beautiful planted among perennials and shrubs. Currants and gooseberries make good hedges to block out street noise or unsightly views. You can even train a dwarf apple tree on a trellis against a sunny garage wall, or grow grapes along the top of your backyard fence.

Fruit at the Feeder

A handout of fruit at your feeders is a sure draw in most areas, especially in the fall, winter, and early spring, when natural fruits are scarce. For example, try putting out an apple in the winter and watch the birds work at it until nothing's left but a hollowed-out skin.

It may take up to two weeks before fruit-eating birds zero in on the new source of food. During your start-up phase, you may have to toss the untouched fruit into your compost pile after a few days and put out fresh. Once the birds get the idea, they'll leave little behind.

Birds can make surprisingly quick work of fruit treats. To fill your feeders without straining your budget, buy blemished or over-ripe peaches, apples, or citrus at local orchards, and ask your grocer to keep past-their-prime fruits for you.

To learn more about growing fruit for birds and using fruit at your feeders, turn to Berries, Bird Feeding, Brambles, Cherries, Crabapples, Fruit Trees, Grapes, and Mulberries.

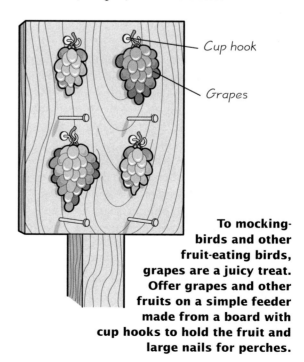

Cup hook

Grapes

To mocking-birds and other fruit-eating birds, grapes are a juicy treat. Offer grapes and other fruits on a simple feeder made from a board with cup hooks to hold the fruit and large nails for perches.

FRUIT TREES

Fruit trees are for the birds, as many a dismayed backyard orchardist has discovered. When cherries, peaches, or other fruits swell to juicy perfection, birds are often on the scene before you are—almost as if they've been watching from a distance, waiting for the big day. If a bountiful harvest is your main reason for having fruit trees, then you'll need to protect the fruit with netting or bird-scare devices. But if attracting birds is your goal, pull up a lawn chair and enjoy the show.

Caring for Fruit Trees

Two or three fruit trees, or even a well-chosen single tree, will bring plenty of birds flocking when the juicy treats are ripe. And caring for a fruit tree intended for birds is easy. For example, pruning is much simpler when you're growing a crop for customers that can fly. One of the main reasons to prune a fruit tree is to keep it to a manageable size, where fruits are in reach for easy picking. Since no ladders are required when the fruit pickers have wings, you can let your trees grow to their natural heights (leaving plenty of low branches for your own fruit-eating pleasure).

Choosing Fruit Trees

Crabapple trees and some cultivars of apples are a good choice for birds, because the fruits hang on the branches well into winter. You'll notice that the fruits continue to attract birds no matter how shriveled and unappealing they look to us. To find out more about choosing and growing crabapples, turn to Crabapples on page 89.

With today's modern dwarf varieties of cherries, apples, plums, and other fruits, there's no need to relegate these bird-beloved plants to a separate "orchard" section of your

Birds That Flock to Fruit Trees

Fruits are irresistible to birds, but just like us the different species have their preferences. Cherries are the number one fruit for birds, probably because they are small and have soft flesh, which makes them easy for birds to eat. Plant a cherry tree, and you're bound to attract birds.

Catbirds, grosbeaks, mockingbirds, robins, thrashers, thrushes, and cedar waxwings have a taste for apples, apricots, sweet and sour cherries, pears, plums—all the hardy tree fruits except for peaches. Bluebirds also love to nibble at apples, once frost has softened the fruit. Bluebirds, vireos, and flycatchers join the feast, along with the usual crowd of suspects, at crabapple trees and mulberries.

Cherries and plums will also attract bushtits, cardinals, jays, finches, woodpeckers, and quail. Peaches have a more limited appeal, attracting mainly house finches, orioles, robins, and mockingbirds. Orioles like citrus fruit the best.

yard. Let a dwarf apricot tree add a drift of white blossoms to your perennial garden, plant a thorny hedgerow of beach plums for privacy, or accent your doorway with a dwarf apple tree. The idea is to keep the fruit trees up close, where you can watch the birds they bring.

When it comes to fruit trees, you have plenty of choices to make, even after you decide what kind of fruit you want to grow. Tree size, hardiness, disease resistance, and pollination requirements are some important factors to ponder when you select fruit trees for your yard.

Size. For most backyard gardens, dwarf fruit trees make the most sense. For example, a dwarf apple tree stays at a very manageable height of 8 to 12 feet, whereas an unpruned standard-size apple tree can stretch to 40 feet tall. Semidwarf apple trees reach about 20 feet tall.

Hardiness. You can grow all the familiar fruit trees—apples, pears, plums, cherries, apricots, and peaches—just about everywhere in the United States except for the hottest and coldest climates. Peaches and nectarines have the most restricted range, doing best in Zones 6 to 9, but many tree fruits are cold-hardy to Zone 2. Because climate and conditions can vary so widely across the country, you'll need to choose a cultivar that's suited to your area. Your local garden centers carry varieties that are suited to your own conditions, but if you're selecting from a catalog, pay attention to the regional recommendations.

Fruit trees that bloom early in the spring, such as peaches and cherries, often fall victim to late cold snaps that freeze the swelling buds or blossoms, preventing fruit set. If spring weather is unsettled in your area, plant these trees on the north side of your house, where they'll be less prone to blooming early.

Disease problems. Pears are probably the least troubled by disease of all the major tree fruits; cherries and plums are notorious for problems, and peaches are close behind. Many fruit tree diseases are problematic only in limited regions or under certain conditions. Pears are usually untroubled by diseases except for fire blight, which is prevalent mostly in the South (although it can strike anywhere during a mild, wet spring).

There are three important techniques that help prevent disease problems: applying dormant oil in late winter to smother insect larvae, cleaning up dropped leaves and fruits in fall to remove the overwintering places of insects and diseases, and pruning out dead or diseased branches.

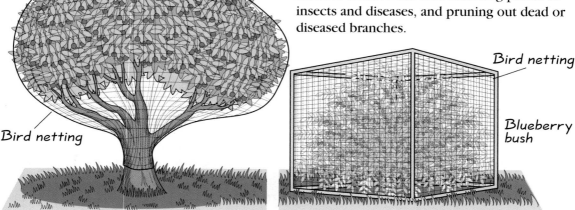

Cherry tree

Bird netting

Bird netting

Blueberry bush

To prevent birds from plucking fruit from your fruit trees and bushes, cover your plants with inexpensive, garden-center bird netting. Just drape it over the tree and fasten it tightly closed, or spread it over a rigid metal frame. Be sure there are no gaps that birds could squeeze through, or they may get trapped inside the netting.

Excellent disease-resistant cultivars of many tree fruits are available. The pears 'Harrow Delight', 'Harrow Sweet', 'Harvest Queen', 'Seckel', and 'Stark Honeysweet' show excellent resistance to fire blight. 'Freedom', 'Jonafree', 'Liberty', and 'Priscilla' apples shrug off most troublesome apple diseases.

Pollination. In many cases, fruit trees need a second tree growing nearby to pollinate their flowers. Sour cherries, peaches, and most apricots are exceptions—a single tree planted alone will bear loads of fruit. 'Golden Delicious' apple is one of the few apples that needs no pollinator. Many pears are self-fruitful but bear better with a pollinator. Most plums need a pollinator, but the Japanese plum cultivar 'Catalina' and the European plums 'Stanley' and 'Mount Royal' are self-pollinating.

FUCHSIAS

Fuchsias will dress up your garden or your front porch all summer with their 3-inch-long, dangling "lady's earrings" flowers in vibrant shades of purple, violet, red, pink, white, or flashy two-tones. The tubular flowers of fuchsias (*Fuchsia* × *hybrida*) are sure to entice hummingbirds, who often claim territorial rights to an individual plant and fend off competing hummers with dazzling displays of aerial warfare.

If you garden in a cold-winter area, you'll treat these tender perennials as summer plants, usually bought for the season and then discarded. Although some fuchsias can withstand Zone 6 winters, most cultivars are hardy only to Zone 8 or 9. Mild-winter gardeners can also grow shrubby hardy fuchsia (*F. magellanica*), which reaches the size of a forsythia bush in warm climates. Hardy fuchsia can tolerate winters as cold as Zone 6—it may die back to the ground in cold winters, but new growth quickly sprouts when warmer weather returns.

Keeping fuchsias flowering. To keep your fuchsias flowering and the hummingbirds humming, set fuchsia plants in light shade and in average to fertile soil. You can also grow them in hanging baskets or in containers. Keep the soil evenly moist, and feed them every 10 days with a balanced liquid fertilizer, such as compost tea or fish emulsion, to keep them blooming.

All fuchsias are easy to propagate by stem cuttings. In cold regions you can pot up and bring the plants indoors in fall, or overwinter cuttings in a jar of water and pot them up in late winter.

Hang a basket of brightly colored fuchsias outside a window, and enjoy watching hummingbirds come to dine.

GOLDFINCHES

Although they aren't the rarest birds you'll see at your backyard feeder, the sight of goldfinches pecking happily at a tube full of niger seed will bring a smile to your face every time. Clad in bright yellow and singing prettily, goldfinches are cheery-looking songbirds that are delightfully easy to attract to your feeders.

Getting to Know Them

An old name for goldfinches is wild canaries, and these golden birds do resemble the caged pets. The 5-inch-long males have buttery yellow bodies with gleaming black wings accented by white bars, and wear a jaunty black beret on their heads. Females are soft olive green and subdued yellow. Like other songbirds, male goldfinches molt into drabber winter colors that resemble the female's quiet plumage. (See the illustration on page 169 for a comparison of goldfinch coloring in winter and in the breeding season.)

You can time spring's passage just by glancing at the male goldfinches. About the time pussy willows show their sleek, furred catkins, goldfinches begin to sport a blotchy look, their yellow plumage coming in bit by bit. By the time the tulips bloom, they're back to their rich, bright color.

These cheerful birds brighten cities and countrysides across the United States and into southern Canada. Goldfinches prefer the open spaces of backyards and fields. They nest in all areas except for a strip of the far western mountains and the extreme South and Southwest, although those areas are part of their vast winter range. Listen for their cheery *per-chick-oh-wee* (some translate it as *potato CHIP*) calls

as they fly across open spaces in their trademark swooping curves. During spring migration, goldfinches often gather at hospitable feeders in large numbers, filling any nearby trees with their sweet, ecstatic warbling songs.

Unlike other birds, which spend most of spring and summer raising families, goldfinches nest only once, very late in the season. The rest of the time, these vivid yellow birds live in small flocks, flitting from one stand of seeds to another. In early spring, they feast on dandelion puffs; in summer, they swing from garden plants of cosmos and zinnias; and in between, they're regulars at the feeder.

If you miss a thistle seed when weeding, goldfinches will find it as soon as the flowers go to seed. They'll gobble the seeds as fast as they ripen. The olive-backed female bird (right) will also take some thistledown to line her nest.

When you see thistles going to soft white puffs of down, it's goldfinch nesting time. The cup of fine grasses and moss, usually built low, is lined with a comforter of softest thistledown, or occasionally cattail fluff. The female bird sits on a clutch of four to six pale bluish white eggs.

Attracting Goldfinches

Seeds of a wide variety of common garden plants and weeds are popular with goldfinches. Plant sunflowers, zinnias, tickseed sunflower, coneflowers, coreopsis, and cosmos and they'll attract droves of goldfinches as the flower heads go to seed. At the feeder, offer black oil sunflower seed and stock tube feeders with niger seed.

Foiling House Finches

If hordes of hungry house finches overrun the niger tube feeders you've put out to attract goldfinches, there's a simple alternative. Either buy a feeder with perches above the holes or turn your feeder upside down. Acrobatic goldfinches will have no problem feeding upside down, but house finches will give up in frustration.

JUST FOR GOLDFINCHES

■ One surefire way to attract goldfinches is to plant a big patch of lettuce and let it go to seed.

■ Water is a big draw for goldfinches, who like to bathe daily. They prefer a low, wide, shallow bath to splash in and sip from, although they'll also use pedestal-type birdbaths.

■ Once you've seen a flock of goldfinches feeding on dandelion seeds, you'll be less vigilant about running for the dandelion digger when you spot these weeds in your lawn.

■ Many weed seeds, including goldenrod, burdock, and thistles, are favored goldfinch foods.

■ Plant chicory, beets, and catnip, whose seeds they adore. These three plants make an appealing combination in the garden: The sky blue flowers of the chicory complement the red-tinged leaves of the beets; the catnip's gray-green foliage and billowy shape help soften the combo.

■ Goldfinches also come to backyards to eat the buds of birches, conifers, and other trees.

GOURDS

Imagine planting a single seed and harvesting a dozen birdhouses! When you grow birdhouse gourds, you can do just that. Birdhouse gourds (*Lagenaria siceraria*) are like Jack's bean stalk: They grow and grow. A single gourd vine can sprawl 20 feet or more along a backyard fence, and at summer's end, it'll be hung with lots of long-handled, round-bellied gourds, the perfect size and shape for making birdhouses. Swallows, purple martins, chickadees, and wrens will all take to gourd houses.

Birdhouse gourd vines have white flowers with a soft, crepe-paper texture. And the vines themselves are covered thickly with lush, large, green leaves all season. When grown on a trellis, birdhouse gourds make a shady bower that's perfect to shelter shade-loving flowers and to linger under on a hot afternoon.

Growing Birdhouse Gourds

Birdhouse gourds grow best in well-drained soil in full sun. In the spring, just sow three or four seeds in a slightly raised hill of soil. Or plant them in a wooden half-barrel on your deck and let the large-leaved vines clamber along the railings. In the garden, be sure to give your vines a support that's tall enough to keep the gourds off the ground so that they'll develop straight necks. Birdhouse gourds are fairly drought-resistant, but if you water them regularly, you'll harvest more and bigger gourds.

All gourds, including birdhouse gourds, need a long, hot summer to grow to good size. In areas with a short growing season, start seeds indoors in early spring and transplant the seedlings outdoors after the last frost. Also, once your first few gourds set fruit, pinch off any new flowers that form. This makes the plants put all their energy into ripening the fruits before the first frost.

Making Gourd Birdhouses

After frost kills the vines, snip off all the gourds. To keep sooty mold from discoloring your gourds, wipe each one with a sponge dipped in a solution of ½ cup household bleach and 2 quarts of water. Then lay the gourds in a warm, dry place. For example, you can spread them on the floor near your furnace. Turn them weekly so all parts dry well. If mold forms on the gourds while they're drying, rub it off with a cloth.

By springtime, your gourds should be dry and ready to turn into birdhouses. The dry gourds will feel much lighter than when you picked them. Shake them hard to loosen the seeds inside, or whack them (carefully) against a hard surface to break the seeds free.

The first step in making a gourd house is to use a carpenter's pencil to outline an entrance hole. The size will vary depending on the type of bird you want to attract—see "A Birdhouse for Every Bird" on page 40 for specification of entrance hole sizes.

Using a ¼-inch drill bit, drill a series of holes through the penciled circle. Then finish cutting the entrance hole with a sharp, sturdy, serrated knife. Shake the seeds out through the hole.

Drill a hole through the neck of the gourd near the stem end and insert a strip of plastic twine to hang it by. If you want decorative gourd birdhouses, first coat the outside of the gourd with exterior latex paint. Then paint on your design using acrylic paint. You can make the gourds look like animals, toadstools, or thatched cottages.

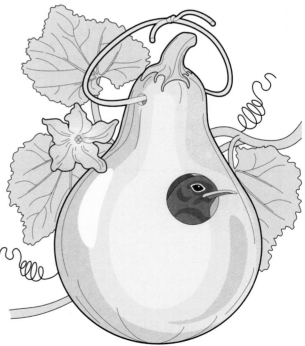

Wrens will quickly take to nesting in a gourd birdhouse. Making birdhouses from gourds you've grown yourself is a simple and satisfying do-it-yourself project.

GRACKLES

When you hear a bird cry that sounds like the creak of a rusty gate, you're hearing the harsh voice of a grackle. I used to think that common grackles got their name from their call note, a loud *graack!* or *chaack!* but in fact the word is from the Latin *graculus,* a "jackdaw," or European blackbird.

Glossy Grackles

Grackles are regal birds that strut about on lawns with a dignified gait, their iridescent head held high. Some species of grackles are as large as 16 inches. Their glossy black plumage has a sheen of purple, green, bronze, or blue, depending on the species and the light. Their tails are long and sweep the ground like the train of Cinderella's gown.

East of the Rockies, the common grackle is common indeed, congregating in huge flocks to feed or roost, except during nesting season. In the Southeast and along the eastern and Gulf coasts, the boat-tailed grackle, which has a wingspan of close to 2 feet, claims its territory. In Texas and the Southwest, it's the great-tailed grackle, which has a very long slender tail.

You can tell a grackle in flight just by looking at its tail. Unlike other birds, grackles hold their tail feathers in a V—like a boat's keel—when they're airborne.

Grackles often nest in colonies that can number in the dozens. Male boat-tailed and great-tailed grackles each mate with several of the noticeably smaller and less glossy females of their species. The female grackle builds the nest—a loosely constructed cup of stems and grasses, lined with feathers and fine grasses—into which she lays three to six pale greenish white eggs scrawled and splotched with darker colors.

Grubs for Grackles

The eating habits of grackles aren't much appreciated by songbirds, because nestlings are high on the menu. These big blackbirds also kill adult birds, especially house sparrows. But gardeners will be happy to know that grackles also eat thousands of grubs, beetles, grasshoppers, armyworms, flies, and other tidbits plucked from the ground. For variety's sake, they also dine on snakes, crayfish, crabs, minnows, frogs, salamanders, and snails—they will even pick through trash. The huge boat-tailed grackle is so bold it snatches crayfish from the beaks of large waterbirds like the glossy ibis.

A patch of lawn grass is all the invitation grackles need to visit your backyard. They like open spaces, usually near water. You may prefer not to make your yard more welcoming to grackles, but if you have a dense spruce or other conifer in your backyard, chances are you're already hosting at least one pair. At the feeder these birds enjoy cracked corn and bread.

Good news for gardeners: Hungry grackles like to grab the grubs of pests like Japanese beetles!

GRAPES

Growing grapes for the birds is much easier than growing them to harvest for yourself. Birds don't care if grape vines are neatly tended. All they want is the fruit. Grapes attract rose-breasted grosbeaks, catbirds, thrashers, mockingbirds, wrens, downy woodpeckers, robins, bluebirds, thrushes, vireos, tanagers, orioles, and waxwings.

If you want to grow grapes just for the birds, you can put down your pruning shears and simply let your vines ramble high over a trellis or up in a tree. Even if the lower parts of the vines are shaded and don't bear fruit, there'll still be plenty of grapes at the top.

Growing Great Grapes

The key to carefree grape growing is to choose varieties that bear well even when neglected. Most species and cultivars grown in America are hardy to Zone 7. Grapes need full sun and well-drained soil, and bear fruit best when they have a long growing season. When birds feast on grapes, they leave sticky, partly eaten grapes behind, which may attract yellow jackets. Choose a site for bird grapes that's well separated from your backyard patio.

Plant the vines as you would a shrub or tree, as shown on page 248. Most grapes are self-pollinating, so you can plant just one vine and still get fruit. The vines begin bearing fruit two to four years after planting.

Grapes for the Birds

American grape (*Vitis labrusca*), which is also called fox grape or skunk grape, is a strong, fast-growing vine that easily climbs trees and is hardy from Zones 4 to 7. Birds will eat these fruits on the vine and also on the ground (the fruit drops after frost). 'Concord' is a favorite for juice and jelly making. Birds also love these small, fragrant, intensely flavored blue-black fruits. 'Fredonia' is good for southern gardens because it grows as far south as Zone 9. Like 'Concord', the large, blue-black fruits of 'Fredonia' are coated with a dusty white "bloom."

Vigorous muscadine grape (*V. rotundifolia*) varieties, such as 'Carlos', 'Doreen', and 'Magnolia', grow well in Zones 7 to 9, tolerate high humidity, and are very disease resistant. These grapes produce unusual, bronze-colored fruits with a sweet, musky flavor. Some muscadine grapes require a pollinator, so ask your supplier about pollination requirements.

Northern gardeners can plant riverbank grape (*V. riparia*) or chicken grape (*V. vulpina*), which produce small blue-black fruits and can even survive winters in Zone 2.

Let a grape vine ramble over a trellis or arbor. Be sure to choose a sturdy trellis to support the heavy, long-lived vines.

GRIT

When you're feeding the birds, put out some grit along with the seeds. A scattering of gritty coarse sand and small pebbles will appeal to nearly all of your backyard birds. To find out why, just watch a cardinal eating whole dry corn, or a wood duck or wild turkey eating acorns and hickory nuts. You'll see that the birds gulp these foods down, hard shell and all.

Grit for the gizzard. It's a wonder that birds can digest such tough fare, having no way to chew it first. Their secret is a special digestive organ called a gizzard. All birds have gizzards—a muscular part of their stomachs that works like an internal food processor to grind hard foods like seeds and grain into digestible pieces.

Gizzards are designed to work best when they're full of gritty grinding stones, and that's where you can help. You can buy inexpensive boxes of commercial bird grit or fine undyed aquarium gravel in the pet aisle of discount stores and in pet supply shops. If you're looking for a real bargain, you can collect fine gravel from streams or buy coarse sand like that sold in bulk at building supply stores.

Grit for calcium. During the nesting season, all birds will eat calcium-rich grit to strengthen the developing eggshells and bones of their young. You can buy calcium-rich grit like crushed oyster or clam shells at pet shops, and you can also make your own by crushing eggshells saved from your breakfast table. Crossbills, evening grosbeaks, purple finches, and pheasants especially enjoy crushed shells like these.

A little grit goes a long way, so dole it out sparingly, a handful at a time, to keep it from being wasted. Offer sandy and calcium grit in separate piles on a tray feeder so that birds can eat only as much of each as they need, or sprinkle it on the ground along with seed you put out for ground-foraging birds.

GROSBEAKS

Big, beautiful grosbeaks are backyard favorites everywhere, even though their eager eating habits have earned them the affectionate nickname "grosspigs" among some birdwatchers.

Getting to Know Them

The five common species of grosbeaks are all gorgeous, and they have vocal talent to match their looks. Their voices are sweet and rich, with the melodious songs offered in a clear whistle.

Grosbeaks are about the size of a cardinal, and their beaks are just as big and tough. As you can tell from that heavy-duty beak, grosbeaks are seed eaters. But they also devour millions of insects, including some of the worst garden and farm pests, like weevils, grasshoppers, cutworms, and squash bugs.

Except for the evening grosbeak, which may build its nest as high as 70 feet, grosbeaks nest within 15 feet of the ground in willows, deciduous trees and shrubs, or conifers. They weave shallow, bulky nests out of twigs and pieces of root, with a soft inner lining of hair or roots and a few finishing touches: Blue grosbeaks use bits of snakeskin, pine grosbeaks use rabbit fur and lichens, rose-breasteds include straw and horsehair, and evening grosbeaks prefer no embellishments. Their eggs are greenish, from blue-green to gray-green, with brown speckles for pine and rose-breasted grosbeaks, and no speckles for evening and blue grosbeaks.

Attracting Grosbeaks

The arrival of grosbeaks in your backyard is cause for celebration. It's also time to lay in 100-pound sacks of sunflower seeds, because these birds are big eaters. Sunflowers will keep them happy at the feeder, and berries and seeds will tempt them to linger or nest in your garden.

One of the most endearing things about grosbeaks is that they're unusually tame. If you move slowly, you can easily approach them without scaring them away. Pine and black-headed grosbeaks may fearlessly eat sunflower seeds out of your hand even the first time you try it. It's easy to win the trust of the other species, too.

Grosbeak Checklist

Each grosbeak species has a distinct range and habitat (though ranges overlap). Part of the grosbeak's job is to disperse tree seeds, which it does quite well. They're all business as they go about feeding, gobbling berries or splitting the pods or husks of tree seeds to free the meaty morsels inside. Catalpa seeds are a favorite of evening grosbeaks. They twist and stretch their bodies to nibble at the long, skinny pods, releasing a shower of chaff that drifts down from the tree like big, light tan flakes of snow.

Evening grosbeak. Evening grosbeaks look like oversize goldfinches in hues of antique gold rather than sunny yellow. Males are brighter colored, with females decked in mostly olive. They pal around in flocks that can number in the dozens, nibbling seeds and buds of maple, alder, and box elder, along with the usual pinecones. They nest across lower Canada, in New England, Minnesota, and in the West, south to California and the Southwest. They have a distinctive throaty voice that you'll soon come to recognize if grosbeaks come calling: it sounds like *peet, peet.*

Rose-breasted grosbeak. The male rose-breasted grosbeak is elegantly decked out in black and white with a glorious crimson breast patch. The female is dark brown above, with a streaky brown-and-white belly. These grosbeaks spend their time at woods' edges and streamsides, in roadside thickets, and in parks and backyards with big trees. They dine on the buds, blossoms, and seeds of deciduous trees and enjoy eating caterpillars, grasshoppers, and small moths in the warm months.

Rose-breasted grosbeaks stay in the eastern half of the country. They breed from Canada to central Oklahoma and New Jersey and south through the Appalachians to Georgia. Like the other grosbeaks, they turn up in backyards in a much wider area during spring and fall migration. The long-lasting beautiful song sounds a lot like a robin's voice, warbling varied phrases. Female birds sing a shorter version of the male's song.

JUST FOR GROSBEAKS

■ Grosbeaks are big on berry-bearing bushes and vines, so plant a variety, including their particular favorites—bittersweet, blackberries, elderberries, and barberries.

■ Plant shade or ornamental trees with grosbeaks in mind. Grosbeaks love the fruits of crabapple, mountain ash, hawthorn, and mulberry.

■ Seeds are another important food source for grosbeaks. Conifers, maples, birches, box elder, white ash, and catalpa produce the seeds they crave.

■ If grosbeaks are fighting for space at your feeders, scatter some sunflower seeds on the ground as well for more peaceful feeding.

If you put out sunflower seeds at your feeders, you're almost sure to have evening grosbeaks (shown) and other grosbeaks visit, even if it's just a brief stopover during migration.

Black-headed grosbeak. The male black-headed grosbeak has a black head setting off rusty orange underparts and striking white wing patches. The female is streaky brown, with a striped head. This grosbeak takes over in the West, where the rose-breasted leaves off, and nests across most of its range. Its favorite haunts are deciduous trees and shrubs, as well as broad-leaved evergreens like rhododendrons. Along with seeds, these birds enjoy blackberries and other small fruits, caterpillars, grasshoppers, and other insects. The long, varied song is performed in a clear, trilling whistle.

Blue grosbeak. The lovely blue grosbeak, which is deep blue with rusty wing bars (females are dull brown with tan wing bars), nests from central California to southern New Jersey, south to the oceans and Mexico. You may see blue grosbeaks in trees, but the best place to look for them is on the ground or close to it. They often hop around looking for grasshop-

pers, beetles, and other insects. Blue grosbeaks are easy to overlook unless they're in good light; out of direct sun, they look black. If you hear a bird singing a particularly sweet song from the top of a shrub or from a fence post or utility wire, it may be a blue grosbeak. The whistled phrases of the song sound somewhat like the purple finch and indigo bunting.

Pine grosbeak. Rosy-colored pine grosbeaks, which are deep red-pink with white wing bars (the female is brown or grayish brown), are birds of the Far North, ranging south into the mountains of the West and wandering southward across the northern third of the country in winter. In their summer homelands, pine grosbeaks live along openings in coniferous forests, but in winter they frequent any area where they can find food. Pine and other conifer seeds are favored foods, along with seeds of maples and birches, buds of deciduous trees, weed seeds, berries, and insects. Their song is short but sweet, a few warbled notes that sound like *tee, tee, tew*.

Whenever you spot the white webbed shelters of tent caterpillars, keep an eye out for rose-breasted grosbeaks, who seem to find these caterpillars especially delectable.

GROUNDCOVERS

Instead of feeling like a Saturday morning slave to your lawn mower, fill the spaces of your backyard with groundcovers. These spreading plants offer cover for ground-dwelling birds, and many of them bear bright fruits or flowers that attract hummingbirds, sparrows, towhees, and other birds.

Besides saving labor and befriending birds, groundcovers also are great landscape plants. You can use a groundcover like periwinkle or cotoneaster to tie together isolated trees and shrubs for a more finished look.

Groundcovers keep your bird-friendly backyard looking tidy. When fruits and seed pods drop from trees and shrubs, they'll disappear into the camouflaging foliage of the groundcovers (but hungry birds can still find them).

Establishing Groundcovers

When you're ready to plant groundcovers, buy vigorous young plants—they'll spread faster than older plants. Clear grass and unwanted plants from the site, then mulch with 4 inches of shredded bark, wood chips, gravel, or chopped leaves. Pull back the mulch and make planting holes with a trowel for each plant, at the spacing recommended by the nursery. Set plants at the same depth they occupied in the nursery pots.

Once the groundcover is established, it will shade and crowd out most weeds. Tree seedlings, however, will crop up in your groundcovers, planted there by visiting birds. Pull tree seedlings by hand, before they get big enough to get a roothold. For easy removal, wrap a seedling around your hand and twist it as you pull upward.

Evergreen Groundcovers

Evergreen groundcovers are undemanding, hardy, and beautiful. Most grow from Zone 5 and colder regions to warm areas like Zones 7, 8, and 9. They grow in well-drained soils with moderate rainfall and no fertilizer, in full sun to part shade. Evergreen groundcovers are favorites of the birds because the dense, waxy foliage sheds rain and winter snow and their berries arrive at the end of summer when other bird foods dwindle.

Bearberry. The small shiny leaves of bearberry (*Arctostaphylos uva-ursi*) cover its mat of woody stems. Thrushes, wrens, mockingbirds, robins, bluebirds, and waxwings eat its bright red berries. Bearberry thrives in Zones 2 to 6, and in Zones 7 and 8 in shade.

Cotoneaster. For a fast-growing groundcover that looks good all year, try cotoneaster (*Cotoneaster dammeri, C. horizontalis, C. adpressus,* and others). Its glossy dark green leaves are dotted with red berries from fall into winter in Zones 4 to 8, depending on the species and cultivar. Rockspray cotoneaster (*C. horizontalis*) and creeping cotoneaster (*C. adpressus*) are favorites of thrashers, catbirds, mockingbirds, waxwings, robins, and other birds.

Juniper. Sparrows and juncos like to nest in creeping junipers (*Juniper horizontalis* and *J. conferta*). Waxwings, finches, robins, flickers, mockingbirds, bluebirds, jays, and other fruit-eating birds feast on juniper berries. For more information, turn to Junipers on page 153.

Lingonberry. Thrushes, bluebirds, titmice, orioles, mockingbirds, catbirds, thrashers, and towhees enjoy lingonberries (*Vaccinium vitis-idaea* var. *minus*). This creeping shrub has pink urn-shaped flowers, small oval leaves, and red berries. Hummingbirds visit the flowers. Grow lingonberry in full sun, in well-drained, moist acid soil high in organic matter. It's hardy in Zones 2 to 5.

Prickly pear. The spiny jointed pads of prickly pears (*Opuntia* spp.) can be as big around and as flat as dinner plates. These ever-green cactuses have yellow flowers and egg-shaped red or yellow fruits favored by many birds. The plants shelter nesting cactus wrens, mourning doves, curve-billed thrashers, road-runners, and sparrows. Grow prickly pears in full sun and in infertile well-drained soil. Prickly pears grow throughout Zones 6 to 9.

Deciduous Groundcovers

The leaves of deciduous groundcovers, like wild strawberries, die in winter. Even so, de-ciduous groundcovers retain some stems, branches, and dried leaves in winter, which can provide winter cover for birds.

Running serviceberry. In early spring, run-ning serviceberry (*Amelanchier stolonifera*) forms dense thickets of erect stems about 4 feet tall. It produces white flowers that cover its dense thickets of erect, 4-foot stems, which make an excellent bird-friendly cover for a slope. The flowers attract insects, which in turn attract warblers, orioles, and other insect-eating birds. The purple-black berries are favorites of a wide range of birds. Grow running serviceberry in either sun or shade, in Zones 4 to 9.

Strawberry. The small red fruits of wild straw-berry (*Fragaria virginiana*) and beach straw-berry (*F. chiloensis*) are a big favorite with bluebirds, robins, thrushes, thrashers, mock-ingbirds, waxwings, quail, grosbeaks, catbirds, wrens, and many other birds. Grow these mat-forming perennials in full sun and well-drained fertile soil in Zones 4 to 9.

Birds that forage for food at ground level, such as thrashers, catbirds, mockingbirds, waxwings, and robins, love a yard that in-cludes groundcovers. Groundcovers range from grasses like fountain grass to vines like Virginia creeper. Even cactus can be a groundcover!

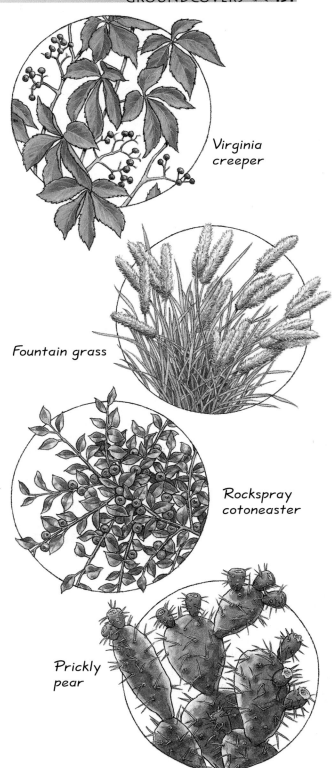

Virginia creeper

Fountain grass

Rockspray cotoneaster

Prickly pear

HAND TAMING

Having a wild bird land on your hand of its own free will is an incredible thrill. When those few feathered ounces land on your palm for the first time, the feeling of connecting with a wild creature will give you the biggest grin.

Getting a bird to eat from your hand—or your hat—requires only one thing: patience, and plenty of it. The technique itself is simple: Let the birds get used to you at the feeder and eventually they'll trust you enough to take food from your fingers.

When to Tame Wild Birds

You'll get results fastest by taming wild birds in winter, when they are most dependent on your feeder. The morning after a big snow- or ice storm, when food sources are at a premium, you can tame birds in 20 minutes or less just by slowly approaching a snowed-in feeder holding out a heaping handful of food. Birds are difficult to hand-tame in late spring and summer, when natural food is abundant and parents are looking for a quick source of calories to feed themselves and their hungry nestlings.

Simple Steps to Hand Taming

If you have more than one feeder, empty all but one the night before you plan to try taming. An unroofed tray feeder works best, because you can rest your hand in it and wait. Take a handful of nuts, seeds, or other treats and lay your hand in the feeder, palm up. Sit or stand as still as you can and avoid the temptation to make eye contact with any birds that approach. Even a motion as slight as moving your eyes can startle birds.

You'll notice that birds will fly toward the feeder as usual, then quickly veer away when they spot you. Chickadees and others will probably scold you, but don't get flustered—stay stock-still but relaxed. In as little as 20 minutes, or as much as two hours, a brave bird will land on the feeder, and soon others will join it. After that it won't take long before they're eating out of your hand. If you reach the limits of your patience before birds approach your hand, leave your post, moving slowly and quietly away, and try again when you're ready.

Practice in the morning or late afternoon, when birds are feeding actively. They'll soon learn to associate you with food, and you'll find that you can move about without scaring the birds away. When you reach that point, start carrying around bird treats in your pocket and offer them to your feathered friends whenever you encounter them in the garden.

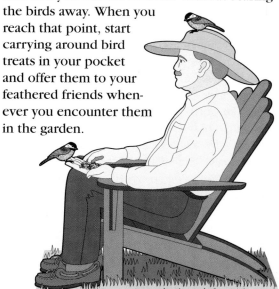

A hat is a great accessory for taming wild birds. Place nut meats or other tidbits around the brim or on the crown and sit still—you'll have a chickadee hood ornament in no time. Put some food in your hand, and the birds will feed from there, too.

HAWKS

Whether it's a hawk soaring overhead or perched high in a treetop, the sight of these beautiful birds of prey is an exciting experience that never seems to lose its thrill. Perhaps it's because hawks are among the only predators that nature really lets us get a good look at.

Hawk Habits and Habitat

Up close, hawks are even more impressive than at a distance. They are handsome birds with strong, curved beaks, sharp talons, and piercing eyes that reflect their hunting habits. But it's not often that you get to study a hawk at close range: Most hawk visits to the backyard are of the eat-and-run type.

Hawks usually stay away from humans, and no wonder. Although shooting hawks is against the law, it still occurs. Unless you have a very large, very wild piece of property, you're unlikely to host nesting hawks. Most hawks prefer to build their large, coarse-looking but well-constructed nests high in the trees in a wooded area. The American kestrel, a small, slim falcon, is the exception: This beautiful bird will accept nest boxes mounted relatively close to human comings and goings.

Almost any hawk can turn up in a bird-friendly backyard, especially during migration, when food is a top priority. If your feeder birds are lying low, and there's no bustle of activity at prime-time hours, look in the trees for the silhouette of a perched hawk.

Cooper's and Sharp-Shinned Hawks

These look-alike hawks are beautiful birds. Sharpies are a little bigger than the average pigeon, although much more svelte. Cooper's hawks are bigger birds—not quite crow size. The males of both species have a blue-gray back and a chestnut-striped belly and breast. But while the end of the sharp-shinned hawk's tail is blunt, the Cooper's hawk's tail is rounded at the tip. Females, which are

Help Songbirds Hide

Hawks are quick to spot a meal on the wing, and the feeding station in your backyard may be too much for them to resist. Unfortunately it's not the seeds and suet that tempt these stream-lined predators. It's the feeder guests themselves that hawks eye hungrily.

I try to give my feeder birds a fighting chance by offering dense cover close to the feeder for fast getaways. Hemlocks and spruces are perfect; a discarded Christmas tree or a pile of branches and other brush serves well as a temporary measure.

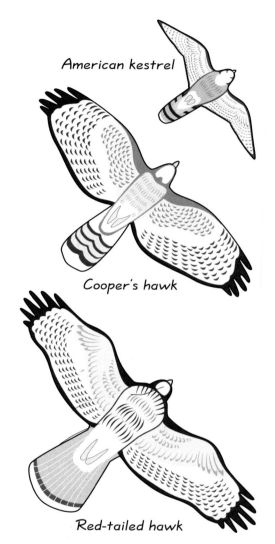

American kestrel

Cooper's hawk

Red-tailed hawk

Even when soaring high overhead, a hawk's size, shape, and markings offer clues about its identity.

bigger than the males, have a deep brown back and a streaky underside.

Both of these hawks feed mainly on other birds, with some small mammals thrown in for good measure. They're among the swiftest of the hawks, and they can twist and turn in midair.

Cooper's hawks and sharpies stay mostly in and along the edges of woods. But in winter, Cooper's hawks and sharp-shinned hawks turn up in backyards wherever there are bird feeders. They sometimes adopt a route of feeders, going from one to the other.

Red-Tailed Hawk

Found across the country, the red-tailed hawk is a big, heavy bird with wide wings. Instead of swift darting pursuit, redtails depend on their sharp eyesight to spot prey on the ground be-neath them. Dark brown birds, 1½ feet tall with a 4-foot wingspan, redtails have snowy white bellies crossed by a streaked band of brown.

The adults have a gorgeous red tail that shines chestnut when lit by the sun.

Redtails prefer small mammals, although they do occasionally snack on birds. If mice or voles live in your gardens, one of these hawks may stop by for a quick lunch.

American Kestrel

The male kestrel is an elegant small falcon with long pointed blue-gray wings, a warm chestnut back, and a set of Elvis-style black sideburns. The somewhat larger female looks the same except that her wings are chestnut instead of blue-gray. Kestrels range across North America and are commonly seen perched on utility wires and poles or roadside fence posts.

Kestrels are top-notch grasshopper eaters, so be thankful if one takes up residence in your neighborhood. They also eat mice, as well as crickets, frogs, and snakes. Kestrels are also called "sparrow hawks," because they eat small birds as well.

If you have a meadow or a yard bordering on open spaces, you may attract kestrels with a nest box (see Birdhouses on page 36 for dimensions). Mount it on a tree or pole with a good view of the wide-open spaces.

HEMLOCKS

Graceful, soft-textured hemlocks are one of the best bird plants you can add to your garden. Even newly planted hemlocks have dense foliage that offers birds excellent camouflage from predators and protection from the elements.

Goldfinches often take to hemlocks when it's time to build their thistledown-lined nests. Juncos, robins, jays, and other birds also like to nest in the security of these trees.

Hemlock seeds are a favorite for several kinds of backyard birds. Chickadees, crossbills, pine siskins, and other birds will patiently sit and pick seeds out of hemlock cones, eating each one before reaching for the next.

Growing hemlocks. Hemlocks are stately additions to any yard, reaching up to 100 feet tall and 60 feet wide. Hemlocks are hardy in Zones 4 to 7, but they prefer cool summers and require deep, moist, well-drained soil to grow their best. The trees tolerate some shade but growth may be sparse if they don't get enough sun. In some areas of the East, hemlocks are plagued by an insect pest called the hemlock woolly adelgid, which looks like small white waxy blobs on needles and twigs. Their feeding causes needles to drop and can even kill the trees. To control this pest, spray affected trees with horticultural oil (follow label directions).

Hemlock choices. Eastern hemlock (*Tsuga canadensis*), also called Canadian hemlock, grows to 80 feet tall and thrives in Zones 3 to 8. It has a loose pyramid shape; small, soft needles; and a graceful, drooping habit. Carolina hemlock (*T. caroliniana*) tops out at 70 feet and is hardy only in Zones 5 to 7.

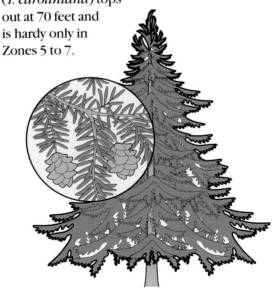

Hemlocks produce a multitude of seed-filled cones that birds love. Their drooping branches offer a safe haven for nesting and protection from wintry winds.

HERONS

Long necked, long legged, and extremely long beaked, herons add a look of living sculpture to backyard ponds and pools. It's fascinating to watch the single-minded manner in which they stalk fish and frogs.

Getting to Know Them

The great blue heron and its pure white, slightly smaller look-alike, the great egret, are statuesque birds. They both stand about 3 feet tall and have a wingspan of 5 to 6 feet; sexes look alike. White great egrets are the strong, silent type, rarely vocalizing with their hoarse croak, but great blue herons are squawkers, holding forth or calling alarm with loud, croaking cries.

Great blue herons and great egrets nest in colonies near bodies of water but visit backyard ponds, pools, and streams before and after the breeding season in search of fish and other water-garden animals. In the winter, if all the bodies of water are frozen over, herons may also resort to eating small mammals like mice.

Great blues range widely over the United States in all seasons, retreating from the colder top half of the country in winter. Great egrets are less widespread, found mostly in the South and West along the coasts and in the Midwest.

Green herons are more common visitors to backyard water gardens. This dark green-blue bird is roughly crow size, with a hunched posture and bright orange or yellow legs. Sexes look alike. If there aren't any fish or frogs in your pond or stream, green herons will happily dine on crayfish, dragonflies, water bugs, earthworms, and other residents of wet areas, as well as mice.

Green herons are common in summer in the eastern half of the country, west through the Southwest, and along the western coast; in winter they retreat to the very edges of the southern United States.

Herons and Water Gardens

Any size and shape of water garden may attract herons. If your backyard pool is full of prize koi or your children's pet frogs, you may not want herons to visit. To discourage herons from coming near your water garden, try dangling aluminum pie pans or fluttering strips of white cloth from a string suspended across the pond. The sound and motion may scare the birds away. Sheets of plastic netting draped above the surface of the water are also effective (black wide-mesh net is least noticeable to human eyes). If you use mesh, keep a close watch on your pond. The net might entangle the legs of an unwary heron who drops in for a meal.

A water garden provides many favorite foods for great blue herons. Fish are tops on the menu, but these birds also relish frogs, salamanders, snakes, and aquatic insects.

HOLLIES

Hollies have it all, as far as birds are concerned. Their red, yellow, or black berries fill many a hungry bird's belly in fall and winter. Prickly holly leaves offer birds protection from climbing cats and other predators, and the dense foliage hides nests and sheds rain and snow like a million little umbrellas.

Hollies are hardy, easy-care trees and shrubs that add four-season interest to a garden with their dark, glossy foliage. Most hollies are evergreen, but a few kinds are deciduous—they lose their leaves in winter. Berries of deciduous hollies draw bluebirds like a magnet. Robins, thrushes, mockingbirds, waxwings, and flickers devour the fruit of both evergreen and deciduous hollies.

Most hollies grow well in Zones 5 to 8. They set fruit in full sun to light shade, but do best when grown in deep, moist, well-drained soil. Keep in mind that hollies are male and female—each type of plant bears only male or female flowers. To get female hollies to bear heavy fruit, plant one male holly as a pollinator for every three females. You can prune hollies in late spring to improve their shape or limit their size.

Hollies for the Birds

The American holly (*Ilex opaca*) is a slow-growing, red-berried evergreen tree that eventually reaches 30 feet. It grows as far south as Zone 9 and prefers acid soil. To protect its leaves from cold damage, shelter American holly from drying winter winds. Longstalk holly (*I. pedunculosa*) is an evergreen holly that grows 15 feet tall or more. It has smooth-edged leaves and bright red berries that dangle from its long stems.

Good shrub hollies for birds include the red-berried Chinese holly (*I. cornuta*), which

reaches 10 feet tall, grows from Zones 7 to 9, tolerates almost any soil type, and withstands drought and heat. Meserve hybrids (*I. × meserveae*), commonly called blue hollies, are lustrous, dark-foliaged shrubs that reach 15 feet tall and have red berries. Hardiness varies according to cultivar, but most blue hollies grow well in Zones 5 to 7. Winterberry (*I. verticillata*), also called black alder, is an extremely hardy deciduous shrub that will grow in Zones 3 to 9. Winterberry reaches 10 feet or taller, and bright red berries cover the bare stems in fall. Japanese holly (*I. crenata*) tops out at about 8 feet tall and bears small black berries.

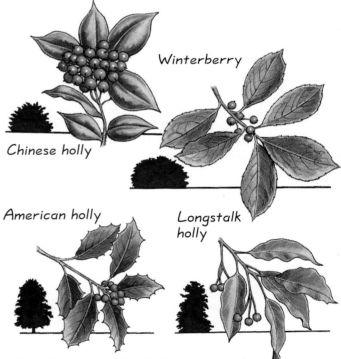

Winterberry

Chinese holly

American holly

Longstalk holly

All hollies are a hit with the birds, and they're a wonderful addition to foundation plantings or shrub borders. You can choose from elegant holly trees like American holly or dense shrub hollies like Chinese holly.

HONEYSUCKLES

From a bird's-eye point of view, honeysuckles are real winners. Catbirds, cardinals, song sparrows, and other birds nest in the tangled vines. Honeysuckles produce bold clusters of tubular, nectar-rich blossoms that draw hummingbirds and orioles. And the blue-black berries are a favorite of robins, waxwings, chickadees, and many others.

But from a gardener's viewpoint, honeysuckle can be a thug. Some honeysuckle vines spread rampantly. Birds contribute by sowing the seeds far and wide. So choose honeysuckles with care and plant them where they won't choke out less vigorous plants.

Growing Honeysuckles

Honeysuckles are ideal for disguising unsightly fences and outbuildings. Honeysuckle vines can reach heights of 30 feet with support. They're as happy scrambling over shrubs and dead or fallen trees as they are climbing a trellis, and many grow as well in filtered shade as in full sun. When your honeysuckle vines get too rambunctious, just cut them back as drastically as you need to—you won't harm the plants. But wait to prune until the vines finish blooming, so you don't deprive the birds of their beautiful, nectar-filled flowers.

Honeysuckles for the Birds

Trumpet or coral honeysuckle (*Lonicera sempervirens*), native to the East and South, and Arizona honeysuckle (*L. arizonica*), a Southwest plant, both have showy, mildly fragrant orange-red flowers and bright red berries. The vivid flowers attract hummingbirds and orioles.

Trumpet honeysuckle (Zones 4 to 9) is evergreen in the South and semievergreen in colder regions. This native of woods and shady roadside thickets does well in both sun and shade. Arizona honeysuckle is hardy only in Zones 6 to 8. Arizona honeysuckle is deciduous and grows best in full sun. Both species tend to grow into shrubs unless you encourage them to climb by tying the vines to a trellis as they grow.

The heady fragrance of Japanese honeysuckle (*L. japonica*) on a summer night has inspired many gardeners to add this vine to their garden, where it is indeed a delight. Each flower cluster includes both white and yellow flowers—white blossoms are newly opened, yellow are older. But heed my warning: If you plant Japanese honeysuckle, keep your pruning shears handy. When it outgrows its trellis or arbor, Japanese honeysuckle can take over any plant in its path. In one year, every branch tip of this highly vigorous vine can grow 6 feet or more.

Brightly colored orioles make a stunning sight sipping from the neon-bright flowers of a trumpet honeysuckle vine. The flowers also attract hummingbirds, and many birds will eat honeysuckle berries or nest in the lush vines.

HUMMINGBIRDS

Hummingbirds are living jewels. Their shimmering feathers gleam like burnished metal when the sun hits them. They come in gorgeous colors of green, bronze, purple, blue, red, pink, and orange. Hummingbirds are also high-octane bundles of energy that seem to be always in motion. Between their beauty and high-energy antics, it's no wonder that hummingbirds are such a favorite among backyard birdwatchers.

Getting to Know Them

Hummingbirds are talented fliers: They can move forward, backward, and sideways, or remain stationary while beating their wings so fast they make a humming noise. They feed on both nectar and insects. Because of their supercharged metabolic rate, hummingbirds must be on the wing and feeding almost constantly all day long.

Males are the beauties among hummingbirds. Females of all species are mostly green above, whitish below. The spectacular color at the male's throat is a patch of tiny feathers called gorgets. Just think of "gorgeous," and you'll know where the word comes from.

These tiny treasures live only in the Americas. Most species are found in Central and South America, and except for some areas of the Plains states, just about every part of the United States is graced by hummingbirds. In winter, hummers migrate southward, returning in spring in a migration that follows the spring flowers. Birdwatchers at migration points such as Hawk Mountain in eastern Pennsylvania have noted hummingbirds zipping along the same route as hawks and monarch butterflies.

The courtship maneuvers of hummingbirds are a treat to watch. The male, always a show-off, performs death-defying feats of flying, swinging like a pendulum or twisting in arcs to impress the female. Mating hummingbirds join together, spinning in tight, dizzying circles just above the ground.

Hummingbird nests are tiny, amazing feats of construction. The birds use lightweight materials like plant down and feathers bound with spider silk and use their saliva to fasten the nest to a small tree branch. Most species stud the outside of the nest with tiny bits of lichen. The inside diameter may measure less than an inch across.

Attracting Hummingbirds

The first step in bringing hummingbirds to your yard is to put out a plastic nectar feeder. Buy the gaudiest feeder you can find, with plenty of splashy red plastic—red is the best color for catching the birds' attention. Once hummers are accustomed to visiting your feeder, you can replace it with a more sedate model.

If you spot a hummingbird with a green back and whitish belly at its tiny nest, it's most likely the female, like this female ruby-throated hummingbird.

Fill the feeder with sugar water: 1 part sugar to 4 parts water. Regular granulated sugar melts quickly in boiling water; superfine sugar dissolves easily in cold water. Let water cool before you fill the feeder. Avoid using red food coloring to tint the water. It's not necessary, and may be harmful to the birds.

Sometimes hummingbird feeders also attract house finches. If finches start to hog your nectar feeders, you can discourage them by switching to a nectar feeder without perches and without a flared-out base, so that the finches (literally) can't get a grip.

Hummers in the Garden

While hanging up a sugar-water feeder will attract hummingbirds to your yard, the best way to get to know these tiny bundles of energy is to plant a garden for them.

Flowering plants will entice hummingbirds to linger in your garden, and you'll get to see all kinds of behavior you miss out on if hummers are just making fast-food stops at a feeder. Watch for hummers driving away butterflies, wasps, and bees from flowers, using those dagger beaks to show the competition they mean business. They'll also drive off other birds, or even people, when they're claiming territory for food sources or nearing their nests. Keep an eye on the hummers in your garden and you may see them chasing jays, waxwings, and even mockingbirds.

The best flowers for hummers have tubular blossoms, like honeysuckle, salvias, and bee balm. For ideas on what to plant, see the illustration on page 141.

Hummingbirds often visit spiderwebs in the garden. They steal tiny insects—and sometimes the spider itself—from the web for a meal. During nesting season, hummers also

The Wild World of Backyard Birds

Tiny hummingbirds fall victim to all kinds of oddball mishaps, from getting tangled in spiderwebs to getting stuck on thistles. Margaret Heffner of Steinsville, Pennsylvania, witnessed one such hummingbird happening.

One day Margaret was returning to the house for her noon meal when she found a hummingbird in quite a predicament. There was a big bowl of red zinnias on her kitchen table, and apparently the bright color had caught the little fella's eye. He'd tried to make a beeline for the flowers but ended up stuck by the beak in Margaret's screen door. His beak was on one side and he was on the other!

Working with infinite patience, Margaret maneuvered him free. He rested a moment in her hand, then zoomed off to the garden.

gather the strands of sticky spider silk for their nests.

Hummingbirds will even bathe on the fly, so if you use a fine-mist spray head on your garden hose, you may be visited by a hummingbird seeking a bath.

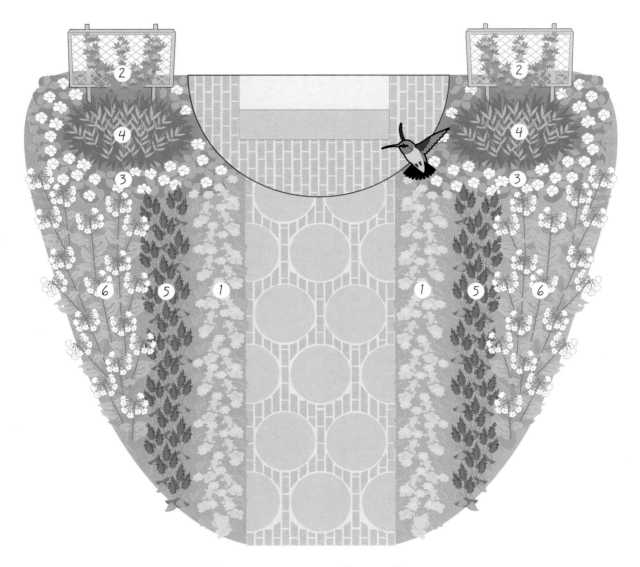

A Hummingbird Hello Garden

1. Apple-scented geranium *(Pelargonium sp.)*
2. Trumpet honeysuckle *(Lonicera sempervirens)*
3. White-flowered impatiens *(Impatiens wallerana)*
4. Pineapple sage *(Salvia elegans)*
5. Scarlet sage *(Salvia splendens)*
6. Flowering tobacco *(Nicotiana sylvestris)*

Hummingbird Checklist

Only one species, the ruby-throated humming-bird, nests east of the Great Plains. Occasional strays of other species may show up though, especially the rufous hummingbird, which occasionally visits the Gulf Coast and South Atlantic area in winter.

Ruby-throated hummingbird. Male ruby-throated hummingbirds have green backs, white bellies, and lovely deep pink-red throats. The ruby-throated nests from Nova Scotia south to Florida, and west to the Dakotas and east-central Texas. You'll find illustrations of the ruby-throated hummingbird on pages 83 and 139.

Hummingbirds of the West. Rufous hummingbirds are common in the Pacific Northwest. The male has a lovely chestnut back and a bright orange throat. Allen's hummingbird is found along the coast of California. This bird has a red throat and rusty brown lower back and tail. Anna's hummingbird is common west of the Sierras. It has a green back and a bright red-pink throat the color of a neon highlight.

In the western mountains, look for the well-named black-chinned hummingbird. Other hummingbirds' throats may look black until the light hits them, but then their bright colors show. The black-chinned's throat is black even in the best light. You'll find an illustration of the black-chinned hummingbird on page 80.

The broad-tailed hummingbird, with a solid red-purple throat and green back, is also common in the western mountains. The tiny calliope hummingbird occurs occasionally in western mountains. It's an itty-bitty 2¾-inch green bird whose red-purple throat has a distinctive striped appearance.

Hummingbirds of the Southwest. The Southwest is heaven for hummingbird lovers—at least eight more species of hummers live there. The blue-throated, at 5¼ inches, is the biggest, with a gorgeous cobalt throat. Almost as large is the magnificent hummingbird, whose violet crown, bright green throat, and deeper green back and belly live up to its name.

Purple is the outstanding color of several of the southwestern species: The head of Costa's hummingbird is a rich violet; the Lucifer hummingbird has a violet throat; the violet-crowned has a white throat and a rich purple cap; and the white-eared wears a purple cap and a brilliant green throat.

Whenever we go camping in the Southwest, I take along a nectar feeder and some instant nectar mix (available at bird supply stores and discount centers). I hang the feeder near our campsite picnic table so we can enjoy the show.

Hummingbirds can't resist the attraction of a nectar feeder, especially one with lots of red. The rufous hummingbird is a common sight at feeders in the Pacific Northwest.

IDENTIFYING BIRDS

Knowing the identity of the birds that visit your feeders and plants is key information for planning the most bird-friendly yard you can. If you spot a little gray-and-yellow bird flitting through your young oak tree in April, all you can do is admire it. But if you identify that bird as, for example, a yellow-rumped warbler, you can do a little research and discover that planting a bayberry bush is sure to entice the bird to return in fall or winter.

You don't have to know the name of every bird you see, but even a general working knowledge—like recognizing a bird as a sparrow or wood warbler—will make you feel more connected to the feathered visitors who share your home place. It's like knowing the names of the flowers in your garden: It makes them seem more like friends.

Narrowing the Search

Pick up a field guide for the first time, and you're bound to be baffled. How do you find that brown bird you just spotted among the hundreds of birds in the book? Looking through page by page will do the trick, but that could take an hour or more. Besides, by the time you narrow the possibilities to "sparrow of some kind," you're likely to realize that you don't have enough information to do any better. Did the bird you saw have white bars on its wings? How about yellow spots on its outside tail feathers? Chances are, you didn't notice, and you certainly won't remember them clearly.

Long before you get to such details, you need to learn a few tricks for narrowing the search. If you trust your memory for details, make mental notes as you observe birds and answer the following questions. I find it's safer to jot the pertinent details on a scrap of paper, or even make a quick sketch with arrows pointing to important details. After you've noted everything you can about the bird, and have it fixed in your memory, then consult your field guide. At first, you may have to flip

Paintbrush or Camera?

When you go shopping for a field guide, you'll find that some guides feature artists' illustrations of birds and others have bird photos. Photos are great for studying the details of a bird's markings or tail shape, for example, but I find drawings more helpful when I'm trying to identify a bird.

A drawing can show all the features of the bird that give you clues about its identity: the white spots in a prothonotary warbler's tail, for instance. But a photo only shows the pose of the bird at the time the camera snapped. Photo field guides can show you the general setting for the bird, though: pine tree or grassland, for instance (some artist-illustrated guides include typical plants with the birds, too).

I keep both types of field guides: illustrated guides to get the initial fix on a bird, and photo guides to give me another look at it in a typical posture and a real-life setting.

through a lot of pages to find your bird. As you become familiar with the book and add birds to your list, the process will become much quicker. You'll know from the start, for example, that your bird is probably a sparrow, or a blackbird, or a warbler, and can limit your search to just that section of the guide.

Here's how to systematically gather the information you need to identify a bird with certainty. **Check the size.** To quickly judge a bird's size ask yourself: Is it roughly the size of a robin? Or is it more like a sparrow? That answer immediately narrows the possibilities.

Several common types of birds are about the same size as a robin, including tanagers, orioles, grosbeaks, thrushes, waxwings, jays, blackbirds, starlings, and some woodpeckers.

Among the sparrow-size birds are finches, buntings, wood warblers, vireos, chickadees, titmice, wrens, gnatcatchers, kinglets, and larks.

Notice the colors. Pay attention to the overall color of the bird, and the colors of various body areas. (For more about using color details for identification, see "Noticing Field Marks," on the opposite page.)

◆ What color is its back?
◆ What color is its underside?
◆ What color are its wings and tail?

Study the tail. The tail is often a giveaway to a bird's identification. Not only can the tail give you a general idea of bird family, but it also can help you tell one type of sparrow, swallow, or other look-alike bird from another.

◆ Is the tail long, stubby, or somewhere in between?

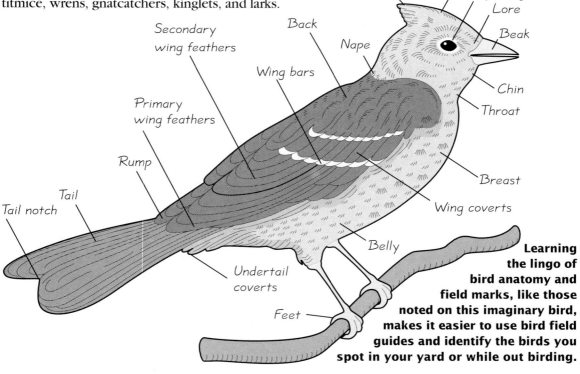

Learning the lingo of bird anatomy and field marks, like those noted on this imaginary bird, makes it easier to use bird field guides and identify the birds you spot in your yard or while out birding.

◆ Does the tail have a deep fork or a notch in the middle?

◆ Is the tip of the tail pointed, rounded, or square?

Zero in on the beak. If you're close enough to see the bird's beak, or if you're using binoculars, you have a great advantage, because beak color and shape are distinctive features.

Look for a crest. Check the top of the head for a crest. It may be in the lowered position and easy to miss at first glance.

Notice the surroundings. Although birds can and do stray from their usual haunts, most stick to surroundings they're comfortable in. Shy birds like sparrows stay in the brush or weeds, or on the ground among them. Field birds seek out open space, and woodpeckers are almost always clinging to a tree trunk or branch. You can check this information against the habitat description in your field guides. (When you look up habitat information, check the range map to make sure the bird in question occurs in your area.)

Watch the bird's actions. Some birds flit their tail frequently, either from side to side or up and down, like a nervous tic. Others may flick their wings or spread their tails.

Listen. Bird songs are hard to remember from the time you hear them until the time you pull out the field guide, but they can be helpful. The first time I spotted an olive-sided flycatcher, a new bird to me, I noticed its song was three loud whistled syllables, repeated after a brief interval. When I tracked down the bird in my field guide, I had to laugh at the translation: *Quick, three beers!* my bird was apparently demanding.

Noticing Field Marks

Field marks are the details of plumage that can make or break an identification. The illustration on the opposite page shows several types of field marks.

Once you get in the habit of looking for field marks, you'll have a much easier time identifying birds. And if you're anything like me, don't trust your memory—jot down key field marks on whatever scrap of paper you have handy.

After a while, looking for these trademarks of particular birds becomes a snap. Here are the main points to notice when you're in your yard trying to get a fix on a bird.

◆ Are there streaks or dots on its breast and/or belly, or are these areas plain in color?

◆ Are there thin stripes or wide bars, either dark or light in color, on its wings or tail? Is there a single wing bar or two bars?

◆ Does the tail have a different-colored band at the very tip? Or white outer feathers? Or white or colored spots?

◆ Does the bird have a white patch just above its tail on its rump?

◆ Is there a stripe at the eye?

◆ Is there a distinct ring around the eye?

◆ Does the crown of the head have a cap or patch?

◆ Do the wings show white patches when the bird flies? Where are the patches?

Learning to identify birds is just one small step from keeping a mental or written list of what you've seen, and that's the start of a lifetime of learning, not to mention a possible obsession that will have you peering into every bush you pass, scanning the sky overhead, listening to peeps and tweets, and planning treks to birding hotspots so you can add more names to the list. If these activities sound intriguing, you can learn more about them by reading Birding, Birding Hotspots, and Life List.

IMPATIENS

Impatiens brighten shady places with bloom from spring through frost with never a letup, and bring hummingbirds calling wherever you plant them. Impatiens are a well-loved favorite for flowerbeds, but bird-loving gardeners should also plant pots or hanging baskets of impatiens for a close-up look at the hummingbirds that feed at the nectar-rich flowers. As a bonus, when impatiens go to seed, you can watch rose-breasted grosbeaks, sparrows, finches, and buntings feed on the seeds.

Impatiens are a tender perennial usually treated as an easy-care annual. They come in enough colors to suit any color scheme. Plant a six-pack of impatiens, and the plants will quickly fill out into mounds of lance-shaped green or bronze leaves from 6 to 12 inches tall, covered with hundreds of 1- to 2-inch-wide cheery flowers.

Growing Impatiens

There is simply no better flower for shade than impatiens (*Impatiens wallerana*). They also grow in sun, but may wilt in dry soil and midday heat. Plant impatiens in soil that's well amended with organic matter, and keep the soil moist. Space compact types 6 to 10 inches apart, and larger varieties 15 to 20 inches apart. It's faster to use starter plants, because seeds are slow to germinate (as long as three weeks) and grow. To multiply your impatiens, simply snip cuttings from mature plants and insert them into moist soil, where they'll quickly root.

New Guinea impatiens (*I. hawkeri*) are taller and flashier than regular impatiens. They have dazzling, boldly striped leaves of green, bronze, pink, red, and yellow. New Guinea impatiens reach 2 feet tall, and the pink, red, orange, purple, or white flowers are 3 inches across.

Old-fashioned garden balsam (*I. balsamina*), also called touch-me-not because its seed pods burst open when ripe, is another favorite of hummingbirds and seed-eating birds. The elegant, lance-leaved plants reach 24 to 30 inches tall and have snapdragon-shaped flowers in pink, lilac, fuchsia, red, or white. It's easy to start balsam from seed sown in the garden. Once there, it self-sows—if any of the seeds escape the scrutiny of hungry birds.

For a hummingbird garden in a pot, combine impatiens with trailing verbena, red geraniums, and bronze-leaved coleus. Once the impatiens go to seed, you'll also enjoy the visits of seed-eating birds like finches, buntings, and grosbeaks.

INSECTS AND BIRDS

If it weren't for insect-eating birds, gardeners might become an endangered species. Caterpillars and grasshoppers would strip the leaves from our favorite plants, ants would be everywhere we step, and wood-boring beetles would turn tree trunks into sawdust.

Birds are major players when it comes to keeping insects in check, both in and out of the garden. Early spring to early summer is the prime time for birds to hunt insects, when they have lots of hungry nestlings clamoring

for high-protein meals. During the two weeks that a brood of meadowlarks is being fed in the nest, the parents will feed the nestlings up to 10,000 grasshoppers, not to mention all the other kinds of bugs they catch.

Some birds depend so heavily upon insects for food that they'll starve if cold weather causes the insect population to disappear. Migrating birds like purple martins and swallows may retreat southward if a bout of late-spring cold sets in and keeps the flying insects they eat out of the air. Sadly, early-nesting bluebirds may starve if a late-spring snow hits when they have young to raise.

Six-Legged Snacks

Birds are a flying SWAT team when it comes to insects. When you welcome birds into your garden, they'll thank you by eating hundreds of these pests each day—even more during their spring nesting season.

Insects	*Birds That Eat Them*
Ants	**Flickers, wood thrushes and other thrushes; swallows eat swarming ants on the wing**
Bees and wasps	**Flycatchers, kingbirds, tanagers, and many other birds**
Cicadas	**House wrens, crows, cardinals, and many other birds**
Cutworms	**Bobwhites, robins, cuckoos, catbirds, brown thrashers, and many other birds**
Flies, gnats, and midges	**Flycatchers, swallows, martins, gnatcatchers, and many other birds**
Grasshoppers, crickets, and locusts	**Many insect-eating birds**
Leafhoppers	**Wrens, chickadees, warblers, and many other birds**
Long-horned beetles	**Woodpeckers**
Mosquitoes	**Almost all birds**
Treehoppers	**Flycatchers, blackbirds, vireos, kinglets, and many other birds**

Good Bug or Bad Bug?

Birds aren't discriminating when it comes to snatching insects to eat. They'll devour beneficial garden insects right along with insect pests. To hungry birds, there's no such thing as a "good" bug—to birds, all insects are high-protein snacks. Bluebirds, which eat a fair share of plant-damaging grasshoppers and crickets, will also eat plenty of beneficial ground beetles, which ordinarily prey on insect pests.

During the early years of this century, the federal government sponsored studies conducted by Foster E. L. Beal. He studied bird diets, comparing the percentage of "good" bugs to "bad" bugs. His study of Carolina wrens revealed that they dined on boll weevils, stinkbugs, flea beetles, orange scale insects, and dozens of others. The Carolina wren was a beneficial bird, he concluded, because it ate insects that were harmful to crops.

Beal's research and similar surveys were intended to show farmers which birds were their friends. Wheat farmers in North Carolina were delighted with one census that showed native sparrows ate wheat aphids at the astounding rate of 1 million a day on a single farm. Wildlife managers still use the information from these studies to select plants that will create good habitats for birds in their areas.

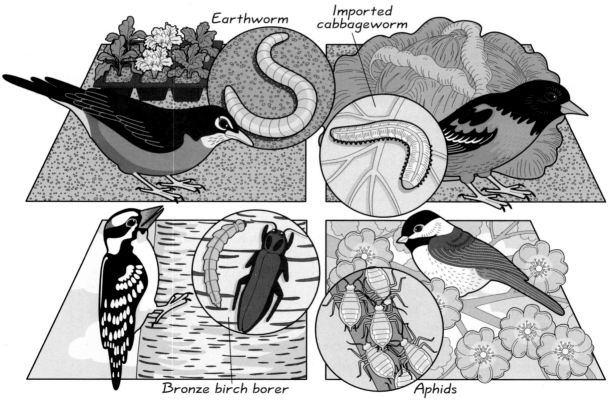

Earthworm

Imported cabbageworm

Bronze birch borer

Aphids

On the wing, in the trees, and in your garden, backyard birds help with organic pest control by eating huge quantities of insect pests. While they also eat earthworms and beneficial insects, bug-eating birds are definitely a plus in the garden.

Jays

Big, bold, and beautiful, jays are the most brazen of backyard birds. Because they're so noisy, they're a good bird to practice your birding skills on. Whenever you hear a bunch of jays screaming, check it out. Their fury is often directed at birds of prey, so jays have helped me get excellent close-up looks at great horned owls, barn owls, screech owls, and many hawks. Also many songbirds will attempt to drive off jays, knowing that they're a threat to eggs and young. Watching these interactions can give you clues about where birds' nests are hidden in your backyard.

Getting to Know Them

Jays of one kind or another cover almost every part of the United States. Blue jays are the most widespread, living year-round in the eastern two-thirds of the country and ranging into the Northwest in winter. The elegant deep blue Steller's jay is a bird of the West, where it overlaps with the western scrub jay and pinyon jay; the gray jay is a bird of the North and the western mountains.

With a length approaching 12 inches, jays would be hard to overlook, even if they weren't always shrieking *Look at me!* in their harsh, unmusical voices. Their blue color catches your eye as they flash across open space or swoop into the feeder, and the crests that top the heads of the blue jay and Steller's jay add a regal finishing touch.

Whether they're eating or playing, jays like to hang around with their buddies in small congenial groups. They're active birds, and make no attempt to be secretive except during the nesting season, when they suddenly become as

invisible as a Stealth aircraft. If it seems like all your jays have disappeared in spring, keep an eye out for that telltale flash of blue in the trees and shrubs. Watch for jays tenderly courting with soft, chuckling love songs and a neat little bowing, bobbing dance on a branch overhead, or collecting twigs from beneath your shrubs and trees for building materials.

Jay nests are messy-looking masses of twigs, pieces of root, moss, and bark, with a neat lining of fine roots or grasses and sometimes feathers and hair. The nests are often built not far off the ground, only 10 to 15 feet high, in a tree or shrub, but may occasionally

Blue jays enjoy sumac berries, as well as a wide variety of other berries, seeds, and nuts. Gardeners as far west as Texas may host these jays year-round. Some western gardeners may find blue jays in their neighborhood in the winter.

be much higher, up to 50 feet. Eggs vary in color depending on species, but are typically blue-green to pale grayed shades of either color. The eggs of blue jays, gray jays, Steller's jays, and scrub jays are freckled with brown; pinyon jays lay unmarked eggs.

The appetite of a jay shows its heritage as part of the crow family: Like crows, jays will eat just about anything. They consume tons of insects, seeds, nuts, fruit, and berries, supplemented with such treats as salamanders, spiders, snails, fish, mice, and bats. They'll also eat eggs and young birds. Jays are also gardeners of a sort: They often bury acorns and nuts for later use, and end up planting trees for the future.

Attracting Jays

At the feeder, keep your jays happy with handouts of sunflower seeds, peanuts, nuts, corn, bread, doughnuts, dog food, chick scratch, and chopped suet.

When jays arrive at the feeder, less assertive birds like sparrows and chickadees make themselves scarce. To keep all your guests happy, add an open tray feeder on a post for the jays, so the little birds will have a better chance of dining uninterrupted.

Plant oaks, beeches, pecans, walnuts, and other nut trees to bring jays to your garden. Jays love berries, too, including sumac berries, blueberries, grapes, cherries, and serviceberries.

To appreciate the playful side of these birds, put out some shiny trinkets and watch the birds discover them. Set out broken mirror bits, shiny dimes, rhinestone jewelry, silver-colored safety pins, and any other bright, shiny objects you can find. Jays will quickly approach and carry off the treasures to hide or bury.

The Wild World of Backyard Birds

Like a bunch of mischief-loving youths on the street corner, jays hang out in groups most of the year, just waiting for a chance to tweak the tail of a sleeping dog, harass a trespassing owl, or scatter the songbirds at your feeder. Their dining habits are not above reproach, either: They may feed on songbird eggs or even nestlings.

But in spite of all these strikes against them, jays can be a delight. They're intelligent creatures who seem to have more awareness of the world than the average songbird. And they definitely have a sense of humor. One way-too-early-morning, while on vacation in a California campground, we were awakened from a sound sleep by somebody dropping something on the canvas roof over our heads. When I investigated, I found we were under bombardment by a bunch of scrub jays who were sitting in an oak tree above our tent, dropping acorns one by one onto our heads. I swear I almost heard them laughing.

Many birdwatchers think Steller's jay is the most beautiful species of jay. Found west of the Rockies, this handsome bird prefers coniferous forests but may show up in your backyard if it includes plenty of evergreens.

Jay Checklist

Jays with various arrangements of blue feathers reside all across the country. In certain areas you can also find a gray-feathered jay.

Blue jay. The blue jay is the only jay that appears in the East. Bright blue on top and white below, the blue jay sports a black-outlined crest and white wing accents. As with all jays, the sexes look alike. Blue jays can appear at any time of year from Canada to Texas and eastward. In winter, blue jays also venture westward into Washington and New Mexico.

Steller's jay. This striking bird of the West and Northwest is a deep, rich midnight blue on its back and head, with brighter blue tail, wings, and belly. It has a big, prominent crest. Like other jays, it's a great mimic, specializing in hawk calls.

Gray jay. The gray jay is a bird of the north woods of Canada and the northern tier of the United States, also ranging south into the western mountains. Folks there often refer to it as the "camp robber" because of its habit of nabbing items left about, including soap and toothpaste. Easily tamed, this soft gray jay lacks a crest. Its white forehead, chin, and collar and dark nape of the neck make it look something like a giant chickadee.

Other jays. Scrub jays, Mexican jays, and pinyon jays lack crests, making them look something like overgrown bluebirds. Scrub jays hang out in the scrub-oak regions of the West. They have a blue head, white belly, and gray back, and their rich blue tail and wings are easily visible in flight.

Mexican jays, found in oak and oak-pine areas of the Southwest, look like scrub jays that have been washed a few times too many. Their blue is faded instead of shockingly bright.

Pinyon jays are common in arid regions of the West. In silhouette they look more like starlings than jays, thanks to their stubby tail. They're gray-blue all over and have a soft mewing voice instead of a loud holler.

Sometimes called "blue squawkers," scrub jays like to snack on the berries of wax myrtle (*Myrica cerifera*) and other berry-bearing shrubs.

JUNCOS

If ragweed makes your allergies act up, say a big thank-you to the next junco you see. Almost a third of a junco's winter diet consists of ragweed seeds and seeds of smartweed, another bane of the gardener's existence. Of course juncos don't know they're doing us a favor. They seek the seeds because they're high in protein and oils.

Getting to Know Them

Juncos have distinct whitish pink beaks that stand out against their gray faces. They belong to the sparrow family, and they're sparrow size—5 to 6 inches long. Their white outer tail feathers make them easy to identify at a glance when they fly. Female juncos are a bit paler than the males. Listen for their jingly, trilling voices and their sharp *clink!* call note. Juncos build their nests on the ground, laying pale, speckled eggs. Juncos range across the entire United States in winter. They're one of the top five most common feeder birds in winter nationwide.

There are four common types of junco. They are all considered different "races" of a single species called the dark-eyed junco. The four types are called slate-colored juncos, white-winged juncos, Oregon juncos, and gray-headed juncos.

Slate-colored junco. Affectionately called "snowbirds," slate-colored juncos show up all across the United States in winter, with bellies as white as fresh flurries and backs the color of a snow-laden sky. These sparrow-size birds are a familiar sight at feeders and in backyards, where they hop about on the ground, picking up seeds. They nest far north in Canada and Alaska.

Oregon junco. The Oregon junco wears a snazzy black hood and has a rusty brown back. This western bird nests along the coast and in the Northwest; in winter, its range extends to the Plains. Occasional strays wander far outside their normal haunts, showing up at feeders to delight those of us used to the plain gray-and-white snowbirds.

Gray-headed junco. The gray-headed junco, a gray bird with a dashing chestnut cape across its upper back, reigns in the Rockies. The yellow-eyed junco (which is a separate species) looks much like the gray-headed except for the color of its eyes, but is found only in high mountains of the Southwest.

Attracting Juncos

Juncos are ground-level birds, so give them a low platform feeder or sprinkle seed on the ground. They like millet, and in cold weather appreciate a handout of fine-chopped suet. They'll check your flower garden, too, for seeds of cosmos, zinnia, and tickseed sunflower (*Bidens aristosa*).

Look for slate-colored juncos feeding on the seeds of weeds or garden plants in winter.

JUNIPERS

When berries appear on junipers, it's a race among over 50 kinds of birds to see who gets the bonanza of round blue fruits. Bluebirds, thrushes, flickers, yellow-rumped warblers, robins, and other birds compete for juniper berries.

Growing Junipers

Junipers are tough, adaptable evergreens that provide excellent nesting sites and winter shelter for birds as well as food. They also bring year-round beauty to gardens. Tall junipers make excellent windbreaks or screens. Shrubby junipers are a good choice for hedges or to accent a garden, especially if you pair their short needles and fine texture with bird-attracting broad-leaved evergreens such as bayberries or hollies. And low-growing junipers make beautiful, low-maintenance groundcovers for sunny spots. Select ones with space below their branches, such as creeping juniper (*Juniperus horizontalis*), so birds can find shelter at ground level.

Most junipers grow from Zones 3 to 9. Cultivars may vary greatly in hardiness and plant form, so read plant tags or catalog descriptions before buying. Grow junipers in full sun and in average, well-drained soil (they'll also tolerate poor soil). Except for western red cedar (*J. scopulorum*), the junipers described below have separate male and female plants. Plant one male juniper as a pollinator for every three to five female plants—only the female plants will produce fruit.

Upright junipers. Chinese juniper (*J. chinensis*) is a slender tree that grows 50 feet tall or more, but some cultivars are much smaller. 'Hetzii' and 'Hetzii Columnaris' reach only 15 feet tall.

Eastern red cedar is another slender tree that reaches 20 feet tall or more. The cultivar 'Grey Owl' tops out at 3 feet tall and 8 feet wide. 'Manhattan Blue' has dark blue-green needles and grows 10 to 12 feet tall and nearly as wide.

Western red cedar, also called Rocky Mountain juniper, grows in Zones 3 to 7. It can reach 30 feet tall, but its silvery-needled cultivars, including 'Gray Gleam', 'Moonglow', and 'Skyrocket', reach only about 15 feet.

Low-growing junipers. Creeping junipers form a thick groundcover of green or blue-green needles even in hot, dry conditions, and set abundant fruits.

Shore juniper (*J. conferta*) and its cultivar 'Emerald Sea' have the added benefit of being salt tolerant. These dense-growing junipers stay from 1 to 2 feet tall and will grow in Zones 5 to 9.

Junipers range from upright trees like this eastern red cedar to shrubs and low-growing groundcovers. Their "berries" attract cedar waxwings, bluebirds, and many other birds.

KILLDEERS

In early spring, listen for the sound of killdeers returning home from their winter vacation in the southern half of the country and in Mexico. Their call is a high, keening *kill-deee! kill-deee!* that you may hear during the day or at night as the birds fly overhead.

Getting to Know Them

Robin-size but long-legged killdeers look as though they'd be right at home on an ocean beach. That's no coincidence, since their closest relatives are shorebirds like plovers and sandpipers. But unlike their kin, killdeers make their homes in meadows, pastures, parking lots, and suburban driveways, often far away from water.

Killdeers nest across the United States and most of Canada. Except they don't exactly "nest": They merely carry a few weed stems or pebbles to a shallow depression on open ground, then lay four well-camouflaged and heavily blotched buff-colored eggs right out in the open.

These birds are well camouflaged, too, thanks to dark stripes that break up the silhouette of their head and neck. The adult killdeer wears a double collar of dark bands around its neck, while the juvenile bird sports only a single dark band. When they fly, killdeers reveal an otherwise hidden patch of rich deep orange just above their black-and-white-tipped tail feathers. Their backs and wings are gray brown, and their underparts are pure white. This color combination is so effective that killdeers are nearly impossible to see when they're sitting motionless on their nest full of eggs. Both killdeer parents take turns at this task.

If you get too close to a killdeer nest, you're in for quite a show. To distract your attention from

the eggs or baby birds, the parent will flutter away, pitifully dragging its apparently broken wing. Even when you know it's all an act, it's hard to resist the impulse to follow the adult bird.

Killdeer babies hatch fully fluffed and are ready to run about and find their own food in about an hour or so. Their blotchy plumage gives them good protective camouflage, but if they have to flee from danger, they're speedy little critters that are remarkably adept at evading pursuers. It takes more than three weeks, though, before the young birds can fly.

Attracting Killdeers

Feeding stations and berry bushes won't lure these birds, because insects make up about 98 percent of their diet. Killdeers patrol lawns for grubs and earthworms, and they may take up residence in a meadow garden or near a backyard pond. Relatively undisturbed areas of gravel, bare soil, or short grass attract killdeers when they're nesting, because these sites provide the most camouflage for their eggs.

Like robins, killdeers are likely to turn up on open areas of your lawn, where they'll search for grubs and earthworms to eat.

154

KINGBIRDS

Kingbirds are either the bravest songbirds or the most foolhardy. Their Latin name, *Tyrannus,* is a perfect fit for their self-appointed role as guardians of the neighborhood, where they protect their nests from crows, ravens, hawks, owls, and cats.

Most of the day kingbirds perch on fences or other lookouts to keep an eye on things, then zip out to ward off any intruder that happens along. Clocked at better than 20 miles per hour on the wing, they're agile fliers.

Getting to Know Them

Kingbirds are medium-size flycatchers that often perch out in the open. Both sexes look the same. Kingbirds perch much of the time, waiting to dart out after passing bees, moths, grasshoppers, and other insect prey (or after intruders). They also eat berries and wild fruits. These birds have sputtering, often startlingly loud voices.

A post-and-rail fence along a meadow garden or other open space in your yard gives eastern kingbirds and other kingbirds a great perching place.

Kingbirds nest in isolated trees or shrubs. They build a rough, deep cuplike nest of twigs, straw, rootlets, and feathers lined with fine grasses, hair, wool, or small roots on a branch anywhere from 2 to 60 feet above the ground. They lay three to five white or pale buff eggs, marked with brown splotches.

Attracting Kingbirds

Because kingbirds are insect eaters, you can't tempt them with birdseed at a feeder. But they do like berries, so plant viburnums, brambles, elderberries, hawthorns, and grapes to attract them. They also like a fence or other good perch from which they can hunt insects. Large water features, such as ponds or streams, are also a draw.

Kingbird Checklist

The two most common kingbirds, the eastern and the western, like to hang out at the edges of towns or farms where there's lots of open space.
Eastern kingbird. The eastern kingbird, which ranges across the country except for the Southwest, has a charcoal black topside and white underparts, with a teeny strip of red on the crown and a white tail band. Look for this bird in open farm fields and in suburban areas.
Western kingbird. The western kingbird, found in the western half of the United States, has a beautiful yellow belly, gray upper parts, and a white throat. It's common around homesteads and farms and along streams and rivers. The western kingbird may build its nest on a utility pole, on a ledge above a door, or against a fence post.
Cassin's kingbird. The Cassin's kingbird lives in the Southwest. It looks like the western kingbird but lacks that species' white outer tail feathers and has a dark olive green throat between the white chin and yellow belly. It likes brushy areas or woods.

KINGLETS

Tiny kinglets are easy to overlook, although they're common birds and their range covers the entire country. One of the reasons they're not often noticed is their smaller-than-a-chickadee size: They just top the 3-inch mark from tip of beak to end of tail. The other reason is they spend most of their time flitting or hovering about the tops and branch tips of conifers and other trees.

Getting to Know Them

Kinglets are nervous little bundles of energy, always in motion. There are two species of kinglets in the United States: the golden-crowned and ruby-crowned. The two species look nearly the same: Both have gray-green bodies and two white wing bars. The difference is head color, as their names suggest. Ruby-crowned kinglets have a bright red patch on the top of their heads, and golden-crowned kinglets have a dash of butter yellow. But at a distance, these patches of color on the male birds' heads are hard to see.

You can also tell one kinglet from another by checking some other features. For example, the golden-crowned kinglet has a strongly striped head, whereas the ruby-crowned kinglet has a plain head. On the other hand, the ruby-crowned has a white eye ring, and the golden-crowned doesn't. And the ruby-crowned has a habit of constantly flicking its wings, which the golden-crowned doesn't.

In wintertime, kinglets join mixed flocks of chickadees, titmice, nuthatches, brown creepers, and downy woodpeckers to patrol the trees. Listen for the high, thin *zee-zee-zee-zee* calls of the golden-crowned kinglet, or the similar *zhee-dit* of the ruby-crowned. In spring you may hear the startlingly loud song of the ruby-crowned kinglet, who whistles out *liberty-liberty-liberty*.

The ruby-crowned builds a small hanging nest, usually in spruces. The golden-crowned builds a tiny domelike nest with an opening at the top, so small that it has to lay its tiny brown-marked white eggs in two layers.

Attracting Kinglets

In most of the United States, kinglets are winter visitors only. Other than planting elderberries, all you need to do to lure kinglets is to plant insect-harboring trees where they can search for food. Hemlocks, spruces, oaks, and pines are good choices.

When you find kinglets, you'll notice they're unafraid of humans. Hold out a leafy branch and a kinglet will ignore you to focus on exploring the foliage. If the bird is in reach, it may allow you to stroke it lightly with a finger.

Both the ruby-crowned kinglet (shown) and the similar-looking golden-crowned kinglet are insect eaters. You may spot them hunting for aphids, caterpillars, bark beetles, and other insects in trees and shrubs.

LAWNS

Your lawn can be a terrific setting for back-yard birding. An open area like your lawn is a natural place to set up feeders and birdbaths in strategic spots so you have a clear view from your favorite birdwatching windows. As long as there are sheltering shrubs or trees nearby, most backyard birds will stop to feed or bathe.

Some birds find a lawn appealing even without added attractions. Robins, flickers, starlings, killdeers, grackles, and other birds know that lawns can be prime hunting grounds for the soft foods they crave: earthworms and grubs. In spring and fall, migrating robins and flickers often show up on lawns in large numbers to refuel on these high-protein morsels. Starlings are adept at pulling the plump larvae of June beetles and Japanese beetles from their underground tunnels. After a troup of starlings has worked the lawn, you can sometimes see the puncture marks made by their beaks.

Other turfgrass critters including spiders, ants, centipedes, sowbugs, and crickets are also favorite treats for many kinds of birds. To attract nesting bluebirds, wildlife experts recommend facing bluebird houses toward an open area, such as a lawn or meadow, which will not provide camouflage for predators.

If you can tolerate your yard looking a little seedy, you can tempt some dazzling birds to land on your lawn. Let a few dandelions go to seed, and the fluffy seeds will attract brilliant blue indigo buntings, bright yellow-and-black goldfinches, house finches, purple finches, white-crowned and white-throated sparrows, and other birds.

In late spring, seed-eating birds like indigo buntings and goldfinches gather on lawns where dandelion flowers have turned to seedy puffs, while robins, flickers, and other birds probe for worms and grubs. Add a birdbath and a couple of feeders, and your lawn will attract an exciting variety of songbirds.

Organic Lawn Care

It's easy to grow a healthy, handsome organic lawn. The first thing you'll want to do is set your mower an inch or two higher than the recommended cutting height for your type of grass. Mowing higher keeps you from damaging the growing points, or crowns, of the grass with your mower blades. You can mow taller grass as often as you like without damaging it. Fact is, the taller your grass grows, the healthier it becomes. You'll notice brown spots go away over time as the turf becomes more drought tolerant and freeze resistant, because taller grass has more leaf area for converting the sun's energy into nutrients.

Using a mulching mower and leaving clippings on your lawn also make it healthy because the clippings are a natural fertilizer that adds nitrogen to the soil as they decompose. Of course, it's okay to gather clippings once in a while if you like using them as mulch on your flower or vegetable beds.

If you water your lawn, water it deeply to encourage roots to penetrate deeper into the soil. That way, they'll be more naturally drought resistant, and your lawn will tolerate drought and other stress better.

Thick organic lawns are a joy to care for because they shade out weeds. Keep in mind that most lawns are never entirely weed-free, and organic lawns are no exception. But you can hand-weed as needed and feel good about letting a few dandelions go to seed to feed the birds.

LIFE LIST

Keeping a list of birds you've spotted appeals to the collector in us. Listing the birds you've identified will also help you improve your birding skills. Once you've mastered the basics of easy-to-identify birds, you'll find yourself motivated to detect the differences between those confusing warblers or those confounding sparrows. You'll want your list to keep growing.

Travel list and home list. I keep two lists: my anytime-anywhere list, which includes all of the hundreds of bird species I've identified during my travels around the country, and my at-home list, which includes birds I've seen on or over my yard. While I enjoy ticking off new birds on the big list, I get a bigger thrill out of adding a new bird to the 86 species on my home list. I'm proud to say that list even includes a whooping crane, which flew over a few autumns ago. Though it never touched down, I still counted it, since at least my feet were standing on my home ground.

Hitting the 100 mark. Once you start ticking off birds on a list, you'll find that attaining a list of 100 birds happens faster than you'd expect. You may reach the 100 mark in your first year of birdwatching, with only a little extra effort beyond strolling your yard. Of course, dyed-in-the-wool birders spend years chasing down rare migrants in order to boost their list and achieve the rank of the "600 Club," whose members have tallied at least that many birds.

The checklist in your field guide—or even beside the illustrations—is a good place to start keeping track of your birds. I like to add a few notes that will jog my memory when I refer back, such as "Orchard oriole 5/26/81, singing from ash tree behind shed."

Magpies

Magpies are hard to miss. These big birds have extravagant tails that are longer than their bodies, and a memorable, if not melodious, voice. If you live in magpie range (the western half of the country except for the Southwest and coastal regions), you'll most likely get a visit from these sociable, curious birds, who are always investigating their neighborhoods. Look for them walking around on your lawn or driveway like they own the place.

Long Tails and Loud Voices

From tip to tail, magpies measure 16 to 18 inches long; their tails alone can be 12 inches long. They're colored in a striking black-and-white pattern that you can spot from a long way. Close up, you can see their iridescent greenish black tail feathers and greenish blue upper wings. Males and females look alike.

If you've ever heard of someone who "chatters like a magpie," you have a clue to the vocal habits of these birds. Their repeated, loud, harsh *check, check* cries don't always endear them to their human neighbors.

Black-billed magpies live in the West year-round, from Alaska south to California and northern New Mexico, and east as far as Iowa. Yellow-billed magpies, which live in the farming valleys of central California, look very similar to black-billed magpies, but have yellow beaks. The ranges of these birds don't overlap.

Magpies spend most of their time on the ground. They eat grasshoppers, crickets, ground beetles, and other insects, as well as carrion, mice, snakes, and some fruit. Like their relatives the crows and jays, they also partake of eggs or an occasional nestling.

Like the birds themselves, magpie nests are easy to spot from a distance. Built in trees or shrubs, the conglomeration of sticks and dry plants can reach the size of a bushel basket. Magpie eggs are gray or green, splotched and spattered with purple or brown.

Some folks are less than fond of magpies because the birds chatter so much, but these magnificent birds are part of the super-intelligent crow family, which means they're great fun to watch. Magpies play hide-and-seek with favorite objects, especially their favorite shiny treasures. They'll eagerly snatch up polished coins like quarters, as well as buttons, bright new nails, and safety pins to bury in sand or a crevice or to use in magpie games. They're often easy to hand-tame, with a bit of patience and some grub. Lunch meat, bread, and other leftovers are welcome treats.

Black-billed magpies are birds of the western United States. They prefer a diet of crickets and other insects to the fare at backyard feeders, but shiny objects like coins will attract them. The similar-looking yellow-billed magpie lives only in California.

Manure

Manure makes your plants grow and makes your garden a better place for birds. Dug into the soil or spread on the surface, well-rotted manure encourages earthworms, ground beetles, and smaller insects to call your garden home. Critters like these are favorite foods for robins, thrushes, towhees, and other insect-eating birds. Manure may also contain weed seeds or grass seeds, which small birds like horned larks, snow buntings, and sparrows will search out and snack on.

Using manure safely. If you're using manure around your garden plants, be sure it has aged or composted for about six months before you apply it. Most fresh manure produces ammonia as it decomposes, which can burn plants, stunt their growth, or even kill them. It may also contain disease-causing organisms.

Composted or well-rotted rabbit manure, chicken manure, cow manure, and horse manure all add valuable organic matter and nitrogen to your garden. If you get manure from a stable, it will also likely be mixed in with wood shavings or sawdust bedding, but it still needs to be thoroughly composted before you use it. Never use manure from dogs or cats in your garden.

You can usually pick up as much manure as you need at little or no cost from commercial stables and some farms—check the farm listing in your local paper's classified ads. If you live near a zoo, it may offer some type of zoo animal manure for purchase. Or you can buy commercial bagged composted manure at garden centers.

Martins

Folks who have martins nesting in their backyard feel special, and they should. Although these birds nest across the United States, it can be tricky to attract martins to a new place of residence, even if you provide them with everything it seems they desire.

Getting to Know Them

Purple martins aren't purple at all. They're glossy deep blue, almost black, with a forked tail. Females and juvenile birds have light bellies. They have a rich, warbling twitter that's delightful to listen to through your open windows, or when you work outside in the yard.

These elegant members of the swallow family have an immense appetite for flying insects. Martins traditionally nest in colonies that can number in the dozens, often just yards away from houses and other buildings. Martins build nests of leaves, grass, and feathers to hold their four or five pure white eggs.

Martins patrol the skies near their high-rise apartment houses, swooping and soaring in effortless flight that's a delight to watch. At home they're devoted parents, stuffing countless beakfuls of beetles and flies down their nestlings' gullets and guiding the youngsters on their first tentative efforts to wing it alone.

Attracting Martins

Choctaws, Chickasaws, and other Native Americans knew that martins were fearless enough to drive away hawks who trespassed near their breeding colonies. So they hung hollowed-out gourds around their villages for the martins to nest in. In doing so, the Native Americans were taking advantage of the martins' protectiveness to keep the tribes' flocks of poultry safe. The Indians chose a stout young tree and cut off all the upper branches, leaving

The Wild World of Backyard Birds

An antique martin house in the yard sold Donna deFries on her home near Silver Spring, Maryland. "From the time the martins arrive in April until they leave in summer, I'm never alone in the yard. They're always flying back and forth or sitting on the wires, talking to each other all the time," Donna says. Donna has even taught the birds to snatch duck feathers from her fingers (the birds use them in making nests). Donna points out one drawback to living with martins: "I never get to sleep in anymore," she says. "At the break of day, they start singing, loud."

entrance hole placed 1½ inches above the floor, will suit them just fine. A martin house may have four or more of these compartments, in which the birds will build their nests. Most martin fanciers mount their houses on poles about 15 to 20 feet high, although the birds will nest as low as 9 feet above the ground.

If martins are in your neighborhood, they may be quick to adopt the housing you offer. If martins aren't already resident nearby, you may have years of waiting before a bird shows up to check out your apartment building.

Other than putting out martin houses, there's not much you can do to attract them. They won't visit feeders, because they don't eat seeds. However, crushed eggshells are a hit with purple martins. Scatter the finely crushed shells on the ground below their

stubs from which they hung the gourds. If no tree was handy, they hung gourds from crossbars mounted atop a post. Gourds still work well as martin houses. To learn how to make a gourd birdhouse for martins, turn to Gourds on page 123.

Today you can buy simple aluminum martin houses for under $100, or you can go all out with an architectural wonder that will be the centerpiece of your backyard. The birds themselves aren't too fussy when it comes to housing. A compartment about 8 inches square, with a 2-inch-diameter

About the only time a purple martin stays still is when it visits a nest box—these birds spend most of their time on the wing.

house, or in another open area where they're easily accessible.

Protecting a Martin Colony

Martins face two major problems: finding food during bad weather and being driven from their homes by house sparrows and starlings.

Totally dependent on insects, martins nab their food almost entirely on the wing, snatching flies, mosquitoes, dragonflies, moths, and butterflies out of the air and darting down to pick off cucumber beetles, weevils, and other ground-dwelling insects. The birds even drink while flying, skimming the surface of ponds or streams with open beak. They do alight occasionally to eat ants or other morsels or to gather in convivial flocks on wires or other roosts to preen or rest near their home.

Two or three days of sustained cold weather—or even a prolonged rainy spell, which keeps flying insects away—can be a disaster for a martin colony. Starvation quickly sets in when insects are unavailable, and the birds themselves may suffer and fall ill from the cold. If the birds are already nesting, and if you can afford it, you can buy mealworms and offer them on an open tray feeder or on the grass. Other than that, all you can do is hope that the weather will change.

House sparrows and starlings compete with martins for nest space, and they can be very persistent. If you choose to get involved, you can try to chase the sparrows and starlings away from your martin house, and pull out any nesting materials they bring to the houses.

When martins are looking for a place to nest, they don't care whether it's a group of simple gourd houses (left) or a prefab mini-mansion: Just erect the martin houses in an open area so the birds can swoop in freely.

MEADOWLARKS

If your yard includes a meadow garden, you'll probably get to enjoy the sights and sounds of visiting meadowlarks. Larks are celebrated in song and poetry for their heavenly voices, but only the western meadowlark lives up to the reputation.

Getting to Know Them

Meadowlarks are glorious birds when you see them front-first. Their breasts are shining golden yellow, slashed with a broad black V across the chest. In contrast, their backs are streaky brown and rather dowdy. Meadowlarks are about 8½ inches long and shaped like starlings, with chunky bodies, stubby tails, and short legs. Males and females look alike.

Birds of open grasslands, meadowlarks fly low in short, fluttering spurts. Look for their white outer tail feathers and down-curved wings to identify them in flight. Or watch for them perched on a post, a tall weed, or a clump of grass where they survey their surroundings or sing. They approach their well-hidden nests on foot, which makes it tricky for predators (or curious people) to pinpoint the location. The clever female pulls still-growing grasses over the nest and weaves them together to hide the dark-splotched white to pinkish eggs.

Eastern and western. Eastern meadowlarks cover the eastern half of the country, into Texas and westward as far as Arizona and New Mexico. Western meadowlarks range from the eastern border of the Plains to the Pacific. The birds are almost impossible to tell apart by looks, but as soon as a bird opens its beak, the secret is out. The western meadowlark has a rich, melodious song as liquid as the wood thrush, but sung with a clear whistle instead of a breathy fluting. The eastern species has only a melancholy four-syllable whistle, *tee-you, tee-yair,* and a harsh rattle for an alarm note.

Attracting Meadowlarks

A meadow garden may attract a meadowlark, especially if your yard is a big one or if your property is near farm fields or pastureland. Meadowlarks prefer to live undisturbed, so if you have a meadow, keep part of it free of paths and traffic, both human and canine, so that the birds can feel safe.

Although it's almost impossible to entice meadowlarks to a feeding station near your house, they do appreciate a handout of seed scattered on the ground near their home. They like cracked corn, wheat, and oats and will also eat millet. In summer, they eat insects almost exclusively and are important natural controls for grasshoppers, weevils, cutworms, and crickets.

Eastern meadowlarks feel right at home in a meadow garden, where there are grasses to shelter nests and plenty of grasshoppers and other insects to feed on.

MIGRATION

The best time of year for backyard birdwatchers is spring, when birds return from their winter vacations to sing in the garden and eat at the feeder. One morning, it's the trill of a chipping sparrow that greets our ears; the next, it's the clear whistled song of the first oriole or the rich fluting notes of a wood thrush. As birds stop over in the bird-friendly yard for refueling or to return to nesting territories, the garden is suddenly full of color, song, and life.

Spring migration is the time to grab your binoculars and spend the morning outdoors. This extravaganza of birds hits its peak in April across most of the country. Birds arrive in the South sooner, because it's closer to wintering grounds in tropical America, and the North gets its birds a bit later.

Birds also migrate in the fall, but they're not as noticeable because they're quieter and the males have molted to their winter plumage. Tanagers and orioles wear olive green instead of red, orange, or yellow, and all the wood warblers look just about identical.

Migrating birds are strictly business: eating machines. Food is paramount, to replenish the calories burned during flight. During spring and fall migrations, birds that typically don't visit feeders may surprise you by stopping in for an easy-access bite. Backyard birdwatchers who live outside of the normal range of rose-breasted grosbeaks, for example, know that they can expect an all-too-brief visit from the birds when they're passing through.

Traveling Timetable

Fall migration begins in late summer, with shorebirds, hummingbirds, swifts, swallows, and martins. By October millions of wings are in the air, heading for warmer regions where bugs are plentiful and the air is balmy. In late fall the last of the migrants, mostly large hawks, begin their travels.

In spring the schedule works a little differently. Shorebirds are the first to come back, followed soon after by sparrows, meadowlarks, and kestrels, then hummingbirds, swallows, swifts, martins, and the bulk of the songbirds soon after.

Migration by Moonlight

One of the most unusual methods of birdwatching calls for a pair of binoculars and a full moon. Many songbirds, including thrushes and warblers, travel by cover of night. The darkness keeps them safe from the predators that travel by day—hungry hawks making their own journeys.

Spring is the best time for moonlight birding. Dress appropriately against the chill of night and settle yourself in a comfortable chair, preferably with arms so that you can prop up your binocular-holding elbows. Focus your binoculars at their farthest setting and keep your eye on the moon. If you're patient enough, you may spot migrants silhouetted against its light as they travel.

You can also follow night migrants by voice. Listen for their call notes—usually a sharp *chip!* or soft peeping calls—as they pass overhead. If you're an experienced birder, you may even recognize some of the voices. The calls keep the flock together as they travel.

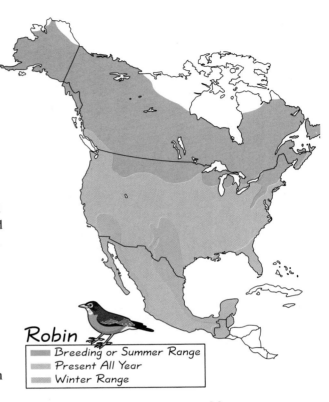

Migrants often appear on exactly the same date year after year. Jot your sightings on a wall calendar, and next year hang the calendar beside your current one. Then you'll know when to expect the first robin or hang out the hummingbird feeder. In my corner of southwestern Indiana, that red-letter day for the first ruby-throated hummingbird is also a red-letter day in another way: It's April 15, income tax day.

Why Do Birds Migrate?

Songbirds migrate southward to escape the cold and lack of food that winter brings to northward climes. Many of them depend mostly on insects, which die off or go dormant before the deep freeze settles in. Hummingbirds, which must have flower nectar to survive, are among the earliest migrants. Instead of risking an early fall frost blackening the blossoms they depend upon, they buzz southward at the end of summer, weeks before the killing frost.

Why don't birds stay in the hospitable south year-round? No one knows for sure. Scientists theorize that migratory habits were set eons ago, when weather patterns were much different than they are today. As proof of this theory, they point out that some birds still follow the routes of ancient watercourses that vanished millions of years ago.

Vacation Hotspots

Most of our American songbirds spend the winter from the southern United States to Central or South America. Some head for islands in the Caribbean or the West Indies. The distances these birds travel are stupendous: The rufous hummingbird, for instance, propels its tiny body across more than 3,500 miles every spring and every fall.

Not all birds are such fearless fliers. Goldfinches, for instance, may not migrate at

Robin
- Breeding or Summer Range
- Present All Year
- Winter Range

Robins are present year-round in most parts of the United States. You just may not see them in winter because they tend to hide in thickets in cold weather.

all, or may move only a couple of hundred miles south of their breeding range. House wrens spend their winter in the southern United States.

Central and South America are home to many of "our" birds in wintertime, and that's one big reason for the drop in songbird populations. As rain forests are decimated and habitat disappears in traditional wintering grounds, the birds suffer.

Other scientists point the finger right back at us: They say that most American migrants winter at the edges of the rain forest or on cut-

Wood Thrush

| | Breeding or Summer Range |
| | Winter Range |

The wood thrush travels far south in the winter, completely leaving its summer range in the United States.

over tracts of forest or disturbed land, and that our own destruction of habitat in North America is more to blame for declining songbird populations.

Flying without a Compass

Migration has been a mystery for hundreds of years, and it's fascinated birdwatchers from the beginning. Early theories pointed to the sun, the moon, and the stars, and indeed, experiments have shown that some birds have trouble finding their way when those guiding lights are hidden from view. Landmarks like mountains and rivers may also serve as naviga-

The Flyway Myth

The concept of "flyways," or main routes by which migrating birds travel, is a long-standing part of migration lore. But flyways aren't fact, say modern scientists. When Frederick Lincoln came up with the idea of four major flyways—the Atlantic, the Pacific, the Central (which follows the Rockies), and the Mississippi—in 1950, he studied only waterfowl migration. Songbirds travel differently.

Songbirds do migrate along flyways, but the reasons have more to do with convenience and geography than destiny. Migrants prefer to fly east or west of the Great Plains, for instance, because there's more food available in wooded parts of the country. As birds funnel up from Central and South America in spring, they naturally spread out across the country; the situation works in reverse for fall migration. Many biologists now believe that songbirds migrate into and out of North America on a broad front, scattered across the entire country. If you've ever traveled the United States at the height of migration—or compared the sightings in your backyard with friends in other places—you know that songbirds crop up everywhere.

tional aids, and research shows that birds do follow geographical features on their travels. Some research also shows that the earth's magnetic fields may help migrating birds find their way.

Millet

Crunchy millet seeds are a high-protein food that's just the right size for the beaks of sparrows, juncos, buntings, and other small seed-eating birds. These tiny, round, golden or rusty brown seeds are a major ingredient in commercial birdseed mixes. Foxtail millet (*Setaria italica*) is the best millet for birds. It produces large seedheads, packed tightly with thousands of small smooth kernels.

It's easy to start your own patch of millet for the birds. Just save some seeds out of a birdseed mix. In the spring when the soil warms, scatter the seeds on a sunny patch of loose soil. By late summer, you'll have a natural feeding place for small birds.

The common weeds known as foxtail grass (*S. viridis* and *S. glauca*) also produce seedheads that attract birds. If you can learn to think of these grasses as ornamental instead, birds will thank you come fall and winter when they feast on the nutritious seeds.

Start a millet patch in your yard to supply a natural source of nutritious seeds for small seed eaters like song sparrows to enjoy in fall and winter.

Mockingbirds

If bird song filters into your dreams on summer nights, look out your bedroom window and you're likely to spot a mockingbird serenading in the moonlight. This gray bird is a gifted mimic. He can't do Jimmy Cagney, but he can imitate cackling hens, barking dogs, human whistles, and dozens of his fellow feathered friends.

Getting to Know Them

Mockingbirds are long, streamlined gray birds up to 9 inches long, with white undersides. Their flashy white wing patches and outer tail feathers are unmistakable in flight. Males and females look alike. Mockingbirds formerly were southern birds, but they've expanded their range to include most of the United States.

If you have a mockingbird in residence, you're in for a show. Mockingbirds are fearless and fiercely territorial. They'll torment any passing cats or may even attack humans who venture too close to their nests. (They usually conceal their nests of brown-splashed blue or green eggs in dense evergreen shrubbery.)

One of the most intriguing mockingbird displays involves the bird's white wing patches, which flash like signal flags when the bird opens its wings. If you see a mockingbird on the ground flashing its wings, watch carefully. The bird may be scaring up insects from the grass or bluffing a snake. Witnesses have also reported seeing the bird flash its wings at a piece of string on the ground. No one knows for sure why mockingbirds do this, but I have a feeling the birds may be mistaking the string for a snake, and they're trying to chase off the slithery white "creature."

Attracting Mockingbirds

Mockingbirds are big fruit eaters, so elderberries, hollies, mulberries, raspberries and other brambles, and many other fruiting plants will bring them to your garden. In summer, they dine mainly on grasshoppers and beetles. To entice them to visit your tray feeders, put out raisins, grapes, dog food, doughnuts, and bread.

In winter, a mockingbird may decide to claim your feeding station. As soon as a hapless chickadee or sparrow settles in, the mocker will dash to the attack, chasing away the smaller birds time after time. One year a mockingbird claimed the wreath of bittersweet on my front door as its own personal bird feeder. For days it was woe to any other bird that ventured near. I finally gave up and moved the wreath to the back door, well away from my feeding station.

Growing blackberries and other berry-producing plants is a good way to lure mockingbirds to your garden. Mockingbirds are great entertainment—they have an incredible ability to imitate bird calls and other sounds.

MOLTING

Feathers don't last forever, so most songbirds shed them at least once a year. The changeover, called molting, takes place after nesting season is over. By the time of fall migration, birds are fully refeathered. Changing plumage takes a lot of energy, so this timing makes sense. The birds are done with the hectic chores of raising nestlings, and there's plentiful food to be transformed into new feathers.

Many songbirds molt a second time, in late winter or early spring, before breeding season begins. This is when male goldfinches, tanagers, and other brightly colored birds acquire the knock-your-eye-out colors that make them such a catch from a female bird's point of view.

The late-summer molt is a total makeover. The bird loses and replaces every one of its feathers, beginning at the head and working toward the tail. You'll never see a bald bird, though, because they shed their feathers gradually. When the crucial wing feathers begin to molt, they do so in matching pairs—one or two from one wing, and one or two from the other, so the bird's flight is still balanced.

The molt into breeding plumage seems more drastic because of the color change, but

typically many fewer feathers are lost—
usually only those of head, body, and tail are
shed and renewed.

It's the change in the length of day that
triggers the hormonal changes that induce
molting. That's why you can tell the season by
glancing at your goldfinches. If the males are
dressed in blotchy yellow and green instead of
their usual glossy black and butter yellow, either spring is nigh or Ol' Man Winter is right
around the corner.

**Goldfinches change color with the seasons. At
breeding time, male goldfinches wear a brilliant
yellow coat (see page 122). In fall, after nesting
is over, they molt to drab olive green (shown).**

Moss

Some gardeners try to get rid of moss in their
yards, but if you're a bird-loving gardener, you can
welcome moss to grow in your garden. Moss is at
the top of the list of nesting materials for many
birds. Various flycatchers use bits of moss to
make a soft lining for their nests. Some sparrows
also put moss in their nests, as do titmice, chickadees, thrushes, juncos, and other birds. Eastern
phoebes build the outer covering of their nests
entirely of mud and moss. The northern parula, a
type of warbler, goes whole hog, often making
its nest in a hanging clump of Spanish moss.

If there's no moss growing in your yard,
just buy an inexpensive bag of dried Spanish-
or long-fibered moss (often labeled as
sphagnum moss) at a craft store. Put the
moss into a bucket or a large bowl of water
and soak it overnight. Spread the damp moss
on your grass for the birds to collect. If you
have leftovers, dry it out and save it to put out
for next spring's nesting season.

Making moss grow. Moss can grow anywhere in your garden where you have a shady,
moist spot. You can even raise a mini-moss
garden in a shallow pot of soil if you sprinkle it
with water often to keep the soil moist.
Starting a moss garden is a snap—all you need
is some moss and a few cans of beer or a
carton or two of buttermilk.

Don't collect moss from the wild—ask a
gardening friend if you can collect some from
his or her garden. Once you have the moss,
fill an old blender jar with stale beer or buttermilk and add a heaping handful of living moss
with a little soil still attached. Blend the
mixture well to distribute the moss spores
throughout the liquid. Then pour a thin layer
of the mixture over stones or garden soil in a
damp, shady location. Mist the mixture often
enough to keep it moist until moss begins to
grow on its own. Depending on how hot the
daytime temperatures are, expect to mist your
moss from once to three times a day for about
a week.

Mud

A plain old mud puddle can be a hotspot for birds when nesting season rolls around. Robins plaster their nests with mud, and many other birds use mud to strengthen their nests.

Homemade Mud

Birds will travel a long way to find a reliable source of "perfect" mud, especially when rain has been scarce. To make an inviting mud puddle, dig a shallow depression in an open area of your yard, about 4 inches deep at the center and tapering to very shallow edges. Make your puddle about 2 feet in diameter; any smaller and it will dry out too quickly. Soak the area thoroughly with a garden hose, and then get ready to play in the dirt. Fill the depression with water. Using a claw-type hand cultivating tool, scrape the sides and bottom of the hole until you've made a thick slurry of mud—a bit stiffer than the consistency of the mud pies you made as a kid. Spray the mud puddle again with a gentle mist from the hose nozzle, and then make yourself scarce.

It may take a few days for birds to find the puddle, but once they know where it is, watch for phoebes, thrushes, robins, swallows, and other birds coming to gather beakfuls of the precious stuff. Wet down the puddle once every day or so, depending on the weather, so that it doesn't dry out.

Maintain your mud puddle through the summer, to supply mud for birds that nest more than once a year. You'll also attract butterflies to your yard. Cabbage whites and sulfurs, plus many of the big swallowtails, frequent mud puddles to sip mineral-rich liquid. Flycatchers and other insect-eating birds, attracted by the butterfly activity, may also visit to try for a butterfly meal.

Use a hand tool to work up some sloppy mud in a homemade mud puddle that's about 2 feet in diameter. The puddle will supply cliff swallows and other birds with the sticky stuff they need for plastering and strengthening their nests.

MULBERRIES

Birdwatching is supreme at a tree full of ripe mulberries. Pull up your chaise lounge and watch as dozens of birds fly in for the feast. Flashy-colored fruit eaters like orioles, tanagers, grosbeaks, thrashers, great crested flycatchers, and bluebirds settle in the tree for hours, stuffing themselves on the soft, blackberry-shaped fruits. Mulberries also attract flycatchers, vireos, warblers, thrushes, and waxwings. In fact just about every songbird in the area will search out a mulberry tree when the juicy berries ripen in early summer.

Managing Mulberries

Mulberry fruit can be messy, but the trees draw so many birds in such incredible quantities that it's worth a bit of creative planning to find a place for a mulberry tree in your yard. Pick a site away from walks and driveways, and surround the tree with a thick groundcover like pachysandra, so that fallen fruit "disappears." If your yard is small and doesn't have an appropriate isolated spot, try planting a white-fruited cultivar of white mulberry (*Morus alba*) such as 'Tehama' and 'Beautiful Day'. The white berries are just as big a draw for birds, and they won't leave telltale stains on cars or your line-dried laundry.

Mulberries are hardy trees untroubled by pests and diseases. They'll grow in any sunny spot in any type of soil, as long as it's well drained. Seedlings can sprout like weeds, so keep an eye out for volunteers "planted" by birds and pull them out while they're small.

Mulberry fruits are sweet and tasty for humans to eat, too. If you'd like to harvest some for yourself, spread a clean cloth on the ground below the tree, and shake branches to make the fruits drop. If you plan to make jam or pies, harvest the fruit when it's slightly underripe.

Mulberry Choices

Purple-fruited red mulberry (*M. rubra*) is the giant of the mulberry trees, reaching 60 feet tall. Black mulberry (*M. nigra*) is a small, spreading tree of about 20 feet tall that becomes wonderfully gnarled with age. Both thrive in Zones 5 to 8.

White mulberry can have white, pink, or purple fruits, so read plant tags and catalog descriptions carefully when buying. It grows to 60 feet tall and flourishes in Zones 4 to 8.

Mulberries have separate male and female trees, but some female trees will set fruit even if the flowers aren't pollinated. Ask when you buy whether the tree will need a pollinator.

Mulberries have no equal for attracting fruit-eating birds, including Baltimore orioles. White-fruited cultivars of white mulberry will attract just as many birds as purple-fruited mulberries and create less mess on paths and around your yard.

NATIVE PLANTS

Native plants are a natural choice for bird-friendly gardens. When you grow native plants, birds know when the fruits or seeds will ripen, which plants have stems or leaves that make good nesting material, and which plants offer thorny branches or other protection for roosting and nests.

You'll love the beauty of native plants, too, like the spiky blooms of red cardinal flower (*Lobelia cardinalis*), which are sure to draw hummingbirds. Winterberry holly (*Ilex verticillata*) is a wonderful shrub for a foundation planting, and its bright red berries will draw waxwings, thrushes, and bluebirds to your garden in the fall.

Choosing Native Plants

Native plants that are adapted to your region and your local conditions are easy to grow and need no coddling. Natives like white fringe tree (*Chionanthus virginicus*) can thrive in humid summers in the Southeast, while downy hawthorn (*Crataegus mollis*) can weather the frigid cold of Zone 3 winters in the upper Midwest.

Besides being suited to your particular climate, native plants have evolved their own defenses to most insects and diseases. Native American plants only have serious problems when new pests show up from foreign places: the gypsy moth plague, for example, or Dutch elm disease.

The secret to success in choosing native plants is to realize that there's a big difference between being native to North America and being native to your particular corner of the world. Plant a California native in Pennsylvania and it may thrive, if it's an adaptable plant. But it's no more "native" in your area than a plant from the Himalayas.

To choose appropriate native plants, go on some field trips in your area. Take a field guide along so you can identify plants that appeal to you. Jot down which trees grow with which shrubs, what wildflowers grow with which grasses. Imitate these wild plant groupings for a natural look and successful garden.

If your garden's sunny, look for plants that thrive in nearby meadows, fields, deserts, or other bright places. If your home place is shady, look for plants of the woods. If your land is wet, check boggy areas and other low places.

Your well-chosen native plants will thrive with little or no care from you beyond initial watering while they establish new roots. Before long, your garden will be as appealing—to both you and the birds—as your favorite natural retreats.

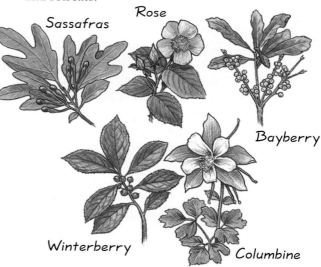

Birds feel at home in your yard when it includes some of the shrubs, trees, and flowers that are native to your region.

FAVORITE NATIVE PLANTS FOR BIRDS

There's an incredible variety of bird-attracting plants that are native to North America. The ones you choose to grow will depend on where you live and the soil, light, and moisture conditions in your yard. Since I've gardened in Indiana, Pennsylvania, and Oregon, this selection of my favorite native plants for birds includes some from both East and West.

PLANT NAMES	BIRDS ATTRACTED	PLANT DESCRIPTION	NATIVE HABITAT	CULTURE AND COMMENTS
Blue flax (*Linum perenne*)	Goldfinches, house finches, purple finches, sparrows, and buntings eat the oil-rich seeds.	Delicate, wiry-stemmed perennial to 18" tall. Short, needlelike leaves; true blue flowers open in morning and close by afternoon.	Prairies and woods' edges east of the Cascade Mountains of Washington, Oregon, and California	Grow in sun, in any well-drained soil. Short-lived perennial that reseeds. Zones 5 to 10
Buttonbush (*Cephalanthus occidentalis*)	Warblers, vireos, gnat-catchers, and orioles hunt insects among the flowers. Finches, sparrows, warblers, and buntings nest in the branches.	Deciduous shrub, 3' to 6' tall, but can grow 15' tall in the South. Pointed, oval leaves. Creamy powder puff–like flowers in summer are followed by balls of seeds that last through winter.	Marshes, ponds, and other wet sites from New Brunswick to Florida, and west to Minnesota and central California	Grow in moist or wet soil, in sun to shade. Combine with grasses or rushes to fill in for the twiggy-looking shrub in winter. Zones 5 to 10
Crested iris (*Iris cristata*)	Native sparrows, thrushes, towhees, and other woodland birds move freely through the protective foliage.	Perennial, 6" tall, with lavender blue flowers. Not a solid ground-cover; it has spaces between tufts for birds to navigate freely.	Woodlands from Maryland south to Georgia, and west to Missouri	Grow in partial to full shade, in well-drained soil. Spreads rapidly by roots. Great for a shade garden. Zones 3 to 8
Crossvine (*Bignonia capreolata*)	Hummingbirds drink nectar from the flowers. Catbirds may nest in the foliage.	High-climbing evergreen vine with long, pointed leaves that turn a rich bronze-maroon in winter. Clusters of trumpet-shaped flowers are dark orange outside, golden inside.	Woods and river bottoms, from Virginia to southern Illinois, and south to Florida and Louisiana	Grow in full sun to full shade, in moist, well-drained soil. Let it climb up a deciduous shade tree, where it can decorate the trunk and branches in winter. Zones 6 to 9
Desert marigold (*Baileya multiradiata*)	Native sparrows and finches eat the seeds. Plants make good cover for native sparrows and buntings in dry areas.	Tender perennial grown as annual that forms tufts of gray foliage topped by stems of golden yellow, double-flowered daisies. Heat- and drought-tolerant.	Mesas and dry plains in the Southwest and Mexico	Grow in full sun, in well-drained soil. Good naturalizer for dry gardens in the Southwest and Southern California.
Downy hawthorn (*Crataegus mollis*)	A wide variety of birds eat the fruits. Warblers and vireos eat insects when flowers are in bloom. Robins, tanagers, cuckoos, and other birds may nest in the branches.	Deciduous tree, 20' to 30' tall, with a rounded, wide-spreading shape. Grayish bark, leaves are woolly when young, turning yellow to bronze red in fall. Strong-smelling clusters of white flowers in spring are followed by red fruits in late summer.	Woods' edges and hedgerows, from southern Ontario south to Virginia, west to South Dakota and Kansas	Grow in almost any soil, in sun to part shade. Makes an attractive small tree for a partly shady backyard. Zones 3 to 6

(continued)

FAVORITE NATIVE PLANTS FOR BIRDS—CONTINUED

PLANT NAMES	BIRDS ATTRACTED	PLANT DESCRIPTION	NATIVE HABITAT	CULTURE AND COMMENTS
Drummond's phlox, annual phlox (*Phlox drummondii*)	Hummingbirds visit flowers for nectar; flowers draw butterflies, which bring flycatchers, phoebes, and other birds.	Annual that grows up to 18" tall, with clusters of red, pink, lavender, or white flowers in spring.	Open ground and grasslands in Texas	Grow in full sun, in well-drained soil. Self-sows. Plant in masses for best effect.
White fringe tree (*Chionanthus virginicus*)	Robins, thrushes, bluebirds, catbirds, orioles, thrashers, mockingbirds, waxwings, tanagers, vireos, titmice, downy woodpeckers, and grosbeaks eat the fruits.	Shrub or small tree up to 10'. Long, pointed oblong leaves with slight gloss, and fleecy clouds of flowers with long, dangling, ribbony petals in late spring to early summer. Hanging, small, dark blue, oval fruits are hidden by foliage.	Stream banks, edges of swamps, roadsides, or woods' edges from southern New Jersey to Florida, west to Texas	Grow in full sun to part shade, in moist, fertile soil. Also thrives in average garden soil. Easy to grow. Zones 3 to 9
Giant four-o'clock (*Mirabilis multiflora*)	Hummingbirds come to flowers for nectar; the plant provides cover for sparrows, buntings, and wrens in dry gardens.	Perennial to 2' tall, spreading to 3' or wider, with tubular bright magenta flowers from late spring through summer.	Mountains or open grasslands of southern Colorado to Mexico, west to California	Grow in full sun, in sandy or otherwise very well drained soil. Grow in a raised bed if you have heavy soil. Zones 5 to 9
Hay-scented fern (*Dennstaedtia punctiloba*)	Towhees, quail, bobwhites, native sparrows, juncos, and other ground-dwelling birds take shelter and nest in the fronds.	Delicate, spring green lacy fronds spread by roots to cover a large area.	Woods' edges and clearings in eastern North America	Grow in sun to light shade, in moist, acidic soil with plenty of organic matter. An excellent groundcover for an open woodland garden. Zones 4 to 8
Indian blanket flower (*Gaillardia pulchella*)	Finches, buntings, and sparrows enjoy the seeds.	Drought-tolerant annual with downy leaves and 2" to 3" daisylike flowers with rich orange-red middles and yellow-tipped petals.	Grasslands and open spaces from Florida to Colorado, south to Mexico	Grow in full sun, in any soil. Sow seeds in early spring for bloom in less than two months.
Possumhaw (*Ilex decidua*)	A wide variety of birds eat the fruits; native sparrows, towhees, and thrushes may nest in the plant.	Multistemmed shrub or small tree, 6' to 15' tall, with dense branches and beautiful glossy dark green, small, pointed oval leaves. Orange to red berries stud the branches, singly or in clusters of two or three, in early fall.	Moist woods, from Virginia to Florida and west to Texas	Grow in full sun to partial shade in moist, acidic soil high in organic matter. Excellent dense shrub for cover. Good for hedges. Zones 4 to 9
Virginia sweetspire (*Itea virginica*)	All perching birds seek shelter in the evergreen foliage. Warblers, vireos, and orioles seek insects attracted to the flowers.	Evergreen shrub, usually 5' but can reach 10'. In shade, has upright form; in sun, wider and more densely branched with pointed oval leaves. Spikes of tiny white, fragrant flowers open in summer, and mature to attractive seed spikes.	Streamsides and wet places from New Jersey to Florida, west to Missouri and Louisiana	Grow in sun to full shade in moist to average soil; also tolerates wet soil and drought. Plant near a path where you can enjoy the fragrant flowers. Zones 5 to 9

NECTAR

Nectar is the reward that bees and beneficial insects, as well as hummingbirds, seek when they buzz from one blossom to the next. As they collect nectar, the insects also collect pollen and pollinate the flowers. Tubular flowers, like those of honeysuckle and trumpet vines, and the long-spurred flowers of columbines are typically rich in nectar. To taste the clear "honey," pinch the end of a honeysuckle flower, draw out the pistil, and touch it to your tongue. You can also see shiny drops of natural nectar in the bottom of flat-topped flower clusters of plants like dill and Queen-Anne's-lace.

Making Nectar

Homemade nectar is nothing more than a solution of sugar and water, but when you offer it in a plastic feeder, it's irresistible to hummingbirds. Nectar feeders, particularly those with orange trim, also attract orioles.

To make nectar, bring 2 or 3 cups of water to a boil in a small saucepan. Stir in ½ cup of white, granulated sugar. Continue stirring until all the sugar is dissolved. Cool the solution and pour it into a clean hummingbird feeder. Don't use honey to make nectar—it's sweet, but it can cause bacterial and fungal diseases in hummingbirds.

If you're trying to attract hummingbirds for the first time, use the more concentrated version of the formula (½ cup sugar to 2 cups water). Make sure your feeders have red or orange trim or decorations—the color helps attract the birds. There's no need to add food coloring to the syrup, and it may not be good for the birds. Once you have regular customers at your feeders, reduce the sweetness of your homemade nectar, because that's better for the birds' long-term health.

In some areas of the country, woodpeckers, house finches, and other birds have learned to use nectar feeders. It seems to be a regional adaptation, and it will be interesting to see how quickly the behavior spreads.

If you feed birds homemade nectar, keep in mind that nectar breeds bacteria easily, especially in warm weather. Be sure to empty your feeders twice weekly. Clean each feeder by pouring boiling water through it, then refill with fresh solution. To learn more about feeding hummingbirds and other birds, see Bird Feeders and Hummingbirds.

The orange trim on some nectar feeders mimics the color of fruit in the orange groves of Florida, California, and Texas, where orioles peck the oranges to enjoy the sweet juice. For hummingbirds, choose a feeder with red trim.

NESTING

Nesting season is a busy time for birds, and a delightful time for backyard birdwatchers. There are all kinds of activities to observe, from parent birds collecting twigs, grasses, and other building materials to nest construction and the raising of the adorable, loudly cheeping babies. By learning the signs of the season, you can enjoy every step of the process and gain a better understanding of your birds and their behavior.

A bird nest is "home" only while parent birds are raising babies. Once the young leave the nest, the birds don't return. Many songbirds raise more than one brood a year, and usually they build a new home for each. A few birds may reuse an old nest more than once: Robins, for example, sometimes recycle their sturdy mud-lined cups for another batch of babies, or even use the old nest the following spring.

Some birds don't build what we think of as the typical bird nest. For example, many woodpeckers chisel an opening inside a dead tree and lay their eggs directly on whatever chips of wood accumulated from their work. Killdeers lay their eggs right on bare ground or gravel. Kingfishers and bank swallows use burrows in an earthen bank to raise their families.

Watch for the Signs

Birds usually nest from very early spring to late summer, which gives the youngsters time to mature before the demands of migration or cold weather. In mild-winter areas, a few birds such as mourning doves may raise families year-round.

Courtship and mating are your first clues that nest building is soon to come. Listen for birds singing regularly from the same perches: a sign that they've staked out their territory. Watch for the behaviors that mean love is in bloom (see Courtship on page 85 for descriptions). Then keep your eyes open for birds gathering nest materials.

When you see a bird with a twig or a piece of grass or string in its beak, see if you can figure out where it's taking the material. You probably won't be able to pinpoint the location the first time, because birds work fast and cautiously. But you'll get a general idea of the nest location. Watch that spot and you're bound to see the bird leave with an empty beak or return with another piece of material. The number of trips a nest-building bird makes going back and forth for materials is truly staggering. It takes more than 1,000 trips for a barn swallow to carry enough mud to make its home, and about the same amount of travel for a song sparrow to collect the grasses and feathers it uses during nest construction.

During nesting season, you may spot birds carrying grass, twigs, feathers, mud, or, in the case of indigo buntings, even bits of snakeskin in their beaks. Every bird has its own special tastes in nest furnishings.

Always stay at least 15 feet away from any nest under construction when you're doing your surveillance work. Birds will abandon a nest site in its early stages (before eggs are laid) if they realize they've been observed—to them, you're a potential predator, not an interested observer.

Where Birds Nest

Ever wonder why bird nests are so hard to find until winter, when trees and bushes are bare? It's because birds are careful to select a well-hidden place where the family can safely grow to fledgling stage. Shrubs with dense foliage are a favorite for many birds, thanks to the camouflaging greenery that shelters the nest from view. Prickly leaves or stems are an extra asset—only a determined cat or raccoon will brave a tangle of thorny blackberries or reach its tender paw into the well-armed interior of a shrub rose.

Birds that nest in trees often build their homes far out on the branches, near the very tip. Look at the tips of overhanging branches next time you travel a road that's lined with big trees and you're likely to spot an oriole nest suspended from the very tip of a high branch. The road beneath has nothing to do with the placement of the nest; it's just coincidence. But the placement of the nest at the branch tip is deliberate: any climbing predators or heavy-bodied owls and hawks will be reluctant to approach or land on a thin branch that dips alarmingly under their weight and makes them lose their balance.

It's the female bird that usually decides where home should be. Males may offer selected sites, or even build nests to show the female, but the final decision is usually a spot she selects alone. It's also usually the female who does most of the actual building, though the male may help by lugging some or all of the nest materials home. In some species, nest building is a shared proposition—woodpeckers, some swallows, and waxwings share the duties equally.

Nest making is a complicated job—all those sticks and grasses to weave together, let alone the plastering!—but when songbirds turn their singleminded attention to their work, it's completed relatively quickly. Nest building usually takes less than a week and often just a few days. Even woodpeckers manage to hollow out nesting holes in less than a week.

Nest Construction

It's fascinating to examine the wondrous nests that birds make out of nothing more than a handful of dead sticks and a few tufts of grass. Keep in mind that "possessing" bird nests is against federal law, so don't remove nests from

Birds may nest high or low in your yard, so step carefully during nesting time! Birds like sparrows may have set up house-keeping in a clump of mint or other dense foliage among your herbs or perennials.

The Best Nest

Orioles win the prize for superior nest building among American songbirds. Their strong, deep, hanging cradles woven of plant fibers are true wonders of the natural world. They're so well made that despite the weight of heavy nestlings inside, they never fall apart.

Orioles build their nests fairly high in trees, so it's not always easy to spot them at work. If there are orioles in your neighborhood during nesting season, try using string to lure the birds. Cut some white string into short lengths and drape it on shrubs in your yard. Watch for the orioles to take the string, and then follow their flight. You may see them head to their nest-in-progress, and then you can use binoculars to study their amazing nest-building skills for yourself.

If barn swallows live in your area, you may find them raising a family in an outbuilding or barn. They use mud to fasten their nests under eaves; it's easy to get a close-up view of the parents feeding the babies.

shrubs or birdhouses to examine them. You can see plenty with just a close-up look. It's important to leave nests in place because button-eyed deer mice and other small, furry animals often use old bird nests for shelter from wintry cold and snow—or as hiding places for a store of berries and seeds. A few birds use their nests for more than one season, too, or build new ones on the old foundation.

Size and shape. The size of a nest depends on the size of the bird that builds it. Hummingbird nests are miniature wonders—only an inch across and an inch deep. Believe it or not, these toy-teacup–size nests are big enough to contain the pea-size eggs and the belly of the

parent bird who nestles herself down into the snug little cup with her beak and tail jutting over the rim. At the other extreme are osprey and eagle nests, which are immense complexes that the birds return to year after year, adding new material each year. Over time, the nests can reach weights of a ton or more, and can cause the tree or utility pole on which they're built to come crashing to the ground.

Larger songbirds like thrushes, tanagers, and other robin-size birds make nests that measure about 6 to 8 inches across; smaller sparrow-size birds build smaller homes, about 4 inches across. Some birds make a nest with very wide walls, so that the nest overall is twice as big as the custom-size interior which fits the bird's body snugly (the tight fit helps keep those eggs warm when Mom is on the nest). **Straw or sticks.** Birds are smart when it comes to choosing nest-building materials—they select materials that help camouflage their precious home. If you look at a collection of bird nests in a museum, you'll probably find it easy to guess what kind of habitat the nest comes from, even without checking the labels.

◆ Grassy cuplike nests are for ground-dwelling birds, such as grasshopper sparrows, that live in fields and nest on or very near the ground.
◆ Lichen-covered nests, like hummingbird nests, are plastered on a lichen-covered branch, where they're easily mistaken for a natural bump or knot in the wood.
◆ Twiggy platform nests, like those of mourning doves, blend in with the network of slim branches of the tree or shrub in which they're placed.

◆ Nests with dead leaves worked in could belong to birds that dwell on the forest floor, like ovenbirds, or from tree-nesting birds like wood thrushes.
◆ Nests with one flat side are fastened to walls, usually using mud as a glue. Chimney swift nests are an exception. They attach their bare-bones stick nests to the inside walls of chimneys using their gluelike spit.

Helping Out

Most birds don't need help with nest building or raising their families, except for cavity-nesting birds like bluebirds, finches, and woodpeckers. You can help these birds find safe spots to nest by putting up birdhouses around your yard. To learn more about them, turn to Birdhouses on page 36.

Once birds are nesting in your yard, you may have the experience of finding baby birds on the ground. To learn what to do if this happens, turn to First Aid for Birds on page 110.

NIGER

Want a yard full of goldfinches? Tempt them with niger. Tiny, black niger seed is unsurpassed at attracting finches of all kinds. High in fat and protein, niger seed looks like very small grains of wild rice, and it has become an instant classic for backyard bird feeding. There are even special feeders with very small openings, like the one shown on page 222, that allow birds to feed on the seed without spilling it.

Niger has another name—thistle seed—that makes some birdwatchers hesitate to offer it. They're afraid they'll end up with a yard full of prickly plants sprouting from the spilled seeds. But never fear—niger is not a

thistle at all. It's the seed of niger plant (*Guizotia abyssinica*), an annual flower that's native to Ethiopia. Also, niger seed sold as birdseed is heated to prevent it from germinating because the plants can become pests in areas that have sunny, dry conditions. In California farming country where niger is raised commercially, yellow niger flowers are a common roadside sight.

Niger seeds are like candy to finches, but they're also nibbled by towhees, pine siskins, juncos, mourning doves, and many sparrows. Except for siskins, these birds prefer to feed on or near the ground. To give them a treat, scatter niger in small amounts directly on bare soil or a flat rock, or offer it in a low, open tray feeder.

NUTHATCHES

Nuthatches are endearing birds that have the unusual habit of traveling head-first down tree trunks. This queer posture allows them to search bark crevices for insects and insect eggs overlooked by other birds who move along the trees head-up.

Unusually tame, nuthatches are unsuspicious around people. They'll fly to a tree trunk or feeder even if you're standing just a few feet away. In fact, you can even train them to feed from your hand.

Getting to Know Them

Nuthatches are dapper little birds, dressed in a costume of blue-gray above, white beneath. Head markings vary depending on the species, but all nuthatches look as neat as if they're dressed for a formal ball. Males and females look alike. Nuthatches are talkative, keeping in touch with others of their kind by calling frequently as they forage through the trees. In winter, they keep company with chickadees, titmice, brown creepers, and downy woodpeckers.

The word *nuthatch* is from the Middle English for "nut hacker." Watch a nuthatch eat and you'll see how this bird got its name. It flies off with a seed or nut, wedges it into a crevice of bark or a cranny of the bird feeder, and whacks it with its beak to split and shell the nut meat.

Red-breasted nuthatches have the mysterious habit of smearing pine pitch around the entrance to their nest cavity. Often they renew the pitch daily, but what the purpose of the sticky paint job is, no one knows for sure. Inside the cavity, nuthatches add a layer of strips and chips of bark, topped off by a cozy lining of moss, feathers, rabbit fur, or other soft material. The white eggs are dotted with brown and purple. Nuthatches believe in big families: White-breasted and pygmy nuthatches usually raise eight babies, whereas red-breasted and brown-headed nuthatches care for five or six.

Attracting Nuthatches

Nuthatches help keep trees healthy by eating tons of beetles, caterpillars, wood borers, and other insects. These birds also feed on nuts and seeds.

To keep nuthatches happy, plant conifers and nut trees in your yard. At the feeder, the birds love suet, sunflower seeds, and nut meats. White-breasted nuthatches also enjoy corn.

Nuthatch Checklist

There are almost two dozen species of nuthatches in the world, but only a few are found in North America.

White-breasted nuthatch. The white-breasted nuthatch, which ranges across nearly

JUST FOR NUTHATCHES

■ Nuthatches nest in cavities and come readily to a nest box. Mount the box about 15 feet above the ground.

■ Want to attract white-breasted nuthatches? They are very fond of beechnuts, acorns, hickories, and other nuts.

■ Red-breasted nuthatches eagerly devour seeds of pines, spruces, firs, hemlocks, and other conifers.

■ It doesn't take much coaxing to hand-tame a nuthatch—just try offering some shelled nuts on your open hand.

Try luring a red-breasted nuthatch to your hand with shelled walnuts (black walnuts are particularly appealing). If you stand quietly for a few minutes, the bird may approach to eat out of your palm.

all of the country except for a strip down the Plains to Mexico, is the largest of the tribe. It measures 5 inches from the tip of the pointed beak to the end of its stubby tail. Common in deciduous woods, the birds are usually year-round residents. The male and female are a de-voted couple, staying together summer and winter until death. You'll often hear their nasal call note, a distinctive *yank, yank, yank,* as you wander through the woods at any time of year.

Red-breasted nuthatch. The white belly of the adorable red-breasted nuthatch is flushed with a rusty tint. These birds have a bold white stripe above the eye, and a black stripe through the eye, making them easy to identify. Red-breasted nuthatches breed in the far North and in the West, but some years they spread southward across the country in irreg-ular migrations, presumably when food is scarce in winter.

Their voices are unmistakably nuthatchy, with a strong nasal quality that some people liken to short blasts on a tin trumpet. (If you're not old enough to remember what tin trum-pets sound like, imagine the bird saying *kng, kng, kng* in a high-pitched, pinched-nose sound effect.) These tiny birds measure barely 3½ inches in length.

Other nuthatches. The brown-headed nuthatch of the South and the Atlantic coast area indeed has a brown cap on its head and black eye stripe. Otherwise, it resembles other nuthatches. Its soft call is unlike that of other nuthatches.

The pygmy nuthatch lives in the western mountains; it looks like the brown-headed nuthatch but has a gray head.

White-breasted nuthatches put some of their food aside for later, carrying off pea-size nuggets of suet or seeds to hide in cracks of bark or other secret places.

NUTS AND NUT TREES

Nuts are extra rich in fat content as well as in protein—exactly the kind of snack hungry birds crave. Jays, titmice, chickadees, woodpeckers, and many other birds are crazy about nuts. They peck at them on the spot or carry them off to store for later use. Small birds like juncos and sparrows scavenge below nut trees looking for bits of fallen nut meats.

Growing Nuts

Most nut trees grow 50 to 100 feet tall, offering shade and beauty along with a big crop of appealing food. Nut trees are easy to grow and are mostly trouble-free—they need no pruning, spraying, or other fussing to produce a plentiful harvest. (For tips on planting nut trees, consult Trees on page 246.)

Plant nuts that you enjoy eating, too—once the tree starts to bear, there will be plenty for both you and the birds. Named cultivars of nut trees, such as 'Ashworth', 'Colby', and 'Hansen' English walnut (*Juglans regia*), usually have the best flavor.

Keep in mind that it takes from three to as long as seven years before the nut trees you plant begin bearing a crop. Most nuts need cross-pollination, too, so you'll need to plant two trees of each type to get a harvest.

Nut Choices

Pecans (*Carya illinoinensis*) have thin shells that are easy for birds to crack. Pecans are common in gardens of the upper South, growing in Zones 6 to 9.

Hickories (*Carya* spp.) grow from Zones 3 to 8, their foliage turns a rich gold in the fall, and their nuts are a winter staple of woodpeckers. Bushy filberts or hazelnuts (*Corylus* spp.) have delicious, easy-to-crack nuts. They grow in Zones 2 to 8 and make an excellent hedge when planted in rows. In the mild climates of Zones 7 to 9, almond trees (*Prunus amygdala*) offer beautiful flowers in spring and are ideal for small yards, reaching only 30 feet in height.

If you have a large yard, you may want to plant a black walnut tree (*Juglans nigra*). Black walnuts are very easy to grow in Zones 5 to 9, and their nut meats are delicious. But the tree's roots give off a toxic substance that stunts and even kills many ornamental plants. Birds can't break the hard shells, but you can store the nuts and break them open to serve at feeders, as shown below.

Peanuts are also popular with birds, but they come from annual plants, not from trees. For more information on feeding peanuts to backyard birds, see Peanuts and Peanut Butter on page 191.

The hard shells of black walnuts are impossible for birds to crack. Collect the nuts when they fall and store them in metal cans until winter. Then split the shells open with a hammer and pile the broken nuts in the feeder so birds can pick out the treats.

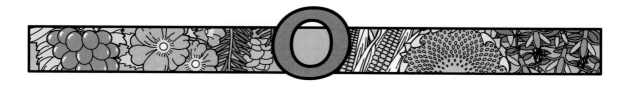

OAKS

Stately oak trees produce pounds of acorns, one of the best winter bird foods. Dense oak foliage can host a cornucopia of caterpillars and other insects, most of which will be invisible to you, but not to hungry birds. Many kinds of birds eagerly search oak leaves and bark for a meal of insects. During the spring migration of wood warblers, the branches of oak trees are the best places to look for these tiny, fast-moving birds.

Oaks in the Landscape

Stout-limbed imposing oaks grow well in most parts of the country. Small oak trees will reach up to 45 feet tall, with branches spreading up to 35 feet wide. Large oaks may tower 100 feet tall with a canopy 80 feet wide. They make fine shade trees and are usually trouble-free. Oak trees require full sun, and while they tolerate a variety of soil conditions, they'll thrive if you plant them in moist, humus-rich, well-drained soil.

If you live in the North, you're accustomed to seeing the canopies of oaks turn red or brown in the fall before dropping their leaves. Most northern species of oaks are hardy from Zone 6 to as far south as Zone 8, with hardier species like northern red oak (*Quercus rubra*) surviving Zone 4 winters. In the South and in mild-winter western states, many oak species are evergreen—most of these live oaks, as they are commonly called, are hardy in Zones 7 to 10.

Best Oaks for Birds

When choosing oaks for your yard, start with those that are native to your region, because they're naturally adapted to your climate and soil. In the Northeast, try northern red oak, scarlet oak (*Q. coccinea*), or white oak (*Q. alba*). If you live in the Plains or prairie states, good choices include bur oak (*Q. macrocarpa*) and post oak (*Q. stellata*). In the South, Canyon live oak (*Q. chrysolepsis*) and southern live oak (*Q. virginiana*) are classic landscape features.

Swamp white oak (*Q. bicolor*), Gambel oak (*Q. gambelii*), and bur oak will thrive in gardens in the western mountains and high deserts. On the northern Pacific Coast, start with California live oak (*Q. agrifolia*), blue oak (*Q. douglasii*), Oregon white oak (*Q. garryana*), or California black oak (*Q. kelloggii*). California live oak, blue

Northern red oak

California live oak

In northern areas, oaks drop their leaves or turn brown in fall, but in the milder South and far West, many oaks are evergreen. No matter where you live, oaks will draw birds and wildlife to feast on acorns.

oak, and Emory oak (*Q. emoryi*) are good choices for Southern California and low desert areas.

If all these choices are overwhelming, try leaving your oak choices to nature. Simply wait for birds and squirrels to plant your oak trees for you. If you allow part of your backyard to grow naturally, without disturbing the soil between plants, you're bound to see some oak seedlings crop up here and there from acorns that were buried and forgotten by jays and squirrels. Trees that sprout in your garden are likely to flourish and grow as strong and healthy as any store-bought specimen you would plant.

You can also try collecting a few acorns when you walk in a local wooded area. Plant the acorns about an inch deep, or bury them under moist leaf mold. In spring you should see strong young shoots emerge.

ORIOLES

Orioles aren't shy of people; they frequently take up residence in an inviting backyard with shade trees and other food sources. But because orioles tend to stay in the treetops, it's easy to miss seeing the orioles in your yard. Listen for their loud voices to help pinpoint their whereabouts, and then watch for a glimpse of the male's magnificent colorful feathers.

Getting to Know Them

Males are the showboats among orioles, decked out in brilliant orange or bright yellow with gleaming black hoods, wings, and tails. Females are dressed in greenish garb, washed with a hint of yellow or pale orange. Orioles have a harsh, chattering alarm call or scolding call, plus a beautiful whistled song that's often interspersed with the rattle.

Orioles are related to blackbirds, but instead of staying close to the ground like their dark-colored kin, they spend their lives in trees. Their nests are amazing creations, finely knitted of plant fibers and other soft materials and suspended from a tree branch where they sway gently in the breeze. Orioles usually build their nests near the tip of a branch, where the eggs and baby birds are safe from climbing predators. Orioles lay whitish or pastel eggs that are scribbled, splotched, or flecked with brown and purple.

Insects are the mainstay of an oriole's menu. Caterpillars, especially the delectable spiny or hairy types, are tops on the list. Weevils, beetles, moths, aphids, and a wide range of other critters add diversity to the diet. Orioles have quite a sweet tooth—they love to eat

JUST FOR ORIOLES

■ To make your yard more tempting to orioles, plant blackberries, cherries, elderberries, mulberries, strawberries, and figs.

■ Want a surefire oriole attractant? An arbor of grapes will draw these fruit-loving birds like a magnet.

■ Flowering agaves, aloes, cacti, rose-of-Sharon, and hibiscus have nectar-rich flowers to satisfy an oriole's sweet tooth, along with small insects for the birds to snack on.

■ Drape shrubs and lawn with short lengths of white string in spring for nesting orioles. Watch where the birds carry the string, and you'll find the nest.

■ Orioles enjoy nibbling on bread or other baked goods at feeders.

fruit and drink nectar from tubular flowers like honeysuckle or from nectar feeders.

Attracting Orioles

One large shade tree may be all you need to make your yard inviting to orioles. To increase the chance of attracting these beautiful birds, add a variety of flowers and fruiting shrubs to your yard.

At the feeder, offer orange halves and homemade nectar in a plastic feeder with perches, like the one shown on page 175. Orioles may also patronize suet feeders or eat ground suet from a tray feeder.

Oriole Checklist

Orioles have such showy coloring that they look like they belong in the rain forest. These exotic birds do winter in Central and South America, but during the breeding season, they add glamour to backyards across the country.

Baltimore oriole. The beautiful orange-and-black Baltimore oriole resides in the eastern half of the United States. It has a pretty, clear whistled song and a harsh chattering call. At one time, scientists classified both the Baltimore oriole and the Bullock's oriole as one species called the northern oriole. Since then, they've reclassified the birds as two separate species, but your field guide to birds may list them under "northern oriole."

Bullock's oriole. West of the Great Plains, Bullock's oriole takes over where the Baltimore leaves off. Bullock's orioles have large white wing patches and a black cap instead of the Baltimore's hood. Its song sounds like the Baltimore's. Like hummingbirds, Bullock's orioles collect nectar from flowers with tubular blossoms, such as salvias; they also eat tiny insects that these flowers attract.

Hooded oriole. In the Southwest, the hooded oriole reigns. This orange bird lacks a full

hood but has an extended black patch from its chin to its breast. The male's song is a mix of rough chattering calls and sweet throaty whistles. Like other orioles, hooded orioles are common in backyards.

Scott's oriole. Scott's oriole is another southwestern bird, but he's yellow-and-black instead of orange. Take a close look at this guy's tail: Instead of being all black like other orioles, Scott's has patches of yellow in his outer tail feathers that flash when he opens his tail.

Orchard oriole. The striking russet-and-black orchard oriole occurs east of the Great Plains, but isn't as common as the Baltimore. This bird's whistle is similar to that of other orioles, but his melody is choppier, with pauses between.

The brightly colored male Baltimore oriole (right) is much snazzier than the female. These birds build an ingenious nest that closes like a drawstring purse when it's occupied by a parent bird or growing youngsters.

ORNAMENTAL GRASSES

Birds would have a hard time getting along without grasses. Grass plants shelter nests, grass seeds sustain birds through fall and winter, and dry grass leaves are the perfect material for nest construction. Grasses also offer birds plenty of insect delicacies, from grasshoppers and crickets to aphids.

Gardening with Grasses

Grasses are simple to grow. Most of them need full sun, although a few, like purple-top (*Tridens flavus*) and northern sea oats (*Chasmanthium latifolium*), flourish in shade. Most grow well in average, well-drained soil, and usually need no fertilizer or watering. Many have long-lasting foliage that bleaches to a creamy white in fall and stays attractive throughout the winter. The only maintenance most

ornamental grasses require is a yearly "haircut" with pruners or a string trimmer in early spring to cut off dead foliage.

When you plant ornamental grasses in your yard, think big. For example, cover a slope with a mix of grasses of different sizes to give birds plenty of elbowroom for collecting nesting materials and seeds. Try adding short grasses under shade trees to give cover to ground-feeding birds.

Grasses and shrubs make great combinations for beauty and for birds. In the fall the soft tans and golds of grasses are stunning against the flaming red leaves of bushy sumacs. And adding ornamental grasses to flowerbeds will give birds yet another place to feed and nest. Even after your perennials die back in winter, the seedheads of the dried grasses will continue to attract birds.

Indian grass

Little bluestem

Burning bush

Bearberry

Sparrows, juncos, and other seed eaters will flock to ornamental grasses to eat the plentiful seeds. To add more cover and food choices, try combining grasses with shrubs and groundcovers.

BEST GRASSES FOR BIRDS

Despite their delicate appearance, ornamental grasses are hardy plants that adapt to most parts of the country. No matter what size garden you have, there's a grass that's right for your garden and your bird friends. The grasses described below range in size from petite 1'-tall purple-top to towering 10' cattails.

PLANT NAMES	BIRDS ATTRACTED	PLANT DESCRIPTION	CULTURE
Big bluestem (*Andropogon gerardii*)	Sparrows, meadowlarks, blackbirds, and other birds eat seeds. Sparrows and other ground-nesting birds build nests in the clumps.	Clumps grow 4' to 7' tall, with narrow foliage that emerges silvery blue in spring and turns bronze in winter. Branched seedheads look like a turkey's foot.	Plant in full sun in well-drained soil. Tolerates heat, humidity, and drought. Zones 4 to 10
Common cattail (*Typha latifolia*)	Foliage shelters nests of red-winged and other blackbirds. Wrens, vireos, and chickadees pick fluff of ripened cattails to line their nests.	Coarse, strappy blades grow 6' to 10' tall, with equally tall stems topped by cigar-shaped, brown seedheads. Foliage turns yellow-brown in fall and winter.	Plant at water's edge or in water up to 12" deep, in full sun or part shade. Spreads rapidly. Zones 3 to 10
Deer tongue grass (*Panicum clandestinum*)	Sparrows, finches, buntings, and other small birds enjoy seeds.	Forms low-growing clumps of bamboolike foliage with delicate sprays of seedheads at tips of arching stems. Foliage turns yellow in fall.	Plant in moist, humusy soil in shade. Zones 4 to 9
Indian grass (*Sorghastrum nutans*)	Small birds forage below plants when ripe seeds drop.	2'- to 3'-tall clumps of grass with feathery wands of flowers rising 2' to 3' above strappy leaves. Foliage turns yellow to orange in fall.	Plant in sun to part shade. Tolerates drought, clay soil, wet soil, or dry soil. Zones 4 to 9
Indian rice grass (*Orysopsis hymenoides*)	Many kinds of birds eagerly eat seeds.	1' to 2' tufts of narrow, delicate-looking foliage and many tall flower stems topped with delicate seedheads. Foliage is tan in summer, green in winter.	Plant in full sun in well-drained soil. Grows best in the arid West. Zones 8 to 10
Little bluestem (*Schizachyrium scoparium*)	Birds take shelter and nest against clumps. Sparrows, juncos, and other small birds eat seeds.	Upright clumps grow 2' to 5' tall. Flower-topped stems emerge in summer, followed by fluffy plumes of seedheads. Foliage turns orange in fall and winter.	Plant in full sun; won't tolerate wet soils. Zones 3 to 10
Purple-top (*Tridens flavus*)	Finches, sparrows, buntings, and other birds eat seeds. Foliage and old stems are popular nest material.	Low clumps of foliage grow to 1' or taller, with taller stems of drooping, red-purple flowers. Foliage turns tan in winter.	Plant in full sun to shade. Self-sows. Zones 5 to 9
Switch grass (*Panicum virgatum*)	Native sparrows, juncos, and other birds eat seeds. Foliage is used for nest building.	Clumps of spiky foliage produce clouds of delicate flowers and seedheads that catch the light. Leaves turn ruddy red or golden in fall, beige in winter.	Plant in full sun. Grows well in most soils. Self-sows. Zones 5 to 9

OWLS

Because owls go where the food is, you never know exactly who-o-o-o may show up in your backyard. Most owls are forest birds and stay near the sheltered stretches of conifers or deciduous trees they prefer. But if you have a woods nearby, you may get a visit, especially in winter, when owls range farther afield to find mice and other small mammals to eat. Also keep in mind that the small birds in your backyard can also be menu items for owls.

In the daytime, owls usually roost in thick woods or stands of pines or other conifers. Under cover of darkness, though, they may sweep through your yard or perch in your trees, watching for any small creatures that are out and about. Keep an eye out for the trademark calling card of owls: an elongated grayish lump, known as a pellet, consisting of the regurgitated undigestible fur, feathers, and bones of a previous meal.

Occasional dropped feathers also indicate an owl was in the neighborhood. If you find a large, soft feather—usually striped and brown and white—hold it so its surface catches the light. If it looks softly furred instead of shiny and sleek, you can bet it's an owl feather.

Form Follows Function

We can only guess at what goes on behind an owl's golden eyes, but it's probably a single-minded concentration on where the next meal is coming from. Owls need good vision to find prey in the dark, and their unusually large eyes are a great aid. They can see in the daytime, but the bright light is annoying to their unprotected eyes, so they draw a special third eyelid over their eyes like an opaque window shade to keep out the sun.

Not Exactly Night Owls

Not all owls limit their flights to the nighttime. Although some, like barn owls, are sound daytime sleepers, other owls work the daylight hours instead of the night shift. Here are owls to look for before the sun goes down.

- The small burrowing owls that inhabit Florida airports and stretches of midwestern prairie are active during broad daylight. Look for them bobbing up and down among the residents of prairie dog towns, or spot them perched on fence posts or hovering over the ground.

- If you live near a wooded area in the eastern half of the country, listen for the hooting of a barred owl in the late afternoon or on a gray, overcast day. These common owls are often active at dawn or dusk, and also on cloudy days.

- Short-eared owls come out to hunt in the afternoon, even on sunny days. Look for them scouting for rodents over fields and meadow gardens, with their wings held in a V (in flight, you may mistake them for a northern harrier, or marsh hawk).

- The snowy owl, a huge and regal white bird, also hunts by day. In winter, it may show up anywhere in the northern half of the country. This owl usually perches near the ground in open areas, but sometimes sits on utility poles even in the middle of cities.

But owls can't hunt by sight alone. They also depend on their keen ears, which are holes in the sides of their heads. Look at an owl and you won't see the ear. It's usually covered by feathers, which the bird can shift and form into a funnel that channels even the slightest sound. The round shape of an owl's face also improves its hearing. This "facial disk" works like a satellite dish to capture and focus any stray bits of sound in the bird's surroundings.

Noiseless wings are another adaptation that helps owls hunt successfully after dark. Great eyesight and terrific hearing would be worthless if owls made a racket going after their prey. That's why the front edge of an owl's first long wing feathers are softly serrated. The saw-toothed edge lets air pass over the wing without even a whisper.

Owls in the Backyard

Owls look like the wise old men of the forest. Their eyes are set on the front of their wide face instead of the sides of the head, and they stare head-on with the intensity of a pair of headlight beams. Their slow, deliberate movements, so different from the quick flutterings of songbirds, and their attitude of alert concentration make them unique among birds.

Barred owl. Common year-round in the eastern half of the country and across southern Canada, this big bird measures about 1½ feet tall and has a wingspan approaching 4 feet. As with all owls, the sexes look alike; barred owls have a dark, dull brown back, spotted and striped with white, and a pale belly, streaked with brown. It's one of only two owls with dark eyes (the other is the barn owl).

The barred owl nests in cavities in trees or in abandoned crow or hawk nests; it may also use an old squirrel nest. Barred owls have a varied diet featuring mostly mice but also including chip-munks and squirrels, foxes, rabbits, opossums, and birds, from cardinals to crows. Salamanders, frogs, and grasshoppers round out the list.

Screech owl. This common and familiar small owl ranges across most of the country year-round. The screech owl is only 8 inches tall, with wings that spread to about 2 feet. Screech owls come in various colors: chestnut ("red") or gray in the eastern two-thirds of their range, and brown in the West. The owl's big, chunky head is decorated by two upright tufts referred to as "ears" (although they're not ears at all; the real ear openings are concealed on the sides of the owl's head). The screech owl's unearthly quavering whinny has a descending tone and is easy to imitate, which usually causes the owl to

If you're out in your garden at dusk or on an overcast day, listen for the call of the barred owl: *Who cooks for you? Who cooks for you all?* **Try mimicking its call and there's a good chance you'll see the owl as it flies in for a closer look.**

move closer and investigate. Mice, shrews, and insects are tops with this owl, which also snaps up chipmunks, flying squirrels, frogs, snakes, lizards, cecropia moths, starlings, sparrows, and many other birds. Put up a flicker-size nest box in your yard and you may attract a house-hunting screech owl, which nests in cavities—often those abandoned by woodpeckers.

Great horned owl. This big owl is common all across the country. It stands almost 2 feet tall and has a wingspan approaching 5 feet. Its streaky, finely striped feathers are brown on the back, paler on the belly, with a collar of darker streaks. The great horned owl's call is classic: long drawn-out, low-pitched hoots. Copy this call and you may draw the bird in, especially during nesting season, which begins in winter.

Great horned owls build enormous stick nests in trees. The nests are used year after year and are visible from far away. Great horned owls nest everywhere from wilderness to suburbs and downtown.

Their favorite food item is skunk, and their feathers often carry a skunk scent. They also eat mice, rats, rabbits, foxes, groundhogs, and big snakes, as well as cats, waterfowl, other owls, crows, and other birds. If you hear crows making a commotion, check it out: They often pester roosting great horned owls during daylight hours, when the owl usually perches in a dense conifer.

Long-eared owl and short-eared owls. Both of these owls are a little more than a foot tall, with a wingspan slightly wider than 3 feet. They have streaky, finely striped feathers and paler plumage on the underparts. The long-eared owl is a darker, duller brown on its back, while the short-eared wears a warmer brown color. The long-eared owl has distinctive tufts of feathers on its head. But the short-eared owl has no noticeable "ears." Both have light-colored underwings with dark patches near the bend of the wing, and both hunt at dusk, dawn, or on bright moonlit nights. The short-eared owl sometimes flies in the afternoon.

Voice and habitat separate these two similar owls. Long-eared owls softly hoot *quoo-quoo-quoo.* Short-eareds sound like a yappy little dog: *yak! yak! yak!* or sometimes a rapid-fire *toot-toot-toot-toot-toot* repeated up to 20 times. Both owls are found across the country in winter, and nest in the northern states. But the short-eared is a "ground owl" that spends a lot of time sitting on the ground. It even nests on the ground. The long-eared owl is a secretive woodland bird that perches in trees. It adopts old crow or hawk nests. Both eat mice, along with shrews, bats, squirrels, rabbits, and the occasional songbird, beetle, or snake. Short-eareds also eat many insects, especially grasshoppers and cutworms.

Barn owl. The barn owl is an uncommon but beautiful bird with a rusty-golden back and ghostly white front and white heart-shaped face. Fourteen inches long with wide, almost 4-foot wings, this owl has unusually long legs and small, dark eyes. It frequently lives in barns, factories, and abandoned buildings. Unlike other owls, this bird doesn't hoot—it wheezes. The barn owl eats mice, rats, rabbits, and other rodents, and sometimes birds, including blue jays, starlings, and sparrows.

Attracting Owls

Putting up big birdhouses with owl-size entry holes (3 inches for a screech owl; 6 inches for a barn owl) may bring an owl to your yard, if a squirrel doesn't adopt the box first. Dense conifers like firs, spruces, and hemlocks attract owls. These hunters may visit if your yard has places for mice, shrews, and rabbits to make their homes, so naturalistic landscaping is a plus in welcoming these remarkable birds.

PEANUTS AND PEANUT BUTTER

Birds love peanuts and peanut butter, and they'll eagerly devour these nutritious foods year-round. Titmice, chickadees, nuthatches, woodpeckers, and bluebirds are all extraordinarily fond of peanutty delights, including raw and roasted peanuts and smooth and chunky-style peanut butter.

Pricey Peanuts

Peanuts are fairly expensive, as bird treats go, but you can stretch your supply by chopping the nuts into sundae-topping-size bits. You can chop peanuts 1 cup at a time in a food processor or put several cups in a plastic bag, fasten the bag with a twist tie, and carefully hammer it with a heavy coffee mug until the nuts are broken.

If you plan to feed peanuts regularly, buy them in bulk—the price per pound is considerably less. You can buy raw, hulled peanuts at hardware stores and garden centers, or you can buy chopped nuts in bulk from wholesale restaurant suppliers—try asking your local ice cream parlor for a source. Store your peanut supply in the refrigerator so they don't turn rancid.

Peanut hearts. Peanut hearts sound like they're the best part of the peanut, but the opposite is true. Peanut hearts are a by-product of peanut-butter manufacturing, removed before the peanuts are processed.

You'll find peanut hearts at some bird supply stores and as an ingredient in some bagged "premium" seed mixes. They're not cheaper than peanuts, so I don't recommend buying them. Chickadees scorn peanut hearts, but they love chopped peanuts. On the other hand, I've noticed that starlings seem to love peanut hearts.

Peanut Butter

Endear yourself to your feathered friends by buying your peanut butter in bulk—the bigger the container, the better. If you keep a giant jar or institutional-size can of peanut butter on your pantry shelf just for the birds, it's easier to be generous when you dole it out.

There's some controversy about whether birds can choke on peanut butter. Experts at Cornell University have assured me that it's perfectly safe to feed peanut butter to birds straight, and I've been feeding straight peanut butter to birds for 20 years without a casualty or visible signs of distress.

Nevertheless, if you don't want to take chances, you can mix your peanut butter with cornmeal or rolled oats. Mixing peanut butter with fillers like these also makes the peanut-butter supply stretch a little further.

To make peanut buttery bird treats, stir ½ cup of peanut butter into 2 cups of uncooked cornmeal or rolled oats. Spoon the mixture onto a tray feeder and stand back as chickadees, song sparrows, and woodpeckers flock to the feast.

PERENNIALS

Perennials are the backbone of the garden, returning year after year to provide colorful flowers, attractive foliage, and dinner for the birds. Some perennials like coneflowers offer tasty seeds, whereas coral bells and others provide nectar for hummingbirds. But the biggest benefit of perennials to birds isn't their seeds, it's the plants themselves. Perennials provide excellent cover so that birds can move safely through the garden, and their foliage holds insects, caterpillars, slugs, snails, and other ready-to-eat goodies.

Growing perennials is a treat for gardeners, too. Most are easy to grow, and you only have to plant them once for years of pleasure. Watching the first perennial shoots poke through the ground in spring is like seeing old friends returning. And throughout summer and fall, you can enjoy watching their buds and flowers unfold.

Perennials for Birds

Many easy-care perennials are ideal for the bird-friendly garden. Goldenrods (*Solidago* spp.), especially cultivars like 'Crown of Rays' and the dwarf 'Cloth of Gold', make handsome clumps of leafy foliage and have lovely yellow flower plumes. Chickadees, titmice, sparrows, buntings, and many other birds visit goldenrods regularly, looking for aphids and other delectable insect treats. Ripe goldenrod seeds are a draw for sparrows. Gall wasps lay eggs on goldenrod stems, which create a ball-shaped swelling that chickadees probe for larvae to eat in winter.

Perennials with nectar-rich tubular flowers, such as anise hyssop (*Agastache foeniculum*), attract hummingbirds and butterflies when in bloom, and when they go to seed, finches or sparrows will nibble at the seed spikes. When small, orange-and-black pearl crescent butterflies gather on garden

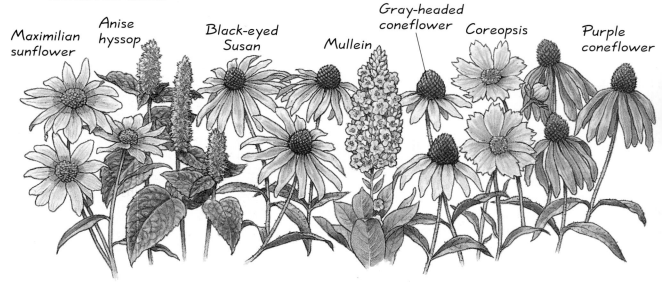

Maximilian sunflower • Anise hyssop • Black-eyed Susan • Mullein • Gray-headed coneflower • Coreopsis • Purple coneflower

Easy-care perennials are a joy to have blooming in the garden. They're also a year-round pantry for birds, who will eagerly pick insects and seeds from the plants.

phlox and black-eyed Susans, you'll know that flycatchers and cuckoos are close behind.

Be sure to include the basic bird-attracting perennials—sunflowers and purple cone-flowers—in your garden. Then fill in the rest of the space with plants that appeal to you. For example, in a sunny spot you could plant bird-attracting boltonia 'Pink Beauty' (*Boltonia asteroides*). Sparrows, buntings, and other small birds eagerly patrol boltonia for spiders and insects. Check "Perennials for the Birds" on page 194 for more planting suggestions.

An "untidy" perennial garden that's not snipped down at the end of the season is inviting to birds, which will feel protected among the plants. You'll discover birds gleaning seeds along with insects, insect eggs, and larvae that are over-wintering on the dried foliage or in the stems.

Planting and Care

You can buy bareroot perennials through the mail or look for potted plants at garden centers and nurseries. Just choose plants that are a match for your light conditions, soil, and climate.

Plant bareroot perennials in spring, while they're still dormant. You can plant container-grown plants anytime, as long as they have at least six weeks to spread their roots before the first hard freeze. To get perennials off to a fast start, fill the planting hole with water and let it drain before you plant. Water newly planted perennials deeply at least once a week for their first two or three months in the garden.

Perennials will grow bigger if you give them fertilizer, but nearly all perennials do just fine without it. To pamper your plants, spread an inch-thick layer of aged manure or finished compost around them in spring. Mulch perennials with a couple of inches of grass clippings, compost, or chopped dead leaves to keep weeding to a minimum in summer.

Homegrown WISDOM

PERFECT PERENNIALS FOR BIRDS

"Winter is when I most need to see birds in my garden," says Betty "Birdie" Gillihan of Wilkes-Barre, Pennsylvania. "When everything is bare outside, I want to see life when I look out the window." A perennial garden for birds gives Birdie—and her backyard birds—just what they need.

A few years ago, Birdie gave away many of her favorite plants to make room for more bird-friendly perennials in her garden. Birdie added coneflowers and perennial Maximilian sunflowers for their seeds, and then looked around to see what else the birds liked. "I saw how the birds gathered at wild goldenrod, so I ordered some goldenrods for the garden. The very first spring, I had an indigo bunting nesting in it." In the winter, tree sparrows, song sparrows, white-throated sparrows, and white-crowned sparrows came to eat the seeds, making the goldenrod the busiest spot in Birdie's garden.

Birdie was surprised by some of the plants that turned out to be bird favorites. For example, mulleins attracted birds daily to pick insects off the flowers. "Come winter, a downy woodpecker adopted it and pecked at bugs hiding in the stems. That plant self-seeded, and now I'm never without a few mulleins," Birdie says.

PERENNIALS FOR THE BIRDS

While birds may enjoy almost any dense perennial garden because it provides good shelter and nesting sites, they'll be more likely to visit gardens that include some of the perennials listed below. You can also learn about more great perennials for birds by reading Bee Balm, Columbines, Coneflowers, Coral Bells, Salvias, and Sunflowers.

PLANT NAMES	BIRDS ATTRACTED	PLANT DESCRIPTION	CULTURE
Coreopsis (*Coreopsis lanceolata* and other perennial spp.)	Flowers attract butterflies, which attract spiders and other insects eaten by many birds. Sparrows and finches eat seeds.	Mounds of lance-shaped or feathery-looking leaves topped by daisy-shaped gold flowers; species and cultivars range from 1' to 3' tall.	Grow in full sun, in average-to-rich, well-drained soil. Drought-tolerant. Zones 3 to 10
Goldenrods (*Solidago* spp.)	Seeds attract sparrows; chickadees and other birds forage for insects on flowers and stems.	Clumps of leafy stems topped by plumes of tiny golden flowers from midsummer to fall. 18" to 6' tall, depending on species.	Grow in full sun in average, well-drained soil. Zones 3 to 10
Anise hyssop (*Agastache foeniculum*)	Flowers attract bees and humming-birds; finches and sparrows eat seeds.	Scalloped, gray-green leaves topped by branching spikes of tiny blue-purple flowers; 2' to 3' tall; plant smells like licorice.	Grow in full sun, in average-to-poor, well-drained soil. Zones 5 to 9
Yellow giant hyssop (*Agastache nepetoides*)	Flowers attract hummingbirds; finches, buntings, and sparrows eat seeds; in winter, downy wood-peckers, chickadees, titmice, and yellow-rumped warblers eat insects and larvae overwintering in stems.	Beautiful vertical plant with stout, erect stems topped with branched spikes of tiny, green-yellow flowers.	Grow in shade to part sun in soil rich in organic matter; also grows in clay. Zones 3 to 8
Mulleins (*Verbascum thapsus* and other spp.)	Goldfinches and other small birds eat seeds; in winter, downy wood-peckers, chickadees, titmice, yellow-rumped warblers, bluebirds, and others eat insects and larvae overwintering in seedhead stalks.	Gray, fuzzy leaves grow in a ground-hugging clump, from which rises a 3'- to 6'-tall spire covered in tiny, yellow or white blossoms.	Grow in full sun in average-to-poor, well-drained soil. Zones 3 to 8
Garden phlox (*Phlox paniculata, P. maculata*)	Flowers attract butterflies, which attract spiders and other insects, which are eaten by many birds. Nesting site for sparrows and buntings.	Strong clumps of foliage topped with showy flat-topped or domed clusters of fragrant flowers. Pink, rose, lavender, or white flowers often have a contrasting-colored center. 3' to 4' tall.	Grow in full sun, in average-to-fertile, well-drained soil. Zones 4 to 8
Smartweed (*Polygonum* spp.)	Finches, sparrows, and other small birds eat oil-rich seeds.	Long-blooming spikes of pink or rosy red flowers top clumps of smooth foliage, which may turn red in fall. Various species range from a few inches to 6' tall.	Grow in partial to light shade, in moist soil rich in organic matter. Zones 3 to 8

PEST CONTROL AND BIRDS

Birds are your garden's best friend when it comes to keeping a natural balance between pests and plants. Hungry birds devour literally tons of grasshoppers, cucumber beetles, stinkbugs, aphids, and other common garden pests. If you discover an outbreak of insect pests on a plant, chances are birds have already found it. Birds may take a bit longer to get the problem under control than a spray or dust would, but if you give them a little time, birds will soon restore the balance.

Many widely available lawn and garden chemicals can be harmful to birds, or can upset the natural order of things so that your backyard is no longer inviting. Abundant insect life in the landscape is a big attraction to birds. Eliminate the bugs and you eliminate the birds.

If you must step in to control pests, take the organic approach: Monitor your plants for outbreaks, and if birds or naturally occurring predator insects don't take care of the problem fast enough, start with the least intrusive control methods. Snip off an aphid-infested branch, for instance. Plunk clumsy Japanese beetles into a jar of soapy water. Smash cucumber beetles between your gloved fingers. You'll be able to control most outbreaks with easy steps like these.

If your plants need more protection than hand-picking can provide, turn to an all-purpose, bird-safe, organic spray: insecticidal soap. A simple squirt will help keep many insects under control.

Red-Flag Warning

You may not realize it, but you're not doing birds a favor when you turn to "natural" controls that kill insects by making them sick. For example, BT (*Bacillus thuringiensis*) kills caterpillars and milky disease spores kill lawn grubs. Think about what you're doing when you apply these materials. BT kills "leaf-eating caterpillars": That's pretty much all of them! If you kill every caterpillar on a young oak tree, for instance, what will orioles feed their nestlings?

Be a Friend to Birds

In the end, the choice is yours. If you truly want a bird-friendly yard, let the birds take care of pest problems as they arise, or give them a hand with a little hand-picking. If your goal is a picture-perfect garden, then your birds will stay mostly at the feeders. (See Vegetable Gardens on page 251 for more about pest control.)

Laying a board in your garden creates a cool, moist daytime hiding place for slugs. Just turn over the board to reveal an inviting slug banquet for oven-birds and many other pest-eating birds.

PHEASANTS

It's exciting to see and hear a pheasant suddenly fly out from a tangle of grasses. These regal birds, with their beautiful shining feathers and absurdly long tails, aren't native to America; they were brought here from Asia. They've managed to survive in the wild in some areas of the country, and they're also released periodically from special ranches that raise them as game birds.

Getting to Know Them

Male ring-necked pheasants have a gleaming chestnut breast, golden sides, a glistening green head, and a startling red patch of skin near the eye. These bright markings are accented by a prim white collar around the neck. Their feathers are gorgeous up close: some tipped with black, others marked with intricate multicolored patterns. They measure up to 3 feet from tip to tail. Females are soft tan, with barred and spotted feathers.

Pheasants live in brushy places or in fields of tall grass, so a meadow garden will appeal to them. Females build a grassy nest on the ground to hold their dark olive greenish eggs. Chicks, which usually number about 10 to 12, can fend for themselves soon after hatching.

Ringnecks are ground-dwelling birds, rarely taking to the air unless threatened. In spring you can hear the loud *kock-cack!* crowing of the male from quite a distance. If you listen hard enough, you'll hear the muffled sound of rapid wingbeats. Both behaviors are part of the pheasant's territorial or courtship display. If a competing male enters a pheasant's home grounds, you may witness a cockfight. The birds rear and strike at each other, feet first, in a burst of flapping wings and loud cries, until one gives up and retreats.

Attracting Pheasants

Pheasants eat grasshoppers and other insects, and they delight in dried corn, wheat, and other grain. Scatter whole or cracked corn or wheat directly on the ground. The birds also appreciate crushed eggshells. A planting of buckwheat may also bring these birds to your backyard.

You can even build a special lean-to shelter to provide an open area for scattering feed where it won't be buried by winter snow. See the illustration of a shelter like this on page 216.

Pheasants shelter under dense evergreens in winter. The coloring of the female (left) can't compare to the male's. He has a green head that shimmers blue and purple in the sunlight.

PHOEBES

Fee-bee, fee-bee, fee-bee is the unmistakable call of the eastern phoebe. When you hear phoebes call, you know spring is starting. Phoebes arrive at their breeding grounds in March and early April.

Getting to Know Them

Phoebes are flycatchers with medium-size, slim beaks and longish tails. They're about 6 inches long, and males and females look alike. When the bird is perched, the tail constantly flicks downward in a leisurely, cat-twitching-its-tail manner. Like other flycatchers, phoebes perch alertly in erect posture, loop out to nab passing insects in flight, then return to the perch until the next tidbit-on-the-wing comes by.

Beetles, flies, moths, and dozens of other creepy-crawlies make up the menu for phoebes. Along with their usual flycatcher food-gathering technique, they also pick up insects in swooping flight near the ground.

Phoebes often nest on house eaves or above a window, wherever a shelf will support their nests of mud and moss or plant fibers. They lay four or five white eggs spotted with red-brown. In wilder areas, phoebes fix their nests to rocks on cliffs or to supports beneath bridges. Being insect eaters, phoebes retreat to the southern United States and southward in winter.

Attracting Phoebes

The seeds in your bird feeders won't interest phoebes. Plentiful bug life—which appears naturally if you grow a wide variety of flowering plants—will attract phoebes to your yard; so will a small pond or other water source. To encourage nesting, build a simple open shelf and mount it on a protected wall of the house or an outbuilding.

Phoebe Checklist

Three phoebes with very different dress cover the United States. If you see a bird perched in perfect-posture flycatcher fashion, watch for the tail twitch—then you'll know it's a phoebe.

Eastern phoebe. Ranging from the Atlantic coast to the foothills of the Rockies, the eastern phoebe is common in rural areas, where it hangs out near buildings, along streams, and near bridges. Its body is an understated grayish green, with a white throat and dark gray head.

Black phoebe. In the Southwest, you'll see the black phoebe, a striking bird in simple dress of black above, snowy white beneath, like an oversize junco. The black phoebe also hangs out in the countryside, but it sometimes visits city lawns, too. Another water lover, it's often attracted by a backyard pond or pool.

Say's phoebe. This pretty brownish gray bird has a belly blushed with orange-pink. In the western half of the country, it's common around buildings or bluffs.

The female eastern phoebe appreciates a supply of white feathers and sphagnum moss for her nest in early spring. Phoebes may visit a backyard mud puddle when they need mud for nest building.

PHOTOGRAPHING BACKYARD BIRDS

The trick to good bird photography is to know where to find the birds, and to have patience. Professional bird photographers spend countless hours crouching in cramped, hot shelters, waiting for birds to appear in just the right spot in precisely the right light. But you don't need to go to such lengths to enjoy photographing birds in your yard or while on vacation.

If you know where birds are likely to hang out, you can hang out there, too, camera in hand. The easiest way to photograph birds is to sit quietly by a bird feeder and wait for the birds to come and feed. Another approach is to look for nesting birds and, very quietly and carefully, wait for the birds to feed their young. (However, if you see any signs that the birds are disturbed by your presence, it's better to leave them alone. How important is that picture, anyway?)

Getting Started

Photography can be an expensive hobby, and if you're just starting out, you may not want to sink lots of money into equipment. But although you can use any kind of camera to photograph birds, you may not be satisfied with the photos from an instant camera or disposable camera. Chances are the birds will only show up as small specks in photos taken with cameras like these.

To take good bird photos, use a 35mm single lens reflex (SLR) camera, such as the ones made by Nikon, Canon, Pentax, and Minolta. Mount the camera on a tripod—the tripod keeps your camera stock-still, so your photos will be in focus. Auto-focus cameras are a good choice since birds tend to be so active.

Professionals invest tens of thousands of dollars in equipment, especially lenses, but you don't have to invest a fortune to be able to take amazing bird pictures. You'll just have to work a little harder and figure out a way to make the birds come close to you. This is easier than you think. If you have a

Stuff a pair of jeans and a shirt with newspaper to make a dummy and prop it in place where you intend to take pictures of birds. Let the birds get used to it for a few days, and they probably won't notice when you take the dummy's place.

feeding station or a birdbath or pond, you already have birds accustomed to visiting a certain place.

The photographer's dummy. One way to get birds used to your presence near a feeder or birdbath is to sit there frequently, as described in Hand Taming on page 132, or to let a dummy do the work for you, as shown in the illustration on the opposite page. Or you can set up a simple hiding place called a blind. If you hide behind a blind when you photograph, the birds won't scatter every time you move your arm to click the shutter.

A homemade camera blind. Use your ingenuity to come up with a blind. If your driveway is close to the feeding area, your car is ideal (instead of a tripod you can use a window bracket—available at good camera shops—to hold your camera steady). If your feeders are near a window, you can even sit inside the house to shoot through the opened window. A big appliance box can make a good blind, too, especially if you decorate it with branches and other green camouflage. You can fashion a more elaborate hiding place from PVC pipe and cloth, or with a drape of leaf-bedecked camouflage netting, sold at hunting supply stores.

Technical Tips

As you become more serious about a bird-photography hobby, it pays to learn more about the technical workings of your camera. Here are some basics you should know. Knowledgeable salespeople at camera shops can also be helpful in explaining the technical aspects of taking photos.

Film. Your main consideration when choosing a film is the ISO, or film speed. The best choice is print film in the 200 to 400 range. Faster film than this tends to be "grainy," which causes a slightly out-of-focus effect when the picture is enlarged, but is fine for snapshots. Slower film than ISO 200 requires more light and slower shutter speeds. Since birds tend to be very active,

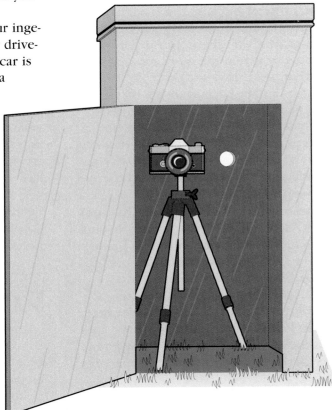

You can make a camera blind out of an appliance box. Just cut away one wall so you can set up your camera inside, and cut a small opening on the opposite wall for viewing the birds.

it's harder to get a clear picture with slow-speed film—any smidgen of movement will show up as a blurred area in the photo.

Professional bird photographers often use slide film (also called color transparencies) because this film reproduces better in magazines and books. High-quality slide films have terrific, rich color. One problem with slides is that they're difficult to view at home unless you have a projector. It's not the same as thumbing through a handful of snapshots. Another problem with slides is that the top-quality slide films are slower than ISO 200. Professionals know how to work with these slow films, but they might shoot several rolls of film in order to get one excellent photo. It's not easy.

Lenses. The most important piece of equipment for bird photography is a big lens—at least 400mm, if possible. These big lenses aren't cheap. Good-quality lenses made by companies like Sigma, Tamron, Tokina, and Vivitar start around $600. (Professionals use lenses that cost anywhere from $2,000 to $8,000 per lens.)

A less expensive alternative is to use a 200mm or 300mm lens in the $200 to $500 range. You'll be surprised, however, to see how tiny the birds look in your viewfinder, even with lenses like these. You can add a "tele-extender" for $100 to $200 to increase the magnification of the lens, but these tend to make photographs look less crisp. Better-quality extenders can be expensive.

The Natural Look

Pictures of birds at the feeders are fun to look at, and a good way to record who was there, but if you want photos of birds in a more natural setting, try this great tip from professional photographers that produces perfectly natural results.

"Plant" a good-size dead tree limb, wrist-thick or better, somewhere in your yard where the background view is appealing and there's room nearby for you to set up a camera blind. When you have the branch in the right spot, drill a hole an inch or more wide and about an inch deep into the side of the branch. Make sure the hole is invisible from the front.

Fill the hole with peanut butter and set up your blind near the branch. Then just wait, and let the birds discover the hidden treat. After a few days, the birds should be approaching the branch freely. Now's the time to stalk them with your camera. You'll get great natural-looking shots as the birds swoop in, or while they're clinging to the branch, or even between pecks at the peanut butter.

PINES

Pine trees give birds just what they need most: year-round shelter from the elements, protected places to build their nests, a variety of insects to eat, and a long-lasting supply of nutritious seeds. Pines may harbor insects like scale, sawflies, and borers, which attract such welcome visitors as nuthatches, kinglets, chickadees, and wood warblers. Pinecones bursting with seeds bring in many more birds for the winter feast, including crossbills, jays, evening and pine grosbeaks, juncos, wood-peckers, and more nuthatches and chickadees.

Pine trees are good news for gardeners as well as birds, because these long-needled ever-greens bring year-round beauty and structure to the garden. Pines can shade your house in summer and block cold winds in winter. Pines are very hardy, flourishing from Zones 2 or 3 to Zones 6 and warmer. They grow in tough sites where most other conifers won't, but they do best in a site that has full sun and well-drained, slightly acid soil. Pines can grow to 80 feet tall, so give them plenty of room in the landscape.

Pines for Birds

Eastern white pine (*Pinus strobus*) is a beauty in middle age, when it reaches a full, feathery, pyramidal shape 20 to 40 feet across. But for its first 8 to 10 years, eastern white pine is as gangly as a teenager, with wide spaces between the branches. By the time it reaches its full height (50 to 80 feet), the tree develops open spaces between its limbs once again. This pine grows in Zones 3 to 8, and although it prefers fertile, moist soil, it will also grow in a dry, rocky soil.

Scotch pine (*P. sylvestris*) is a popular choice for a Christmas tree, and because it is uniformly dense and has handsome, short, blue-green needles, it's also a good choice for home landscapes. Scotch pine reaches 30 to 60 feet tall at maturity, and as it ages, the lower branches die and drop from the tree. Try planting several trees of shorter cultivars like 'Watereri', which tops out between 10 and 25 feet tall, as a windscreen or hedge. Scotch pines need full sun, and although they prefer good, well-drained, acid soil, they tol-erate rocky, poor soils.

A good pine for southern gardens is the loblolly pine (*P. taeda*), because it thrives in Zones 7 to 9, but you'll need binoculars to see the birds in a mature loblolly. Loblollies stretch 60 to 90 feet tall, dropping their lower branches as they mature. They grow best in acid soil that's moist and poorly drained, so they're popular as fast-growing screens in sites where other pines won't grow.

Japanese black pine (*P. thunbergiana*) is a truly versatile tree. It's hardy in Zones 5 to 8 and is heat-, drought-, and salt-tolerant. This pine prefers moist humusy soil, but will grow in poor soil and even on sand dunes. Japanese black pine starts out as a neat pyramid-shaped tree with dark green needles, and gains char-acter as it matures, with open spaces between drooping branches. The tree usually reaches 20 to 30 feet tall, but with favorable conditions it can grow another 20 feet or more.

Scotch pines and other pines shelter birds from summer rains and winter snows. Ruby-crowned kinglets and other birds will search pine branches for insects to eat. In the winter many kinds of seed-eating birds pick pine nuts from the cones.

PREDATORS

Birds have a great natural-defense system—they can fly out of reach at a moment's notice—but they still fall prey to a variety of predators. While you may wish you could keep your backyard predator-free, it's worth remembering that predators are part of nature's balance. And some bird predators, such as owls and hawks, are fascinating subjects for birdwatching in themselves.

In the big picture, bird predators play a vital role in the survival of their prey. The easiest adult birds for a predator to catch are the weakest: birds that are sick, old, or stressed. By removing these birds, predators strengthen the bird population by preventing the spread of diseases. It's survival of the fittest: If a bird is healthy, watchful, and quick to escape a predator, it won't get eaten, and will pass these desirable traits to its offspring.

Birds have lots of babies, and some even raise more than one set of babies in a season. There are predators who eat bird eggs, too, but enough hatch for some to reach adulthood. Besides, at the rate they're born, if all nestlings survived, not only would we be knee-deep in nuthatches, we'd also be taking out second mortgages to pay for birdseed for our feeders.

Who preys on birds? Bird predators fall into three groups. There are the pursuers, mainly hawks, which swoop down on their bird prey and nab them in midair. The pouncers include perching hawks, cats, snakes, and other animals that sneak up on unwary or roosting birds. Nest thieves include owls, jays, crows, and raccoons, which raid nests looking for eggs, young, or even parent birds.

If you'd like to know more about bird predators, see Cats, Crows and Ravens, Hawks, Jays, Owls, and Snakes.

PUMPKIN AND MELON SEEDS

When you carve a jack-o'-lantern or scoop out a dessert melon, don't throw the seeds into your compost pail—save them to make great bird treats. Rich and nutty tasting, the seeds of pumpkins, squashes, watermelons, and other melons are a favorite delicacy of backyard birds like cardinals, jays, nuthatches, and chickadees.

Once you get in the swing of saving pumpkin and melon seeds to feed the birds, try saving other kinds of seeds, such as cucumber and pepper seeds—even the poppy seeds that drop from your breakfast bagel. If squirrels are a problem at your feeders, seeds from hot peppers may help. Birds seem to

enjoy the seeds of hot peppers with no ill effects, but they're a great deterrent to pesky squirrels and other small varmints, who have more sensitive palates.

When you're preparing squash, melon, and other vegetables at mealtime, scoop out the seeds and rinse them in a colander to remove any clinging bits of pulp. You can scoop them onto a tray feeder to offer them fresh, or if you have a lot of seeds, you can dry them for storage. To dry veggie seeds, spread them in a single layer on several sheets of newspaper in a sunny spot outdoors. They'll be thoroughly dry in a few days. Mix the dried seeds together if you like, and then pour them into a jar or a plastic bag. Seal the container and store it in a cool, dark, dry place, like a kitchen cupboard shelf.

QUAIL

With their hurried, scurrying stride and bobbing heads, quail look like birds straight out of a cartoon. These bottom-heavy birds are part of the pheasant family.

Getting to Know Them

Quail are plump, short-tailed birds about 8 inches from stem to stern. These fast-running birds only take to the air when necessary. They nest on the ground, filling a shallow depression with leaves, sticks, grasses, and sometimes feathers. The nest may hold as many as 20 of their creamy white or brown-blotched eggs. Their voices are clear whistled tones that can carry for up to a mile.

If you live in the Plains states or eastward, the only quail you'll see is the Northern bobwhite. Bobwhites show intricately patterned plumage in rich browns, accented with white and black edgings. Its call is a loud, clear whistle that sounds like its name, *bobwhite*. In the wild, bobwhites prefer brushy areas, old fields, and woods' edges. If any of these habitats borders your yard, bobwhites may visit your meadow garden or feeding station.

California quail, Gambel's quail, and mountain quail live in the western states and look similar to one another. They have a black face and throat outlined with a necklace of white, a dark gray back, white streaks or stripes along its sides, and a teardrop-shaped topknot.

California quail are a common backyard bird from Southern California to the Pacific Northwest. Gambel's quail are common in the Southwest and eastern Colorado.

Mountain quail live in mountainous areas from Nevada to California.

Attracting Quail

A grassy or weedy patch in your garden will attract quail; so will a spread of sunflower seeds and millet or mixed birdseed. Most quail like fruit, especially grapes, elderberries, hackberries, and other berries. Some eat acorns or seeds of pinecones. These ground-dwelling birds eat lots of insects, too, including ants, beetles, caterpillars, and many others. A shallow garden pool will draw quail. Linked plantings of shrubs and grasses will give the birds cover so they can travel safely about your yard.

Quail, including Northern bobwhites, are a gardener's friend. They'll eat the seeds of pesky chickweed, ragweed, pigweed, clover, and grasses.

Raisins

Raisins are delicious treats for birds that like to eat fruit, but it may take some ingenuity on your part to launch a raisin-feeding campaign. Mockingbirds, bluebirds, robins, tanagers, thrushes, and other birds that eat mainly soft foods are the best customers for raisins, but these birds aren't regulars at bird feeders. They're used to plucking fruits from the branches of plants rather than from a feeder. **Make a "raisin tree."** You can try putting out raisins in an open feeding tray, but if birds don't discover the raisins within a week or so, try this trick. Choose a shrub or tree with stiff, slender, twiggy branches, such as a plum tree.

Impale raisins on the branch tips, using as many of the tiny fruits as you have the patience to attach. Another strategy is to make dangling clusters of raisins by stringing them with a needle and thread, and then hanging the raisin garlands in tree branches. You can also make raisin wreaths by poking raisins onto a length of wire, as shown on page 75.

Birds are apt to investigate strange objects in their usual haunts, and your raisin art will certainly get their attention. Once they discover that it's food, you can draw their attention further by scattering the raisins on the ground near the "raisin tree." From there, it's just a short step to enticing the raisin fanciers to visit your tray feeder.

Roadrunners

In the hot, dry backyards of the desert Southwest, the greater roadrunner often replaces the common robin as the lawn bird in residence. The roadrunner is a big bird, measuring almost 2 feet from tip of beak to tip of tail, and its long legs make it a pro at chasing fast-moving lizards.

Getting to Know Them

Roadrunners have a streaky brown back and a snowy white belly. A feathered crest and bright patch of blue and orange-red bare skin decorate its head. The roadrunner's long tail aids its balance and maneuvering. Male and female birds look alike.

Though it looks more like a barnyard fowl than a songbird, the roadrunner is actually closely related to cuckoos, those secretive treetop birds of woodlands and shaded back-

If you live in the Southwest, include prickly pears in your garden. The juicy fruits of these easy-to-grow cacti are a favorite with roadrunners.

yards. You can hear the connection in the roadrunner's low, hoarse *coo, coo, coo, ooh, ooh, ooh.*

Roadrunners live year-round from Southern California to Louisiana and north to southern Kansas. They mate for life and build their big nests low in small trees, thickets, or clumps of cacti. The nests, which can be more than a foot across, are roughly constructed of sticks lined with leaves, grasses, feathers, snakeskin, and bits of dried cow or horse manure. They lay three to five plain white eggs, which sometimes have a faint yellow tinge.

Attracting Roadrunners

Roadrunners are great birds to have in your yard because they eat a wide variety of insects, including many pests such as ants, grasshoppers, and cutworms. Their menu also includes mice, gophers, rattlesnakes, snails, scorpions, and lizards. Roadrunners like to hunt among flowerbeds and mulch for such delicacies. Rocks in the garden where reptiles can bask may in turn attract roadrunners, too.

It's great fun to watch roadrunners in action. They're single-minded when it comes to pursuing their prey, twisting and darting about at full speed. It doesn't take much imagination to envision puffs of dust as the bird speeds along or screeches to a stop. Roadrunners may nab an occasional bird egg or nestling, but the good points and fascinating habits of these big birds redeem them as valued residents of the backyard.

ROBINS

The American robin is a symbol of spring. With its ruddy orange-red breast and gray-brown back, the robin is a common sight on lawns in every state from the Atlantic to the Pacific.

Getting to Know Them

Although almost everyone can identify a robin by sight, far fewer folks know the beautiful song of this familiar bird. Listen for the rich *cheer-up, cheer, cheer, cheer-up* at dawn and dusk, when the song isn't mixed with dozens of other singers.

Robins are about $8\frac{1}{2}$ inches long. Female birds have a paler belly than the males, and during nesting season they may show a bald patch on the breast. This "brood patch" keeps eggs cozy against the warm bare skin.

Robins live year-round in most parts of the country, but the birds you see in your garden

The female robin often builds her nest in dooryard shrubs, or even over the door itself. The mud-lined cup of grasses holds the bird's pastel eggs (robin's-egg blue, of course).

JUST FOR ROBINS

- Give robins a safe place to find earthworms by keeping your lawn mowed and free of pest- and weed-killing sprays.
- In spring and summer, keep a mud puddle available for nesting robins.
- Compost piles and mulched beds provide a bounty of wrigglers for hungry robins, especially when summer drought has hardened the soil in lawn areas.
- In winter, cut some apples in half and lay them in a tray feeder or on the ground, cut side up. Robins will quickly clean out every bit of delectable apple flesh.

in winter are usually migrants that have moved in from more northerly areas, while the summer residents have moved south. During winter, robins in cold-winter areas move into thickets or hang around fruit trees such as crabapples or hollies, where they're protected and have a ready source of food.

Insects and fruit top the menu for robins. They like earthworms best, but they also eat beetles, termites, grasshoppers, caterpillars, and other insects. Robins hunt by sight, not by feeling vibrations from the worms beneath their feet or by listening to them. Watch robins as they forage, and you'll notice they cock their head frequently so they can get a better look at earthworms peeping from their burrows.

Robins aren't shy about nesting close to people. The birds often nest more than once a season and are quick to take advantage of a simple shelf nailed to a protected wall.

Attracting Robins

Make your yard inviting for robins by adding bayberry, elderberry, grape, crabapple, and other fruit-producing shrubs and trees. Robins may visit feeders for raisins, grapes, currants, and other fruits, or for bread.

ROSES

Birds don't care a whit about which rose smells best, but they do appreciate the prickly canes, which can keep their nests safe from cats and other prowlers. Birds also enjoy feasting on the tasty orange or red fruits called rose hips, which can provide a winter's worth of nourishment.

Find a species rose like rugosa rose (*Rosa rugosa*), or one of the dozens of old-fashioned bushes, ramblers, and climbers, and chances are you'll find a song sparrow or cardinal nesting in its thorny branches, and dozens of other birds stripping the clusters of rose hips in winter. Climbing rose cultivars, like 'Golden Showers' and brilliant red 'Blaze', are favorite nesting sites for cardinals, which often return to the same rosebush year after year to raise their family.

Caring for Roses

The roses that birds love best, the species roses and old-fashioned roses, are also some of the easiest roses to care for. These plants are hardy, disease-resistant, and require pruning only to keep their growth in bounds. These large rose plants generally bloom only once, in early summer, so plant them where their thick, glossy foliage will form a background for a bed of summer-blooming perennials.

Roses grow best in a site that gets at least half a day of direct sun, with open space around them for good air circulation (this helps prevent disease problems). Plant roses in average to slightly acidic, well-drained soil with plenty of organic matter worked in, and mulch with a couple of inches of compost each spring. Birds should help keep any insect pests in check. If aphid or mite problems build up, knock them off plants with a strong blast of water from a hose or spray with insecticidal soap. You can easily hand-pick and dispose of pests like Japanese beetles and slugs.

Bird-Worthy Roses

Rugosa roses produce clusters of plump colorful fruits, sometimes as big as cherries, that decorate the plants like Christmas ornaments well into winter, or at least until birds discover them. Available with single or multipetaled flowers in shades of white, pink, purple, and red, these tough-as-nails roses thrive on neglect. They grow as well in poor soil, in sandy, salty conditions, and during droughts as they do when planted in a pampered garden setting. Their stiff, pleated-looking leaves are a beautiful shade of deep green. You can plant them alone as a garden accent in a mixed hedge with other plants. These ultra-hardy roses thrive in sun or part shade from Zone 7 to as far north as Zone 2.

The prairie rose (*R. setigera*) and the pasture rose (*R. carolina*), which is also called Carolina rose, are a pair of excellent native American roses with simple, single-petaled pink blossoms and fat, red rose hips. Both grow well in sun or part shade and adapt to most soils in Zones 4 through 8.

Other good roses to grow for bird snacks and shelter include the hardy meadow rose (*R. blanda*), which grows in Zones 2 to 7 and has rosy, single flowers and pear-shaped red hips. Sweetbrier (*R. eglanteria*, also called *R. rubiginosa*) is hardy in Zones 4 to 8 and produces pale to deep pink flowers. The trailing or climbing memorial rose (*R. wichuraiana*), which grows in Zones 5 to 9, has pristine white, multipetaled flowers and orange to dark red fruits. Don't overlook old shrub rose cultivars, such as the frilly, multi-petaled pink 'Konigin von Danemark', which have dense branches and tasty rose hips.

In the spring the dense, thorny canes of rosebushes make a burglar-proof nesting place for Eastern towhees and many other songbirds. Roses that produce fat fruits (called hips) also provide a good food source for birds.

SALVIAS

Salvia blossoms are tailor-made for hummingbird beaks. The vividly colored, small, tubular blossoms of both annual and perennial salvias add long-lasting color to your garden and provide a feast for nectar-seeking hummingbirds.

Salvias run the gamut in size, form, and flower color. They have square stems, showing that they belong to the mint family. But unlike mints, salvias don't spread rampantly. Some cultivars, such as 'East Friesland', are neat plants that stay in a compact mound about 1 foot tall. At the other end of the scale are salvias like clary sage (*Salvia sclarea*) that stretch out into 3-foot shrubs. Be sure to give sprawling salvias like these plenty of room and support them and string stakes if the plants flop.

Many salvias are native to the western deserts, so they prefer well-drained, light or loose soil, and an open, airy location. However, some salvias grow as well in average garden soil as they do in less fertile soil. All salvias do best in full sun. In cold areas, grow the more tender salvias as annuals, or bring potted plants or rooted cuttings indoors before the first frost to overwinter on your sunniest windowsills.

Serving Up Salvias

If you want to advertise a garden buffet to hummingbirds, start with three fire-engine red salvias: scarlet sage (*S. splendens*), pineapple sage (*S. elegans*), and Texas sage (*S. coccinea*). These sages will reach from 1 to 3 feet tall when grown as annuals. Scarlet sage and pineapple sage are tender perennials that can reach up to 8 feet high in Zones 9 and 10. Autumn salvia (*S. greggii*) is a perennial salvia that grows from 1 to 3 feet tall and is hardy enough to overwinter in Zones 7 to 10. Pineapple sage and autumn salvia bloom very late in the season, so protect them from early frosts by covering the plants with a sheet on cold nights.

Red doesn't have to be the only salvia color on your hummingbird buffet. If you like blue flowers, salvias are definitely the way to go—some of the hardiest perennial salvias have intense blue flowers. These include blue sage (*S. azurea*), pitcher's sage (*S. azurea* var. *grandiflora*), and meadow sage (*S. pratensis*), which overwinters as far north as Zone 3. Clary sage (Zones 5 to 10) is a branching plant that grows up to 3 feet tall, with large leaves and blue-and-white or blue-and-pink flowers. Bog sage (*S. uliginosa*) has lovely blue flowers, and can grow 4 to 5 feet tall, but is hardy only to Zone 9.

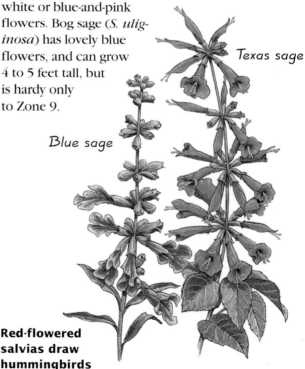

Blue sage

Texas sage

Red-flowered salvias draw hummingbirds like a magnet. Once hummingbirds find your garden, they'll eagerly feed from any kind of salvia. Flower colors range from blue and purple to white, pink, and coral.

SAPSUCKERS

The yellow-bellied sapsucker is an unusual member of the woodpecker family. Unlike other noisy woodpeckers, it's a quiet, shy bird. The only noise it makes is an occasional soft squeak. If you spot it, it usually quickly hitches around the trunk of a tree to escape from view.

Getting to Know Them

Seen from the back, sapsuckers look mostly black—they don't have the black-and-white markings of the more familiar downy and hairy woodpeckers. Sapsuckers are moderate-size woodpeckers, about 7½ to 8½ inches long. Several species of sapsuckers cover the continent, wintering in the Southwest and the eastern half of the country.

Both male and female yellow-bellied sapsuckers have a red patch on the crown of their black-and-white-striped head; males also have a red throat. That famous yellow belly is more of a dirty yellowish white.

In the West, the yellow-bellied bird may interbreed with the red-breasted sapsucker, a glorious bird with a brilliant red-orange head and hood and a bright yellow belly. The yellow-bellied sapsucker may also interbreed with the glossy black Williamson's sapsucker, which sports big white wing and rump patches and a sunny yellow belly.

Horizontal rows of small, closely spaced holes on a tree trunk are evidence of sapsucker drilling. The birds bore holes into the inner bark. The holes ooze sap, which the sapsuckers return to lick or suck up with brushy tongues.

Sapsucker trees are a great place to look for beetles, butterflies, hummingbirds, chipmunks, and other creatures that also enjoy a sweet treat. Experts are divided over the question of whether sapsucker drilling can damage trees, providing entry for insects or disease. Sapsuckers eat many insects destructive to trees and bark, though, so they're not all bad.

Sapsuckers seem to prefer to lay their five or six white eggs in holes in live aspens or dead birches or elms. They build no nest, except for whatever stray sawdust may soften the floor of the cavity.

Attracting Sapsuckers

As you might expect, sapsuckers love a sweet treat at the feeder. The birds may horn in on your hummingbird or oriole nectar feeder. Suet is another favorite food, as are jelly doughnuts stuck on a nail or hung by a string. They may also move into a woodpecker nest box, built to red-bellied woodpecker specs, though they usually prefer to find their own natural home site.

Sapsuckers are shy, so you may see sapsucker holes in your trees more often than you see the birds. To tell a male yellow-bellied sapsucker from a female, check the throat—the male's throat is red.

SCARECROWS

Do scarecrows really keep birds away? Not for long it seems, but even so, they're fun to make and they add a cheerful "human" touch to your veggie garden.

Most garden birds quickly become accustomed to a scarecrow or any other object that doesn't move, no matter how fearsome it appears at first. Passing crows that spot your scarecrow will raise an alarm when they cruise by, especially if your figure includes flapping black cloth, which apparently looks to them like a crow in trouble. But resident sparrows, thrashers, catbirds, and other garden nibblers will soon realize that that guy (or gal) in the garden never moves an inch. (If you'd like to know about reliable ways to keep bird pests away from your berry bushes, fruit trees, or vegetable garden, check out the crop-protection techniques described in Fruit Trees and Vegetable Gardens.)

A Recycler's Dream

Constructing a scarecrow is a great garden project for kids and adults. This is recycling at its finest: a pair of broomsticks or that broken hoe handle for a skeleton; some dowdy duds from your closet (this could be just the time to reincarnate that prom dress you've been moth-balling); straw for stuffing; and of course, a fine chapeau.

Nice for Nesters, Too

Your scarecrow may turn out to be a great bird attractant. Any house sparrows in the neighborhood will soon be fishing stems of straw out of its sleeves. Orioles will unravel any dangling threads at nest-building time. And a tattered straw hat is great raw material for sparrow and wren nests. Speaking of wrens, don't be surprised to find house wrens taking up residence right on your scarecrow. Scarecrow pockets have sheltered many a family of these tiny-but-fearless birds.

Robins and other birds quickly get used to a scarecrow's presence in the garden. In spite of their name, scarecrows aren't all that scary, but they're fun to make and can provide nesting materials for your feathered friends.

SHADE AND WOODLAND GARDENS

Woodsy gardens tend to take care of themselves, and that means they're especially inviting to birds. Birds feel at home in areas where they can forage and nest undisturbed. Creating woodland habitat for birds is important in the grand scheme of things, because woods are disappearing fast in many parts of the country, making way for highways, shopping malls, and housing developments. Although your woodsy backyard may seem like a drop in the bucket, it will be welcomed by shade-loving birds.

Birds on the Shady Side

A backyard with lots of shrubs and trees to cast cooling shade won't limit the numbers or kinds of birds that visit your feeding station. In fact, the cover of shrubs and trees will make most birds more comfortable when they move in and out of the feeding area to grab a snack and then return to their home base.

You'll want to include birdseed feeders, nectar feeders, fruit feeders, and suet feeders in your shady garden, but be sure you choose plants that do double duty as well. Add berry-producing shrubs to your shady patch, and fruit-loving birds will stick around to clean them off. Nut trees and oaks offer valuable high-energy foods, and the foliage and bark of all shade-loving plants will also attract birds, thanks to the creepy-crawlies tucked among the leaves or hiding in the crevices.

Keep Looking Up

Many of the birds that like a shady garden will be over your head—literally. If your yard includes any tall shade trees, be sure to look up into the branches frequently to see who's moving around in the tree canopy, especially during spring and fall migrations. A single tree can host dozens of bird species foraging for insects, fruit, or nuts, and unless you crane your neck every now and then, you may miss them.

A combination of native wildflowers, like Jack-in-the-pulpit and wild ginger, with groundcovers, shrubs, and trees will shelter a variety of woodland songbirds such as thrushes.

Creating a Shady Garden

A shady woodland garden has the feel of a natural woods. It depends on a multilevel arrangement, with tall trees like oaks or maples underplanted with midsize trees like sassafras and younger tall trees, then small trees like redbuds and dogwoods. Beneath the trees is a layer of shrubs, with a layer of wildflowers and ferns covering the ground. I like to stick with native plants in a woodland garden, because I want my little piece of heaven to look as much like the natural woods as possible so that birds feel at home in my garden. I'm not above sticking in a few exotic perennials or selected shrubs with better berries, though, as long as the natives carry most of the garden.

Leaf litter is a natural part of such a garden, doing duty as a soil replenisher and natural mulch, so your woodland garden needs little or no leaf raking. Paths of wood chips, bark, or root mulch will look for all the world like deer trails or footpaths meandering through a forest.

If your backyard includes one or more big trees, you have the perfect foundation for a woodland or shade garden. If your backyard has that new-subdivision look, don't despair: You can create a woodsy feel with young trees and shrubs while you wait for your plants to mature.

Start small, choosing your shadiest patch of yard to begin your garden. If you have no trees to cast a convenient pool of shade, place your garden on the north side of your house, or in a section of yard shaded by the neighbor's garage or your privacy fence. If your yard is truly sun-baked, you can erect a trellis to shield part of it from the brunt of all-day rays.

Build around existing woody plants, or choose a few favorites like a maple, dogwood, or redbud, shown in the garden design illustrated on the opposite page. Deciduous hollies bring a bounty of red berries—and birds—in fall. Add evergreen shrubs like azaleas and a fast-growing hemlock for that necessary all-year greenery, pleasing to the eye and sheltering to the birds. Ferns also add good cover, not to mention beautiful softening texture. And don't forget to indulge in wildflowers while you're planting.

Shade Lovers for Birds

Plant these shade-loving perennials, wildflowers, and small trees to create a natural-looking carpet of vegetation that will make forest-dwelling birds like thrushes, fox sparrows, and towhees feel at home. When flowers fade or plants become dormant, mulch thickly with chopped fallen leaves.

Pinxterbloom azalea. Pinxterbloom azalea (*Rhododendron periclymenoides*) is a branching, 4- to 6-foot-tall deciduous shrub that's hardy from Zones 3 to 8. The clusters of fragrant pale to deep pink spring flowers attract hummingbirds. The dense foliage attracts nesting songbirds.

Virginia bluebells. The spoon-shaped leaves of Virginia bluebells (*Mertensia virginica*) appear in bunches in early spring, followed by 2-foot stems of blue, tubular flowers and pink buds. The plants, which are hardy in Zones 3 to 9, go dormant after blooming. Grow it in moist, humusy soil, in partial to full shade.

Dutchman's breeches. Spreading swiftly from small underground tubers, Dutchman's breeches (*Dicentra cucullaria*) soon forms large colonies. Its lacy, gray-green leaves are topped with arching wands of dangling, ivory pantaloon-shaped flowers in spring. Dutchman's breeches is hardy in Zone 3 to 9 and goes dormant after blooming. Grow it in moist, humusy soil, in part to full shade.

Cinnamon fern. Cinnamon fern (*Osmunda cinnamomea*) has clumps of upright green

A Shady Garden for Birds

1. Mature shade tree
2. Pinxterbloom azalea
   (*Rhododendron periclymenoides*)
3. Virginia bluebells (*Mertensia virginica*)
4. Dutchman's breeches (*Dicentra cucullaria*)
5. Cinnamon fern (*Osmunda cinnamomea*)
6. Hosta (*Hosta* spp.): dormant here
7. Mayapple (*Podophyllum peltatum*)
8. Eastern redbud (*Cercis canadensis*)
9. Downy serviceberry (*Amelanchier arborea*)

fronds, 3 to 5 feet tall, surrounding rusty brown fertile fronds. The green fronds turn a rich reddish brown color in fall and are hardy in Zones 2 to 10. Grow cinnamon fern in moist, humusy, well-drained soil.

Hosta. Hostas (*Hosta* spp. and cultivars) are wonderful foliage plants with dramatic leaves ranging from gray-green, chartreuse, rich green, or green with edgings or central stripes of contrasting white or yellow. Sizes range from miniatures 6 inches in diameter to giants with huge crinkled leaves that may reach 1 foot long—each! Flower stems topped with tubular lavender or white flowers in late summer attract hummingbirds. Hostas are hardy from Zones 3 to 9, depending on species and cultivar. Give the plants a few years to reach full size in the garden. Grow hostas in rich, well-drained soil with plenty of organic matter, in partial to full shade.

Mayapple. The ground-hugging green umbrella-shaped leaves of mayapple (*Podophyllum peltatum*) open like parasols in early spring. Waxy white flowers nod demurely from the stems. Mayapple is hardy in Zones 3 to 9. The plants grow in moist, humusy, well-drained soil, in part to full shade, and colonize by spreading roots.

Redbud. Redbud (*Cercis canadensis*) is a graceful small tree that grows 20 to 30 feet tall and is hardy from Zones 4 to 9. The dark, bare branches are studded with long-lasting small, deep pink, sweet-pea-shaped blossoms in spring. Chickadees relish the seeds of the dangling small, dark brown pods. Grow it in well-drained, moist soil in full sun to shade.

Serviceberry. The bare branches of serviceberry (*Amelanchier arborea* 'Princess Diana' or similar tree-form amelanchier) are covered in a cloud of white flowers in spring. Serviceberries reach 15 to 25 feet tall and are hardy in Zones 4 to 9. The flowers attract insects, which attract vireos and warblers, and many birds eagerly eat the blueberry-like fruits. Grow it in well-drained, moist, acidic soil, in sun to shade.

Birdwatching in the Shade

A garden that's left to its own devices, as are most shade or woodland gardens, is a little sanctuary for birds to move about in to feed and raise their young just as they would in a natural woodland. Keep an eye out for these shade-loving birds after your shady garden is established and undisturbed.

Bird	Where to Look for It
Blue-gray gnatcatcher	In tree canopy
Cuckoo	In tree canopy; shrubs
Flycatchers (small)	On exposed perches and on tree branches
Fox sparrow	On ground, or in low branches of shrubs
Gray-cheeked thrush	In shrubs and small trees
Great crested flycatcher	In tree canopy
Jays	In tree canopy; occasionally on the ground
Tanagers	In tree canopy
Thrushes	On ground or in shrubs
Towhees	On ground or in low shrubs
Veery	On ground or in shrubs
Vireos	In tree canopy or in shrubs
Wood pewees	In tree canopy
Wood warblers	In tree canopy or in shrubs
Wrens	On ground or in low shrubs

SHELTER

When it comes to shelter, a bird's motto is "more is better." They prefer a large group of shrubs, or a big patch of meadow garden, or a hedgerow to a single shrub or a small flowerbed.

Birds don't just need shelter from the weather, they need to hide from the always-watching eyes of cats, hawks, and other predators. Not many birds are comfortable on a wide-open expanse of neatly mown lawn, except for robins, blackbirds, and occasionally flickers and killdeers.

Shelter from the Storm

If you've ever endured a night in a wet down sleeping bag, you know what feathers are like when they get drenched: They're heavy, soggy, and don't help keep you warm at all. The same goes for birds. Their feathers are superb insulation, but their usefulness disappears when they get soaking wet. Keeping dry, or at least dry enough, is a priority for birds, which can quickly fall ill after a feather-drenching chill.

When the weather turns rainy, windy, cold, snowy, or otherwise nasty, birds seek shelter in shrubs and trees with dense foliage and layered branches that shed the brunt of the moisture and draft. That rhododendron you planted along the front of your house may be just an ornament to you, but to birds seeking shelter, its broad, leathery leaves are a virtual life preserver.

Protection from Predators

Dense shrubs and trees are also a bird's refuge from predators. Nimble little birds can negotiate the nooks and crannies in the interior of woody plants, but to hawks and four-footed predators, there's no way to get in. Birds are much more likely to visit your feeders and birdbaths if there are sheltering plants nearby for a quick getaway.

Homegrown WISDOM

USEFUL YEWS

"I despised the yew bushes in front of my house from the day I moved in," says James Stanton of Darien, Connecticut. "They were so blah, the same green lumps that my parents had had in front of their house." James put getting rid of the yews at the top of his to-do list.

"It's a good thing I'm a procrastinator, because when the weather turned cold, I found out those yews were the favorite nighttime shelter of every bird in the neighborhood." As James watched, he saw cardinals and sparrows fly into the bushes one after another. "I had to laugh picturing the scene inside," James says. "But I guess all those bodies kept things cozy inside!"

Once James realized how important the yews were to the birds in his neighborhood, he abandoned his plans to remove them and made them part of his overall garden plan instead. As James points out, "My lumpy bushes are really the Hilton in disguise."

Shelter Suggestions

Here are a few good ways to increase the shelter for birds in your yard.

◆ Include evergreen shrubs and trees and deciduous shrubs with dense branches in your garden plan, so that birds can seek protection all year-round. You'll find recommendations of specific trees and shrubs that shelter birds in Evergreens, Shrubs, and Trees.

◆ Look for plants like spruces with sharp needles that repel predators or plants like rhododendrons and camellias with broad leaves that shed rain like a shingled roof.

◆ Consider adding a brush pile to your garden: Simply make a domed pile of wind-downed branches and prunings. Native sparrows, juncos, and other small birds stay safe within such a jumble of twiggy branches.

◆ You can expand on the brush-pile concept by building a plywood framework and turning the area underneath into a feeding station for birds like pheasants, as shown in the illustration below.

◆ For quick shelter while you're waiting for shrubs and trees to grow, plant fast-growing grape vines (Concord's a good choice) to cover an arbor. Autumn clematis or annual climbers like hyacinth bean or moonflowers also work well.

◆ Even a single eastern red cedar (*Juniperus virginiana*) provides excellent shelter. Its dense, extremely prickly branches are tops with birds seeking a safe roost for the night. Rare is the predator that will brave the spiky needles to reach the birds sleeping inside.

◆ If you have a large, open yard, cast-off Christmas trees make great instant shelter for birds. Try staking the trees upright to metal pipes hammered into the ground. A few strategically placed trees near your bird feeders offer comforting cover, and will greatly increase the bird traffic at your feeders.

Use sturdy 2 × 4s to prop up a sheet of plywood at a 45-degree angle to make a winter feeding shelter for pheasants and other ground-feeding birds. Camouflage the shelter with evergreen boughs and brush.

SHRUBS

From the chipping sparrow nesting in the yew to the robin waiting out the rain in the lilac, birds give shrubs their seal of approval. Shrubs are ideal places for birds to nest, sleep, and hide from predators and bad weather.

Shrubs are also a delicatessen of bird delights. Birds will scour your shrubs in all seasons looking for insects, egg masses, or cocoons hidden among the branches or dangling from twigs. The leaf litter beneath your shrubs is a happy hunting ground for sparrows, thrushes, grackles, and other birds who scratch or sift through the leaves and humus to find tasty insects. The flowers of shrubs attract yet more insects, and their fruits and berries add the crowning touch.

The Shrub Advantage

Plus, shrubs are so vital to birds that you could plant nothing but shrubs and still attract more birds than you could with a yard full of trees and flowers. Shrubs like barberries and burning bush provide safe cover for foraging for food and nesting materials. The twiggy branches and dense foliage shield birds from predators like hawks, which can't get into the dense interiors of the bushes. If your yard is thickly planted with shrubs, birds will feel at ease there and move about freely.

Shrubs with dense, overlapping foliage shelter birds from wind and rain, and shrubs of all kinds also offer a cool respite of shade. The twiggy, sheltered interior of a shrub is a perfect spot for a nest. Birds that spend most of their time on or near the ground, including song sparrows and other native sparrows, buntings, and thrushes, often build nests in backyard shrubs. Shrubs also offer a jackpot of nesting materials like dead twigs and leaves.

Fruiting shrubs like viburnums are the best bird magnet there is. The birds they attract are often unusual beauties—bluebirds, waxwings, grosbeaks, and others. But it's not only berries that provide food for birds. Flowering shrubs provide nectar for hummingbirds. Blossoms and leaves attract tiny insects, which in turn attract warblers, vireos, and other bug eaters. When songbirds are feeding nestlings, a garden full of shrubs is as popular as a fast-food restaurant.

Planting and Caring for Shrubs

Shrubs are great garden bargains. They're inexpensive to buy, costing as little as a few dollars. They grow fast and live practically forever. Rarely troubled by disease or severe insect outbreaks, shrubs just keep growing

Red osier dogwood has berries that attract birds, and insect-eating birds like fox sparrows will find plenty of treats in the leaf litter at the base of the shrub.

Plenty of interesting birds may nest in your yard when you plant dense, sheltering shrubs. Gardeners in the eastern United States may spy a black-billed cuckoo nesting in their American cranberry bush.

year after year, providing the garden with permanent color and structure.

Shrubs are generally easy to establish in your yard. They put out new roots quickly and begin sprouting healthy new growth even in their first season. There's no need to fertilize, but be sure to water shrubs when rain is scarce during their first year, especially in late fall when they need a good drink to get them through winter. For step-by-step planting instructions, see Trees on page 246.

While a single shrub will attract birds, a group of shrubs has a lot more appeal. There's safety in numbers, and a grouping, hedge, or corridor of shrubs helps birds feel more secure. When birds are less nervous about predators, they're much more likely to linger in your backyard.

For the most pleasing landscape look, plant your shrubs in groups of two or three of one kind. Stagger the shrubs, rather than plant them in a regimented line, especially when you're planting a hedge of privet or other shrubs. When you plant a group of shrubs, arrange the taller shrubs in the rear of the planting, and group shorter ones in front. Keep each species in a separate group rather than mix them all up, but overlap the groups a bit for a more natural-looking planting.

Be sure your home landscape includes evergreen shrubs like juniper. Carolina wrens and other small birds will seek shelter inside the protective cover of the dense foliage.

SHRUBS FOR BIRDS

Choosing shrubs for birds is difficult, not because there are few choices, but rather because there are so many! This short listing is just a quick sampling of shrubs that offer shelter, nesting sites, and food for birds. You'll also find information on more great shrubs for birds in Bayberries, Berries, Brambles, Evergreens, Hollies, Junipers, Native Plants, Roses, and Viburnums.

PLANT NAMES	BIRDS ATTRACTED	PLANT DESCRIPTION	CULTURE
Cotoneaster (*Cotoneaster* spp.)	Insect- and fruit-eating birds are lured by insect-attracting flowers and berries.	Species and cultivars vary from groundcover types to 10'- to 15'-tall shrubs; evergreen or semievergreen with bright red or black fruits	Grows best in moist, well-drained soil; some tolerate dry soil; all need full sun. Most types hardy in Zones 3 to 7
Gray dogwood (*Cornus racemosa*)	More than 100 species of birds are lured by insect-attracting flowers and berries; shelters roosting and nesting birds.	10'- to 15'-tall, multistemmed deciduous shrub with pointed, oval leaves, gray branches in summer; clusters of white berries on crimson stems in fall and winter	Grows in wet and dry soil, in sun to full shade. Sprouts from the roots to form clumps. Zones 4 to 8
Red osier dogwood (*Cornus sericea* [formerly *C. stolonifera*])	A wide range of birds is lured by insect-attracting flowers, berries, and nesting sites.	7'- to 9'-tall, multistemmed deciduous shrub with pointed, oval leaves that turn reddish purple in fall; deep red bark on young stems and clusters of white berries in winter	Grows in almost any soil, including wet places, in full sun to shade. Spreads by underground stems. Zones 2 to 8
Winged euonymus, burning bush (*Euonymus alata*)	Fruit-eating birds relish berries; many birds use it for nest sites and shelter.	10' or taller, deciduous shrub shaped like a large, flat-topped, mounded bush; brilliant red fall foliage; small dangling fruits have orange-red seed coats that peel away from red berries	Thrives almost anywhere, except waterlogged soil, in sun to full shade. Zones 4 to 9
Oregon grape holly (*Mahonia aquifolium*)	Insect- and fruit-eating birds are lured by insect-attracting flowers and berries; also offers shelter.	Evergreen 4'- to 6'-tall shrub with lustrous, hollylike leaves; clusters of bright yellow flowers; beautiful, blue-black berries	Grows in moist, well-drained, acidic soil; grows best in partial to full shade but tolerates sun if protected from drying winds. Zones 4 to 8
Common privet (*Ligustrum vulgare*)	Insect-eating birds are lured to insect-attracting flowers; provides shelter and nest sites.	Dense, semievergreen shrub 12' or taller, with small, leathery, dark green leaves and creamy flowers with strong aroma; birds ignore the shrub's black berries	Grows almost anywhere, except wet soil, in sun to shade. Zones 4 to 7
Weigela (*Weigela florida*)	Nectar-rich flowers attract hummingbirds; many birds use it for nesting sites.	Deciduous shrub, 6' to 9' tall, forms a wide, arching mound, with trumpet-shaped pink or red flowers in summer. Best grown in hedges because of its undistinguished shape.	Grows in well-drained soil, in full sun. Zones 4 to 9

Pruning Shrubs

Shearing shrubs is popular, but birds won't care whether your shrubs look neat and tidy. In fact they'll probably prefer shrubs that grow in their natural form. I don't prune my shrubs more than I absolutely have to. I remove dead and crossing branches, and occasionally I remove some branches from an older shrub to make its shape more open. Sometimes I cut off the lower branches of shrubs and shape the top into shorter, more compact branches to make a small tree out of a shrub.

Here are two simple rules to help you figure out when to prune: Prune shrubs that bloom in early spring (like forsythia and quince) soon after blooming, so that there's plenty of time for new branches to grow and form flower buds before next spring's flowering. Prune shrubs that bloom in summer (like weigela and butterfly bush) in late winter or early spring, and they'll bloom that same summer. But if you can't keep these rules straight, stick to pruning all your shrubs right after they flower and you won't go wrong.

SISKINS

Siskins are uncommonly tame backyard birds. You can walk right up to them, and they're easy to hand-tame at the feeder. Listen for their distinctive high-pitched *tit-a-tit* calls as they fly about the garden.

At close range it's easy to confuse these 4-inch, streaky brown birds with a female house finch—until they open their wings, that is. Then you can see patches of yellow in each wing and at the base of the tail.

In summer, pine siskins nest in Canada and Alaska and south to Mexico through the western mountain ranges. Their nests, built in the branches of coniferous trees, hold three to six brown-speckled, pale greenish blue eggs. In winter, siskins head south, showing up in every state of the lower 48.

Leave a patch of weeds like lamb's-quarters standing in winter to attract siskins. In spring, gone-to-seed dandelions will draw migrating siskins. They also like the seeds of birches, alders, and other trees. At the feeder they relish niger and sunflower seeds.

Pine siskins love the seeds of arborvitae, which they dig from the cones with painstaking effort. In winter, these active little birds often flock together in evergreens for food and shelter.

SNAKES

When it comes to their relationship with birds, snakes have a place at both ends of the food chain: They're predators, but they're prey as well.

Many snakes, including the beautiful green snakes that live in the treetops and the common garter snake, prefer to dine on insects or mice and pose no danger to birds. Nevertheless, a snake of any kind will probably frighten any bird that spots it. You can use this to your advantage if hungry birds are raiding your vegetable garden or berry bushes—even a fake snake spells danger to most birds and thus can make an effective bird deterrent.

Large tree-climbing snakes, such as the black snake, the blue racer, and the pilot black snake, are a major threat to nesting birds. They can climb a 50-foot tree with ease. If it isn't driven away by the parent birds and nearby allies, the snake will swallow any eggs or nestlings it can reach. The hog-nosed snake, which prefers to stay on the ground, is a danger to sparrows and other birds that nest in the grass.

Neighborhood Watch

Birds band together to drive off snakes. If you hear blue jays raising a ruckus, or the alarm calls of other birds, follow your ears to the commotion and watch the birds to see what has them so upset. Chances are your investigation will lead to the discovery of a climbing snake and a nest that you probably didn't even know was there. When a parent bird raises the alarm, all the other resident birds in the neighborhood will rush to join in the defense. Their efforts are often effective, causing the snake to retreat from the scene.

Sometimes, if the attack is intense and the snake feels in danger, it may lose its grip on the tree and suddenly drop to the ground. Once a snake finds a nest, though, it can be persistent, and unless the parents are vigilant, tragedy can result. Adult birds that are unwary or come too close become victims, too.

Snakes on the Menu

On the other side of the coin, some large birds eagerly devour small snakes. Snakes are among red-tailed hawks' favorite foods. Slithery snakes are also a delicacy to roadrunners, which pursue them with a burst of speed that can reach 18 miles per hour. The burrowing owl of southwestern deserts also occasionally dines on snakes.

SODA BOTTLES

Before you bag those plastic soda bottles for the recycling center, set a few aside to use for bird-attracting projects. I love working with soda bottles, because they're free, easy to cut to size, and adaptable for several purposes including nectar feeders and niger feeders. You can also use soda bottles as a squirrel deterrent by stringing them along a clothesline and then hanging your feeders from the line (this technique is illustrated on page 229).

Making a Nectar Feeder

A simple one-step project starts with a 2-liter soda bottle and a trip to the bird supply store, where you can find a plastic nectar feeder that simply screws onto the bottle. Hang the bottle upside down and you'll have a nectar feeder that will serve lots of hummingbirds before running dry. (If woodpeckers, house finches, or other thirsty birds have commandeered your hummingbird feeder, a few of these giant-size sugar-water bottles will keep them happy for days.)

Making a Niger Feeder

You can also make a decent niger feeder from an empty 2-liter soda bottle like the one shown at right. Though it won't last as long as a commercial feeder, a soda bottle feeder is a gratifying and simple project that will satisfy birds for the season.

To start, use a large nail to poke a ring of four holes in the bottle about 3 inches up from the bottom of the bottle. Make two of the four holes about ½ inch higher than the other two holes. Make a second set of four holes in a similar pattern about 5 inches above the first set.

Insert a ¼-inch-wide, 6-inch-long dowel through two opposing holes in the bottle. Do the same thing with three more dowels.

Using a small, sharp pocketknife, cut a small vertical slit above each hole. Make the hole about ⅛ inch high and very thin, so that the birds can grasp the tiny niger seeds and withdraw them one or two at a time. If you're not sure how big to make the holes, try checking the slits on a commercial tube feeder for comparison.

Fill the bottle with niger seed and screw the cap on tightly.

Wrap a length of florist's wire around the neck of the bottle several times and then fashion a loop in the end of the wire for hanging.

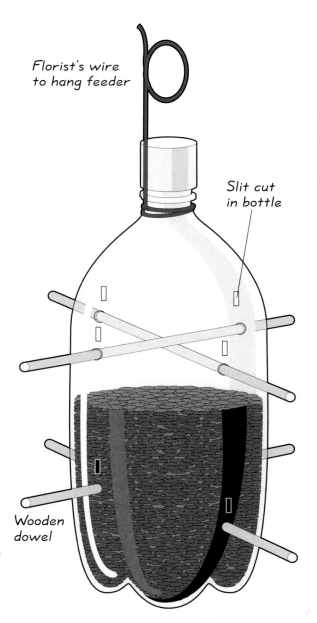

Florist's wire to hang feeder

Slit cut in bottle

Wooden dowel

A soda bottle feeder is one of the cheapest and easiest types of feeders to make. All you need to make a niger feeder from a soda bottle is some wooden dowels and florist's wire.

SONGBIRDS

If it sings and it's a bird, it must be a songbird, right? Not necessarily. To ornithologists, a "songbird" is a member of a grouping of birds they call the Passeriformes, or perching birds. Also known as "passerines," these birds are a diverse group. They vary in size from the imposing raven to the dainty tree swallow, live in all areas of the world, and may be insect eaters, seed eaters, fruit eaters, or meat eaters. But they have one thing in common: their feet. No, it's not a glass slipper that's the clue to these Cinderellas: It's the three-toes-front, one-toe-back arrangement that gives them their place in the world of birds.

The feet of perching birds are made for, well, perching. Ever wonder how a bird manages not to fall off its perch when sleeping? Their leg muscles and tendons are so specialized that they automatically tighten if the bird begins to lose its grip.

The passerines include some of the best singers in the bird world. Thrushes, wrens, and thrashers are legendary songsters, with beautiful voices and the ability to sing intricate melodies. But each of the species of perching birds has its own distinct vocals, and the beauty of the song is in the ear of the beholder. To many backyard birdwatchers, a chickadee's familiar cheery call is just as welcome as the most wonderful wood thrush serenade.

SPARROWS

Sparrows are charming little birds and a welcome addition to a backyard bird garden. While nearly every garden hosts sparrows, identifying which sparrow has come to visit is a challenge. Most types of sparrows look nearly alike, but you can tell them apart by their songs. Sparrows have incredibly diverse voices, from the insectlike buzz of the grasshopper sparrow to the lovely melody of the song sparrow and the plaintive *Old Sam Peabody, Peabody, Peabody* of the white throat. (By the way, give "Peabody" the Yankee pronunciation of "Peabiddy" to get the sparrow's rhythm right.)

Getting to Know Them

Except for a few striking exceptions, most sparrows are small, streaky brown birds, about 4½ to 5½ inches long. Males and females look alike. Native sparrows are generally reclusive birds, probably thanks

Even a small yard with only a single shade tree or a yew at the corner of the house can host a sparrow: the tiny chippy, or chipping sparrow.

Sparrows are a good friend to have in your garden. White-throated sparrows and their relatives consume bushels of seeds, especially those of weeds and grasses.

to their position near the bottom of the food chain. They're favored prey of kestrels and other hawks, as well as of roaming cats. Native sparrows usually hide in brush or weeds; they rarely sit out in the open long enough for you to tick off the field marks that give a sure clue to their identity. Just when you're checking the tail for length or sorting out the head stripes, the bird flits back into sheltering cover—just another LBB, or "little brown bird," as bird-watchers call them.

Most sparrows shun deep woods, preferring meadows and fields or shrub plantings and hedgerows. They spend much of their time on the ground, where their streaky coloration blends in with their surroundings. Spotting sparrows takes patience and a quick

eye with the binoculars. To watch sparrows, sit in a comfortable place near brush or tall grass or weeds and stay motionless. Before long, you'll hear quiet *chip!* calls coming from the vegetation, and eventually a bird will flit into view. Persevere with the wait-'em-out technique and the bird will finally show enough of itself for you to figure out what it is. If sparrows are reluctant to come out of hiding, try making squeaky noises by sucking on the back of your hand, or purse your lips and say *psh, psh, psh:* They may be curious enough to investigate.

Sparrows tuck their grassy cupped nests in places you may pass by every day: Strawberry patches, beds of mint, and plantings of pachysandra or other groundcovers are favorite nesting sites. Built low or on the ground, their nests are easy targets for raccoons, opossums, cats, dogs, and other predators. Most sparrows lay four or five creamy white to pale green eggs liberally speckled and splashed with brown.

Sparrows by Habitat

Which native sparrows you have in your backyard depends on two things: the habitat you provide, and the part of the country in which you live. Here's a guide to sparrows and their habitats.

◆ A meadow garden, weedy field, or patch of prairie wildflowers and grasses in just about any area may host grasshopper, savannah, and vesper sparrows.
◆ Add a few shrubs in the field, and you invite the song sparrow.
◆ Plant a hedgerow along the field and you've got the right conditions for white-crowned and tree sparrows, or lark sparrows west of the Mississippi.

◆ Change the grassy field to sagebrush, and the Brewer's sparrow feels at home.

The cast of characters in a sparrow-friendly backyard changes with the seasons, just as with other songbirds. Most sparrows have separate ranges for winter and summer. Plump, cinnamon-colored fox sparrows, for instance, may spend the fall and winter in southern backyards, but come spring they move to nesting grounds north of the Mason-Dixon line.

A few sparrows, including the common song sparrow, appear in their range year-round. The birds you see in winter, however, are most likely not the same birds that nest there in summer; they're usually birds who summered farther north and have moved southward for the cold months.

Attracting Sparrows

Leave a weedy or unmown grassy area in a corner of your yard to shelter a variety of sparrows. These little birds peck at pigweed, goldenrod, ragweed, foxtail grass, and other common weeds, from the time the seeds ripen on through winter. At the feeder, sparrows enjoy the small, nutritious seeds of millet.

The English Invader

The most common sparrow, the house sparrow (once called the English sparrow), is an imported bird that belongs to a different family than the 30 or so species of native sparrows that roam the United States. Brought to America about 1850, house sparrows have gained a reputation as a nuisance across America. They're found everywhere from big cities to farmyards, where they hang out in noisy flocks, constantly cheeping and squabbling.

House sparrows are notorious for displacing bluebirds and purple martins from their nest holes or nest boxes, and building nests there for themselves. They also build freestanding nests in hawthorns and other small trees. Their nests are immense globes of sticks, grasses, string, strips of plastic and paper, feathers, cigarette butts, and anything else the birds can find.

There's no way to get rid of house sparrows, so you may as well learn to enjoy them. You can discourage them from visiting feeders by offering only large striped sunflower seed, which they have a hard time cracking. If you decide to welcome them, try putting out bread, cracked corn, millet, and other small seeds.

JUST FOR SPARROWS

■ In the flower garden, plant zinnias, bachelor's-button, cosmos, sunflowers, and other annuals with abundant seeds to attract sparrows.

■ Naturalistic plantings, such as meadow and prairie gardens, will also draw sparrows to your backyard bird habitat to feast on their bounty of seeds.

■ Step carefully if you venture off the paths of your meadow garden during nesting season. Sparrows often hide their tiny nests in tall grass.

■ House sparrows bothering your bluebird houses? Try mounting a martin house, or an A-frame-type nesting box with two or three rows of apartment cubicles under the eaves of a garage or shed. The sparrows may prefer using it, and leave your bluebird boxes alone.

Spring Almanac

Birdwatchers know that spring arrives long before the first robin makes its grand entrance. The new season is ushered in by owls, titmice, and chickadees, whose fancies turn to love even before winter gives its final gasp. If you're lucky enough to have a patch of woods in your yard or nearby, start listening in late winter for the deep-throated booming hoots of great horned owls, which begin raising a family in February or even earlier.

Closer to home, tune your ear to the high-pitched whines of chickadees and titmice. The screechiness of these love calls makes some people cringe. Both titmice and chickadees have other love songs up their sleeves, and they start singing even before the first pussy willow breaks free of its brown shell. Whenever I hear the clear *pe-ter! pe-ter!* whistle of the tufted titmouse, my heart lifts, because I know spring is on the way no matter what the thermometer says.

At the Feeder

Breakfast at the feeder window is always an adventure in spring. One day you may find a rose-breasted grosbeak, resplendent in snow white, shining black, and crimson breeding plumage, cracking sunflower seeds; the next morning, brilliant indigo buntings may sparkle in the sunlight. These bird-feeding hints are sure to please spring visitors.

◆ Put out the hummingbird feeder for early arrivals. Look for them when spring-blooming red flowers like wild columbine, flowering quince, or red flowering currant begin to blossom.
◆ Stock up on soft foods for insect eaters that return in spring. Mealworms are a welcome treat for bluebirds. Suet is a favorite with many birds, including yellow-rumped warblers. Blackbirds, robins, and jays will appreciate bread.
◆ Freshen up the area below your feeders with a 2-inch layer of bark mulch to cover the winter's accumulation of seed hulls.
◆ If a late snowstorm hits your area, stock up with bread, and head out in your car. Leave pieces of bread along the road near hedgerows where robins are sheltering. Include some dark bread so it's easily visible from a distance or to a bird flying overhead. Robins and some other birds need soft foods, and the lifesaving bread holds them over until the snow melts.

In the Garden

Of course spring will find you planting annual flowers, which birds will enjoy in summer (because of the insects) and fall (for the seeds). But there are other spring gardening activities that are fun for you and good for the birds.

◆ Now's the time to add a garden bench—or another one—so that you can sit in the thick of things with your morning cup of tea and your binoculars at the ready. Watch for motion among the branches and stems, and don't forget to watch for secretive birds, like wood thrushes, fox sparrows, and towhees, that stay low to the ground in thick shrubbery.
◆ Offer a reliable source of water in your garden—it's one of the best ways to attract birds. Spring is a good time to add a small pool, a bubbling spring, or other water feature.
◆ Have a little fun with mud: Create a nice sloppy puddle for robins, swallows, and other birds to use in nest building. Create a nice sloppy mud puddle for birds to use in nest building, as shown on page 170.
◆ Drape short lengths of white string over your shrubs for orioles, and scatter white feathers, dog combings, or other soft materials. Birds will pick them up to line a cozy nest.

◆ Don't plant just flowers! Berry bushes, evergreens, and other shrubs and trees for food and shelter top the list for a bird-friendly garden.

◆ Early spring is the time to put up more birdhouses or nesting shelves so there's plenty of prime real estate waiting and ready when wrens, phoebes, and woodpeckers are looking for a home.

The Spring Scene

When days begin to lengthen and spring migration starts, you'll spot delightful surprises as migrants filter through the garden. In spring you never know who you might find at the feeder, the garden pool, or among the grasses and shrubs in the garden.

Migrating birds like warblers are quick to take advantage of a welcoming yard, especially if it offers a bounty of food, a ready pool of fresh water, and sheltering shrubs and grasses for a safe rest from traveling. While it's exciting to spot unusual migrants, you'll also enjoy seeing familiar friends returning, too, like the pair of bluebirds that adopted a nesting box in your yard the year before.

Remember to raise your eyes now and then to catch birds on the wing. Look overhead to catch a host of wood warblers and vireos flitting through the tender new leaves of oaks and maples. If you haven't already, now's a good time to start keeping notes on your bird sightings. Compare your notes from year to year. Birds are amazingly punctual: They often show up on the exact same day, year after year.

Love on the Wing

By midspring, courtship maneuvers are happening everywhere you look. Male and female birds are pairing off, and behavior is changing as males begin performing dances and songs to show off for their lady loves.

Watch for the mourning doves that nibbled millet all winter at the feeder to begin billing and cooing, with head bobbing and bowing that can go on for hours. Birds that once shared the yard and feeders in friendly groups, like cardinals, jays, and chickadees, turn territorial in spring as they claim nesting areas. Look for skirmishes as male birds chase each other from their own territories.

It's great to be alive in spring, and birds proclaim it every morning with a waterfall of song that begins even before the sun peeks above the horizon. Set your alarm for the ungodly hour of 4:30 A.M. and sit outdoors in the middle of the concert hall. See how many singers you can identify before the chorus melds into a multitude of voices.

Nesting birds appreciate extra supplies for building and lining their homes. Offer short pieces of string and yarn, pet hair, dried grass, twigs, and straw—and watch doves, robins, orioles, and other birds choose their favorite items.

SQUIRRELS

Squirreling away food for a rainy day—or a lean winter—is an admirable habit, but it's hard to admire squirrels when they're hauling off your expensive birdseed.

While dealing with thieving squirrels can be one of the frustrating parts of bird-watching, there are lots of innovative gadgets and devices for outwitting these bushy-tailed rascals. Many a penny has been invested in so-called squirrel-proof feeders, with varying degrees of success and frustration. Some work well for just a short time—hungry squirrels are clever squirrels—while others offer reasonably good feeder protection on a long-term basis.

But squirrel watching is fun, too. "If you can't beat 'em, you may as well learn to love 'em" could be the best motto for dealing with backyard squirrels. Although squirrels don't exactly eat like birds, their antics are worth their weight in dried corn, which just happens to be the most economical treat you can offer the bushytails in your neighborhood.

Feeding Squirrels

Once you start feeding squirrels, you'll discover that they eat fast! To slow down their greedy corn consumption, push whole cobs of corn onto stout nails, so they have to nibble it off the cob (you can make a nail feeder like the one shown in the illustration on this page).

If you're feeding more than a couple of animals, buy your corn in quantity at a feed mill. Cracked corn is one of the cheapest feeds available, costing just a fraction of sunflower seeds. Squirrels will eagerly eat it from a tray feeder. I've found that as long as I keep the corn feeders stocked, the squirrels rarely bother the bird feeders. Of course, the pres-

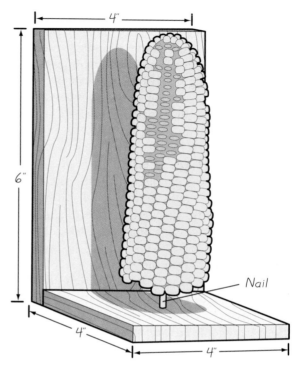

To make a corn feeder, hammer a large nail through a 4-inch-square piece of 2 × 4 board. Fasten on a second piece of board for a backboard that you can mount on a pole or tree.

ence of two squirrel-chasing dogs helps, too: The squirrels prefer to eat at their feeder near the getaway trees.

Squirrel Slowdowns

If squirrels are raiding too many of your feeders too often, try some of these tactics to save your birdseed for the birds.

◆ Mount your feeder on a smooth metal pole surrounded by a metal baffle. One type of ingenious sliding baffle has a sleeve below it that slides downward, baffle and all, when the squirrel grabs on and tries to climb it.

◆ Put a dome-shaped plastic baffle over a feeder.

◆ Make sure your feeders are more than a squirrel's-leap away from any overhanging tree branches, eaves, or other launching areas.

◆ Try a tube feeder within a metal cage. The cage keeps squirrels out while the space between the bars allows finches, chickadees, and other small birds to pass in and out.

◆ Removing the bottom spill tray from hanging tube feeders makes it harder for squirrels to hang on.

Undercover Squirrels

When your bird feeder is mysteriously emptied at night, the list of suspects is a short one: raccoon, opossum, or flying squirrel. Flying squirrels are endearing little critters with huge dark eyes, delicate features, and flat 4-inch tails that aren't at all like their daytime relatives' fluffy brushes. Folds of skin that stretch between front and back legs open like parachutes when these animals execute their graceful, soaring leaps.

To reveal whether flying squirrels are raiding your feeder under cover of darkness, set up a stakeout. Shine a strong flashlight beam on the feeder every half-hour or so, especially between 10:00 P.M. and midnight. You'll probably see a palm-size squirrel in the feeder, eagerly eating birdseed.

The Dark Side of Squirrels

Unfortunately squirrels don't dine exclusively on nuts, corn, and birdseed. Squirrels also rob bird nests of eggs and sometimes nestlings. All the nesting birds in the neighborhood will join together to try to drive off a squirrel when it threatens a nest.

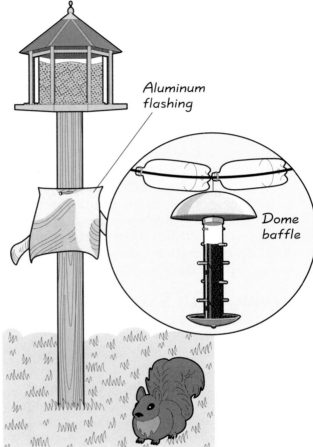

Aluminum flashing

Dome baffle

To foil squirrels, hang a bird feeder from a clothesline that has plastic soda bottles strung on it. A plastic dome mounted over the feeder helps too. For pole-mounted feeders, use aluminum flashing to make a baffle that squirrels can't climb over.

If your neighborhood is overrun by squirrels, you may worry about whether birds will survive. Don't worry; balance usually returns quickly—squirrels are at the prey end of the food chain, too. Owls and hawks savor these plump critters.

STARLINGS

Starlings didn't ask to come to America. They were released in the United States in the late 1800s in a misguided attempt to introduce all the birds mentioned in the works of Shakespeare.

Welcome or not, these unwanted immigrant birds aren't going to go away. Like house sparrows and house finches, starlings have managed to thrive outside their native region. Their range covers all of North America, and they flock in numbers that can reach the tens of thousands.

Not only are starlings a little too numerous, they're also messy, noisy, and not particularly pretty. Add their harsh calls and screeching cries and you have a package that's not easy for a backyard birdwatcher to love.

Coping with Starlings

Since starlings are here to stay, we may as well learn to appreciate them. Their love songs aren't as melodious as the musical notes of a wood thrush or robin, but starlings are just as enthusiastic as any spring singer. Cousins of the myna, starlings are also excellent mimics that can imitate the whistle you use to call your dog, as well as other birds' songs.

Starling plumage has a subtle beauty that changes with the seasons. In spring and summer, their feathers are black with gleaming purple and green highlights. In winter, starlings show light-colored flecks at the tip of each body feather, like a field of stars scattered on the dark plumage. One glance at a starling beak will tell you the season as sure as any calendar: Dark in fall and winter, their beak changes to bright yellow in spring and summer.

Starlings nest in cavities and will quickly adopt a bird box. They're also quick to take over holes made by flickers or other birds, perching nearby while the woodpeckers do

the excavation work, then moving in as soon as the homemaker turns its back. The solution? Add more birdhouses to your garden so there's a place for everybody.

A Starling Menu

Starlings like open areas, especially lawn, where they can waddle about searching for grubs. One plunge of that sharp, pointy beak and another future Japanese beetle is history. To their credit, starlings dine on garden pests other than grubs as well. They're also the main predator of the clover weevil, and they munch down bunches of beetles and cutworms.

At the feeder, starlings gobble millet, bread, and just about any other soft foods. They love berry bushes, too. Dry dog food or chicken scratch are economical choices if you're hosting a lot of starlings. If starlings hog your suet feeder, simply add more feeders for your other feathered visitors.

No matter where you live, you'll probably play host to starlings. While they're not the prettiest of backyard birds, they do help out by dining on Japanese beetle grubs and cutworms.

STUMPS AND SNAGS

A tree stump is one of the best bird attractants you can have in your garden. Dead wood is a favored site for nest holes, and it's also a banquet table for birds. Of course you'll want to remove any hazardous dead branches that dangle over pathways, lawn, or your house, but an upright dead tree poses little danger and makes a great birdwatching spot.

Working with Wood

Soft, rotted snags (standing dead trees) are perfect for construction work when a beak is your only tool. Woodpeckers, chickadees, titmice, and bluebirds all favor a snag for home building, and wood ducks, owls, and squirrels may sublet holes for their nests.

The larvae of beetles and other insects are often tucked inside the wood of stumps and snags, providing great snacks for woodpeckers. Carpenter ants and other adult insects make a meal for flickers, nuthatches, chickadees, the brown creeper, woodpeckers, and any other bird that happens along. When an old cottonwood tree in my town was cut down, robins feasted for weeks on the termites that were exposed at its stump.

Bringing in Dead Wood

If your garden doesn't have any dead wood in it, you can import some with the aid of strong-armed friends. Tree service companies are often willing to donate a big chunk of wood and may even deliver for a small fee. Keep your eye out, too, for trees being cleared along power lines or on construction sites. Major logs are often free for the asking. Use crowbars to maneuver the log into position in your garden.

"Planting" a Snag

If you want to "plant" a dead tree, have a tree-raising party and invite all your friends. To start, use a posthole digger to excavate a hole about a third of the length of the snag. Pour 4 inches of gravel into the bottom of the hole for drainage. Hoist the snag into position and fill the hole with a foot of soil.

With friends supporting the snag, fill the hole with dry quick-setting cement mix and add water as per the instructions. Use a hoe to smooth the cement into a mound sloping away from the snag at its center so that water doesn't collect around the wood. (Wash the hoe immediately afterward to remove cement residue.)

The snag should remain erect by itself, but if it shows a tendency to keel over, have all your friends lean against it, holding it erect until the cement sets, which will take only 10 minutes or so.

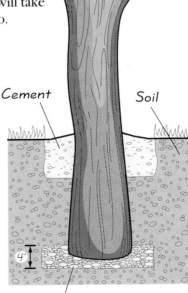

You can "plant" a section of dead tree in your yard, securing it in place with quick-setting cement. Woodpeckers, flickers, chickadees, and many other birds will come to feed or nest.

Cement *Soil*

Gravel

SUET

A chunk of suet in a net bag or wire cage is the ultimate low-maintenance bird feeder. You refill it only once every few weeks, you never need to scrub the feeder, and you can leave it in your yard year-round.

From a bird's point of view, suet is pretty perfect, too. Because their metabolism is set on fast-forward, birds never have to worry about eating too many calories. A ready supply of calories from solid suet helps birds conserve precious energy. That's important because birds use up tremendous amounts of calories in their never-ending search for insects, seeds, and other foods.

Feeding Suet

True suet is the white fat surrounding cow or sheep kidneys, but I use the term loosely to describe any kind of animal fat. You can buy suet in plastic-wrapped square packages that cost about a dollar and slip inside a commercial feeder so neatly that your fingers barely get greasy. But if you're feeding lots of suet eaters, it's more economical to buy suet by the pound at the meat counter of your supermarket.

Wire baskets are ideal for feeding suet, and they're available at home and garden centers for only a few dollars. You can also make your own suet feeders. A cheap, easy way to feed suet is to stuff fat trimmings into a plastic mesh onion bag. Tie the bag closed with a piece of string and hang it from a tree branch.

If you want to really pamper your birds, spread ground or chopped suet in a tray feeder. Suet or fat is easy to chop in a blender, food processor, or even a hand-crank meat grinder. Just freeze it until it's stiff but not solidly frozen to keep it from clogging the machine. Some supermarkets will grind suet for you.

A Feeder Favorite

Almost all birds will eat suet. Acrobatic types like chickadees, titmice, nuthatches, and woodpeckers feed easily from hanging suet feeders, and their beaks are strong enough to pound away at frozen suet. Bigger birds like mockingbirds and jays like a stationary chunk of suet that won't swing when they hammer it with their beaks.

Tuna can

Suet

Homemade suet feeders don't have to be fancy, but they do need to be sturdy. Try using a tuna can hung from a string, or drill holes in a small log and smear suet in the holes.

Ground-dwelling birds like sparrows and juncos that have weaker beaks appreciate ground or finely chopped suet in a tray feeder. I've noticed that bluebirds, robins, and other birds that aren't regular customers at the feeder are quick to spot the white pieces of chopped suet as well. My guess is that to birds, the suet bits look a lot like tasty grubs.

Suet for All Seasons

At the winter feeding station, suet can mean the difference between life and death for birds, especially when a sudden cold snap streaks in from the north. When a winter storm falls in my area, I chop up half-frozen hunks of suet with a sharp chef's knife and keep the feeders filled from early morning until the sun goes down. Birds also enjoy suet in spring, summer, and fall. Keep a suet feeder in a shady spot for summer feeding, so the fat doesn't melt in the sun. Suet can take on a less-than-appealing coating of black mold in summer, but the birds don't seem to mind.

A summer suet feeder will bring you one of the most delightful bonuses of feeding backyard birds. When the babies of your suet-feeding regulars leave the nest, one of their first stops will be your suet feeder. You may see young chickadees, nuthatches, woodpeckers, or titmice gathered for a serving of suet.

SUMAC

The lemony-tart berries of sumac are a favorite with birds, who gobble the berries straight from the branch. The tightly packed, cone-shaped berry clusters ripen to deep red in fall and stay on the plant through the winter, attracting thrushes, including bluebirds and robins, as well as starlings, mockingbirds, and sundry berry eaters.

Sumacs are perfect for a natural garden. These shrubs thrive in poor soil as well as fertile and grow well in full sun to part shade. They spread by the roots to form colonies, so give them plenty of room to roam.

Sumacs reach about 15 feet tall, and have bare stems at the base crowned with dense leafy branches. In fall, sumacs grab the garden spotlight with their flaming red leaves.

Experiment with sumacs that are native to your area, or try cold-hardy (Zones 3 to 8) staghorn sumac (*Rhus typhina*), named for its open, branching form and velvety branches. Smooth sumac (*R. glabra*) is extremely cold-hardy, growing in Zones 2 to 9. Shining sumac (*R. copallina*) has wonderful glossy leaves and grows in Zones 4 to 8.

Poison sumac (*R. vernix*) and poison oak (*R. radicans*) can cause severe dermatitis or produce poisonous berries, so be sure you know what you're planting.

Smooth sumac and other sumacs have dramatic foliage and red berries for the birds.

SUMMER ALMANAC

Early summer is family time for backyard birds. Parent birds actively search all nooks and crannies of the garden for insect morsels to feed their constantly demanding babies. Soon nestlings make the leap to fledglings, flying on a learner's permit as they learn the fine points of handling their wings.

Mid- to late summer is a transition time, as birds finish with raising families and migratory songbirds begin the changes and preparations needed for the long journey they face in the fall to their wintering range.

At the Feeder

Traffic at your bird feeders slows down in summer, mostly because birds have plenty of natural foods to eat, and because they don't require as much food during warm summer days as they do during cold winters and the hectic spring nesting season.

◆ Now's a good opportunity to scrub the feeders with a weak bleach solution (1 part bleach to 10 parts water) and let them dry in the purifying sun.

◆ Continue feeding birds, but cut down on the amount of seed you put out so it stays fresh. Even the best sunflower seed can't compare with a nice fat caterpillar or ripe dandelion seeds.

◆ Check stored seed in cans or bags weekly for signs of bug problems. Throw out infested seed in the trash to prevent perpetuating problems.

◆ Clean hummingbird feeders thoroughly every time you refill.

◆ The birdbath or garden pool may draw more birds than the feeders. Keep it brimming full with fresh water. Clean it frequently as shown in the illustration below.

In the Garden

Summer is a great time for birdwatching. Find a shady spot where you can sit with your binoculars and enjoy the abundant birdlife in your garden.

◆ To locate nests, listen for the rhythmic peeps of baby birds (Baltimore orioles are especially noisy) as you stroll the garden or sit

Use a plastic dish scrubber to keep your birdbath in an appealing condition. Don't use harsh cleansers—just put a handful of sand in the bottom of the bath to provide a natural abrasive when you scrub.

quietly on a bench, and watch for the parents carrying food.

◆ Take inventory of nesting birds in your backyard, and write down nests and locations, along with nesting dates, in a notebook so that you can compare it from year to year. Maps of your yard are fun to draw, too, and kids love to help.

◆ Some birds, including doves, robins, and chipping sparrows, nest more than once a year. They may reuse the first nest or build a new one, so continue putting out nesting materials.

◆ Watch for birds, like tanagers, grosbeaks, and orioles, that usually stay in the treetops to come down to garden level for caterpillars and other insects.

◆ Don't be too quick to adopt an "orphan." Many birds leave the nest before they can fly, hiding in shrubbery or garden undergrowth for a few days until their wings are ready.

◆ On rainy days, watch for baby birds to leave the nest. I think the parents know that wet weather keeps prowling house cats and other predators away, and encourage the birds to leave home.

◆ Enjoy the bounty of volunteer sunflowers planted courtesy of the birds.

◆ Fix yourself a tall, cool glass of iced tea and park the chaise lounge under a mulberry or wild cherry tree or beside a patch of elderberries, blueberries, raspberries, or blackberries. Morning, afternoon, or evening, you can enjoy the scene as vireos, grosbeaks, tanagers, orioles, and other birds feast on summer fruits.

Change of Seasons

In midsummer, when late nesters like goldfinches and cedar waxwings are still working on weaving their nests, other birds

---

Looking Up to Birds

For a wonderful new perspective, try birdwatching from a hammock beneath some big trees in your backyard. Sink a couple of 4 × 4s into the ground to hang the hammock from, then lie back in it and relax. You won't believe how much activity goes on over your head that you never noticed! Birds chase each other through the trees, hunt down insects with single-minded focus, collect spider silk for their nests, weave grasses and twigs into snug homes on branches overhead, and even carry out courtship rituals in the branches above you.

---

are already beginning to congregate in pre-migration flocks. Watch for swallows perching on utility wires in ever-growing groups, and flocks of grackles and other blackbirds crossing the sky before sunset.

Plumage changes take place as birds undergo "post-nuptial molt" after the breeding season. It's fun to try to identify feathers that you find in your yard (but don't keep a collection of found feathers—possessing a bird, nest, egg, feather, or any other part of a bird protected by the Migratory Bird Treaty is a federal offense).

Enjoy a last concert of morning bird song. As birds' hormone levels change after nesting, they sing less and less. By late summer, very few birds are still singing, especially in the heat of the day.

SUNFLOWERS

Sunflowers are the number one plant for a bird-friendly backyard. They're easy to grow, and birds will begin feasting on the seeds while the sunflowers are still blooming—as soon as the meaty kernels plump up. Cardinals, jays, finches, buntings, sparrows, chickadees, woodpeckers, grosbeaks, nuthatches, and titmice will harvest the seeds for months. At season's end, you can harvest sunflower heads and hang them from a porch post for birds to eat, or use them to make festive bird treats like the ones shown on page 76. Sunflowers can be tall, proud giants, with stems as thick as your wrist and dinner-plate-size seedheads that bow under their own weight. But there are plenty of other members of the sunflower tribe, including tough perennials and a host of annuals with both single-stemmed and branching forms, and white, russet, or two-tone flowers as well as the classic sunny yellow.

Sunflowers Galore

Sunflowers thrive in well-drained soil and full sun, and the perennial types can also take part shade. Sow annual sunflowers (*Helianthus annuus* and *H. debilis*) every few weeks from spring to early summer to supply seeds for birds from midsummer through late fall. Giant-flowered cultivars like 'Gray Stripe' are great along a fence line or bordering the veggie patch. For fun and variety, try heirloom sunflowers, like white-seeded 'Tarahumara White'. 'Autumn Beauty' hybrids are winners with branching stems and mixed russet, bicolor, and gold flowers. Shorter types like 'Floristan' with its pinwheels of russet and gold are perfect for the foreground of a sunflower patch.

Only a few of the many species of perennial sunflowers are available for sale at garden centers or through mail-order companies. Most perennial sunflowers spread enthusiastically, so plant them in a naturalistic garden or a meadow. They bloom from midsummer to as late as November in my Zone 6 garden. Free-running Maximilian sunflower (*H. maximilianii*) and clump-forming saw-toothed sunflower (*H. grosseserratus*) are two of my favorites. Maximilian's blossoms cluster along the top 18 inches or so of its tall, willowy stems, while each stem of saw-toothed sunflower holds arching bouquets of blooms above its deep green foliage. Both grow 8 feet tall in my garden, even without any fertilizer.

A sunflower garden is a great living bird feeder. Plant short bushy sunflowers in the front of the bed to screen the bare lower stems of traditional tall sunflowers.

SWALLOWS

Swallows are the Ferraris of the bird world. Lean back and look up on any day in summer and you're apt to see these streamlined birds dipping and gliding above your head, even if you live in the city. The swallows that swarm across every corner of the country are super insect eaters. Without them, we'd be plagued with hordes of mosquitoes, giant clouds of gnats, and enough flies to make any picnic miserable. Swallows also snatch up countless beetles and other insects.

Getting to Know Them

Swallows are built for speed and maneuvering, with long, pointed wings and slender bodies. Most are about 5 inches long; the barn swallow is 6 inches. Males and females look alike. Their short legs and weak feet aren't built for perching in leafy treetops; that's why you'll usually see swallows congregating on roadside utility wires or other open sitting spots. Their legs aren't built for walking, either: Swallows rarely come to the ground except to gather mud for nest building. They eat and drink on the wing, darting after insects and swooping down to skim a beakful of water from ponds and puddles. Their songs are high-pitched twitters, *kvit-kvit-kvit*, or buzzy twitters.

Attracting Swallows

A large pond may attract these birds to your yard, and tree swallows and violet-green swallows will readily accept birdhouses with a 1½-inch entrance hole. A big mud puddle can tempt nest-building swallows into landing in your yard. Create it in an open area where the birds can easily get airborne. Soft white breast feathers of chickens or ducks, scattered on open lawn, are another temptation that the birds find hard to resist during spring nest building.

Swallow Checklist

You'll see this insect-eating tribe of birds mostly in the air. Swallows generally live in colonies that can range from a few pairs to dozens of birds.

Barn swallow. Midnight blue barn swallows, with their rusty orange underparts and deeply forked tails, range across North America. They nest in barns or outbuildings near farms, plastering a deep cup of mud to beams or doorsills. Straw, dried grass, and horsehair strengthen the nest, and a soft layer of white feathers keeps the four or five white eggs cozy.

Cliff swallow. Cliff swallows, which also range across the country, look like barn swallows, with a bright rusty orange rump and light-colored collar on the back of the neck. They glue their bulbous mud nests in groups

Barn swallows are deep blue on top with a rusty orange underside. These insect eaters play an important role in controlling flies, beetles, and other pests.

under sheltering layers of cliffs, under bridges and dams, or on adobe or stucco buildings.

Tree swallow. Tree swallows are shining deep green on top with snowy white underparts. They are common in most of the United States, except for the southern parts. They like to nest near water. If you have an inviting pond nearby, you may find these cavity nesters adopting your bluebird boxes.

Violet-green swallow. Gleaming green wings, a purple head and tail, and pure white underparts make this the beauty queen of swallows. West of the Great Plains, the beautiful violet-green swallow is a common sight, especially in the mountains; it also appears in some towns. It's another cavity nester that will readily take to a birdhouse if a dead tree isn't available.

SWIFTS

From the first light of dawn to the last rays of twilight, swifts are in the air. These agile, cigar-shaped birds not only eat and drink on the wing, they also court their mates and collect sticks for nests while in flight. Considering that some species of swifts fly at up to 200 miles per hour, their in-air abilities are truly remarkable.

Swifts are from 5 to 7 inches long, but their wingspan is about 1 foot. It's easy to recognize their "cigar on wings" silhouette in flight. Swift voices are as energetic as their lifestyles: They call in twittering bursts of high, rapid *chips*.

If you live east of the Missouri River, you'll see chimney swifts, which range from Canada to Florida. They're deep gray above and below. Their beaks are tiny, but they're hinged to open wide, acting like a scoop for catching insects as they fly.

West of the Great Plains, white-throated swifts and the less common Vaux's swift take over where the chimney swift leaves off. Vaux's swift looks much like a chimney swift with lighter-colored underparts. The white-throated swift has striking white markings on its sides and throat that make a bold contrast with the rest of its black plumage. White-throated swifts nest in crevices of cliffs and buildings; Vaux's swifts look for chimneys or tall hollow trees.

Swifts glue their crude stick nests to walls or cliffs with sticky saliva. If you have an uncapped chimney that's not lined with a slick metal liner, chimney swifts may use it as a nesting place. Long-established colonies number in the hundreds, even thousands. Other than a hospitable chimney, the insects in the air over your yard are the only thing that will attract swifts.

Chimney swifts may follow the light shining up a chimney at night and land on your hearth. If they do, carry them outside and launch them with a gentle upward toss.

TANAGERS

Tanagers look like they'd be more at home in a rain forest than a backyard bird garden. These birds have brilliant red, crimson, or yellow-and-red feathers. Even so, they're a common visitor to wooded areas in North America in spring and summer. In winter, they retreat to Costa Rica, South America, and other warm areas.

Getting to Know Them

Tanagers have large but thin and pointed beaks that identify them as insect and fruit eaters. Tanagers range from 6 to 7 inches long, and are tree dwellers that don't often come down to our eye level. Unless you spend a lot of time birdwatching from a hammock, it's easy to overlook them. I used to think tanagers were rare birds indeed, but that was before I learned to identify them by their hoarse, robinlike song.

The male scarlet tanager is brighter than the best bottle of red nail polish, with gleaming black wings and tail for accent. As with other tanagers, the female is olive drab fading to yellow. Scarlet tanagers range across the eastern half of the continent, keeping to deciduous woods or mixed oak and pine woods. Like other tanagers, they place a shallow, loosely built saucer-shaped nest made of twigs, small roots, grasses, and other materials out on a tree limb. They lay three or four pale blue or green eggs speckled or splotched with brown.

Summer tanagers are red (verging on crimson) over their entire body. They are common across the southern third of the country, ranging as far north as the Great Lakes in the eastern half. The hepatic tanager is also all red, but it appears only in the mountain canyons of the Southwest.

In the West, the tanager to look for in conifers or aspens is, naturally enough, the western tanager. This bird has a bright red head, goldfinch yellow body, and black wings and tail. Bold white bars accent the wings.

Attracting Tanagers

Tanagers enjoy fruit, so plant grapes, cherries, mulberries, serviceberries, Virginia creeper, and dogwoods to attract them. In fall, tanagers often feed in groups on berry plants.

At the feeder, tempt tanagers with bread and doughnuts, mealworms, or chopped bananas. They also appreciate a spread of peanut butter mixed with cornmeal to make a crumbly dough. The sound of water will lure tanagers. I loop a hose over a branch above my low clay-saucer birdbath to create a slow drip that attracts their attention.

The female scarlet tanager (back) is less colorful than her mate, but this helps hide her as she sits on her nest in a dogwood or shade tree.

TERRITORY AND RANGE

Birds can't build fences, but they do stake out territories that they'll defend against invaders. During the nesting season, all songbirds establish a breeding territory for themselves and their mate. They don't allow any other birds of their own species to cross its boundaries. Male birds assert their ownership by singing along the borders of their little piece of the world. They quickly rush to the attack should a trespasser step—or fly—over the line.

You'd be surprised how many birds can set up overlapping territories in your yard. While your yard may only be big enough to host one pair of robins, it may also host a pair of blue jays, mourning doves, indigo buntings, and cardinals. For examples of where birds like these might set up home base, see the illustration on the opposite page.

Fighting for Food

Birds can also get territorial over a source of food. Hummingbirds may defend a single hanging basket of nectar-rich fuchsias, driving off any bird at all that blunders near. In winter, the resident mockingbird in my neighborhood claims the red-berried deciduous holly bushes in my front yard as his own—and sometimes he also claims the bird feeder, even though he rarely eats there. Even blue jays take flight in a hurry when the mocker swoops upon them in a rage.

The size of a bird's territory depends mainly on the ease of finding food. Red-tailed hawks may claim 300 acres as their territory, whereas a song sparrow may need as little as half an acre. No matter what the size of the territory, the bird regularly patrols its borders to keep up defenses.

Ruling the Roost

Keeping snug at night is a priority in cold-winter areas, and some birds may get feisty about sharing a roosting hole. Downy and hairy woodpeckers, which work hard to excavate a special sleeping hole separate from their nesting hole, return to the same place night after night. After all that work, it's every woodpecker for himself. Other birds that roost in a pile of warm feathered bodies, like bluebirds, don't mind sharing their space with others; the more, the cozier.

A territory may be temporary, its defenses forsaken after nesting is over. Territories can also change their boundaries from season to season. If food is scarce, a bird may expand to a larger area to fill its needs; if competing birds move into the area, a breeding territory may shrink under the pressure of the newcomers.

Roaming the Range

Range is the word used to describe the area that a bird lives in or hunts in, but which it doesn't defend against others, of its own species or other species. In winter, for instance, chickadees band together in flocks and roam the woods to forage together. Generally, a bird's range in this sense is larger than its defended territory, which may be limited to the area immediately around the nest.

Range can also refer to the entire region in which a species of bird is found. For example, the nesting or summer range of the wood thrush is from South Dakota to Maine, south to Texas and northern Florida; its winter range is mainly from South Texas and Mexico to Panama. Nesting range can overlap winter range, or be entirely separate.

Breeding Territories around the Yard

1. **Oak tree with nest box**: *Scarlet tanager, Baltimore oriole, red-eyed vireo, blue jay, chipping sparrow, downy woodpecker*

2. **Red maple**: *Yellow-shafted flicker (in nest box), least flycatcher or cedar waxwing (on high branch), rose-breasted grosbeak, goldfinch (on low branch)*

3. **Woodland garden**: *Mourning dove, wood thrush, rufous-sided towhee, ovenbird, veery, song sparrow*

4. **Water garden**: *Yellow warbler (in pussy willow tree), red-winged blackbird or common yellowthroat (in rushes)*

5. **Perennial border**: *Field sparrow, indigo bunting, common yellowthroat, bluebird (in nest box by open lawn), house wren*

6. **Rosebush**: *Song sparrow (low in bush), brown thrasher (higher in bush)*

7. **Lilac bush**: *Robin*

8. **Conifer shrub**: *Cardinal, chipping sparrow* **Spruce or fir**: *Grackle, house finch, robin, mourning dove*

9. **Bramble patch**: *Indigo bunting, chestnut-sided warbler, field sparrow*

10. **Grape arbor**: *Catbird, yellow-billed cuckoo*

THRASHERS

Thrashers look like they were put together by the designer that created the tail-fin cars of the '50s: Their tails are ludicrously long, and their beaks are equally outrageous. Voice-wise, the birds exaggerate, too. Thrashers believe in saying things not just once, but at least twice: *shuck it, shuck it; plow it, plow it; hoe it, hoe it* is one of the simpler translations of their call.

Getting to Know Them

Thrashers are big birds (about 10 inches long), beating their relative the mockingbird by at least an inch of tail feather. Look for thrashers on the ground searching for food, or perched in shrubbery or small trees. A great friend to gardeners, thrashers eat lots of pests: Japanese beetles, June beetles, grubs, rose beetles, tent caterpillars, cutworms, and many more. They're also fond of berries, small fruits, salamanders, lizards, and snakes.

Watch for thrashers pulling off dead leaves of fine-textured grasses, such as fescues and fountain grass, or collecting twigs to use in building their large, bulky cupped nest. Eggs are blue-green, usually with fine spots of brown.

Attracting Thrashers

Attract thrashers to your garden with berry plants, such as hollies, brambles, and blueberries. These birds also enjoy the fruits of cacti, strawberries, and figs, and the nuts of hazels and oaks. At the feeder, scatter bread crumbs on the ground. Keep the birdbath filled, too; thrashers are fond of a splashing good time.

Thrasher Checklist

Among the various species, there's a thrasher in almost every part of the country. In winter, the western species retreat to the Southwest, while the brown thrasher heads for the southern third of the United States, from Texas east.

Brown thrasher. The brown thrasher ranges over the eastern two-thirds of the country. It lives in brushy thickets, at woods' edges, or in well-shrubbed backyards. Males and females look alike: rich cinnamon colored on top with a streaked white breast and a gleaming golden eye. The long tail widens at the tip.

Other thrashers. In the sagebrush country of the West, the sage thrasher makes its home. This bird has a shorter tail and a more modest beak than other thrashers. At the other extreme are the California thrasher, the curve-billed thrasher, Le Conte's thrasher, and the Crissal thrasher. These birds have enormous down-curving beaks and long tails. Each of these grayish tan thrashers occupies particular habitats, from fertile valleys to sparse desert scrub.

Like its relatives, the brown thrasher feeds mostly on the ground. It "thrashes" about with its long, down-curved bill in leafy debris to find beetles and other morsels.

THRUSHES

It's easy to overlook thrushes—until they open their beaks to sing. Then out pours the most beautiful music in birddom. More easily heard than seen, thrushes are quiet-colored birds that tend to sneak about near ground level. Their brown backs and spotted breasts blend right in with the plants and leaf litter on the forest floor, where they spend their time looking for insects or berries.

Getting to Know Them

Thrushes are robin-size birds of forests and woodland that spend most of their time on the ground. Except for the gorgeous gold-and-blue varied thrush, these birds are varying hues of brown, from vivid chestnut to rich umber, with snowy white bellies freckled at the throat and breast with dark brown spots. Males and females look alike.

Renowned songsters, thrushes (including the most common one—the robin) are among the first to greet the day in the morning and the last to sing it to sleep at dusk. If you hear a bird singing a lovely solo at twilight, after the last notes of sparrows and other birds have died away, you can bet it's a thrush.

Robins have a pretty song, but the thrushes of the woodland, including the hermit thrush and the veery, are the best singers. Their voices are rich and clear, and their songs rise and fall like flowing water. There are thrushes in all parts of the United States in the summer. In winter, most thrushes depart for Central and South America.

Most thrushes build their nests on the ground, concealing them under small trees, shrubs, or clumps of ferns. The nests are bulky, well-woven cups of twigs, grasses, bark, rootlets, and leaves lined with soft plant fibers, fine pieces of roots, or other cozy materials. Wood thrushes and Swainson's thrushes, which usually nest low in trees, also add mud to the foundation of the nest. Like robins, thrushes lay beautiful blue or blue-green eggs, generally three or four. The eggs of the varied and Swainson's thrushes are speckled with brown.

Attracting Thrushes

Entice thrushes to your yard by providing plenty of cover. They feel at home in multilevel plantings of trees, tall shrubs or small trees, and shorter shrubs. Take a lesson from Mother Nature and mimic the natural growth of your area woodlands, whether it's redbuds, dogwoods, and spicebush, or sword fern, salal, and huckleberries.

During spring and fall migration, thrushes will stop almost anywhere for berries and fruits. To draw them to your yard, fill your garden with berried trees and shrubs, including hollies, deciduous hollies, serviceberries, elderberries, blueberries, viburnums, and grapes, among others.

You'll have the best success attracting nesting thrushes if your yard adjoins a woods. The wood thrush also feels at home among mixed plantings of trees, shrubs, and groundcovers.

TITMICE

These bold little birds are as much fun to watch as chickadees, and almost as easy to hand-tame. Titmice can be demanding customers at the feeding station, though: Run out of seed and they'll scold you roundly the next time you step outdoors!

Getting to Know Them

Titmice are gray birds with paler bellies, often blushed with pink at the sides. These $4\frac{1}{2}$- to $5\frac{1}{2}$-inch birds also wear a jazzy crest atop their bright-eyed heads. Males and females look alike. Though their name may evoke a snicker or two, it makes sense when you understand its roots: *tit* is from an Icelandic word meaning "small," and "mouse" is an adaptation of an Anglo-Saxon word, *mase,* meaning a kind of bird.

These busy birds forage over the bark and twigs of trees to snatch beetles, ants, and other insects from their hiding places. They peck apart galls on leaves to get at the insect larvae within. Titmice are also gluttons for seeds: Favorites include acorns, beechnuts, pecans, weed seeds, tulip tree and alder seeds, and pinyon nuts from between the scales of pinecones. Fruits and berries fill out the menu.

Titmice nest in cavities in trees or in bird houses, where they build a soft nest of grasses and moss, lined with feathers, fur, and plant down. They lay five to eight white eggs covered with fine brown speckles.

Attracting Titmice

Even if your yard doesn't have large trees, you'll find that titmice are easy to attract. Just plant berry-bearing shrubs, and from summer through winter, titmice will join with other backyard birds to eat the fruits of bayberries, sumac, serviceberries, brambles, blueberries, and wild cherries.

If a titmouse is anywhere in the neighborhood, it'll soon become a regular visitor at your feeder. Favorite foods include sunflower seeds, suet, peanuts, and bread.

Titmouse Checklist

Not only do titmice act like chickadees, they also are frequent companions, roaming backyards and woodlands in mixed groups that stay close together. The three species of titmice found in the United States live year-round in the same region, though their nesting territory may differ from their winter grounds.

Tufted titmouse. The tufted titmouse is the bird you see east of the Great Plains. Slightly bigger than other titmice, the tufted titmouse has a medium gray back and head, with pale underparts prettily flushed with pink along the sides of the lower belly. The black-crested form of this species is a very similar-looking bird with a pointy little coal black head. It makes its home in Texas and Oklahoma.

Tufted titmice live in the woods as well as in bird-friendly backyards. These active and engaging little birds will feed on serviceberries and other fruiting shrubs.

Bridled titmouse. The most striking member of the clan is the bridled titmouse. This bird's head is decorated with strong lines of black. These black lines outline its crest and form an open triangle on the sides of the face, meeting under the bird's sharp little beak. The bridled titmouse has a limited range: oak and juniper woods in the Southwest mountains.

Other titmice. There are two closely related species in the West, the oak titmouse and the juniper titmouse. They look very much like the tufted titmouse. Besides geography, the best way to tell them apart is to listen. Both western species have a typical clear, loud two-note whistle, but they also say *chick-a-dee-dee*.

JUST FOR TITMICE

■ Fill your gardens with sunflowers and titmice will feed happily for months.

■ Let a few lamb's-quarters or ragweed plants go to seed in an unobtrusive corner; a weedy patch will provide welcome food in winter.

■ Titmice are particularly fond of peanut butter—just smear some straight onto the roof of a feeder, and titmice will quickly come to feed.

■ Going broke keeping up the demand for peanut butter? Mix it with inexpensive cornmeal to make it last longer.

TOWHEES

When you hear a voice announcing *toe-WHEE!* from a brushy hedgerow or the edge of a woods, you know you're hearing a rufous-sided towhee.

Getting to Know Them

Towhees are actually giant-size sparrows. These 6- to more than 7-inch-long birds have long tails, rounded at the tips. Females are brown, with streaky underparts; males are either warm buffy brown, grayish, or tricolored.

Like sparrows, towhees live close to the ground, scratching about in leaf litter to find insects and seeds.

Towhees build bulky nests of twigs, grasses, and plant stems lined with hair and other softer materials. You may spot their nests on the ground or low in shrubs, small trees, or tangled vines. Eggs are white or creamy white speckled with brown, except for California and canyon towhees, whose eggs are pale blue or pale green with black or dark brown scrawls and spots.

Attracting Towhees

While towhees visit feeding stations regularly, they often prefer to search under the feeders instead of perching in the tray. Offer towhees crumbled bread, millet, chicken scratch, and wheat or oats. Fruit and berries will also lure them to your yard, so plant mulberries, hollies, viburnums, bayberries, strawberries, and blueberries.

Towhee Checklist

Towhees of one kind or another appear year-round across most of the country. One exception is the far North, from which the birds retreat for the cold months. You may be familiar with the rufous-sided towhee, which scientists reclassified in 1996 as the eastern towhee (in the East) and the spotted towhee (in the West).

Eastern towhee. The male eastern towhee has a black back and hood, reddish orange sides, and a snowy belly. The female has warm brown feathers in place of the black. They also have white-tipped outer tail feathers and gleaming red eyes. In the Southeast, the bird may have orange or even white eyes.

Spotted towhee. The male spotted towhee resembles the male eastern towhee, but sports a sprinkling of white spots and dashes across its wings and shoulders. It ranges from the Rocky Mountains west to the Pacific.

Towhees of the West. The green-tailed towhee has an olive-colored back, wings, and tail; gray sides; a bright chestnut crown; and a clear white chin and underbelly.

California and canyon towhees reside along the Pacific Coast and in some areas of the West and Southwest. They are warm reddish brown birds with short beaks and short tails. In the desert Southwest, Abert's towhee makes life difficult for birdwatchers; it looks very much like the canyon towhee except for its black face and buffy orange-tinted underside.

Eastern towhees (which used to be called rufous-sided towhees) feel at home in a yard filled with well-mulched shrubs where they can scratch about for seeds of grasses and other plants.

TREES

Birds, trees, and gardeners—what a great relationship! It's hard to say which or who benefits most. Trees provide all kinds of food for birds, from acorns to seed pods to berries, plus countless insects. Trees also offer a safe place for birds to roost and build nests.

In return, birds brighten our gardens with color and bird song, and they keep trees healthy and thriving by chowing down on aphids, caterpillars, bark beetles, and other pests that would otherwise reduce our backyard trees to a pile of sawdust.

Starting Out Right

If your yard is a blank slate, with no established trees, you're in luck. You get to start right by selecting trees that match your soil and site conditions, and offer the most bird benefits as well. To choose the tree that's right for your yard, read plant tags and catalog descriptions carefully.

Trees and shrubs are sold three ways: bareroot, balled-and-burlapped, and in containers. Container-grown shrubs and trees are easy to plant any time of year the ground isn't frozen. If you plant a container tree in summer, just be sure to keep the soil evenly moist after planting. For directions on planting a container tree, see the illustration on page 103.

Balled-and-burlapped plants adjust better if you plant them in spring or fall, to avoid summer heat stress. Bareroot plants, which are primarily sold by mail order, do best when planted in the fall or in early spring, while they're still dormant. When you get bareroot

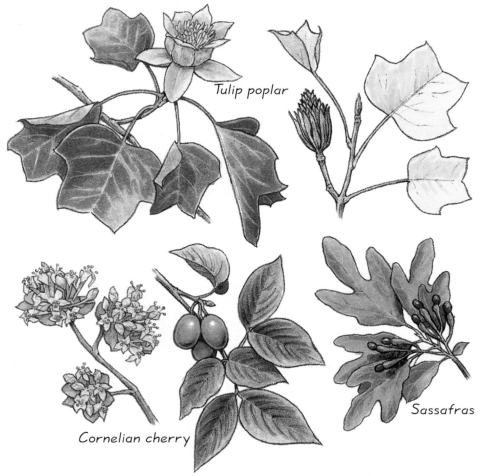

Tulip poplar

Cornelian cherry

Sassafras

Many trees for birds have colorful fall berries or interesting seed pods. Trees for birds range from stately tall tulip poplars to 20-foot cornelian cherries.

plants, unwrap and soak their roots in a bucket of water overnight, and plant them the next day.

Planting Trees

When you're ready to plant, dig a hole at least twice as wide and a little deeper than the root mass you're planting, as shown in the illustration on page 248. Remove any wraps, pots, or burlap from the rootball, trim off damaged or kinked roots, and straighten out any roots that circle the rootball. For balled-and-burlapped plants, make the bottom of the hole flat, so the rootball sits firmly on the bottom of the hole. For a bareroot plant, build a cone of soil in the center of the hole tall enough to let you spread the roots out evenly over it.

Check the hole depth before setting the tree in place. After you set the tree in the hole, hold the plant upright by its trunk and firm soil around the roots until the hole is half full of soil. Water well, and after the standing water drains, finish filling the hole with soil. Take any soil that's left and use it to build a shallow, circular dam around the plant to channel water down to the rootball. Then water well once again.

Establishing New Trees

Mulch your newly planted trees and shrubs with a 3-inch layer of composted wood mulch to keep the roots cool and conserve soil moisture. Spread the mulch in a circle as wide as the tree's branches spread. To avoid disease problems and trunk rot, don't pile any mulch around the base of the trunk. To promote even growth, don't fertilize, but do water your new shrubs and

trees often enough to keep the soil barely moist for the first year.

New trees and shrubs need very little pruning. Just take off broken, dead, or crossed branches. Trees grow faster and stronger without staking, so stake only those that are top-heavy or more than 8 feet tall.

Coping with "Problem" Trees

Having the wrong tree—one that's too big, hard to maintain, or unattractive—can seem worse than having no trees at all. But even a

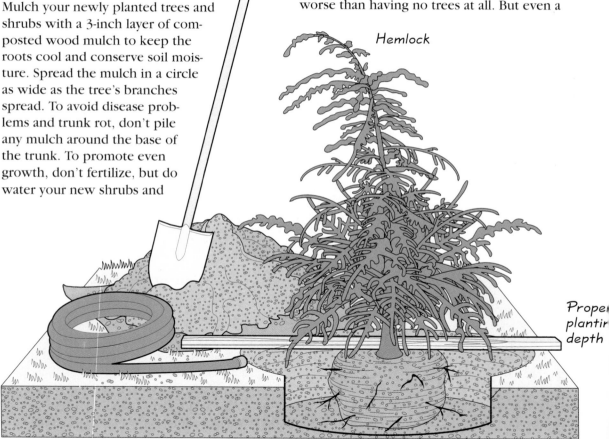

Hemlock

Proper planting depth

It's important to plant trees at the same depth they were growing in the nursery. Use a shovel handle or pole to check whether the base of the tree is at the same level as the surrounding soil.

"bad" tree may be redeemable. Try these tactics before you reach for the chain saw.

◆ If your tree is too big, hire an arborist to cut back the top to a reasonable height and spread, then have the new growth trimmed back to that point every few years.

◆ If a tree dumps massive amounts of leaves every fall, turn the leaf-littered area into a woodland garden.

◆ If you have a tree like Chinese chestnut that drops messy fruits or spiny seed pods, plant a bed of evergreen groundcovers, such as periwinkle, around the tree—the fruits and pods will land out of sight, but foraging birds can still find them.

◆ If your tree has an unappealing shape, you can improve it by thinning or pruning.

Great Trees for Birds

So many trees, so little yard space—make the most of limited yard space by choosing trees that offer birds berries or nuts as well as shelter. You'll also find information on trees that attract birds in Cherries, Crabapples, Evergreens, Fruit Trees, Hemlocks, Hollies, Junipers, Mulberries, Native Plants, Nuts and Nut Trees, Oaks, and Pines.

Cornelian cherry. A spreading tree or shrub of 20 to 25 feet tall, cornelian cherry (*Cornus mas*) is an early bloomer. Its yellow flowers are followed by red, oblong fruits in summer. Grow cornelian cherry in well-drained, fertile soil, in sun to partial shade, in Zones 4 to 8.

White fringe tree. White fringe tree (*Chionanthus virginicus*) is a small tree that grows from 12 to 20 feet tall. Its lacy, fragrant, white flower heads are followed by grapelike clusters of blue berries that birds adore. Grow white fringe tree in moist, fertile soil, in full sun, in Zones 3 to 9.

Black gum. The elegant black gum (*Nyssa sylvatica*) is usually 30 to 40 feet tall, with drooping branches, bluish black fruits, and oval leaves that

Homegrown WISDOM

A TREE MAKEOVER

When Eileen and Dick Matthews bought a house in the Philadelphia suburbs, it came complete with an overgrown 30-foot blue spruce right in front of the picture window. "We hated the thought of cutting it down," says Dick, "but knew we wanted more of a view out our window."

Using a sturdy pruning saw, the Matthewses carefully removed several limbs and shortened others. Then Eileen planted a group of evergreen hollies nearby. She spread bark mulch and added ornamental grasses and white-flowered perennials like columbines.

Birds liked the Matthewses' new "blue spruce garden" so much that the couple even moved their bird feeders close to it to make a complete bird-friendly habitat.

turn scarlet in fall. Grow it in moist, well-drained, acidic soil, in sun or shade, in Zones 3 to 9.

Hawthorn. Thorny-branched hawthorn (*Crataegus* spp.) grows 15 to 25 feet tall. Its clouds of small, creamy white flowers and beautiful, glowing red berries hold great appeal to birds. The long thorns can be hazardous, so don't plant hawthorns if small children play in your yard. Grow hawthorn in well-drained soil, in full sun, in Zones 3 to 7.

Eastern redbud. Fast-growing and trouble-free eastern redbud (*Cercis canadensis*) is a 20-foot-tall American native that's flushed with pinkish purple flowers in early spring. The flowers attract insects, which then attract migrating wood warblers. Flat, dark brown seed pods keep chickadees and titmice happy in winter. Grow redbud in well-drained soil in full sun to light shade, in Zones 4 to 9.

Downy serviceberry. A graceful, often multi-stemmed, small tree, downy serviceberry (*Amelanchier arborea*) grows 25 feet tall and has white flowers in early spring. Its bird-attracting berries turn from green to red, and finally to purplish black. The leaves turn a fine shade of red in fall. Grow downy serviceberry in moist, well-drained, acidic soil, in full sun to partial shade, in Zones 3 to 8.

Sassafras. Sassafras (*Sassafras albidum*) is a handsome shade tree that grows to 30 feet tall or taller. Its large leaves turn gold to flaming orange in fall. Birds will eat the dark blue fruits as soon as they ripen in fall. Grow sassafras in moist, well-drained, acidic soil, in full sun to light shade, in Zones 4 to 9.

Tulip poplar. If you have space for a large shade tree, consider planting tulip poplar (*Liriodendron tulipifera*), which can reach 100 feet tall. It has pointed, lobed leaves and sweet-smelling flowers, with creamy, waxy petals and a green-and-orange central blotch. Flowers mature into pineconelike seed pods, which attract goldfinches, pine siskins, purple finches, cardinals, and evening grosbeaks throughout the winter. Grow tulip poplar in deep, moist, well-drained soil, in full sun, in Zones 4 to 9.

TRUMPET VINES

Trumpet vine shines like a beacon to hummingbirds. When in bloom in mid- through late summer, its trumpet-shaped flowers are constantly buzzing with hummers. The orange, red, or yellow flowers and lush foliage of trumpet vine make a dazzling sight sprawling on a trellis or arbor.

Growing trumpet vines. Hardy from Zones 4 to 9, trumpet vine (*Campsis radicans*) will grow in rich soil or sun-baked clay and just about everywhere in between. Trumpet vine blooms best in full sun but also puts on a decent show in the shade.

Totally untroubled by pests or diseases, trumpet vine can climb as high as 30 feet, but you can keep it short and shrubby by pruning.

From early to late summer, trumpet vine flowers will lure all the hummingbirds in your neighborhood.

Don't be timid with this vine: You can prune it to the ground in early spring and it will be up and blooming by late summer. Wear gloves and long sleeves when you work because all parts of the plant can irritate your skin.

Trumpet vine is a strong, heavy vine that clings to supports with rootlike growths called holdfasts along its stems. If you build an arbor or a trellis for trumpet vines, use sturdy 4 × 4 posts and 2 × 4 crosspieces, because the weight of a mature vine will pull down anything flimsier in a few years. Promptly pull out any volunteer seedlings or suckers that sprout from underground runners.

VEGETABLE GARDENS

Birds eat a lot of bugs, and that's both good news and bad news for vegetable gardeners. The bad news is that most birds don't discriminate between destructive insects like striped cucumber beetles and helpful critters like spiders and green lacewings. The good news is that the balance lands in the gardener's favor. That's because birds come flocking when pests reach destructive levels, such as when aphids cover your pea vines.

If your broccoli or cabbage are overrun with imported cabbageworms, you may spot orioles feeding in your cabbage patch. And if grasshoppers chow down in your vegetable garden, you can bet that a squad of grackles will have the grasshoppers under control in no time.

Jimmy Crack Corn

Vegetables aren't on the top ten list of most birds' menus, except when it comes to corn.

Those sweet milky kernels are prime fodder for blackbirds, jays, and of course crows. Cardinals, woodpeckers, titmice, and other birds also enjoy eating corn, although they usually prefer it dry rather than in the soft-kernel stage.

A scarecrow is the classic solution for hungry birds in the garden, but it only works until the birds figure out it's not human. You can make the effect last a little longer by including moving elements—sleeves or streamers that flap in the breeze, pie pans that bang unexpectedly when the wind blows—and a Halloween latex mask with human features. Moving your scarecrow from place to place in the garden can help, too.

A Snitch in Time

Some birds have a taste for fresh greenery, and that can be an occasional frustration to vegetable gardeners. Blackbirds have a penchant for pulling up seedling corn, and goldfinches may nibble on lettuce seedlings. The house sparrows that live under the eaves of my

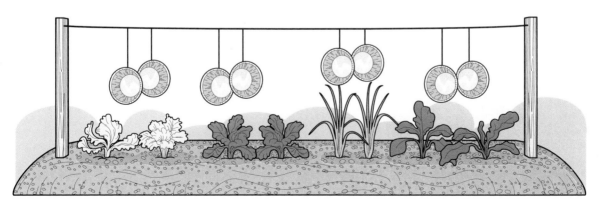

To scare the birds away from tender young crops, hang a line of aluminum pie pans above the plants. Their movement and noise usually keep birds from nibbling on young leaves and buds.

251

garage developed a craving for young pea shoots and quickly decimated the planting.

If you plant sunflowers in your vegetable garden, you may discover that birds don't want to wait for the flowers to grow—they mow the plants down before they barely get started. But there's a quick and easy solution—just cover the row right after planting with a lightweight material called floating row cover. This material, which is available at almost any garden center, lets air, water, and light through, but keeps birds out (see the illustration of this technique below). You can remove the cover once the seedlings have solidly taken root, and the birds will thank you later in the season.

Old-time gardeners often covered their rows with a board to protect the newly sown seeds from birds, but the dark, damp space beneath boards invites slugs and that only compounds the difficulties. I find that the row cover is the best solution for just about all my crops. By the time the plants are pushing up the row cover, they're generally old enough to be unpalatable to birds.

Inviting Birds to the Garden

Since birds are mostly friend, not foe, in the garden, you'll want to do all you can to encourage their presence. Because your frequent presence in the garden is a deterrent to birds, it's important to sweeten the deal to get birds to overcome their initial hesitation. Try a few of these tricks.

◆ Place a pedestal birdbath among the plots and keep it brimming with fresh water.
◆ Mount nest boxes for bluebirds and wrens in and around the garden.
◆ Entice birds with a sour cherry tree at one side of the garden or a patch of strawberries. After they feast on fruit, they'll move to the vegetables to hunt for insects.
◆ If you can, visit your garden at regular times. Birds will learn your schedule and they'll visit when you're not there.
◆ Provide a corridor of shrubs for bird-safe travel to and from the garden. A hedgerow of brambles or blueberries will be hard to resist—and the birds may even share a few handfuls of fruit from it.

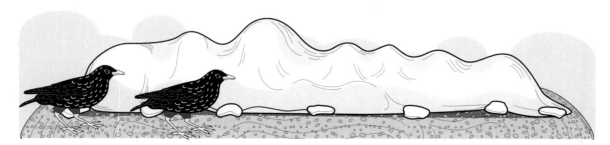

If scare devices aren't enough to keep birds from damaging your vegetables, cover the whole bed with a section of lightweight floating row cover. Be sure to secure the sides with soil, rocks, or a board so birds don't accidentally get underneath and become trapped.

VIBURNUMS

There are over 100 species of viburnums, and birds love just about all of them. Viburnums have dense branches that offer shelter and fine nesting sites. Viburnum flowers attract lots of insects, which in turn attract insect-eating birds like warblers, vireos, tanagers, and others. In the fall, viburnums bear heavy crops of tasty yellow, red, or purple-black berries.

Viburnum Basics

Viburnums are a good choice for gardeners, too. They're vigorous plants that grow fast and need little attention other than regular watering during the first year of growth. Because they're so easy to propagate, viburnums are usually a bargain. You could create an entire bird garden of viburnums. Not all species are a good choice for gardens, but there are more than 35 worthy species and dozens of cultivars to select from.

These deciduous shrubs can range from 2- to 3-foot-tall dwarfs to large shrubs that can top out at 30 feet. Viburnums grow well from at least Zone 5 to Zone 9, and they thrive in any site with well-drained soil, from full sun to shade.

If viburnums have a fault, it's that most of them don't have a dramatic or particularly attractive shape. Selective pruning after the flowers fade can make your viburnums more tidy, but birds will like their unthinned, undistinguished shape just fine.

Try tucking viburnums into a hedgerow, among other shrubs, or at the back of a border where they'll blend in. Viburnums redeem themselves briefly in fall when they turn shades of orange through purple-red.

But to perk them up in winter, combine viburnums with bird-attracting plants like broad-leaved or needled evergreens, hollies, hemlocks, and ornamental grasses.

Viburnums in the Garden

Viburnums have flat-topped or rounded clusters of small, white or pale pink flowers. The flowering season begins with fragrant viburnum (*Viburnum farreri*). This 8- to 12-foot-tall viburnum grows best in Zones 5 to 8 and produces fragrant pink flowers that open about when daffodils bloom in early spring.

Most other viburnums bloom from mid- to late May or a little later. Doublefile viburnum (*V. plicatum* var. *tomentosum*) and its cultivar 'Mariesii' are more appealing than most viburnums with lovely flowers and reddish purple fall foliage.

Explore catalogs and garden centers for more viburnums, and choose those that appeal to you, because the birds will appreciate all of them.

Layered like a wedding cake, the white flowers of doublefile viburnum attract lots of tiny insects for birds to feed on. Later in the season, birds eagerly seek the red viburnum berries.

VINES

Vines are a lush garden accent and a favorite hangout for backyard birds. The tangled stems and dense foliage of vines offer great roosting and nesting places. Fast-growing annual vines provide quick cover for a garden trellis and give birds a range of foods, from berries to insects. Woody perennial vines look beautiful covering an arbor and are sturdy enough to support nests. And the nectar-filled flowers of honeysuckle and other fragrant-flowered vines spice up your garden—some of them attract hummingbirds, too.

Growing and Pruning Vines

Annual vines are real racehorses: Some, like moonflowers (*Ipomoea alba*), can blanket a wall in a single season. Others, such as feathery-leaved cypress vine (*I. quamoclit*), are delicate plants best grown on a trellis or over perennials and shrubs. Annual vines often grow the biggest in long-summer areas, where there's ample heat and humidity. Many types have seeds that germinate slowly. To speed germination, soak the seeds in warm water overnight before planting.

Many types of perennial vines offer food and shelter for birds. You'll need to think carefully about where to plant perennial vines like clematis and grapes, because once they're established, they're difficult to transplant. Erect a sturdy support for your vine before you plant it. You can buy perennial vines, just as trees—bareroot, or bagged, or in containers—and you plant them the same way. For planting guidelines, turn to Trees on page 246. Perennial vines start out slowly, but during their second or third growing season, they may zoom to incredible lengths. Prune them back any time the vines get out of bounds.

Support Systems

Most vines grow best with a support like a fence or arbor. Unless you have a carpenter in the family, it's easiest to buy a ready-made trellis or arbor that you can easily put up in a couple of hours or less. Garden centers have finished trellises and arbors that will do the job. But choose carefully: Some premade trellises are made of thin pieces of wood stapled together. These flimsy trellises will last only a year or two in the garden. For a long-lasting trellis or arbor that's strong enough to hold a heavy vine, shop for one with thick corner posts and crosspieces that are firmly attached with nails, or better yet, screws.

Lattice panels are too delicate to hold up heavy, perennial vines, but make excellent

The exquisite flowers of wild passionflower are gorgeous on a trellis beside a sunny patio. If the vine is in a quiet spot, a catbird or other songbird may decide to nest in it.

supports for lightweight annual vines. Edging the panels by sandwiching them between thicker boards will make them stronger and more finished looking. If you want to put lattice against a wall, frame the panels with 1 × 4s. If you want the panels to be strong enough to stand by themselves, frame them with 2 × 4s, making the vertical end pieces long enough to set in the ground.

If you're growing vines against a wall or solid wood fence, attach sections of wire fencing or chicken wire to it to support the vines. The stems of the vines will twine around the wires, and in no time the foliage will hide all traces of the wire.

Vines for Birds

Sweet autumn clematis (*Clematis terniflora*) offers excellent cover for birds, and is a beauty in the garden with its cloud of fragrant late-summer flowers. It thrives in any well-drained soil, in sun or shade, and in Zones 5 to 9. American bittersweet (*Celastrus scandens*) flourishes in any well-drained soil and full sun. It's a vigorous vine with strong heavy stems, so be sure to grow it on a sturdy trellis, and don't let it invade trees or shrubs. Keep in mind that you'll need to plant both a male and female bittersweet vine for fruit set.

Grape vines (*Vitis* spp.) attract a wide range of birds who eat berries and insects. Honeysuckles (*Lonicera* spp.) and trumpet vine (*Campsis radicans*) are rampant perennial vines that shelter bird nests (they also have beautiful flowers that draw hummingbirds). Virginia creeper (*Parthenocissus quinquefolia*) and its close relative Boston ivy (*P. tricuspidata*) are a little slower growing, but their berries will attract birds, chipmunks, and other small mammals. For

Homegrown WISDOM

A VINY VIEW

Vines make great windbreaks and privacy screens. Martha Breeze of New Harmony, Indiana, used vines to make a privacy screen around her hot tub. To start, she attached simple trellis panels of prefabricated lattice (available at home centers) to sturdy 2 × 4s set in the ground at the corners of the tub. Then Martha planted fast-growing annual scarlet runner beans around the bottom of the trellises, on both sides of each panel. Lush, heart-shaped leaves soon covered the trellis. Then vivid, orange-red flowers bloomed, bringing a show of feeding hummingbirds to entertain Martha while she enjoyed her hot tub.

Annual vines like scarlet runner beans and morning glories can add height while you wait for shade trees to grow. When Pauline Hoehn of Posey County, Indiana, moved into a house with a bare, sunny backyard, she created romantic-looking swags of hyacinth bean vines to frame a sunny garden path. The purple flowers and purple stems of this annual vine swarmed up salvaged, wooden porch columns. Then the vines climbed across chains strung between the two rows of posts to make beautiful deep scallops of greenery overhead.

more about growing these vines, see Grapes, Honeysuckles, Trumpet Vines, and Virginia Creeper.

If you prefer a more restrained vine, try Carolina coralbead (*Cocculus carolinus*), an American native vine that reaches a length of only about 12 feet. Its red fruits appeal to birds. Wild passionflower (*Passiflora incarnata*) is a wonderful vine for birds and for the garden. It's also called maypop, because of its sweet, oblong edible fruit. Catbirds, thrushes, and other birds hide their nests among the stems. The leaves and stems die at the end of the season. You can let the vines stand in winter as a bird shelter or cut them back for a tidier look.

Vines for Hummingbirds

Vines with vivid red or orange flowers will bring hummingbirds to your garden. Transform a trellis with the miniature red trumpets of red morning glory (*Ipomoea coccinea*), cover a deck railing with annual scarlet runner beans (*Phaseolus coccineus*), or encourage the lacy-leaved cypress vine to wander throughout your garden. All are easy to grow in average garden soil in full sun.

In mild-winter areas, create a bower with Chilean glory flower (*Eccremocarpus scaber*), a flame-flowered vine that will overwinter in Zones 9 and 10. In colder areas, you can start seeds of tender perennial vines like this indoors in early spring for bloom in summer.

Another vine with hummingbird appeal is orange-red or orange-flowered trumpet vine or bignonia (*Bignonia capreolata*), a trumpet-vine relative with appealing leaves that deepen to maroon after frost. Bignonia retains some of its leaves through the winter, and is hardy in Zones 6 to 10. Trumpet honeysuckle (*Lonicera sempervirens*) is another red-flowered vine guaranteed to attract hummers (see Honeysuckles on page 138).

Try the stunning flowers of royal trumpet vine (*Distictis* 'Rivers'), which is hardy in Zones 9 and 10; flame vine (*Pyrostegia venusta*), which is hardy only in Zone 10; and cape honeysuckle (*Tecomaria capensis*), which is hardy in Zones 9 and 10.

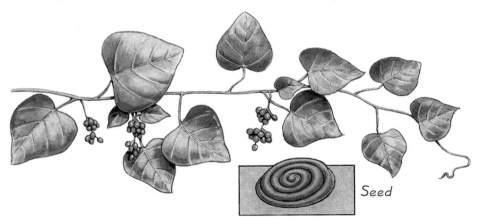

Seed

Carolina coralbead is a native vine that's a moderate grower with lovely flowers and fruits that appeal to birds. It's also called Carolina snailseed because its seeds are shaped like the spiral shell of a snail.

VIREOS

Vireos often sing all day long from spring through summer, but you'll need to look closely to spot them. The olive green feathers of these birds blend perfectly with the foliage of the trees and thickets where they live.

Getting to Know Them

Vireos are sleek greenish birds ranging from 4 to 5 inches long, depending on species. Their bellies are paler than their backs, often with touches of yellow or white that blend into the green. To tell one species from another, look closely at their head markings and check for a colored cap, an eye ring or eye stripe, and the color of the eyes. Females and males look alike.

Slowly and deliberately, vireos move about in treetops and shrubbery, looking for insects, then picking them off. Their style contrasts with the nervous jittery movements of warblers, whom they're often seen with during migration.

The voices of male vireos are a constant in the spring woodland, providing background music to the longer, prettier songs of tanagers and thrushes. Vireos tend to sing in bursts interrupted by short or long pauses.

Vireo nests are beautifully constructed. They're deep, snug cups, woven of fine plant fibers and softened with spider's silk. The soft cup is attached to a fork of slender twigs, so the suspended nest and the brown-spotted white eggs inside it can move gently in the soft summer breezes. Some species of vireos decorate their nests with lichens or leaves, camouflaging the nests so well that it's hard to find a nest for a second time, even if you just spotted it a moment before.

Insects and berries are the main items in a vireo's diet. Like the wood warbler, it's a guardian of the forest, gleaning beetles, caterpillars, and other damaging insects from leaves and twigs.

Attracting Vireos

A garden with plenty of trees and shrubs will draw vireos, especially during migration time in spring and fall. Attract these birds by planting viburnums, dogwoods, Virginia creeper, sassafras, spicebush, brambles, grapes, and other berry-bearing plants. Mulberries and wild cherries are particularly irresistible; find these trees in fruit and watch for a while—you're bound to see vireos.

Vireo Checklist

Wherever you are in the United States, there's vireo territory somewhere nearby. Each of the several species occupies a distinct kind of habitat. **Solitary vireos.** This group of birds includes three closely related species: the blue-headed vireo, Cassin's vireo, and the plumbeous vireo. These birds have gray and green backs

Like all vireos, the red-eyed vireo is a good friend to gardeners, keeping pests like spittlebugs and caterpillars in check.

and soft white bellies. They live in mixed deciduous/coniferous forests. The blue-headed vireo is common in the East; the other two are western species. The song sounds like a robin, but slower and slurred as it moves through the whistled phrases.

White-eyed vireo and Bell's vireo. The white-eyed vireo is common across the eastern half of the country; the similar Bell's vireo is a western bird. Both dwell in thickets, in hedgerows, and at the edges of woods. The white-eyed vireo is easy to identify, thanks to its namesake white eyes. Bell's has the same olive, yellow, and white coloring, but has dark eyes and less prominent wing bars.

Warbling vireo. Listen for this well-concealed fellow singing from shade trees anywhere across the country. The warbling vireo is a drab gray-green bird that sounds like a purple finch. You'll hear him more often than you see him, singing his long, warbling repertoire from tall shade trees and hidden in the foliage. The white belly and white eye stripe are two marks to watch for.

Red-eyed vireo. The red-eyed vireo, at one time the most abundant songbird in eastern woods, was nicknamed "the preacher" because of his incessant singing. You can hear him in deciduous woods from coast to coast, except in the Southwest. This olive brown vireo has a gray cap, a red eye (of course), and a prominent white eye stripe.

VIRGINIA CREEPER

When you find a Virginia creeper vine in fruit, you're bound to find titmice, chickadees, vireos, grosbeaks, and many other fruit-eating birds snapping up the plentiful blue berries. Downy woodpeckers are especially fond of Virginia creeper berries, as are bluebirds, and quail will eagerly search out any berries that drop off the vines.

Virginia creeper (*Parthenocissus quinquefolia*) will bring beauty as well as birds to your garden. In the early fall, its leaves turn a glorious shade of crimson, and the deep blue berries cluster along bright red stems, making a wonderful contrast to the leaves.

Virginia creeper grows in Zones 3 to 9, in full sun to full shade, and in ordinary garden soil. The vines have suction-cup-like structures called holdfasts that will stick to a trellis or other support. These rambling vines can grow 10 feet or more in a single season. Choose a planting site carefully, because it's hard to transplant Virginia creeper successfully. The easiest way to start new plants is to root cuttings taken in late summer.

Plant a rambling Virginia creeper vine where it can cover a fence, wall, or sturdy trellis. Downy woodpeckers, bluebirds, and many other birds will flock to the vine in fall to devour its blue berries.

WARBLERS

Often called the "butterflies of the bird world," warblers are little mites of energy with flashy colors and distinctive voices. However, except during breeding season, warblers don't spend much time singing. When they do sing, most warblers have high, thin, wheezy voices; you'll have to listen carefully to pick them out from the chorus of other spring songsters.

Warbler-Watching Challenges

Only sparrows and shorebirds come close to the identification challenge of these tiny songbirds, especially in fall, when their bright breeding plumage changes to mostly look-alike olive drab. Fifty-six species of these little birds roam the United States. They like to hide in thick vegetation, either in shrubs or in treetops, where their mostly yellow and green plumage blends in like part of the scenery. They're also constantly flitting from one branch to another, so it's hard to keep them in the focus of your binoculars.

In most parts of the country, warblers are visible mainly during migration, in mixed flocks of assorted species. Birdwatchers call these "waves" of warblers, because a flock of a dozen or more birds will suddenly be all around, then disappear as quickly as it came.

Getting to Know Them

Warblers are small birds, many of them measuring about 4½ inches from beak to tail tip. Most are dressed in olive or yellow plumage, with various colorful accents—head caps, eye stripes, wing bars, tail patches—on the males and more subtle variations of these trademarks among the females. Most of the males are deco-rated with flashy splashes of orange, blue, chestnut, or black. Their names often describe their coloration, as in the chestnut-sided warbler, the black-throated blue warbler, and the yellow-rumped warbler.

Warblers nest in all kinds of places, from the ground to shrubs to the highest branches of tall conifers, depending on their species. Almost all warblers build a sturdy, deep, cup-shaped nest. The outer layer of the nest usually includes grasses, bark fibers, and leaves; the inner lining may have moss, plant down, fine grasses, feathers, hair, or other soft materials in it.

They lay three to five small eggs, which are often white or creamy white with brown dots concentrated at the wider end. (The markings often make a kind of wreath around the egg.)

Spring-blooming trees such as crabapples lure migrating warblers; the flowers attract tiny insects for the birds to eat. The Black-burnian warbler (shown) is a showy visitor that gardeners in the eastern two-thirds of the country may spot passing through.

Attracting Warblers

Heavy shrubbery, willow thickets along a pond, or large trees will tempt members of the warbler clan to drop in during migration or in nesting season. When they're on the move, they're looking for fast food, and a yard filled with vegetation or spring-flowering trees like crabapples is a great draw. To attract the wide-ranging yellow-rumped warbler to your yard, plant bayberry bushes; the birds will feast on the berries through the winter.

At nesting season, each warbler has its specific preferences. Canada warblers are fond of rhododendron plantings; pine warblers like pine trees. Warbler names don't necessarily reflect the habitat they prefer—palm warblers live in the sphagnum bogs of the northern part of the country. Whoever dubbed them palm warblers may have seen them in palm trees during migration.

Warbler Checklist

Two of the most widespread species are the striped black-and-white warbler, common in deciduous woods east of the Rockies, and the orange-crowned warbler, common in brushy areas in the West. The yellow warbler is also widespread and commonly spotted. This golden beauty frequents willow thickets and shrubbery across the country.

The yellow-rumped warbler (also called the myrtle warbler) also ranges across the entire country. It's a common resident of coniferous forests all year-round and along the coasts, where it feasts on bayberries in winter. You'll see the dapper, black-capped Wilson's warbler in thickets and willows. The black-masked face of the common yellowthroat pops up in shrubbery from coast to coast (to learn more about this bird, turn to Yellowthroats on page 286).

The Blackburnian warbler, a catch-your-breath beauty with a black back, snowy white belly, and flaming orange throat, nests mainly in spruce-fir forests in the northern tier of the country and into the Appalachians.

Wood warblers are the guardians of our trees, eating enormous quantities of insects along with a few berries and an occasional sip of sap. Most warblers nest in North America and retreat to Central and South America when cold weather hits and threatens their insect supply.

WATER

Keeping a birdbath filled with water is one of the best things you can do for your backyard birds. Water is vital to birds, not only for drinking but also for cleaning their feathers so they can fly properly and stay free from parasites. By providing a source of fresh water in your bird garden, you can attract many species that otherwise would pass you by.

Birds will travel great distances to find water. They drink from anything that's available—puddles, streams, ponds, birdbaths, ditches, livestock troughs, or any other container that holds an inch or two of liquid. Some birds, especially those that live in desert regions, meet some of their water needs by eating juicy insects and green plants.

If you go camping in a desert area, set out a shallow container filled with water at your campsite. You'll attract a host of birds. On one camping trip in Arizona, we set out a saucer of water on the ground near our picnic table and enjoyed watching black-headed grosbeaks, yellow-eyed juncos, hepatic tanagers, Scott's orioles, and other fascinating birds that came to drink.

WATER GARDENS

A water garden is a haven for birds and a soul-soothing retreat for gardeners as well. The sight and sound of water have a wonderfully calming effect, and a view of wild birds sipping or splashing in a garden pool provides hours of pleasure.

A Pool for Any Garden

Songbirds of all sorts, from the commonest robin to the rarest warbler, will eagerly adopt a garden pool or pond as their watering hole and personal bath. A large pond will draw other types of birds, too—such as ducks, stately great blue herons, or a patrol of shorebirds. The good news is that installing a water garden doesn't have to be a major garden project (although it can be if you're game for it). For an easy, reasonably priced water-garden project, try installing a rigid, preformed pool. These are available at many garden centers, nurseries, and discount stores, as well as from a variety of mail-order companies, stores, and catalogs, and the limited demand keeps prices high.

All it takes to install a rigid pool liner is dig a hole that conforms to the depth and shape of the pool, settle the liner in place, and add some rocks and plants around the edges. It's easy to

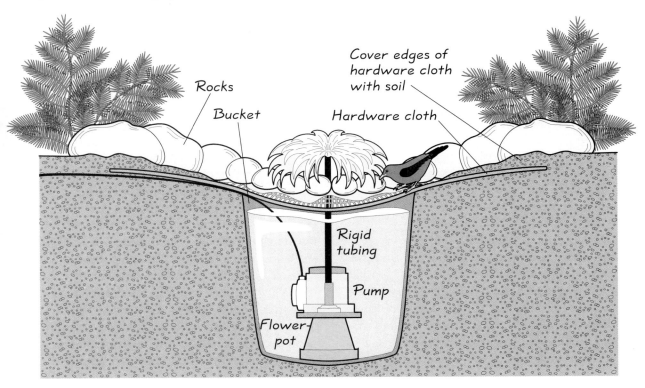

Rocks

Bucket

Cover edges of hardware cloth with soil

Hardware cloth

Rigid tubing

Pump

Flower-pot

If you want the sight and sound of running water to attract birds but don't have room for a full-scale water garden, install a small bubbling spring. All you need is a scrub bucket or other plastic basin, a small pump, a small flowerpot, hardware cloth, and some rocks.

install the whole thing over the course of a weekend. You can put a recirculating pump in the pool if you want to add the liquid gurgle or gentle splash of moving water to the scene.

If you're interested in a more ambitious water garden, you'll probably want to work with a flexible plastic liner rather than a pre-formed pool. With a flexible liner, you can make your pool any size and shape that you like. You can even combine a series of overlapping pools, or make a homemade stream. Thanks to the miracle of plastic, you can now also buy perfectly natural-looking preformed "stone" waterfalls to include in your project. Of course you can still go the natural route and use actual rock to build a small waterfall.

Installing a flexible liner takes time and careful planning. Be sure to get complete instructions on how to prepare the site and ensure that the pool is level. Buy your liner from a reputable dealer, who should be able to give you good advice on installing the liner.

If you have the luxury of a large property, you might choose to have a full-size pond dug. Check the Yellow Pages under ponds, or ask neighbors for recommendations for excavating companies that specialize in ponds.

Landscaping for Water Gardens

Plants add beauty to a water garden, and they make it look more like a natural area, so that birds feel more at home. You'll want to add greenery in all areas of your water garden: in the water, along the edge, and leading up to the pond or pool area, so that birds have a safe corridor to travel along.

Plants growing in the water serve as shelter for visiting ducks and herons and appeal to other birds that like to be near water, such as yellow warblers and red-winged black-birds. These birds will search the flowers and foliage of your aquatic plants for insects to eat.

Gardening around water is a great introduction to plants that like "wet feet." If your water garden is a natural pond or brook, many water-loving plants will spring up there of their own accord, thanks to birds and other animals who bring in seeds on their feet, fur, or feathers. Some of these plants may be just what you want, but you'll probably want to add your own choices, too, like magnificent Japanese irises.

Preformed garden pools hold the water in place without saturating the surrounding soil. Beside these pools, use plants that thrive in wet conditions, but also in drier soil. That may seem like a hard bill to fill, but it actually describes many water's-edge plants like cardinal flower, which in its natural setting must survive seasonal fluctuations in water level, including occasional drought.

Choosing Water-Garden Plants

Although you'll be tempted to landscape the area around your water garden first, resist the urge and start by planting *in* the water. Water plants are vital to helping your water garden achieve the balanced state that prevents algae growth, murky water, and other problems.

Plants that add oxygen. Choose some of the small, less showy aquatic plants for starters. Known as oxygenators, these unassuming plants give off the oxygen that will keep your pool from becoming a stagnant mess. Their roots float free in the water, so you don't really plant them. You just drop them in the water and forget about them. When water plants outgrow their space, just rake them out with a leaf rake covered in cheesecloth.

Waterweed (*Elodea* spp.), which includes several similar plants that range in hardiness from Zones 5 to 11, has long stems and pointed, narrow leaves; it's the basic pond weed that's widespread across America, both in ponds and fish tanks.

Water milfoils (*Myriophyllum* spp.) are more delicate plants, with filmy, feathery foliage. Milfoils are hardy from Zones 3 to 11, depending on species. For variety, try hair grass (*Eleocharis acicularis*), hardy to Zones 4 to 11, which grows in small tufts that look just like hair.

Floating plants. Floating plants on the surface of your garden pond will shade the water, which helps prevent algae from growing. Some of these plants are beauties, like water lettuce (*Pistia stratiotes*), with its rosettes of pale green leaves, and water hyacinth (*Eichhornia crassipes*), which has interesting fleshy green leaves and pretty lavender flowers. Be careful—these two plants can be very invasive in warm-winter areas where they've escaped into natural waterways. (Florida gardeners especially shouldn't use water hyacinth.) North of Zone 8, these plants will die when there's frost, so they're not a problem. (Overwinter a few plants in a tub of water indoors so you have stock for next year.)

More manageable plants include frogbit (*Hydrocharis morsus-ranae*),which your smallest frogs may adopt as a sunning spot. The plants look like miniature water lilies, with white flowers and inch-wide leaves; they're hardy in Zones 5 to 9. Duckweed (*Lemna* spp.), hardy in Zones 4 to 11, will probably start growing on its own, carried in by pond visitors. It has tiny leaves but grows in huge colonies that make a sheet of bright green on the surface.

Aquatic plants. Now for the fun part: the big, steal-the-show aquatic plants like water lilies that have roots anchored in soil. If your pond has a soil bottom, you can plant these plants directly

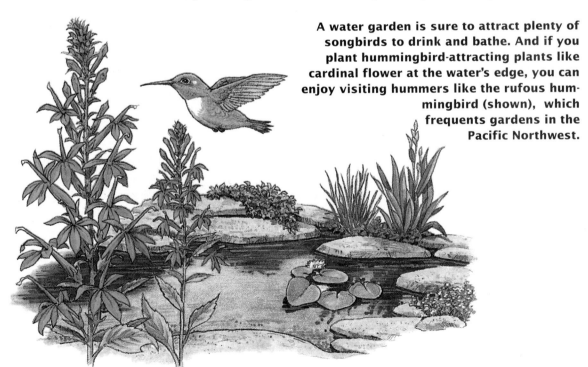

A water garden is sure to attract plenty of songbirds to drink and bathe. And if you plant hummingbird-attracting plants like cardinal flower at the water's edge, you can enjoy visiting hummers like the rufous hummingbird (shown), which frequents gardens in the Pacific Northwest.

in the soil. But for water gardens with plastic liners, you'll "plant" just by submerging the pots. The pots these plants are sold in have slotted sides so that water can freely pass in and out.

For a showy display in deep water, go with 3- to 5-foot-tall golden club (*Orontium aquaticum*), with its stalk of golden yellow flowers, or sweet flag (*Acorus calamus*), whose long, pointed leaves may have ruffled edges like an old-fashioned hair ribbon.

In shallow water or at wet pond edges, try cattails (*Typha* spp.), a familiar standard at wild water places that will make birds feel at home. Be warned, though: Cattails can be pushy sorts, which spread quickly to take more than their share of your precious space.

Other good plants for shallow water or wet soil include umbrella sedge (*Cyperus* spp.), a tender perennial hardy only in Zones 9 to 11, but worth growing anywhere for the eye-catching effect of its bare stems topped by pom-pom or umbrella-like leaves. Soft rush (*Juncus effusus*) and other rushes are also welcome in these conditions, where their clumps of grassy foliage soften the garden.

Bolder-leaved plants include arrowheads (*Sagittaria* spp.), with arrowhead-shaped leaves and white flowers, and blue-flowered pickerel weed (*Pontederia cordata*), which also has arrowhead-shaped leaves. Both of these plants grow well in shallow water and at wet edges. For deeper water and dramatic foliage and flowers, be sure to include water lilies (*Nymphaea* spp.), which offer outstanding showy flowers in white, pink, or red, wonderful fragrance, and those famous "dinner plate" leaves.

Balancing your choices. To balance your water garden, you'll need to include more submerged oxygenating plants and floaters than large aquatic plants whose leaves are held above the water. A good rule of thumb is to select four to six oxygenating or floating plants for every large aquatic plant. For example, for every water lily you put in your pool, you might add two water milfoils, one waterweed, a water hyacinth, and two water lettuces. Catalogs and water-garden supply centers offer other interesting plants you can choose from.

Water's-Edge Plants

Once you've installed water plants in your water garden, you can indulge yourself in choosing annuals and perennials to surround the edges of the garden.

◆ Japanese iris (*Iris ensata*) is a spectacular place to begin. These magnificent plants have bold, strappy leaves and gorgeous, huge blue, purple, pink, carmine, or white flowers like resting butterflies, with petals often veined in contrasting colors. They're hardy in Zones 4 to 9.

◆ Siberian iris (*Iris sibirica*) and yellow flag (*I. pseudacorus*) also have lovely upright foliage and beautiful flowers. All three irises thrive in boggy soil but do just as well in average soil.

◆ Brilliant red cardinal flower (*Lobelia cardinalis*) and its relative great blue lobelia (*L. siphilitica*) also do well in wet or dry conditions.

◆ Monkeyflowers (*Mimulus* spp.) are interesting annuals and perennials that have monkey "faces" on their snapdragon-like blue, red, yellow, or almost orange blossoms. They can stay in bloom for months. Most of them are wet-footers at heart, but they also do well in average moisture.

◆ Dainty blue forget-me-nots (*Myosotis* spp.) make a lovely frothy edging along the water. There are perennial, biennial, and annual types. Annual forget-me-nots will self-sow generously, so you always have a good supply.

A Water Garden for Birds

1. **Purple barberry** (*Berberis thunbergii* var. *atropurpurea*)
2. **Cardinal flower** (*Lobelia cardinalis*)
3. **Narrow-leaved cattail** (*Typha angustifolia*)
4. **Feathertop grass** (*Pennisetum villosum*)
5. **'Palace Purple' heuchera** (*Heuchera* 'Palace Purple')

6. **'Flamingo' maiden grass** (*Miscanthus sinensis* 'Flamingo')
7. **Weeping Japanese maple** (*Acer palmatum* or *A. japonicum* cultivars)
8. **Dwarf mugo pine** (*Pinus mugo* var. *mugo*)
9. **Soft rush** (*Juncus effusus*)
10. **White-flowered water lily** (*Nymphaea* sp.)

◆ Buttery yellow marsh marigolds (*Caltha palustris*) will spread to cover any damp ground along the water with a shining carpet of rounded leaves and bright buttercup flowers.

Away from soggy soil your choices are the same as for any other garden bed, so pick the plants that please you. Ferns of any kind are beautiful near water, and many gardeners like the bold, simple leaves of hostas near a water garden. Be sure to add a shrub or two near the water so bathing birds have a handy place to preen their feathers after splashing.

WAXWINGS

One of the enduring mysteries of the bird world is the red waxy substance that dabs the wings of waxwings. The bright red droplets form on the tips of some wing feathers of both adult males and females, but their purpose baffles scientists.

Getting to Know Them

Waxwings travel together in flocks of a dozen or more, calling to each other in high, thin notes as the flock makes its way through trees or across the sky. The birds typically land in a tree infested with insects, or in a tree or shrub laden with fruit, and methodically clean it of pests or berries. Sometimes they settle in a group in the top of a tree and fly out to nab insects. You'll often spot them feasting on mayflies that are rising in swarms from streams.

During their late-summer nesting period, waxwings pair off to build bulky nests in orchards or shade trees. Their nests hold four to six spotted, pale blue or green eggs.

Attracting Waxwings

Attract these birds to your yard with berry bushes and fruit trees. Waxwings have such a passion for cherries (wild and cultivated) that they've earned the nickname "cherry bird." They also enjoy elderberries, mulberries, crabapples, hollies, hawthorns, and just about any other kind of fruit or berry. One of the most endearing traits of waxwings is their habit of playing "pass the berry." A group will line themselves along a branch, then pass a single berry from beak to beak back and forth down the line, just like a bunch of kids playing party games.

Waxwing Checklist

Two species of waxwings, the cedar and the Bohemian, turn up in backyards across the country. Both are soft shades of fawn, gray, or tawny brown, with a bright yellow band at the tip of the tail. Each has a striking black mask and chin bib, as well as a jaunty pointed crest. Males and females look alike.

Cedar waxwing. Cedar waxwings are relatively small birds, only about 6 inches long. They roam across the United States and Canada, staying mostly in the northern tier of states in summer and wandering southward in winter.

Bohemian waxwing. Bohemian waxwings are bigger, stouter, and flashier than cedar waxwings. They sport white and yellow bars and patches on their wings. The Bohemian waxwing nests in the far North, dropping into the West in winter. Occasionally Bohemians show up elsewhere across the country, usually mixed in with flocks of cedar waxwings.

A generous planting of hollies and other fruiting plants will lure cedar waxwings to your backyard bird garden.

WEATHER AND BIRDS

If your TV weatherperson has been off the mark lately, look to the birds in your backyard for a clue to the forecast.

For birds, gauging the weather is a matter of survival, so I trust their opinions. I always know when the brunt of a storm has passed, thanks to my feathered friends. From the storm shelter in the basement, I listen for the sounds of birds singing outside and I know the worst is over.

Weather Folklore

The reputation of birds as weather prophets is the subject of some wonderful folklore. The catchall name "rainbird" or "raincrow" is linked with several species of birds, including yellow-billed and black-billed cuckoos and spotted sand-pipers, which seem to call more frequently on afternoons when thunderstorms are near at hand. Here are a few other bits of bird weather lore.

◆ See a lark flying high, and fine weather will follow.
◆ When birds stop singing, thunder follows.
◆ When "Mother Carey's chickens" (storm petrels) fly before a wind, prepare for a storm at sea.
◆ When hawks fly low, prepare for a blow.

Perils of Bad Weather

Bad weather can wreak havoc on birds. The legendary winter of 1857–58, when ice and snow and cold gripped the country from New England to Florida, was a disaster for eastern bluebirds, eastern phoebes, house wrens, hermit thrushes, and pine warblers. These birds winter in the Southeast, and when the snow and cold wiped out the insects, thousands of birds starved.

The Wild World of Backyard Birds

In the winter, birds can serve as an early warning system for bad weather, says JoAnn Mueller, who lives in the countryside near Pittsburgh, Pennsylvania. The crowd of chickadees, titmice, juncos, sparrows, cardinals, and blue jays in her yard swells when bad weather is coming. "When I have to refill the feeder in the afternoon," she says, "I know we're in for more than a few inches. So after I put out the seed, I get the snow shovel ready."

Towhees only come to JoAnn's feeders when the upcoming storm will be particularly nasty. "If I see a towhee at the feeder, I start thinking 'No school tomorrow'," says JoAnn (she's a kindergarten teacher). "The snow often starts a few hours after the towhee arrives, and usually it's a humdinger of a blizzard!"

Late-spring cold spells are threatening to early nesters and early migrants like bluebirds, martins, and swallows, which depend on insects to feed themselves and their young. When the weather is rainy and cold, insects are nowhere to be found.

Dry weather can be tough on birds, too, as natural sources of drinking water dry up. It's especially important to keep your birdbath filled during droughts, and also in winter, when many natural water sources are frozen.

Blown Off Course

Strong storms can carry birds far out of their usual ranges. A late April blizzard once brought a red-shafted flicker to my Pennsylvania yard, many states east of its normal habitat. Another time, a flock of 30 cattle egrets—a rare sighting in my area—came in on the winds of a summer storm, landing almost in my backyard.

After a hurricane, some birdwatchers take to the coast to scan for waterbirds blown off course. Unable to fight the force of gale winds, some of those ocean-goers may even show up inland, like the white-billed tropic birds from Bermuda that turned up in Vermont after a hurricane some 60 years ago.

Helping Birds Weather the Storm

Your garden can be a special haven for birds during bad weather. The plants that provide the best shelter against rain, wind, hail, and snow are dense evergreen trees and shrubs. Perched safely in the interior of these plants, birds puff up their feathers for insulation and wait out the storm. Here are a few other ways you can offer a helping hand to birds when bad weather is brewing.

◆ Keep feeders brimming with seed and clear of snow. You may need to go out to sweep off snow every half-hour in severe storms.
◆ Set your alarm clock for the crack of dawn the morning after a winter storm, and get outside to clear and fill feeders. That way food will be ready and waiting when birds begin to stir.
◆ Clear ice and snow from trays and perches.

◆ Scatter seed directly on the ground for easy access, so birds don't have to fight for a turn at the feeder. If snow is soft, sweep a patch bare with broom or shovel before scattering seed so it doesn't sink in and disappear.
◆ Provide a sheltered area for feeding by sticking pine or spruce boughs into snow or soil on the windward side of your feeding area.
◆ If the roads are passable, make a mission of mercy and scatter birdseed along little-traveled roadsides or in open areas. Don't put seeds near busy roadways, where birds might fly into the path of traffic.
◆ Remember that not all birds eat seeds. For thrushes, robins, and bluebirds, provide handouts of bread and other baked goods and raisins. A few loaves of day-old bread torn into pieces and dropped along roadsides can mean the difference between life and death for robins in the aftermath of a blizzard or ice storm.

Try birdwatching right after a summer rainstorm. Many birds, including scarlet tanagers, will come to your garden to sip fresh rainwater that has collected on leaves.

WEEDS

Weed seeds are as irresistible to birds as potato chips are to many of us. It's hard to accept, but no matter how many sunflowers you plant, and no matter how many feeders you fill, you'll discover that the number one attractant for birds is the number one bane of gardeners: lowly weeds.

Plants with Drawing Power

In spring and summer, weed leaves hide many a tasty insect tidbit, and when weed seeds ripen, the bounty draws birds from far and wide. Find a thick stand of ragweed in winter, and you'll also find dozens of cardinals. Look for goldfinches in thistle patches, and indigo buntings, white-crowned sparrows, and other native sparrows wherever dandelions raise their fluffy seedheads. Juncos, sparrows, and finches are fond of lamb's-quarters seeds, and so are titmice, chickadees, and cardinals. In fact I can't think of any weed that doesn't have its takers when its seeds are ripe and ready.

There are some good reasons for birds' love affair with plants that we humans scorn. Most weed seeds are rich in oil and calories, an important consideration when you're a creature whose daily life consists of finding enough food to keep your rapid-fire metabolism on track. Plus weeds are familiar plants. Birds know just where their favorite weeds are likely to spring up year after year. They know when the weed seeds will ripen, and they know just the right technique for foraging the seeds. And weeds tend to grow in dense stands, so that little time or energy is wasted—it's an all-you-can-eat-meal at a single sitting.

Inviting Weeds into the Garden

It goes against the grain for most gardeners but adding weeds to the backyard bird garden is an excellent way to bring in the birds. That doesn't mean you need to rush out and plant weeds—they'll pop up just fine on their own. It does mean that you'll need to shift your perspective a bit. Think of that thicket of lamb's-quarters and dock as sparrow food and junco food.

Of course, in areas like your vegetable garden, you'll want to keep weeds under con-

Backed by a fence and fronted by a neat edging of mulch or bright annuals, a patch of weeds will fit right into your summer garden. Throughout the winter, birds will visit the weed patch to pick the stems clean of seeds.

trol. The magic word for weed control is mulch. A layer of grass clippings, shredded bark, or even sections of newspaper will keep weeds at bay. Organic mulches gradually decompose, so renew yours with a fresh layer as often as needed. Put down a layer of mulch as soon as you set out new plants and you'll stop the weeds in their tracks. You'll still need to hand-weed if you sow seeds in the garden, until your seedlings are big enough to mulch around.

Make weeding easy with an arsenal of the right tools. A long-bladed dandelion fork is great for getting out deep-rooted chicory, burdock, and dandelions. A long-handled hoe can't be beat for slicing off seedling weeds. A hand-tool hoe is handy for weeding in tight quarters or beneath shrubs. To get out tough weeds, including tree seedlings, grasp the weed firmly at the soil surface with a pair of pliers and twist as you pull.

The Top 10 Weeds for Birds

Here are 10 excellent weeds for birds. If they're not on your area's noxious weed list, consider letting a few or all of them take over some space in your garden. The plants on this list are just a small sampling of the great banquet of weeds. Whatever weeds you have growing in your yard will no doubt attract some birds. From low mats of chickweed to thick-branched "trees" of pokeweed, every weed has its fans. Most of these weeds are widely distributed in North America.

◆ Bur marigold likes wet meadows, pastures, and ditches. Warning: If you have a dog, you probably won't want bur marigold in your yard. The seeds stick like crazy in animal fur.
◆ Crabgrass grows best in well-watered, close-clipped lawns and cultivated garden soil. If

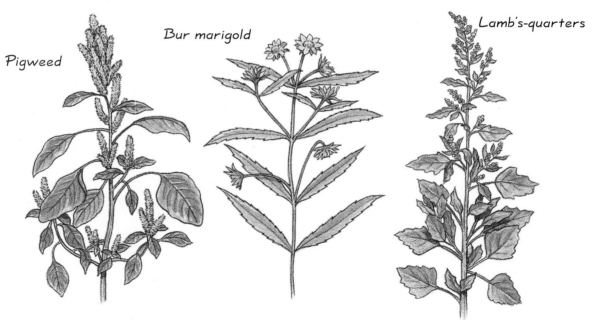

Pigweed

Bur marigold

Lamb's-quarters

To birds, weed seeds are a real delicacy. Learn to recognize their favorites, let a few go to seed, and birds will flock to your garden all winter to feast.

you can tolerate some crabgrass in your lawn or gardens and allow it to go to seed, native sparrows will enjoy feeding on it come fall and winter.

◆ Dandelion grows best in acidic, heavy clay soil, in tilled soil, and in lawns. Buntings, finches, and native sparrows find the seed-filled puffs irresistible.

◆ Dock grows best in moist acidic soil and in lawns. Cut some spikes of the rich brown seeds and put them in a basket for an easy decorative arrangement, but let some seed stems stand for juncos and sparrows to eat.

◆ Goldenrod grows best in fertile, moist soil. In late fall and through the winter, tree sparrows and other sparrows nibble through the fuzzy chaff to reach the tasty seeds.

◆ Jewelweed is common east of the Mississippi River and prefers moist soil and partly shady, woodland conditions. Hummingbirds love jewelweed blossoms; rose-breasted grosbeaks feast on the seeds.

◆ Lamb's-quarters grows best in fertile, tilled soil. By the end of winter, its thick clusters of tiny seeds are reduced to wispy skeletons thanks to the efforts of goldfinches, cardinals, and sparrows.

◆ Mullein is widely distributed, but most common east of the Mississippi River. It grows best in dry, gravelly soil or well-drained garden soil. The seed-packed spikes are a favorite of chickadees and downy woodpeckers, which also probe for overwintering insects.

◆ Pigweed grows best in fertile, tilled soil. The stems take on a maroon tint in the fall, when the fuzzy spikes of seeds attract native sparrows.

◆ Ragweed (both great and common) commonly grows in meadows, fields, and vacant lots. Don't let ragweed grow in your yard if you have hay fever.

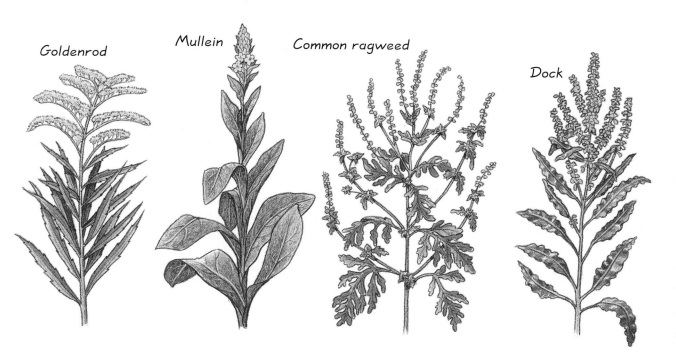

Goldenrod

Mullein

Common ragweed

Dock

WILDFLOWERS

It's only natural that wild birds should love wildflowers. To them wildflowers are living bird feeders that offer the ultimate in dining variety—seeds, nectar, and insects.

Because they tend to grow in dense, spreading colonies, wildflowers also help birds in another way: Dense wildflower foliage keeps birds safely out of sight as they move about on the forest floor or through a meadow.

Wildflower Basics

Many of our favorite garden plants have wild roots, so it's easy to mix wildflowers into your garden with other perennials, annuals, and shrubs. Wiry-stemmed, simple-flowered oxeye daisies, for instance, are a close relative of bigger, more compact shasta daisies. They look great planted together, and both kinds are also fine companions for columbines and bearded irises in a perennial bed.

Most wildflowers adapt easily to life in a garden, as long as you are considerate of their light, soil, and drainage needs. Planting an all-wildflower patch is a rewarding project, too. You may want to try a wild meadow garden like the one shown on page 275. Or if your yard is shady, wildflowers from the woods will light it up, especially in spring. (You can learn more about shade-loving wildflowers by turning to Shade and Woodland Gardens on page 211.)

To choose the best wildflowers for birds, do a little birdwatching first. Visit local fields and woods, and check which native plants have seedheads that attract birds. Be sure to use them as the basis of your garden. Add in some tubular flowers like salvias to attract hummingbirds.

Homegrown WISDOM

A WILD GARDEN WORKS

Mary Dech of Bethlehem, Pennsylvania, discovered by accident that a wild garden attracts lots of birds. Mary alway included some wildflowers, such as oxeye daisies, coreopsis, and black-eyed Susans, among her regular perennials in a neat and tidy garden that took hours to maintain. Butterflies loved the sunny perennial garden, but the only birds that seemed to visit it were hummingbirds and flycatchers (who came to catch butterflies).

But one year, when life got a little too busy, Mary neglected her garden. "The coreopsis, columbines, and oxeye daisies seeded themselves and filled in all the bare spots, and the black-eyed Susans went wild," Mary recalls. "That was all the invitation the birds needed. By the end of summer, I had a pair of indigo buntings working on their second nest among the black-eyed Susans, and song sparrows nesting among the daisies. Goldfinches were here every day, eating seeds of coreopsis and coneflowers, and lots of other birds came to find insects on the plants." Mary realized that birds liked her garden the "wild way," so she changed her ways. She put a comfy bench nearby and now she spends her time birdwatching instead of weeding!

Each part of our country has native wildflowers that are a favorite with the birds of that region. (To learn more about native plants that attract birds, turn to Native Plants on page 172.) By choosing plenty of natives, you're sure to create a bird-pleasing garden. Then add in some spreading wildflowers to provide good cover for the birds.

Wildflowers are perfect for providing cover because they usually reproduce like rabbits. Perennial plants like yarrow and goldenrod and many other wildflowers have spreading roots that create ever-larger colonies of plants. Others, especially annual species such as calliopsis (*Coreopsis tinctoria*), produce prodigious amounts of seed to ensure the survival of their species.

Give your wildflowers plenty of room to roam and they'll fill the available space themselves, just as they do in nature. Over the years, your shady spaces and sunny meadows will become filled with a living tapestry that looks just like Mother Nature designed it.

Starting a Wildflower Garden

If you decide to start a wildflower garden from scratch, you'll need to be sure you start it right. It can be a bit tricky to keep a meadow garden looking like those field-of-flower pictures you see on wildflower seed canisters. The showy annuals that add so much color to wildflower meadows are quickly choked out by perennial plants, like goldenrod and thistles.

To maintain a swath of colorful annual meadow flowers like bachelor's-buttons, poppies, and coreopsis, you'll need to keep the competition in check. That means starting out by preparing the soil thoroughly, and clearing out all bits of perennial weed roots that might sprout. Then each year you'll have to pull weeds that appear, and cultivate the soil so the seeds that drop have open ground to sprout in. It's similar to taking care of a standard bed of annual flowers.

Wildflowers often grow well in areas that other plants don't like. For example, if you have a low swampy spot in your lawn, turn it into an intermittent streambed, and plant moisture-loving jewelweed (left), rushes (center), and great blue lobelia (right) alongside.

For a meadow that maintains itself without so much coddling, switch to perennial flowers that spread fast by roots. They can hold their own among invading weeds. Perennial sunflowers, coneflowers, agastache, bee balm, yarrow, and goldenrod are all pushy enough to keep a meadow garden looking good. (Turn to Perennials on page 192 for information on starting a perennial garden.)

When you're gardening with wildflowers, never dig up plants from the wild. Stick with reputable nurseries or mail-order companies that grow their own wildflower plants. Ask whether they've propagated the plants themselves.

Price is one clue when you're shopping for wildflowers: If it seems too cheap to be true, the plants are most likely wild-collected. Most shade-loving wildflowers in particular multiply slowly, so expect them to be priced accordingly. You're buying natural treasures, after all.

Some Wild Choices for Birds

Wildflowers of the aster family (Asteraceae) are top choices for birds. Sunflowers, coneflowers, coreopsis, and asters produce a bounty of nutritious seeds that sustain birds right through winter—plus they attract butterflies and other insects that birds eat. I include bushy wildflowers, too, to supply shelter and nesting sites.

Purple and yellow is one of my favorite color schemes in nature, so I mimic it in my own garden planted just for the birds (shown in the illustration on the opposite page). All of the plants in this garden thrive in full sun, in average well-drained soil.

New England aster. Fields of asters and goldenrod are favorite places for finches, buntings, and sparrows, and it's easy to duplicate them on a small scale in your yard. New England aster (*Aster novae-angliae*) bursts forth in royal purple glory in late summer. It reaches about 4 feet tall and thrives in Zones 4 to 8. There are many cultivars available, but I prefer the old-fashioned species, with its open, wild look.

Coneflowers. Black-eyed Susan (*Rudbeckia* spp.), with its classic brown-centered golden daisies, and purple coneflower (*Echinacea purpurea*) will keep your goldfinches happy when the seeds ripen in summer. These flowers also attract butterflies, which in turn will bring flycatchers and bluebirds calling to catch and eat the butterflies. Both types of coneflowers reach about 3 feet tall and grow well in Zones 3 to 8.

Calliopsis. Sparrows and finches love the seeds of this annual flower. Calliopsis (*Coreopsis tinctoria*) seeds abundantly, so even if birds come to feast on the seed, there's usually plenty left behind to self-sow for next year's garden. The delicate ferny foliage is splashed with a multitude of daisies in rich gold, burnt sienna, deep mahogany, or two-tone combinations of those colors. Plants can reach 3 feet in rich soil, although they'll often flop over into a graceful billowy mass. Calliopsis is easy to grow in any sunny spot. Try sowing the seeds outdoors in fall—it will bring you earlier bloom the following season.

Sweet goldenrod. Goldenrods are notorious spreaders, and sweet goldenrod (*Solidago odora*) is no exception. But when you combine it with other vigorous perennials that can hold their own, it's gorgeous, making a splash of buttery yellow flowers in late summer. The plants have multiple stems that stand 3 to 4 feet tall and are hardy in Zones 3 to 9. Rub a leaf and sniff—the plant has a delicious anise fragrance.

Great blue lobelia. One for the hummingbirds, great blue lobelia (*Lobelia siphilitica*) grows in a compact clump and bears dense spikes of blue flowers in late summer. It grows to about 2 feet tall and flourishes in Zones 4 to 8. It grows well in wet places, but also thrives in average garden conditions.

Meadow phlox. Another hummingbird favorite, meadow phlox (*Phlox maculata*) has soft pink-purple or white, nicely fragrant flowers. It's more resistant to powdery mildew than other types of tall phlox, and it grows well in sun to shade in Zones 3 to 8, reaching a height of about 3 feet.

Maximilian sunflower. Maximilian sunflower (*Helianthus maximilianii*) holds its bouquets of big golden daisies well over my head—it can reach 8 feet or taller, depending on soil fertility. Even though the plants are large, they have an airy feeling, thanks to their willowy stems and well-spaced leaves. This sunflower spreads too quickly to work well in a perennial border, but it's perfect for a bird garden in Zones 5 to 9, where it can weave its gold among the other plants.

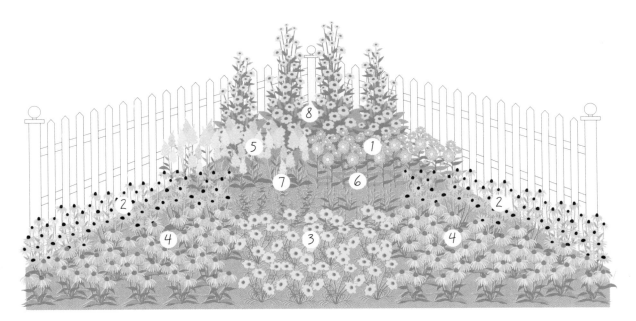

A Wild Garden for Birds

1. New England aster (*Aster novae-angliae*)
2. Black-eyed Susan (*Rudbeckia 'Goldsturm'*)
3. Calliopsis (*Coreopsis tinctoria*)
4. Purple coneflower (*Echinacea purpurea*)
5. Sweet goldenrod (*Solidago odora*)
6. Great blue lobelia (*Lobelia siphilitica*)
7. Meadow phlox (*Phlox maculata*)
8. Maximilian sunflower (*Helianthus maximilianii*)

WILDLIFE

Once you invite birds to your yard by adding shrubs, trees, other plants, and a source of water, you'll notice that other wild creatures are enjoying it, too. Small furry animals like rabbits, squirrels, voles, and shrews will quickly make themselves at home. Ground-hogs and ground squirrels or chipmunks will move into undisturbed areas. Frogs, turtles, toads, and salamanders will seek out moist places. As the lower links of the food chain multiply, predators like raccoons, hawks, owls, snakes, and foxes may pay a visit to seek prey.

Play Wildlife Detective

If you keep an eye out for tracks and other evidence, you'll get an idea of who's visiting or dwelling in your garden. Watch for these calling cards.

◆ Disappearing birdseed in feeders is a sign that you may be hosting flying squirrels. These delightful nocturnal animals are only hamster size, with flat, furred, 4-inch tails and huge black eyes that give them instant appeal.

◆ Emptied feeders can also mean that rac-coons or opossums have been paying a visit. Flash a strong light into your feeders periodi-cally from about 10:00 P.M. to midnight and you may catch them in the act.

◆ Suet holders that are emptied or torn down may be the work of that black-masked bandit, the raccoon. Opossums enjoy a mid-night suet snack, too. Gray foxes, which can climb almost as well as a cat, might also be the culprits.

◆ Tracks in the moist soil around your bird-bath or water garden may belong to visiting

The same fruits and seeds that attract birds to your backyard will also draw other wild visitors, like eastern chipmunks, which enjoy a bounty of tart rose hips.

raccoons, opossums, deer, and other wildlife. Use a wildlife field guide to decide what kind of critter left the tracks.

◆ A splash when you approach your water garden may mean that frogs have moved in. Watch the water, especially near floating leaves, and you may see their bright-eyed green heads poke up in a few minutes.

◆ Nibbled shrubbery is a sign that deer have found your garden. While sweet fawns may be irresistible, deer can quickly eat their way to pest potential. Provide a salt block and a pile of corn to keep them away from your trea-sured plants. But if deer develop a taste for your plants, a fence is the only way to keep them away.

◆ Dropped feathers in early to midfall, when birds are molting, can clue you in to unusual bird visitors. A large mottled or striped brown feather indicates an owl or hawk has been in the neighborhood.

◆ Small food caches of nuts and berries in birdhouses and old bird nests in winter may belong to a deer mouse or other small beastie. When you check for these, you may even come face-to-face with the mouse itself.

Watching Wildlife

Many wild animals are active only at night. But since most of us are inside after dark, we miss all the activity that takes place under the nighttime sky. You can look at your backyard from the dark side by planning a few night visits. Find a comfortable place to sit, where you can remain very quiet and still, and settle yourself at sundown. Dress appropriately for the weather and use insect repellent if you wish, so you can stay outside comfortably for an hour or so. Then see who comes out to play.

Early in the evening, rabbits and groundhogs will creep out to crop grass and nibble plants. You may see bats flitting through the air overhead. Watch for moths at your flowers while the light is fading, and keep an eye out for the sudden swoop of bats diving at the moths.

A late-evening visit is more mysterious because you'll hear much more than you see. Listen for the small stirrings and squeaks of mice, voles, and other rodents, or the booming voice of an owl. See if you can get a sense of who's moving about by the rustling noises you'll hear in the vegetation. You may want to carry a strong-beamed flashlight so that you can shine it on suspects and get a good look.

The Wild World of Backyard Birds

"I was going broke restocking my feeders," says Shirley Johnson of Minneapolis, Minnesota, "because all the seed was disappearing overnight. It wasn't so bad in winter, because the birds cleaned most of it up during the day. But in summer, when I don't have that many customers, I was going through 20 pounds of seed a week."

Shirley finally decided enough was enough. Determined to catch the thief in the night, she sat on her porch near the feeder and waited. In spite of paying close attention, she heard nothing. "I was just about ready to go in to bed," she says, "when I heard a funny squeak in the feeder right in front of me. I quick shone my flashlight on it and there was a mother raccoon with six babies! They were crammed in the feeder so tight that one had been forced overboard and was hanging on by his little black paws. I think that was the one I heard squeak. I still don't know how they all managed to climb in without my hearing them."

WINDOWS

Backyard birdwatchers love big windows for great views of feeding stations and bird gardens, but they also know that windows can be bad news for birds. The reflections in a pane of glass are confusing to birds. They can't distinguish between reflection and the real thing, and so they fly right into what they see as open space, and the resulting collision is often fatal.

Large, unbroken expanses of glass are almost certain death traps for birds. That's why office towers are such a hazard during migration. But even a single picture window can cause the death or injury of dozens of birds every year. From tiny hummingbirds to large-bodied owls, no species of bird is immune to the danger.

The thin wooden strips that divide a window into panes help somewhat, but when the sun is shining just right, the combined effect of the small panes of glass creates the illusion of the wide-open space reflected in them.

Keeping Birds Safe

When birds fly up from a feeder in a panic, as they often do, they can easily fly right toward a large picture window, because all they see is the reflection of the sky and natural surroundings. If your house has large picture windows, either place your feeders far away from the window—30 feet or more—or move them within 6 feet of the window. If the feeders are very close, the birds won't have the chance to get up much speed if they do fly toward the window, and so they're less likely to be injured if they hit the window.

Another solution to the plate-glass window problem is to create a feeding station for ground-eating birds. Put out a very low tray feeder or scatter seed on the ground, and surround the site with sheltering shrubs.

If birds are flying into your windows even though there are no feeders nearby, try to make the windows more visible. I've had good luck with black plastic garden netting, which I drape or tack over the window (I used duck hunter's camouflage netting one year in a pinch). The netting apparently breaks up the reflection so that the expanse of glass is no longer a danger. For other methods, see the illustration below.

Hawk decoy

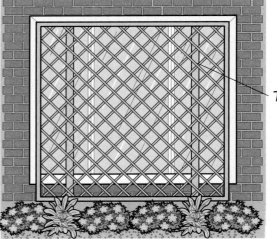

Trellis

To prevent birds from colliding with a window, put up a lightweight trellis—you'll still be able to see out, but birds won't come crashing in. Hawk decoys may also be effective; be sure to stick them to the outside of the pane.

WINTER ALMANAC

Winter is the best time of year to learn to identify birds, because there are fewer birds around and they're easier to see. Instead of dozens of fast-moving migrating birds filling your backyard and flitting through heavy foliage, there's a steady cast of characters visiting your garden and coming to your feeders in full view.

By the time winter settles in, birds have, too. Migration is long over, and winter birds are ranging in groups over large foraging territories.

At the Feeder

Bird feeders are at their busiest in the winter. Suet and seeds disappear quickly. The last of the crabapples and other fruits and berries in the garden disappear fast. Birds still forage in trees and among the remnants of last season's growth for overwintering insects, eggs, and cocoons. As long as the ground is bare of snow, birds also scratch about beneath shrubs and plants to garner dropped seeds and meaty morsels.

◆ High-calorie suet is vital to keeping birds warm in winter. Hang as many suet feeders as you have room for. I like to decorate the strong-limbed shrubs in my front yard with fist-size chunks of suet wrapped in a red plastic onion-bag mesh. If a bird or raccoon rips through the netting, it's no great loss; I just add another.

◆ Keep a supply of suet in the freezer so you don't get caught short. I chop it into manageable chunks before storing so I can take just what I need and not have to wrestle a big frozen hunk.

◆ Lay in a stock of seed in case of emergency. You don't want to get caught short when you need it the most. I keep a 50-pound sack of sunflower seed in the trunk of my car in winter. It serves two purposes: extra traction when the roads are slick, and extra bird food should a blizzard descend.

◆ Run an immersible heater to the birdbath, or try a solar birdbath that uses the sun's heat to keep water from freezing. At the very least, you can put out a shallow pan or clay saucer of warm water once a day. Take it into the house when the water begins to freeze.

◆ Treat birds to home cooking by making muffins, bread, and other snacks with nutritious additions like sunflower seeds and nuts.

◆ Expand the menu by offering chopped nuts, doughnuts, raisins, and fresh orange and apple halves in feeders.

◆ Put out cracked corn and ear corn for squirrels, deer, and other wildlife. Apple peelings are also appreciated.

In the Garden

Any berries or fruits left in your garden won't last long in winter. No matter how unappealing those few shriveled apples clinging to the tree may look to you or me, to birds they're a real find. If you've planted an ornamental flowering crab in your yard, make a note of how quickly the fruit disappears—if it does. I've noticed that birds never touch certain crabapple cultivars, while the fruit of others disappears like candy.

◆ Watch as sparrows, juncos, titmice, and chickadees work the last tiny seeds from flower and weed seedheads, leaving behind a bare stalk or wisps of fiber.

◆ Tree seeds attract the attention of hungry seed eaters now. Look for grosbeaks, cardinals, and finches in your ash trees, tulip poplars, alders, box elders, locusts, and any other tree with seeds still attached. Seeds of catalpa trees are a big favorite with evening grosbeaks, who hang upside down like parrots to extract the seeds from the beanlike pods.

◆ Rose hips are a favorite winter food for birds, so keep an eye on your shrub roses or wild roses at the edge of your yard.

◆ Recycle your Christmas tree as a bird shelter in the winter garden. It'll keep juncos and sparrows snug during storms and on chilly nights.

A Shift in Residence

In cold-winter areas, the inventory of resident birds dwindles to a short list. Insect eaters like vireos and orioles are long gone. Seed eaters like chickadees, titmice, jays, nuthatches, and sparrows are in their element now.

While migratory songbirds move south for the winter, the location of "south" varies from one bird species to another. Birds, like swallows and swifts, that depend on insects to survive must move to reliably warm-winter climes. Seed eaters needn't travel as far. For example, for red-breasted nuthatches from the far North, the Northeast may be south enough; for robins, goldfinches, and blue jays, "south" may be a hundred miles or a few states away.

Birds of the north woods sometimes head south in winter, usually when the pinecone crop is scarce. Evening grosbeaks, redpolls, crossbills, red-breasted nuthatches, and pine grosbeaks at the feeders or in the yard are a good clue that this may be an unusual migration season, also called an irruption year. Winter storms also can cause birds to stray far afield, carried willy-nilly by strong winds. After a bad windstorm or snowstorm, keep an eye out for the unusual.

If a snowstorm hits, create a ground-feeding area to accommodate lots of birds at one time. Sweep away snow first, and scatter seed directly on the ground. Heap up evergreen boughs on the windward side as a windbreak.

WOODPECKERS

Woodpeckers are attention getters: loud, flashy, and instantly recognizable. They whack on hollow trees, they make a wild racket by drumming on metal roofs (usually at the crack of dawn), and their repertoire of peculiar, unmusical whoops and rattles can carry clear across the yard. They're great birds to watch because most love to show off in front of an audience.

Getting to Know Them

Male and female woodpeckers generally look alike, except for the male's head markings. Size varies with species from the 5¾-inch downy woodpecker to the 15-inch pileated woodpecker. Black-and-white wing stripes are common on many species. On many woodpeckers, the wing stripes extend across their backs, an effect called ladder-backed.

Woodpeckers have short legs, with four toes on each foot. Two of the toes face forward and two face backward—a handy arrangement for a bird that spends most of its life clinging to the bark of trees. To make things even more secure, woodpeckers have tail feathers so stiff that the pointed tips can puncture paper. Like a rock climber braced against his ropes, a woodpecker leans against its braced tail. With its strong claws and toes firmly gripping the trunk, the bird can whack and hammer to its heart's content without losing its balance.

Drumming is a woodpecker's way of advertising the boundaries of its territory and serenading its mate. They also communicate with weird whoops, squawks, rattles, and other vocalizations.

Pairs get together late in winter, months before they're ready for breeding and nesting. Look for courtship behavior to start shortly after Christmas. If you see a pair of downy woodpeckers playing hide-and-seek around a tree trunk, you know they've got more on their mind than what Santa left under the tree.

A hole in a tree is a woodpecker's idea of home sweet home. They chisel the holes with their beaks, which can take up to three weeks depending on how hard and thick the wood is. Woodpeckers sometimes reuse a hole the following year, but usually the original owner excavates another home and another tenant moves in. Woodpeckers often use a dead branch or snag year after year, so that it ends up being riddled with nest holes.

Woodpeckers may accept a nest box, if it's mounted on a tree. All species lay plain white eggs, usually four or five in a batch.

Red-headed woodpeckers have a weakness for dried corn on the cob. Lure these birds to your yard by planting a block of field corn and letting the cobs dry in place.

Special Skills

Ever wonder why a woodpecker doesn't have an Excedrin headache after pounding on trees? That's because the bony walls of its skull are extra thick. Superstrong muscles that surround the skull and beak also absorb much of the shock of pounding.

Woodpeckers have special tongues, too. The tongue is about twice as long as the beak so the woodpecker can stick the tip of its tongue way out when it's probing for insects. The tongue is also coated with sticky saliva and tipped with barbs and bristles; not much can escape its determined reach.

Without woodpeckers our trees would be much less healthy. These beneficial birds consume both larvae and adults of wood-boring beetles, ants, aphids, flies, caterpillars, and other pests. Apparently, their sharp hearing lets them zero in on insects moving about in or beneath the bark of trees.

Attracting Woodpeckers

To attract woodpeckers to your yard, tempt them with food, nesting places, and drumming sites. Large trees give your garden great curb appeal when it comes to woodpeckers.

Besides scouring your trees for insects, these birds will quickly become regulars at feeders for handouts of sunflower seeds, corn, and nuts. Many are fond of fruit, too. They will visit mulberry and cherry trees, along with hackberry, Virginia creeper, dogwood, pokeberry, serviceberry, and other fruiting plants.

Woodpeckers also eagerly eat acorns and other nuts—including pecans, walnuts, and beechnuts—off the trees or from a feeder.

Woodpeckers are cavity nesters, so start building nest boxes (for dimensions, see "A Birdhouse for Every Bird" on page 40). For a drumming site, "plant" a dead tree or branch, as shown in the illustration on page 231, and let logs and stumps decay in place. The birds will find other drumming sites to their satisfaction: perhaps your drainpipe or that patch of tin on your shed roof—anything that makes a loud, resonant noise.

Woodpecker Checklist

Every area of the United States has its woodpeckers, with species often overlapping in their ranges. Whatever trees grow in your area, you can be sure there's a guardian woodpecker keeping bark beetles and other damaging insects in check.

Downy woodpecker. Downies are the smallest and probably the most common woodpecker in America. These black-and-white-striped birds range across almost all of the country except for a few areas of the Southwest.

Hairy woodpecker. Big brother of the downy, the hairy woodpecker has the same black-and-white-striped wings and white belly and back. It's a chunkier bird with a much stouter bill, and about $1\frac{1}{2}$ inches longer than the downy woodpecker. It covers the same territory, although it's not as abundant as the downy.

Ladder-backed woodpeckers. The red-bellied woodpecker is common in the East and Midwest. One of the most poorly named species of birds, this ladder-backed woodpecker is bright red on the back of its neck, a marking that stands out like a beacon from a distance. The "red belly" is only a tiny, hard-to-see patch of red feathers on its belly.

In the West, other "ladder-backs" take over, including the golden-fronted woodpecker, the

Gila woodpecker, and the ladder-backed woodpecker, all species found in the Southwest or Texas. The three-toed woodpecker of western coniferous forests has a beautiful yellow cap that contrasts sharply with its shining black-and-white feathers. Another woodpecker with a blurry-looking ladder-back pattern is the famed yellow-bellied sapsucker, a common woodpecker and one of the few migratory species in this family. For more information on this bird, see Sapsuckers on page 209.

Red-headed woodpecker. Ladder-backed woodpeckers are pretty; red-headed woodpeckers are truly dashing. The gleaming black back and wings of this beauty are accented with large, clear white wing patches, a snowy

JUST FOR WOODPECKERS

■ Woodpeckers will eagerly accept a breakfast of doughnuts, corn bread, or homemade bird-treat baked goods.
■ Try a slice of watermelon on a platform feeder to entice the birds in summer.
■ Peanut butter is a guaranteed draw for almost any woodpecker in the neighborhood; suet is also wildly popular.
■ In some areas woodpeckers will drink from hummingbird and oriole nectar feeders.

white belly, and—best of all—a hood of deep, pure crimson. Ranging across almost two-thirds of the country, the red-headed is a locally common bird, but it is uncommon as a species. That means if you're lucky enough to have red-headeds in your neighborhood, they're probably as common as flickers; but step outside of the range of your local tribe and you may have a hard time finding a single one.

Pileated woodpecker. *Pileated* means crested, and this bird sure has one: a swept-back pointy crest that stands up like a bright red signal flag. This bird closely resembles the cartoon character Woody Woodpecker. Even the laugh is the same—a ringing cackle that you can hear for a quarter-mile. Pileateds prefer downed logs and stumps to upright trees, so look for these birds closer to the ground than other woodpeckers. These big birds range across the eastern half of the country and the Northwest all year-round, but they need large, uninterrupted patches of woodland and are sparsely distributed, so consider yourself lucky if you spot one. Other unstriped woodpeckers include the white-headed woodpecker of western pines and firs, and the black, pink, and red Lewis's woodpecker of the West.

Like most woodpeckers, downy woodpeckers are year-round residents of their territories. They enjoy a variety of feeder treats, but suet and peanut butter are among their favorites.

WRENS

These perky little brown birds have a lot going for them: They're endearingly uninhibited around humans, they're enthusiastic singers, and they're great fun to watch. Temperamental at times, wrens are also masters at scolding, especially when you blunder too close to their private birdhouse domain.

Getting to Know Them

Clothed in warm brown with faintly barred backs or wings, wrens are the classic LBB, or little brown birds. Their jaunty tails, however, give them instant appeal. They usually hold their tails erect, often at right angles to their chubby bodies. Their long, slim beaks are slightly down-curved.

Wrens are restless birds, always in motion, hopping about in underbrush or in the garden. Only when they stop to sing—with their tail pointed down and their beak pointed to the sky—do they sit still. But just for a minute.

Attracting Wrens

A yard with plenty of shrubs and beds of perennials and annuals is wren heaven. Throw in a patch of brambles, elderberries, or other small, soft fruits, and you've won a wren's heart. The vegetation will keep the perky birds supplied with plenty of tasty bugs, and the fruit will be a hit with the wrens in the summer.

The number one tactic for attracting house wrens is to put up nest boxes (other kinds of wrens prefer to nest in shrubs, natural crevices, or even in outbuildings). You can mount a nest box right in your garden, because house wrens don't mind humans near their nests. In early spring, offer a selection of feathers, hair, dryer lint, and other soft stuff for nesting material in a tray or on the ground.

You may hear stories about wrens destroying the eggs and nestlings of nearby birds, and unfortunately the stories may be true. When house wrens live close to another songbird's breeding territory, the male wren may puncture eggs or kill nestlings of bluebirds or other wrens in adjacent territories. To try to prevent this, space wren boxes far apart and well away from houses for bluebirds or other backyard birds.

Wren Checklist

Restless wrens patrol the entire country, with house wrens the most widely distributed. Most wrens are common and abundant in their ranges, but familiarity breeds fondness rather than contempt when it comes to these lively birds.

House wren. The diminutive house wren, measuring about 4 inches from stem to stern, is one of the most familiar birds in America. Common in backyards and brushy hedgerows everywhere across the country (except for a patch of Southwest desert), this active little bird has been beloved as a backyard companion for generations. Often known as Jenny wren, the house wren nests anywhere and everywhere: in boots left on the doorstep, in tractor axles, and even in pockets of coats or overalls hanging on a hook. The house wren welcomes nesting boxes, and it will also use natural cavities in trees or fence posts.

Carolina wren. Once limited to the Southeast, the cinnamon-colored Carolina wren has spread northward into New England and the upper Midwest. It's the largest wren in the East, though it's less than 5 inches long, with a warm buff-colored belly and a strong white eye stripe. Carolinas like a yard with plenty of shrubs and vines. Like other wrens, the Carolina wren is a big insect eater, but this bird also visits feeders for small seeds and soft foods. The Carolina wren loudly repeats *tea kettle! tea kettle!* in a loud, clear whistle, along with a repertoire of odd chirring noises.

Carolinas often build their nests in garages or sheds or under the eaves of roofs; they're adept at finding an opening into an outbuilding. Their nests are huge collections of sticks and fibers, which they may add to for years.

Bewick's wren. Bewick's wren is a feather or two bigger than the house wren, with a white belly and a distinct eye stripe. Once abundant from the West through the Appalachians, it's now unusual to spot them east of Texas. You can tell this wren from the rest of the wren clan by its white underparts and its characteristic habit of jerking its tail sideways in a kind of nervous tic.

Like other wrens, Bewick's often lives on or around houses and outbuildings. You can also find it in old pastures and thickets, and in cacti and mesquite. Bewick's wren has a clear, loud voice. Its song, usually a short run of notes followed by a trill, seems to change with every performance.

Winter wren. The winter wren's musical song is the voice of moist, dimly lit forests along the Pacific Coast and in the Rockies, the far North, and the Appalachians. Winter wrens also live in much of the eastern two-thirds of the country, though they're much scarcer than other species. Whenever I see mossy logs, I know the habitat is perfect for these dwellers of damp, woodsy places. If your house adjoins woods and you have a thickly planted yard, winter wrens may come to nest or visit for bread crumbs at your feeder.

Marsh wren. If your backyard holds a large marshy area, you may have the chance to see and hear the marsh wren. Appearing in any area of the country, this 4-inch bird has a long bill and a black back streaked with white and edged with chestnut. Marsh wrens are hard to spot

among the thick growth of cattails or other bog plants, but they're easy to hear. They constantly chatter in musical rattles that vary in pitch.

Other wrens. In the West, look for the small rock wren; it walks about with a characteristic bobbing motion on barren stretches of rocks. If you live close to a canyon, you may enjoy the wonderful descending song of the canyon wren. In desert areas of the Southwest, the cactus wren, a giant at 6½ inches long, is easy to spot as it flies low across the ground. Its thin, down-curved beak and long, cocked tail say "wren" right away, though the bold-spotted breast and heavily streaked back and wings are unlike those of any other type of wren.

The male house wren builds nests before his mate's arrival in spring, hoping she'll accept one. But the persnickety female may insist on starting a new one herself. You may find wren nests anywhere—even in a mailbox left open for an afternoon!

YELLOWTHROATS

If your backyard includes a grassy meadow, an unmanicured flower garden, or lots of shrubs, you're likely to host the "witchety" bird, otherwise known as the common yellowthroat. Common across America, this pretty little wood warbler has a distinctive *witchety, witchety, witchety* call that's easy to recognize.

Getting to Know Them

Yellowthroats remind me of a wren in fancy dress. Frequently holding their tails cocked high, they have the same hyperactive habits as the house wren. They also search for bugs in the same places as house wrens: in gardens, weedy patches, and low shrubs.

Males and females are olive green on top and yellow beneath, and the male has a sporty black mask across his face. The male's belly is bright buttercup yellow; the female is paler. In action, these little birds resemble wrens, darting about and frequently chiding intruders with a scolding *chack!*

Once called "ground warblers," yellowthroats stay in weedy undergrowth and shrubs, rarely rising into trees. Their bulky nest of grasses, dead leaves, weed stems, and strips of grape-vine bark is lined with fine grass and hair. You'll usually find it fastened to weed stems or shrubs at ground level or a few inches above. The collection of four eggs is white or creamy with a splatter of brown dots making a wreath around the wide end.

Attracting Yellowthroats

An abundance of insects in your garden plants will keep yellowthroats happy. A densely planted perennial garden will attract yellowthroats for both dining pleasure and raising a

family. Fall asters, tall garden phlox, perennial and annual sunflowers, mallows, and other branching, dense perennials are the best choices for a yellowthroat-friendly garden. If you can bear to stay out of at least a part of the garden, a pair of yellowthroats may take up residence. Once they do, be prepared for getting scolded every time you intrude too near.

Plantings of ornamental grasses and weedy bramble patches also have great appeal for nesting spots, as do water gardens ringed by willows or viburnums and clumps of rushes or maiden grass. Don't be too quick to cut back all your ornamental grasses and rushes; save the leaves and offer them in spring as nesting material. These determined little birds may use them to weave their nest.

Common yellowthroats often include strips of grape-vine bark in their nests. To attract this distinctive warbler, keep a wild, brushy place in your backyard where they can build their nest.

ZINNIAS

Zinnias are a quadruple delight for bird gardeners. They have abundant, colorful blossoms, and they'll draw songbirds, hummingbirds, and butterflies. And zinnias are super-easy to grow and quick to bloom.

Hummers and butterflies sip nectar from zinnia flowers, which are available in zingy red, yellow, hot pink, orange, pastel, white, and even green. But the real show begins when zinnia seedheads ripen. Finches, cardinals, and buntings will visit from late summer through winter until they pick the seedheads bare. Sparrows and juncos will follow along to clean up any seeds that drop to the ground.

Zinnia Choices

Seed racks and catalogs are filled with all sorts of common zinnias (*Zinnia elegans*), from perky miniature pom-pom-flowered plants to shaggy, 6-inch, cactus-flowered plants that stretch to waist high. These colorful zinnias bloom from early summer through the first frosts. For flowers with an autumn-colors theme, try Mexican zinnia (*Z. haageana*) and its cultivars 'Persian Carpet' and 'Old Mexico'. Narrowleaf zinnia (*Z. angustifolia*) has tiny, daisy-shaped flowers in golden orange or white on 10- to 12-inch-tall plants.

When the soil warms in spring, plant zinnia seeds or bedding plants directly in a sunny patch of well-drained, average soil. Powdery mildew sometimes infects the leaves, causing them to turn white, then brown and drop in late summer, but the disease doesn't affect the flowers. To discourage this fungal infection, plant zinnias in a sunny spot with good air circulation and avoid splashing the leaves when you water them. Try the variety 'Rose Pinwheel', which has good resistance to mildew.

Zinnias are simple to grow and make great bird plants. Their nutritious seeds are as popular as sunflower seeds with birds, and their nonstop flowers will bring you butterflies and hummingbirds until frost. Try planting an entire bed of zinnias using a mix of different sizes and colors.

BIRD SUPPLIES

Your best source of bird supplies may be your local garden center or wild-bird specialty shop. Even discount stores and hardware stores offer birdhouses and feeders. More and more are showing up on the shelves every day. Feed mills are a great source of low-cost birdseed and grains if you buy in large quantity. Fast-dissolving superfine sugar, which melts instantly even in cold water and is great for making nectar, is available at some supermarkets or from restaurant- and bar-supply shops.

Many cottage-industry bird box and feeder makers have entered the market. Check the back pages of any bird or wildlife magazine, such as *Wild Bird* or *Audubon,* for advertisements and places to send for catalogs. You may also want to shop for supplies from the mail-order firms listed below.

THE AUDUBON WORKSHOP
5200 Schenley Place
Lawrenceburg, IN 47025
Phone: (812) 537-3583

DOWN TO EARTH
4 Highland Circle
Lucas, TX 75002
Phone: (800) 865-1996
Fax: (972) 442-2816
E-mail: sales@downtoearth.com
Website:
http://www.downtoearth.com
Makes simple cypress-wood houses and see-through bird feeders and birdhouses that you can attach to your window.

DROLL YANKEES INC.
27 Mill Road
Foster, RI 02825
Phone: (401) 647-3324
Fax: (401) 647-7620

DUNCRAFT, INC.
102 Fisherville Road
Penacook, NH 03303-9020
Phone: (800) 593-5656
Fax: (603) 226-3735
Website:
http://www.duncraft.com

PLOW & HEARTH
P.O. Box 5000
Madison, VA 22727-1500
Phone: (800) 627-1712
Fax: (800) 843-2509

WILD BIRD CENTERS OF AMERICA, INC.
Phone: (800) 945-3247
Website: http://www.wildbird-center.com

WILD BIRDS UNLIMITED
Phone: (800) 326-4928
Website: http://www.wbu.com

SOURCES OF SEEDS AND PLANTS

You can plant-shop from catalogs or in person at nurseries and garden centers. Generally, you'll find larger plants at nurseries than you'll get through a catalog, which is important when you're trying to make your yard inviting in a hurry. When you pick out plants at local nurseries and especially at discount-store garden centers, be sure to choose vigorous plants that show no signs of stress from poor care. I avoid plants that show signs of insects or disease problems, like spotty or sticky foliage or leaves that are yellowing or dropping.

Prices vary widely among plant outlets, so it pays to shop around. I rely on mail-order or patronize the best nursery in town for my unusual treasures, and buy the commoners from chain stores. Some mail-order companies charge a small fee for their catalogs; you'll often get a credit on your first order.

There are far too many mail-order nurseries to list them all; the following is just a small selection. Ask gardening friends what companies they recommend, too.

BUSSE GARDENS
5873 Oliver Avenue, SW
Cokato, MN 55321-4229
Phone: (800) 544-3192
Reliable and beautiful perennial plants that can take cold (but also thrive in milder gardens). Wildflowers, hostas, and heucheras are specialties.

EDIBLE LANDSCAPING
P.O. Box 77
Afton, VA 22920-0077
Phone: (804) 361-9134
Fax: (804) 361-1916
Double-duty plants for you and the birds (and other wildlife). Lots of mouth-watering fruiting trees and shrubs.

FINCH BLUEBERRY NURSERY
P.O. Box 699
Bailey, NC 27807
Phone: (919) 235-4664
Fax: (919) 235-2411
Wide selection of blueberries for your bird garden.

FORESTFARM
990 Tetherow Road
Williams, OR 97544-9599
Phone: (541) 846-7269
Fax: (541) 846-6963
More than 2,000 plants, including wildflowers, perennials, and an outstanding variety of trees and shrubs.

THE FRAGRANT PATH
P.O. Box 328
Ft. Calhoun, NE 68023
Seeds for annuals, perennials, shrubs, and vines that would have been right at home in Grandma's garden.

LILYPONS WATER GARDENS
P.O. Box 10
Buckeystown, MD 21717-0010
Phone: (800) 999-5459
Fax: (800) 879-5459
E-mail: info@lilypons.com
Website:
http://www.lilypons.com
Supplies for creating a water garden, from basic pools and liners to fish and plants.

LOGEE'S GREENHOUSES
141 North Street
Danielson, CT 06239-19399
Phone: (860) 774-8038
Fax: (888) 774-9932
E-mail: logee-info@logees.com
Website: http://www.logees.com
Large selection of greenhouse and exotic plants, including several vines that attract hummingbirds.

LOUISIANA NURSERY
5853 Highway 182
Opelousas, LA 70570
Phone: (318) 948-3696
Fax: (318) 942-6404
E-mail: DEDurio@aol.com
Vines hummingbirds adore, as well as many other trees, shrubs, and perennials.

NICHE GARDENS
1111 Dawson Road
Chapel Hill, NC 27516
Phone: (919) 967-0078
Fax: (919) 967-4026
E-mail: orders@nichegdn.com
Website:
http://www.nichegdn.com
Generous-size plants of grasses, nursery-propagated wildflowers, perennials, and herbs.

PRAIRIE MOON NURSERY
Route 3, Box 163
Winona, MN 55987
Phone: (507) 452-1362
Fax: (507) 454-5238
Native prairie grasses and wildflowers in outstanding variety; also lots of seeds.

PRAIRIE NURSERY
P.O. Box 306
Westfield, WI 53964
Phone: (608) 296-3679
Fax: (608) 296-2741
An excellent source of native wildflowers and grasses, many of them ideal for bird gardens.

SHADY OAKS NURSERY
112 10th Avenue, SE
Waseca, MN 56093
Phone: (800) 504-8006
All kinds of plants that thrive in shade, including wildflowers, ferns, perennials, shrubs, and others.

SUNLIGHT GARDENS, INC.
174 Golden Lane
Andersonville, TN 37705
Phone: (423) 494-8237
Fax: (423) 494-7086
Terrific selection of wildflowers, all nursery propagated, of southeastern and northeastern North America.

TRIPPLE BROOK FARM
37 Middle Road
Southampton, MA 01073
Phone: (413) 527-4626
Fax: (413) 527-9853
Lively catalog of wildflowers and other northeastern native plants, plus fruits and shrubs.

VAN NESS WATER GARDENS

2460 North Euclid Avenue
Upland, CA 91784-1199
Phone: (909) 982-2425
Fax: (909) 949-7217
A complete source of supplies and plants for water gardens.

WE-DU NURSERIES

Route 5, Box 724
Marion, NC 28752
Phone: (704) 738-8300
Fax: (704) 738-8131
Impressive selection of wildflowers and perennials, including lots of woodland plants.

WILDLIFE NURSERIES

P.O. Box 2724
Oshkosh, WI 54903-2724
Phone: (920) 231-3780
Fax: (920) 231-3554
Excellent, informative listing of plants and seeds of native grasses, annuals, and perennials that attract birds and other wildlife. Also water-garden plants and supplies.

WOODLANDERS, INC.

1128 Colleton Avenue
Aiken, SC 29801
Phone/Fax: (803) 648-7522
A fantastic collection of native trees, shrubs, ferns, vines, and perennials, plus other good garden plants. It's a list only, no pictures or descriptions, so if you're a newcomer to plants, pull out a plant encyclopedia to consult as you go.

ORGANIZATIONS AND PROGRAMS

BACKYARD WILDLIFE HABITAT PROGRAM

National Wildlife Federation
8925 Leesburg Pike
Vienna, VA 22184-0001
Free information on developing a bird-friendly backyard; certification program.

NATIONAL AUDUBON SOCIETY

700 Broadway
New York, NY 10003
Phone: (212) 979-3000
Fax: (212) 979-3188
Website:
http://www.audubon.org
Founded in 1905, active worldwide in all kinds of conservation issues as well as birds. Join a local branch to meet other birders and enjoy other bird-related activities.

NORTH AMERICAN BIRD BANDING PROGRAM

Learn how to create your own banding research program or volunteer with other banders.

For U.S. residents, contact:
Bird Banding Laboratory
U.S. Geological Survey—
Biological Resources Division
Patuxent Wildlife Research Center
12100 Beech Forest Road
Suite 4037
Laurel, MD 20708-4037
Phone: (301) 497-5790
Fax: (301) 497-5717
E-mail: BBL@nbs.gov

For Canadian residents, contact:
Bird Banding Office
National Wildlife Research Centre
Canadian Wildlife Service
Hull, Quebec K1A 0H3
Phone: (819) 994-6176
Fax: (819) 953-6612

PROJECT FEEDERWATCH

Winter counts of feeder birds by "regular people" all across North America.

The data collected contribute to scientific understanding of changes in bird populations and distribution.

For U.S. residents, contact:
Cornell Laboratory of Ornithology/PFW
159 Sapsucker Woods Road
Ithaca, NY 14850-1999
Phone: (607) 254-2440
E-mail: feederwatch@cornell.edu

For Canadian residents, contact:
Bird Studies Canada/PFW
P.O. Box 160
Port Rowan, Ontario N0E 1M0
Phone: (519) 586-3531
E-mail: pfw@nornet.on.ca

RECOMMENDED READING

BOOKS

Adams, George. *Birdscaping Your Garden.* Emmaus, PA: Rodale Press, 1994.

Appleton, Bonnie L., and Alfred F. Scheider. *Rodale's Successful Organic Gardening: Trees, Shrubs, and Vines.* Emmaus, PA: Rodale Press, 1993.

Bent, Arthur Cleveland. "Life Histories" of American birds series. Reprint. North Stratford, NH: Ayer Company Publishers.

Bradley, Fern Marshall, and Barbara W. Ellis, eds. *Rodale's All-New Encyclopedia of Organic Gardening.* Emmaus, PA: Rodale Press, 1992.

Cox, Jeff. *Landscaping with Nature.* Emmaus, PA: Rodale Press, 1991.

Harrison, George H. *The Backyard Bird Watcher.* Magnolia, MA: Peter Smith Publisher, Inc., 1996.

Isaacson, Richard T., ed. *The Andersen Horticultural Library's Source List of Plants and Seeds.* 4th ed. Chanhassen, MN: Andersen Horticultural Library, 1993.

Mahnken, Jan. *The Backyard Bird-Lover's Guide.* Pownal, VT: Storey Communications, 1996.

Nash, Helen. *The Complete Pond Builder.* New York: Sterling Publishing Co., Inc., 1996.

National Audubon Society. *The Audubon Society Handbook for Birders.* New York: Charles Scribner's Sons, 1981.

Pettingill, Olin Sewall, Jr. *A Guide to Bird Finding East of the Mississippi.* New York: Oxford University Press, 1977.

Proctor, Rob, and Nancy J. Ondra. *Rodale's Successful Organic Gardening: Annuals and Bulbs.* Emmaus, PA: Rodale Press, 1995.

Roth, Sally. *Natural Landscaping.* Emmaus, PA: Rodale Press, 1997.

Schneck, Marcus. *Your Backyard Wildlife Year.* Emmaus, PA: Rodale Press, 1996.

Stokes, Donald. *Stokes Bird Gardening Book.* New York: Little, Brown, 1998.

Sunset Staff. *An Illustrated Guide to Attracting Birds.* Menlo Park, CA: Sunset Publishing Corporation, 1990.

Terres, John K. *The Audubon Society Encyclopedia of North American Birds.* New York: Random House Value Publishing, 1995.

———. *Songbirds in Your Garden.* Chapel Hill, NC: Algonquin Books of Chapel Hill, 1994.

Thompson, Bill, III. *Bird Watching for Dummies.* Foster City, CA: IDG Books Worldwide, 1997.

Tripp, Kim E., and J. C. Raulston. *The Year in Trees.* Portland, OR: Timber Press, 1995.

Tufts, Craig, and Peter Loewer. *The National Wildlife Federation's Guide to Gardening for Wildlife.* Emmaus, PA: Rodale Press, 1995.

MAGAZINES

Organic Gardening
Rodale Press, Inc.
33 East Minor Street
Emmaus, PA 18098

Birds and Blooms
5400 South 60th Street
Greendale, WI 53129

Bird Watcher's Digest
P.O. Box 110
Marietta, OH 45750

BIRD FIELD GUIDES

Keep a field guide both in your home and in the glove compartment of your car. Page through it whenever you have a few minutes to spare—while you're waiting for cookies to bake, in line at the bank drive-through, or while waiting for your kids after a school event. Just looking at the pictures and the names over and over will familiarize you with birds. And when you see a bird you don't recognize, you'll be surprised how quickly a possible identification pops into your head.

A Guide to Field Identification: Birds of North America by Chandler S. Robbins, Bertel Bruun, and Herbert S. Zim (New York: Golden Press, 1983) shows birds in lifelike poses and on a plant where you're likely to see them. Range maps are inserted at each bird's entry, so you don't have to flip to a separate section in the back of the book as you do with Peterson's. The book includes all birds of North America, which will give you a wider perspective.

The Peterson Field Guide series by Roger Tory Peterson (Boston: Houghton Mifflin Co.) is a set of regional guides, and birds are drawn in flatter, less lifelike poses than in the Golden Press field guide, without any hint of habitat in most illustrations. Peterson uses arrows to point out field marks to look for, for definitive identification.

The Audubon Society Field Guide series (New York: Alfred A. Knopf), another regional set of guides, use photos instead of illustrations. The guides also include a lot of interesting information about each bird.

National Geographic Society Field Guide to the Birds of North America by Jane R. McCauley and National Geographic Society Staff (Washington, DC: National Geographic Society, 1993) has detailed color illustrations, range maps, and species descriptions, including information on behavior and songs.

Stokes Field Guide to Birds: Eastern Region and ***Stokes Field Guide to Birds: Western Region*** by Donald and Lillian Stokes (Boston: Little, Brown and Company, 1996) are two photographic field guides that also offer information on feeding and nesting habits and other behavior.

Note: Page references in *italic* indicate tables. **Boldface** references indicate illustrations.

A

Abert's towhees, 246
Abies balsamea, 102
Acadian flycatchers, 117
Acorns, 1, **1**, 184
Acorus calamus, 264
Agastache foeniculum, 7, 192, **192,** *194*
Agastache nepetoides, 194
Aggression, signs of, 9
Albino birds, 79
Almond trees, 182
Amaranthus caudatus, 2, 4
Amelanchier, **14,** *15*
Amelanchier arborea, 250
Amelanchier stolonifera, 131
American crows
    characteristics of, 92
    eggs of, **99**
    voiceprint of, **55**
American kestrels, **134,** 135
Andropogon gerardii, 187
Anise hyssop, 7, 192, **192,** *194*
Annuals
    as bird attractors, 2–3, **2–3,** *4*
    for birdseed gardens, 52
Anting, for repelling pests, 11–12, **11**
Ants, birds eating, *147*
Aphids, as bird food, **148**
Aquilegia caerulea, 80
Aquilegia canadensis, 80
Aquilegia chrysantha, 80
Aquilegia formosa, 80
Aquilegia vulgaris, 80

Arbors
    grape, as breeding territory, 241, **241**
    for vines, 254
Arctostaphylos uva-ursi, 130
Arrowheads, 264
Arrowwood, 15
Aster novae-angliae, 274
Asters, New England, 274
Autumn. *See* Fall
Azalea, pinxterbloom, 212

B

Baby birds, 5
    all-purpose food for, 113
    behavior of, 11
    feeding, 112–13, **112**
    saving, 111–12, **111, 112**
Bachelor's-button, 2, **3,** *4*
Bacillus thuringiensis (BT), harmful effects of, 195
Backyard, birdwatching in, 42–43
Baileya multiradiata, 173
Bald eagles, hotspots for, 44
Balsam, garden, **3,** *4,* 146
Baltimore orioles, 185, **185**
    eggs of, **99**
Banding, 6
Band-tailed pigeons, 97
Barberries, *15*
Barbs, feather, 11
Barn owls, 190
    beak of, **29**
Barn swallows, 237, **237**
    nests of, **178**
Barred owls, 188, 189, **189**
Bathing. *See also* Birdbaths
    behavior, 11–12
Bayberry, 6, **172**
Beaks
    in bird identification, 145

    as clue to eating habits, 29–30
Bearberry, **186**
    as groundcover, 130
Bee balm, 7, **7**
    spotted, 7
Bees, birds eating, *147*
Beetles, birds eating, *147*
Behavior, 8–13
    aggressive, 9
    alertness for danger, 13
    bathing, 11–12, 19–20
    courtship, 9–10, 85–87
    interpreting, 8
    at mealtime, 8–9, 33–34
    migration, 11, 164–66
    in nesting season, 10–11, 176–79
    during play, 12
    sleep, 13, **13**
    as warning signal, 10
Bell's vireos, 258
Benches, garden, 226
Berberis, 15
Bergamot, wild, 7
Berries, 14, **14,** 15. *See also specific berries*
Bewick's wrens, 285
Bidens aristosa, 4
Big bluestem, *187*
Bignonia, 256
Bignonia capreolata, 173, 256
Billing and cooing, in courtship, 85–86
Binoculars, 16–17, **16–17,** 43
Birdbaths, 18–21
    attracting birds to, 18–19
    for bluebirds, **58,** 59
    choosing, 18
    cleaning, 19, **234**
    de-icer for, **20**
    heating, 279

USDA PLANT HARDINESS ZONE MAP

Average annual minimum temperature (°F)

Zone 1		Below -50°
Zone 2		-40° to -50°
Zone 3		-30° to -40°
Zone 4		-20° to -30°
Zone 5		-10° to -20°
Zone 6		0° to -10°
Zone 7		10° to 0°
Zone 8		20° to 10°
Zone 9		30° to 20°
Zone 10		40° to 30°
Zone 11		Above 40°

This map was revised in 1990 to reflect the original USDA map, done in 1965. It is now recognized as the best indicator of minimum temperatures available. Look at the map to find your area, then match its color to the key at the right. When you've found your color, the key will tell you what hardiness zone you live in. Remember that the map is a general guide; your particular conditions may vary.